T0190359

Communications
in Computer and Information Science   1611

More information about this series at https://link.springer.com/bookseries/7899

Yongtian Wang · Huimin Ma · Yuxin Peng ·
Yue Liu · Ran He (Eds.)

Image and Graphics Technologies and Applications

17th Chinese Conference, IGTA 2022
Beijing, China, April 23–24, 2022
Revised Selected Papers

Editors
Yongtian Wang
Beijing Institute of Technology
Beijing, China

Huimin Ma 🆔
University of Science and Technology Beijing
Beijing, China

Yuxin Peng
Peking University
Beijing, China

Yue Liu
Beijing Institute of Technology
Beijing, China

Ran He
Institute of Automation, Chinese Academy
of Sciences
Beijing, China

ISSN 1865-0929   ISSN 1865-0937 (electronic)
Communications in Computer and Information Science
ISBN 978-981-19-5095-7   ISBN 978-981-19-5096-4 (eBook)
https://doi.org/10.1007/978-981-19-5096-4

This Springer imprint is published by the registered company Springer Nature Singapore Pte Ltd.
The registered company address is: 152 Beach Road, #21-01/04 Gateway East, Singapore 189721, Singapore

Preface

We were honored to organize the 17th Image and Graphics Technology and Application Conference (IGTA 2022). The conference was hosted by the Beijing Society of Image and Graphics and was held at the University of Science and Technology Beijing. Due to the COVID-19 pandemic, the conference was held online from April 23 to 24, 2022. It is a pity that we couldn't meet in person, but we were glad to see the successful continuation of this conference virtually.

IGTA is a professional conference and an important forum for image processing, computer graphics, and related topics, including but not limited to image analysis and understanding, computer vision and pattern recognition, data mining, virtual reality and augmented reality, and image technology applications. The theme of IGTA 2022 was "Cognitive Intelligence, Images, and Graphics". This year, we received submissions from a number of different countries and regions and the selection criterion was competitive. At least two reviewers reviewed each submission. After careful evaluation, 34% of the submissions (26 papers) were selected for oral or poster presentations.

The keynote speech, invited talks, and oral presentations of IGTA 2022 reflected the latest progress in the field of images and graphics. We believe that these provide a valuable reference for scientists and engineers with relevant interests.

As the conference chairs, we would like to thank our committee members and staff for all the hard work they have done for this conference under unprecedented difficulties. Thanks go to all the authors for their contributions and all the reviewers for their valuable suggestions. Finally, we would also like to thank our host, professors, and students from the University of Science and Technology Beijing for their tremendous support. We hope to see you face to face at IGTA 2023!

April 2022

Yongtian Wang
Huimin Ma

Organization

General Conference Chairs

Yongtian Wang   Beijing Institute of Technology, China
Huimin Ma   University of Science and Technology Beijing, China

Organizing Chairs

Yue Liu   Beijing Institute of Technology, China
Yongjin Liu   Tsinghua University, China
Lifang Wu   Beijing University of Technology, China
Bochao Zou   University of Science and Technology Beijing, China

Executive and Coordination Committee

Haibin Duan   Beihang University, China
Hua Huang   Beijing Normal University, China
Qingming Huang   University of Chinese Academy of Sciences, China
Xiangyang Ji   Tsinghua University, China
Chenglin Liu   Institute of Automation, Chinese Academy of Sciences, China
Yuxin Peng   Peking University, China
Weijun Yang   The First Research Institute of the Ministry of Public Security of P.R.C, China
Yao Zhao   Beijing Jiaotong University, China

Program Committee Chairs

Ran He   Institute of Automation, Chinese Academy of Sciences, China
Xucheng Yin   University of Science and Technology Beijing, China
Zhanyu Ma   Beijing University of Post and Telecommunications, China
Zhongke Wu   Beijing Normal University, China
Weitao Song   Beijing Institute of Technology, China

Research Committee Chairs

Xueming Li   Beijing University of Post and
                              Telecommunications, China
Xiaohui Liang   Beihang University, China
Jian Yang   Beijing Institute of Technology, China
Jing Dong   Institute of Automation, Chinese Academy of
                              Sciences, China
Fengjun Zhang   Institute of Software, Chinese Academy of
                              Sciences, China

Publicity and Exhibition Committee Chairs

Xiaoru Yuan   Peking University, China
Lei Yang   Communication University of China, China
Feng Lu   Beihang University, China
Xingce Wang   Beijing Normal University, China
Nan Ma   Beijing University of Technology, China
Jun Yan   Journal of Image and Graphics, China

Program Committee

Henry Been-Lirn Duh   La Trobe University, Australia
Takafumi Taketomi   NAIST, Japan
Jeremy M. Wolfe   Harvard Medical School, USA
Yi-Ping Hung   National Taiwan University, China
Youngho Lee   Mokpo National University, South Korea
Nobuchika Sakata   Osaka University, Japan
Seokhee Jeon   Kyung Hee University, South Korea
Xiaochun Cao   Institute of Information Engineering, CAS, China
Weiqun Cao   Beijing Forestry University, China
Kaichang Di   Aerospace Information Research Institute,
                              Chinese Academy of Sciences, China
Fuping Gan   Ministry of Land and Resources of the People's
                              Republic of China, China
Hongchuan Hou   The First Research Institute of the Ministry of
                              Public Security of P.R.C, China
Yan Jiang   Beijing Institute of Fashion Technology, China
Xueyou Li   National Surveying and Mapping Engineering
                              Technology Research Center, China
Huijie Zhao   Beijing University of Aeronautics and
                              Astronautics, China
Yi Chen   Beijing Technology and Business University,
                              China

Ke Lv	University of Chinese Academy of Sciences, China
Siwei Ma	Peking University, China
Mingzhi Cheng	Beijing Institute of Technology, China
Qingyuan Li	Chinese Academy of Surveying and Mapping, China
Bin Liao	North China Electric Power University, China
Liang Liu	Beijing University of Posts and Telecommunications, China
Yankui Sun	Tsinghua University, China
Yahui Wang	Beijing University of Graphic Communication, China
Yiding Wang	North China University of Technology, China
Cheng Yang	Communication University of China, China
Fengying Xie	Beihang University, China
Hengjin Wang	Tsinghua University, China
Yao Zhao	Beijing Jiaotong University, China
Tao Yang	Beijing Sweet Technology Co., Ltd., China
Guoqiang Yao	Beijing Film Academy, China
Jiazheng Yuan	Beijing Union University, China
Aiwu Zhang	Capital Normal University, China
Runmin Cong	Beijing Jiaotong University, China
Jingfan Fan	Beijing Institute of Technology, China
Xiangdi Han	Journal of Image and Graphics, China
Gao Huang	Tsinghua University, China
Huaibo Huang	Institute of Automation, Chinese Academy of Sciences, China
Yetao Huang	Beijing Fengjing Technology Co., Ltd., China
Fwng Li	China Academy of Space Technology, China
Sheng Li	Peking University, China
Xirong Li	Renmin University of China, China
Bo Meng	The First Research Institute of the Ministry of Public Security of P.R.C, China
Lifeng Ren	Global Saile (Beijing) Technology Co., Ltd., China
Wenqi Ren	Institute of Information Engineering, Chinese Academy of Sciences, China
Xinzhu Sang	Beijing University of Posts and Telecommunications, China
Xiaogang Shi	Beijing Xiaolong Technology Co., Ltd., China
Yong Song	Beijing Institute of Technology, China
Li Tan	Beijing Technology and Business University, China

Contents

Image Processing and Enhancement Techniques (Image Information Acquisition, Image/Video Coding, Image/Video Transmission, Image/Video Storage, Compression, Completion, Dehazing, Reconstruction and Display, etc.)

Multi-resolution Parallel Aggregation Network for Single Image Deraining

Man Qi and Yufeng Huang$^{(\boxtimes)}$

College of Electronic and Information Engineering, Shenyang Aerospace University,
Shenyang 110136, China
651595954@qq.com

Abstract. Single image deraining is an important preprocessing task, as rain streaks awfully reduce the image quality and hinder the subsequence outdoor multimedia issues. In this paper, we explore the multi-resolution representation for rain streaks through parallel hierarchical structure and multi-scale feature extraction and fusion, termed Multi-resolution Parallel Aggregation Network (MPA-Net) in end-to-end manner. Specially, considering the significant role of multi-resolution, we employ the first stage to capture the high-resolution features, progressively introduce high-to-low resolution streams to produce more stages, and then connect all stages in parallel. In each stage, Densely Connected Residual (DCR) block is involved to guide the feature extraction. Besides, Cross-Scale Feature Fusion (CSFF) is first introduced to receive and consolidate the correlated features from different scales followed with Squeeze-and-Excitation (SE) blocks, leading to rich the resolution representations. Extensive experiments demonstrate that our method outperforms the recent comparing approaches on the frequent-use synthetic and real-world datasets.

Keywords: Single image deraining · Multi-resolution parallel · Cross-Scale Feature Fusion

1 Introduction

Images taken from the rainy conditions significantly suffer from degradation, which surely subject to blurring, color distortion and content obstruction. The visibility poor quality severely effects the performance of subsequent multimedia applications. Image deraining thus has become a vital component in the vision tasks and attracts increasing attention in the multimedia area.

In general, the deraining purpose is to recover the clear background B from the obtained rainy image $O = B + R$ with the rain layer R. Since the background and rain layer are usually unknown, the deraining can be considered as a highly ill-posed problem theoretically. To make the problem be well solved, various algorithms have been designed for single image deraining, and previous researches can be mainly classified into two

This work was supported by Innovation project of College students (S202110143005, X202110143128).

categories, including model-based and data-driven methods. Along the model-based line, prior-based model approaches treat rain removal as an optimization problem and typical methods contain Gaussian Mixture Model (GMM) [1], Discriminative Sparse Coding (DSC) [2, 3], low-rank representation [4], image decomposition [5] and filter-based deraining approaches [6–9]. The model-based ways try to make prior and subjective hypotheses on rain streaks, while those methods perform well only in some specific conditions.

Another appealing solution is a data related driven method that considers the deraining question as a non-linear function and searches the suitable parameters to apart the rainy part from the background image [10]. Inspired by the deep learning, numerous data-driven learning methods have emerged for deraining and verified remarkable restoration performance. Fu et al. [11] first employ the related network with multi-layer convolutional neural network to get and remove the rain layer, and then introduce Deep Detail Network [12] that straightly wipe off the rain streaks by decreasing the mapping range. The RESCAN [13] presents a recurrent neural network and convolutional way to apply the contextual information for single image deraining. In [14], Progressive Resnet Network (PReNet) carries out the recursive computer to effectively produce the derained images progressively. Based on the recurrent network, the work of Spatial attentive network (SPANet) [15] is able to get the spatial contextual details and obtain the spatial related information in a local-to-global manner. Jiang et al. [16] explore the multi-scale collaborative to represent the rain streaks and hierarchical deep features. In [17], the convolution dictionary is employed to represent the rain streaks and a proximal gradient descent technique is utilized to simply the deraining model. The above deep learning-based strategies, however, have evident deficiencies in utilizing the comprehensive rain information and representations. Few efforts have been used to preserve the desired fine spatial details and strong contextual information.

In this paper, we proposed a novel parallel architecture namely Multi-resolution Parallel Aggregation Network (MPA-Net), that maintains the multi-resolution feature representations and minimizes the detailed loss for single image deraining. Our main contributions are summarized as follows.

We conduct an end-to-end MPA-Net to handle the single image deraining problem, which can generate a spatially-precise and detailed output by using a novel multi-resolution parallel feature extraction structure, while receiving and consolidating rich contextual information from different scales.

To better illustrate the rain features from different scales, Cross-Scale Feature Fusion (CSFF) is first constructed to effectively exchange and combine the cross scales information, so that the rain streaks distribution can be integrated to characterize in a collaborative manner.

Comprehensive experiments are performed on six challenging datasets (4 synthetic and 2 real-world datasets) and the deraining results demonstrate that our designed method outperforms existing state-of-the-art approaches.

2 Proposed Method

We briefly introduce the proposed MPA-Net, which can properly remove the rain streaks and maximally restore the details in the rainy images. The details of MPA-Net can be described include the overall architecture, the feature extraction and fusion modules, as well as the loss function.

2.1 Overall Architecture of MPA-Net

We design an end-to-end deraining network to restore rainy image using the multi-resolution parallel framework, which is composed of Densely Connected Residual (DCR) blocks and CSFF with Squeeze-and-Excitation (SE) blocks, as illustrated in Fig. 1. In detail, MPA-Net has a parallel multi-resolution structure that the first stage deals with the original scale, and the other two use strided convolutions to down-sample the original input image into the changed scales as 1/2 and 1/4. Next the DCR blocks are involved in each parallel stage to extract and transport the image features. Using the features from different scales, the CSFF then performs the deep feature extraction and fusion after concatenating the multi-resolution feature information. Following the CSFF, SE block is added to adaptively rescale channel-wise features and strengthen the feature hierarchy encoding quality.

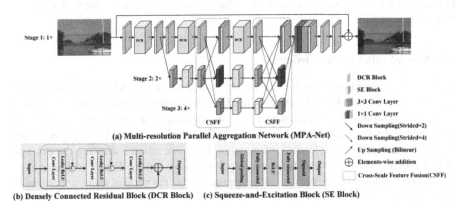

Fig. 1. The overview structure of the proposed MPA-Net framework.

Parallel Multi-resolution Pipeline is the main architecture of MPA-Net, that starts the original resolution as the first stage, progressively involves high-to-low resolution stages to produce more streams and connects all stages in parallel. Hence the later stage contains part of features from the previous stage and an extra low resolution one. As a novel feature extraction model, this structure is effectively used for extracting the fine-to-coarse features with semantically-richer as well as the coarse-to-fine one with spatially-precise feature representations. Let S_{sr} is the stage in the s th stage and r is the resolution index and the latter resolution is $1/2^{r-1}$ of the resolution of the first stage, and the 3 parallel example stages are given as follows:

$$
\begin{aligned}
S_{11} &\to S_{21} \to S_{31} \\
&\searrow S_{22} \to S_{32} \\
&\qquad\quad \searrow S_{33}
\end{aligned}
\tag{1}
$$

2.2 Feature Extraction and Aggregation Module

Our proposed MPA-Net contains two basic backbone blocks: (a) Densely Connected Residual (DCR) block is employed to lead the rain feature extraction and representation, (b) Squeeze-and-Excitation (SE) block is used to aggregate different scale characteristics after CSFF.

Densely Connected Residual Block [18, 19] applies the DenseNet [20] to direct receive and transport features through all the preceding layers and utilities the Residual Net [21] to ensure the features can transport to the deeper layers in a lower computer cost. Based on the advantages of DenseNet and Residual Net, DCR block can obtain a precise negative rain feature to map the corresponding rainy image. Specifically, each DCR block consists of three convolution layers followed by leaky-ReLU with $\alpha = 0.2$ as the activation function, shown in Fig. 1(b).

The Squeeze-and-Excitation Block [22] explores the spatial and channel components, seeking to improve the feature representation capability. As depicted in Fig. 1(c), the SE block is involved to effectively aggregate different scale characteristics. In squeeze step, a global embedding process carries out to exploit feature contextual information. Making full use of aggregated information, the excitation operation is applied to capture feature dependencies efficiently.

2.3 Cross-Scale Feature Fusion

As shown in deraining process, it is an efficient way to get various rain streak components by combining features from different scales. Existing deraining methods usually process each scale separately or just exchange information only in an adjacent manner. Apart from the mentioned methods, the proposed method explores a novel CSFF mechanism to fuse the comprehensive feature information. Here is a scheme showing the example of CSFF unit, which sets the third stage into 3 exchange blocks. Each CSFF unit has 3 parallel convolution layers with an exchange unit across the parallel units, which can be expressed as:

$$
\begin{array}{llll}
S_{31}^1 \searrow & \nearrow S_{31}^2 \searrow & \nearrow S_{31}^3 \searrow & \\
S_{32}^1 \rightarrow C_3^1 \rightarrow S_{32}^2 \rightarrow C_3^2 \rightarrow S_{32}^3 \rightarrow C_3^3 & & & \\
S_{33}^1 \nearrow & \searrow S_{33}^2 \nearrow & \searrow S_{33}^3 \nearrow &
\end{array}
\tag{2}
$$

where S_{sr}^b denotes the convolution layer in the b th block and the sth stage for the rth resolution, and the corresponding exchange unit is C_s^b.

The operation generated reliable feature representations by fusing the multi-scale features produced in the parallel stages. Mathematically, each output is a feature aggregation arriving multiple parallel streams, can be defined as:

$$
\begin{aligned}
s_1^3 &= f_{1\times1}^1\big(C\big(s_{1,2,0}, s_{2,2,2}, s_{3,2,2}\big); \eta\big) \\
s_2^3 &= f_{1\times1}^2\big(C\big(s_{2,2,0}, s_{1,2,1}, s_{3,2,1}\big); \mu\big) \\
s_3^3 &= f_{1\times1}^3\big(C\big(s_{1,2,2}, s_{2,2,1}, s_{3,2,0}\big); \tau\big)
\end{aligned}
\tag{3}
$$

where η, μ, τ are the hyperparameters of the network respectively, and C is the feature map.

According to the final fused features, we can formulate the derained result as:

$$F_{out} = f_{3\times3}\left(f_{1\times1}\left(C\left(s_1^3, f\left(s_2^3\right)_{\uparrow 2}, f\left(s_3^3\right)_{\uparrow 4}, se\right); \theta_1\right); \theta_2\right) + F_0 \qquad (4)$$

where se represents the SE block, $\uparrow$ means the up sampling. $f_{n\times n}(\cdot)$ denotes a convolution of size $n \times n$ and $\{\theta_1, \theta_2\}$ indicates the hyperparameters of the network.

2.4 Loss Function

Generally, the derained output of proposed MPA-Net should be equal to the clean image in certain level. Thus, we adopt two classical loss function provides an efficient way to refine the difference between the derained image and the corresponding clean ground-truth image in the per-pixel level. Besides using per-pixel loss, L_{SSIM} is used to value the structural similarity for the derained process. Finally, the total loss function can be formulated as:

$$L = L_1 + \lambda L_{SSIM} \qquad (5)$$

where λ is the weight parameter.

3 Experimental Results

In this section, we describe the experiment datasets and implementation message in details. Then comprehensive deraining researches are employed to demonstrate the effectiveness of the designed MPA-Net against the current deraining approaches. In addition, ablation studies are conducted to validate the efficiency of our designed model.

3.1 Experiment Settings

Datasets. We carry out rain removal experiments on four updated synthetic datasets: Rain200L/H [23], Rain800 [24], and Rain1400 [12], with numerous rain streaks of diverse sizes, shapes and directions. Besides, some real-world data are collected to assess the presentation of deraining and two related datasets are involved: the first one (called SPA-Data) that the rainy image is real and its ground truth is obtained by human labeling and multi-frame fusion [15], and the other with 167 rainy images collected by Internet. The detailed descriptions are tabulated in Table 1, together with the synthetic and real-world datasets.

Table 1. Datasets description. Values indicate the number of clean/rainy image pairs.

Datasets	Training set	Testing set	Type
Rain200L	1,800	200	Synthetic
Rain200H	1,800	200	Synthetic
Rain800	700	100	Synthetic
Rain1400	12,600	1400	Synthetic
SPA-Data	638,492	1000	Real-world
Internet-Data	0	167	Real-world

Setting. The detailed architecture and parameter settings of the proposed MPA-Net are depicted in Fig. 1 using Pytorch framework. In MPA-Net, the parallel stage number is 3 with the channel dimensions of 32, 64 and 128 at the corresponding resolutions as 1, 1/2 and 1/4, respectively. In the training process, we randomly select 64×64 patch pairs from the training datasets as input, and the loss function weight λ is 0.2. To accelerate the training process, Adam optimization is applied with a batch size of 16, as well as the initial learning rate is 1×10^{-3}, and then multiplied by 0.1 after every 25 epochs. Our model is trained with 200 epochs for the Rain200H, Rain200L, and Rain800 datasets, 100 epochs for Rain1400 datasets and 25 epochs for SPA-Data datasets. All the comparing testing experiments perform with the same datasets and hardware environment on the NVIDIA Tesla V100 GPU (16G).

3.2 Results on Synthetic Datasets

We compare our method with other five state-of-the-art image deraining methods, including RESCAN [13], PReNet [14], SPANet [15], MSPFN [16], and RCD-Net [17]. According to the ground truth in synthetic datasets, we perform the quantitative comparisons using Peak Signal to Noise Ratio (PSNR) and Structural SIMilarity index (SSIM). As shown in the Table 2, our proposed method gets the highest values both in PSNR and SSIM, which reflect the excellent performance and robustness of MPA-Net. The notable increasing scores in Rain200H and Rain800 reveal that our model can properly restore the rainy images especially in the heavy rain with various rainy conditions.

Besides the quantitative results, we further present several challenging examples for visual observation comparisons in Fig. 2. As displayed, the RESCAN leaves too many rain streaks in the derained images, particularly in the heavy rain condition. Clearly, PReNet, SPANet and MSPFN can remove the rain streaks in most of rain cases, while there are still some rain left in the distant or complex sceneries. By observing zoomed parts of image, the main drawbacks of RCDNet are that it tends to blur the contents and fails to reconstruct the scene detail information, and these defects can also be found in the above deraining methods. In contrast, our proposed MPA-Net can deal with majority of rain streaks in diverse rain distribution with complex background. In addition, another benefit can be found is being good at restoring the detailed structure information.

Table 2. Quantitative results evaluate of average PSNR and SSIM metrics on five benchmark datasets.

Datasets	Rain200L	Rain200H	Rain800	Rain1400	SPA-Data
Metrics	PSNR/SSIM				
Input	26.70/0.8438	13.07/0.3733	22.55/0.6850	25.24/0.8097	34.15/0.9269
RESCAN	36.94/0.9812	26.62/0.8415	24.09/0.8412	32.03/0.9314	38.11/0.9707
PReNet	36.28/0.9793	27.64/0.8846	22.83/0.7905	32.55/0.9459	40.16/0.9816
SPANet	35.60/0.9744	26.32/0.8581	24.37/0.8618	29.85/0.9148	40.24/0.9811
MSPFN	36.43/0.9810	27.78/0.8993	25.35/0.8567	32.80/0.9321	39.95/0.9768
RCD-Net	35.28/0.9710	26.18/0.8357	24.59/0.8216	33.04/0.9472	41.47/0.9834
Ours	**38.65/0.9845**	**28.16/0.9042**	**26.33/0.8760**	**33.68/0.9579**	**43.02/0.9885**

3.3 Results on Real-World Datasets

For practical use, we conduct additional comparisons against other deraining related algorithms on the mentioned two real-world rainy datasets. Table 2 in the last column and Fig. 3(a) compare the results on SPA-Data of all competing methods visually and quantitatively. As the natural image are more complex, all the competing methods leave some rain streaks even in the less rain streaks condition. As expected in the SPA-Data datasets, our method still exhibits remarkable performance with the better quantitative values and less rain streaks left.

Furthermore, we choose other two challenging samples from Internet-Data. For fair comparison, all the methods employ the pre-trained model trained on the Rain200H dataset to evaluate. As shown in Fig. 3(b), the rainy picture has complicated spatial space and content with heavy rainy condition. t, all the competing methods fail to remove the rain streaks far from the camera in the complex real rainy scenarios. Zooming the color

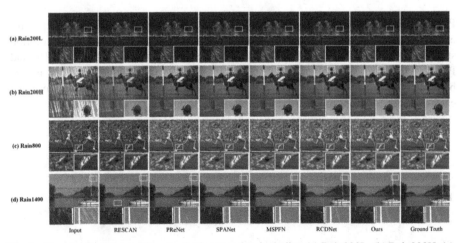

Fig. 2. Visual comparison of four synthetic examples, including (a) Rain200L, (b) Rain200H, (c) Rain800, and (d) Rain1400.

boxes, the other methods loss the details and blur the scene to certain extent. As the various light environment in Fig. 3(c), the above deraining algorithms fail to figure out the rain streaks from the complex surrounding background. It can be observed that the proposed method significantly competes others in removing the majority of rain streaks while preserving image details even in the dark surrounding and light effecting.

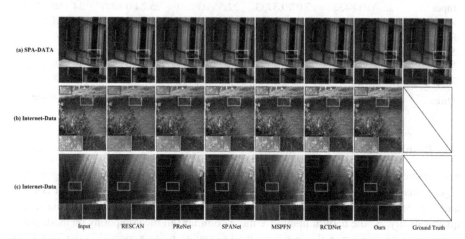

Fig. 3. Visual comparison of all the competing methods on two real-world datasets, including SPA-Data (a) and Internet-Data (b, c).

3.4 Ablation Studies

We study the main component impacts and parameter choices on the final performance. All the following ablation studies are completed in the same situation using the Rain200H dataset.

Parallel Multi-resolution Stages Number. To investigate the different number influences, we implement experiments on different numbers of parallel multi-resolution stages. From the Table 3, the increased parallel stages can lead to higher SSIM and PSNR, which bring a total gain of 2.15 dB and 0.0569 over the one stage that means better deraining performances. To balance the model performances and memory, we choose stages = 3 for our MPA-Net.

Table 3. Ablation study on different number of parallel multi-resolution stages.

Metrics	Stage = 1	Stage = 2	Stage = 3
PSNR/SSIM	26.05/0.8473	27.69/0.8850	**28.16/0.9042**

Feature Extraction and Aggregation Module. We analysis the effect of feature extraction and aggregation module that consist of DCR and SE blocks. The baseline module is constructed by using convolution layers in series. As displayed in Table 4, the greatest performance can be realized by employing DCR and SE blocks both, which can verify its effectiveness in the rain removal tasks.

Table 4. Ablation study on feature extraction and aggregation module.

Modules	M_1	M_2	M_3
Basic block	✓		
DCR block		✓	✓
SE block			✓
PSNR/SSIM	27.74/0.8991	27.95/0.9013	**28.16/0.9042**

Feature Fusion Strategies. We further perform an ablation analysis on feature fusion mechanism and three feature fusion methods as follows: (a) **W/O scale exchange** is no exchange between multi-resolution stages. (b) **adjacent-scale exchange** is only exchange between two adjacent stages. (c) **cross-scale exchange** is our designed method that fuses the features from all the stages. In general, Fig. 4 provides the visual and quantitative deraining results of three stated feature fusion strategies. As shown in Fig. 4(c), the zoomed color boxes perform better in rain removal, texture restoration and less artifact. The evaluation criteria can also reflect the CSFF get the better results under the following pictures.

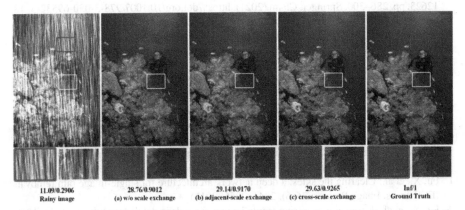

11.09/0.2906	28.76/0.9012	29.14/0.9170	29.63/0.9265	Inf/1
Rainy image	(a) w/o scale exchange	(b) adjacent-scale exchange	(c) cross-scale exchange	Ground Truth

Fig. 4. Quantitative and quantitative comparison of different feature fusion strategies, with the explanation of PSNR/SSIM in the bottom of derained images.

4 Conclusion

In this paper, we propose a multi-resolution parallel aggregation network (MPA-Net) to handle the single image deraining. An original multi-resolution parallel architecture is first utilized to extract and aggregate the multi-scale features, so that the complementary parallel streams are dedicated to spatially-precise generating and provide better contextualized features. In MPA-Net, DCR block is involved to explore the feature extraction and fully propagation. In addition, an innovative CSFF mechanism is introduced to realize comprehensive information exchange, so that the features across multi-resolution stages are progressively fused together for improved representation learning. Experimental results on synthetic and real-world rainy images both demonstrate that our method outperforms other state-of-the-art approaches considerably.

References

1. Li, Y., et al.: Rain streak removal using layer priors. In: Proceedings of the IEEE Conference on Computer Vision and Pattern Recognition, pp. 2736–2744 (2016)
2. Lei, J., et al.: An Image Rain Removal algorithm based on the depth of field and sparse coding. In: 24th International Conference on Pattern Recognition (ICPR), pp. 2368–2373 (2018)
3. Zhang, H., Patel, V.M.: Convolutional sparse and low-rank coding-based rain streak removal. In: IEEE Winter Conference on Applications of Computer Vision (WACV), pp. 1259–1267 (2017)
4. Zhang, L., Zuo, W.: Image restoration: from sparse and low-rank priors to deep priors [lecture notes]. IEEE Sig. Process. Mag. **34**(5), 172–179 (2017)
5. Lian, Q., et al.: Single image rain removal using image decomposition and a dense network. IEEE/CAA J. Automatica Sin. **6**(6), 1428–1437 (2019)
6. Chen, X., Huang, Y., Xu, L.: Multi-scale attentive residual dense network for single image rain removal. In: Ishikawa, H., Liu, C.-L., Pajdla, T., Shi, J. (eds.) ACCV 2020. LNCS, vol. 12623, pp. 286–300. Springer, Cham (2021). https://doi.org/10.1007/978-3-030-69532-3_18
7. Wang, F.L., et al.: When a conventional filter meets deep learning: basis composition learning on image filters. ArXiv, abs/2203.00258 (2022)
8. Zheng, X., Liao, Y., Guo, W., Fu, X., Ding, X.: Single-image-based rain and snow removal using multi-guided filter. In: Lee, M., Hirose, A., Hou, Z.-G., Kil, R.M. (eds.) ICONIP 2013. LNCS, vol. 8228, pp. 258–265. Springer, Heidelberg (2013). https://doi.org/10.1007/978-3-642-42051-1_33
9. Zhang, X., et al.: Rain removal in video by combining temporal and chromatic properties. In: 2006 IEEE International Conference on Multimedia and Expo, pp. 461–464 (2006)
10. Chen, X., Huang, Y., Xu, L.: Multi-scale hourglass hierarchical fusion network for single image deraining. In: IEEE/CVF Conference on Computer Vision and Pattern Recognition Workshops (CVPRW), pp. 872–879 (2021)
11. Fu, X., et al.: Clearing the skies: a deep network architecture for single-image rain removal. IEEE Trans. Image Process. **26**(6), 2944–2956 (2017)
12. Fu, X., et al.: Removing rain from single images via a deep detail network, pp. 1715–1723 (2017)
13. Li, X., Wu, J., Lin, Z., Liu, H., Zha, H.: Recurrent squeeze-and-excitation context aggregation net for single image deraining. In: Ferrari, V., Hebert, M., Sminchisescu, C., Weiss, Y. (eds.) ECCV 2018. LNCS, vol. 11211, pp. 262–277. Springer, Cham (2018). https://doi.org/10.1007/978-3-030-01234-2_16

14. Ren, D., et al.: Progressive image deraining networks: a better and simpler baseline. In: Proceedings of the IEEE Conference on Computer Vision and Pattern Recognition, pp. 3937–3946 (2019)
15. Wang, T., et al.: Spatial attentive single-image deraining with a high quality real rain dataset. In: Proceedings of the IEEE Conference on Computer Vision and Pattern Recognition, pp. 12270–12279 (2019)
16. Jiang, K., et al.: Multi-scale progressive fusion network for single image deraining, pp. 8346–8355 (2020)
17. Wang, H., et al.: A model-driven deep neural network for single image rain removal. In: Proceedings of the IEEE/CVF Conference on Computer Vision and Pattern Recognition, pp. 3103–3112 (2020)
18. Park, Y., et al.: MARA-Net: single image deraining network with multi-level connection and adaptive regional attention. arXiv preprint arXiv:2009.13990 (2020)
19. Wei, Y., et al.: A coarse-to-fine multi-stream hybrid deraining network for single image deraining. In: 2019 IEEE International Conference on Data Mining (ICDM), pp. 628–637 (2019)
20. Huang, G., et al.: Densely connected convolutional networks, pp. 2261–2269 (2017)
21. He, K., et al.: Deep residual learning for image recognition, pp. 770–778 (2016)
22. Hu, J., Shen, L., Sun, G.: Squeeze-and-excitation networks, pp. 7132–7141 (2018)
23. Yang, W., et al.: Deep joint rain detection and removal from a single image, pp. 1685–1694 (2017)
24. Zhang, H., Sindagi, V., Patel, V.M.: Image de-raining using a conditional generative adversarial network. IEEE Trans. Circ. Syst. Video Technol. 30(11), 3943–3956 (2020)

Multi-scale Bézier Filter Based Infrared and Visual Image Fusion

Yu Zhang[1], Jianjun Shen[2], Sheng Guo[1], Leisheng Zhong[3], Shunli Zhang[4], and Xiangzhi Bai[1(✉)]

[1] School of Astronautics, Beihang University, Beijing 100191, China
uzeful@163.com, {gsx,jackybxz}@buaa.edu.cn
[2] Department of Electronic Engineering, Tsinghua University, Beijing 100084, China
sjj20@mails.tsinghua.edu.cn
[3] Naval Research Institute, Shanghai 200436, China
[4] School of Software Engineering, Beijing Jiaotong University, Beijing 100044, China
slzhang@bjtu.edu.cn

Abstract. In this study, we have proposed a multi-scale Bézier filter based method for infrared and visual image fusion. Specifically, we first exploit our developed multi-scale Bézier filter to decompose the infrared image and visual image into a set of multi-scale bright feature maps, multi-scale dark feature maps and a base image, respectively. Then, each scale of bright feature maps and dark feature maps are respectively fused by selecting their elementwise-maximums, then amplified by a scale-related coefficient, and finally integrated as a fused bright feature map and a fused dark feature map. Afterwards, the two base images are fused by averaging their mean values and selecting the elementwise-maximums of their large-scale features. Finally, the fusion image is produced by integrating the fused bright feature map, dark feature map and base image. Extensive experiments demonstrate that our method significantly outperforms the state-of-the-art image fusion methods from both qualitative and quantitative aspects.

Keywords: Infrared and visual images · Image fusion · Multi-scale Bézier filter · Bright feature map · Dark feature map

1 Introduction

Multiple imaging sensors could capture different perspectives of the supervised circumstance, and fusion of the captured multiple images is helpful for fully understanding the corresponding circumstance [1, 2]. For example, multi-modal medical image fusion can help surgeons accurately diagnose diseases [3, 4], and multi-focus image fusion is able to generate a clear all-in-focus image [5, 6]. As for infrared and visual image fusion, it can produce a fusion image that reflects the comprehensive conditions of the supervised circumstance in all daytime, thus has been widely deployed in both the civil and military surveillance systems [7–9]. Therefore, developing new infrared and visual image fusion methods are critical and useful for both civil and military tasks.

Y. Wang et al. (Eds.): IGTA 2022, CCIS 1611, pp. 14–25, 2022.
https://doi.org/10.1007/978-981-19-5096-4_2

In recent years, many image fusion methods have been proposed for fusing the infrared and visual images, and usually can be classified in two categories, *i.e.*, spatial-domain methods and transform-domain methods. The spatial-domain methods firstly segment the source images into multiple regions, and then combine the salient regions together to achieve the fusion image [5, 10, 11]. This kind of methods can hardly achieve accurate segmentation result, thus often yield unsatisfactory fusion effect. While the transform-domain methods are most popular amongst the infrared and visual image fusion methods proposed in the past two decades, such as the pyramid based [12], wavelet based [3] and sparse-representation based methods [13]. These methods extract the salient features from the infrared image and visual image in some domain, and then the salient features in the transform domain, which correspond to the sharp features in the spatial domain, are integrated together to produce the fusion image. Their fusion images are usually pleasant for the perception of human vision systems. However, the fusion images of these methods often suffer from blurring effect or losing much visual image information [14], which would impact the visual quality of the fusion images. More recently, many deep-learning (especially convolutional neural network, CNN) based image fusion methods are proposed. In these methods, CNN is used to extract the image features and reconstruct the fused image [2, 8, 15, 16]. Even though the CNN based methods have achieved great success in the field of image fusion, many of these methods would yield low-contrast defect or other kinds of defects. Besides the above methods, Zhang et al. proposed a quadtree and Bézier interpolation based infrared and visual image fusion method [7], which mainly extracts the salient bright objects from the infrared image and then inject them to the visual image to generate its fusion image. However, there are both bright features and dark features in an image, the fusion image of this method could not reflect the dark features of the infrared image and show the bright features of the infrared image when the corresponding areas of the visual image are over-exposed.

Therefore, in this study, we have further developed a more effective Bézier filter, which is able to extract both bright and dark features from an image. To be specific, the Bézier filter smooths the original image alternatively with the local minimums and local maximums, then the bright and dark features of the image can be obtained from the difference of the filtered image and original image. Furthermore, we propose a multi-scale Bézier filter based image fusion method for fusing the infrared and visual images. The proposed method first extracts the different scales of bright and dark feature maps and generates a base image respectively from the infrared image and visual image, then respectively fuses the salient (bright and dark) features and base images of the infrared and visual images with two different fusion rules, and finally produces the fusion image by combining the fused feature maps and base image together. Owing to our effective Bézier filter, the proposed method can well extract the salient dark and bright features both from the infrared and visual images, and produce one informative fusion image. Extensive experiments verify that our method not only outperforms the state-of-the-art (SOTA) transform-domain image fusion methods, but also can beat the SOTA deep-learning based methods.

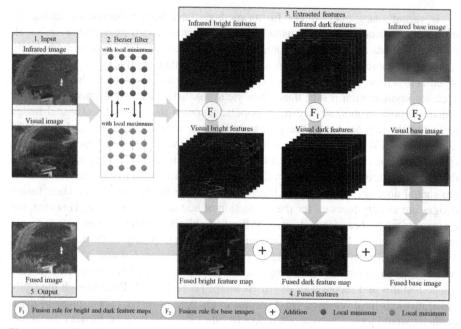

Fig. 1. Flowchart of our proposed multi-scale Bézier filter based infrared and visual image fusion method.

2 Proposed Method

In this study, we propose a novel infrared and visual image fusion method based on the multi-scale Bézier filter. The proposed method mainly consists of four procedures: First, the infrared and visual images are gradually filtered by different scale of Bézier filter, meanwhile the corresponding scale of bright and dark feature maps are extracted respectively from the infrared image and visual image and the final scale of filtered infrared image and visual image are respectively taken as their base images. Second, the bright feature maps and dark feature maps of the infrared image and those of the visual image are fused by selecting their elementwise maximums and enhanced by a scale related coefficient. Third, the base image of the infrared image and that of the visual image are fused by averaging their means and selecting their elementwise-maximum residuals. Finally, the fusion image is generated by integrating the fused bright feature map, dark feature map, and base image. For better understanding our method, we have illustrated the flowchart in Fig. 1.

2.1 Multi-scale Bézier Filter

As is known, there exist bright features and dark features in an image, such as the bright person in the infrared image and the dark hole in the roof corner of the visual image in Fig. 1. In general, smoothing an image and then subtracting the smoothed image from the original image is an effective way to extract the image's bright and dark features [17].

Ideally, the filtered smooth image should remove the bright spots and fill the dark holes in the original image, so that the bright and dark features can be effectively extracted by subtracting the filtered image from the original image.

In [7], Zhang et al. have demonstrated that the Bézier filter is an effective image filter to extract the bright features from the image, but they did not adopt it to extract the dark features and did not extend it to multiple scales. Therefore, we have further developed a multi-scale Bézier filter to solving the problems encountered in [7], the construction procedures of our multi-scale Bézier filter is introduced as follows.

The Bézier filter is essentially a local interpolation operator performed on an image patch, and can be expressed as:

$$Q(u, v) = UMPM^T V^T, \tag{1}$$

where (u, v) denotes the position of the interpolated point, which is represented by the interpolation ratio ranged between 0 and 1. (U, V) denotes the position-related interpolation coefficient, M denotes the constant interpolation coefficient matrix. P denotes the gray values of 16×16 uniformly distributed control points on the image patch. Q denotes the filtered image patch. Specifically, $U = [u^3, u^2, u^1, u^0], V = [v^3, v^2, v^1, v^0]$,

$$M = \begin{pmatrix} -1 & 3 & -3 & 1 \\ 3 & -6 & 3 & 0 \\ -3 & 3 & 0 & 0 \\ 1 & 0 & 0 & 0 \end{pmatrix}, P = \begin{bmatrix} p_{11} & p_{12} & p_{13} & p_{14} \\ p_{21} & p_{22} & p_{23} & p_{24} \\ p_{31} & p_{32} & p_{33} & p_{34} \\ p_{41} & p_{42} & p_{43} & p_{44} \end{bmatrix}.$$

In our study, we exploit the 4×4 control points to reconstruct various sizes (*i.e.*, $(3m + 1) \times (3m + 1)$) of image patches, where m determines the smoothing scale of the Bézier filter. Here we set $m = 2i - 1$, where i denotes the current scale of the Bézier filter. Accordingly, the ith-scale Bézier filter interpolates the gray values of the 4×4 control points to an image patch of size $(6i - 2) \times (6i - 2)$, and $u = v = [0, 1/(6i - 1), ..., (6i - 2)/(6i - 1), 1]$. To effectively smooth the input image, instead of using the original gray values of the 4×4 control points on the image patch, we first reconstruct the image patch with the local minimum gray values of the 4×4 control points to remove the bright spots, then further reconstruct the image patch with the local maximum gray values of the updated 4×4 control points to fill the black holes. The pair of local minimum reconstruction and local maximum reconstruction with Bézier interpolation defines a scale of Bézier filter, and the radius of local region for searching minimum and maximum gray values is set to m in this study.

Let us denote the function of Bézier filter with local minimum gray values by $f_{Bezier,min}(\cdot)$ and that with local maximum gray values by $f_{Bezier,max}(\cdot)$, then smoothing an image patch with our Bézier filter can be expressed as:

$$B_f = f_{Bezier,max}\left(f_{Bezier,min}(B)\right), \tag{2}$$

where B and B_f denote the original input image patch and filtered image patch, respectively. Then, the salient features of the input image patch can be obtained by subtracting the filtered image patch B_f from the input image patch B, and the positive part of $(B-B_f)$ corresponds to the bright features, and the negative part corresponds to the dark features. A demonstration example of the proposed Bézier filter performed on an infrared image

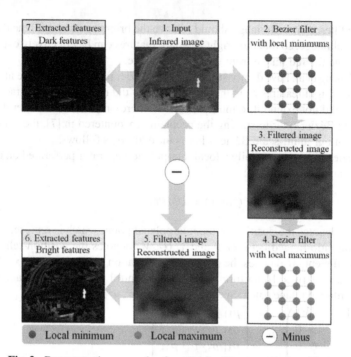

Fig. 2. Demonstration example of our Bézier filter on an infrared image.

is illustrated in Fig. 2, and it shows our proposed Bézier filter could well extract the bright and dark features from the original image.

Afterwards, we extend the Bézier filter to multi scales by iteratively applying the pair of Bézier filter with local minimum gray values and Bézier filter with local maximum gray values according to Eq. (3), and different scales of bright and dark features can be simultaneously extracted from the difference of every two continuous filtered image patches according to Eq. (4) and Eq. (5). Finally, the last scale of filtered image patch is taken as the base image of the original image patch, as shown in Eq. (6).

$$B_i = f_{Bezier,\max}\left(f_{Bezier,\min}\left(B_{(i-1)}\right)\right), \qquad (3)$$

where i denotes the scale of Bézier filter, and i is increased from 1 to n one by one. B_i denotes the ith-scale filtered image patch and B_0 indicates the original image patch B.

$$F_{i,b} = \max\left(B_{(i-1)} - B_i, 0\right), \qquad (4)$$

$$F_{i,d} = -\min\left(B_{(i-1)} - B_i, 0\right), \qquad (5)$$

where $F_{i,b}$ and $F_{i,d}$ are the ith-scale bright feature map and dark feature map of B, respectively.

$$B_{base} = B_n, \qquad (6)$$

where B_{base} denotes the base image of the original image patch B.

2.2 Multi-scale Bézier Filter Based Infrared and Visual Image Fusion

In the previous subsection, we have only taken an image patch for example. As for filtering a whole image, we first resize the original image to $(3km + 1) \times (3lm + 1)$, then decompose the input image to $k \times l$ boundary-overlapped image patches of size $(3m + 1) \times (3m + 1)$, afterwards perform Bézier filtering on each patch, and finally resize the filtered image back to the original size. Further, the current scale of bright and dark feature maps are extracted by subtracting the filtered image from the original image. Following the above method, we have extracted the multiple scales of bright feature maps (denoted by $F_{i,b}^{inf}$) and dark feature maps (denoted by $F_{i,d}^{inf}$) from the infrared image and multiple scales of bright feature maps (denoted by $F_{i,b}^{vis}$) and dark feature maps (denoted by $F_{i,d}^{vis}$) from the visual image, and also generated two base images of the infrared and visual images (denoted by I_{base}^{inf} and I_{base}^{vis}, respectively). Then, we further fuse the high-frequency bright and dark feature maps, and low-frequency base images of the infrared and visual images following two different fusion rules.

As for high-frequency features, we directly fuse the bright and dark feature maps of the infrared and visual images by selecting their elementwise-maximums as:

$$
\begin{cases}
F_{i,b}^{fuse} = \max\left(F_{i,b}^{inf}, F_{i,b}^{vis}\right) \\
F_{i,d}^{fuse} = \max\left(F_{i,d}^{inf}, F_{i,d}^{vis}\right)
\end{cases},
\tag{7}
$$

Like other feature extractors, the proposed Bézier filter cannot extract the entire bright and dark details from the source images, thus we have further enhanced the fused bright and dark feature maps by multiplying each scale of feature maps by a scale related weight:

$$
\begin{cases}
F_{b}^{fuse} = \sum_{i=1}^{n} w_i \cdot F_{i,b}^{fuse} \\
F_{d}^{fuse} = \sum_{i=1}^{n} w_i \cdot F_{i,d}^{fuse}
\end{cases},
\tag{8}
$$

where w_i denotes the scale related weight for the ith scale of bright and dark feature maps. In general, the small scales of feature maps usually correspond to the informative and useful details, thus should be assigned with large weights. In this study, we set $w_i = \zeta^{(n-i)}$, where ζ is a constant no smaller than 1.

As for the low-frequency base images, there might still exist large scales of bright or dark features in them. Thus, we further decompose the base image of the infrared image and that of the visual image in three parts:

$$
\begin{cases}
I_{base}^{inf} = mI_{base}^{inf} + \max\left(I_{base}^{inf} - mI_{base}^{inf}, 0\right) + \min\left(I_{base}^{inf} - mI_{base}^{inf}, 0\right) \\
I_{base}^{vis} = mI_{base}^{vis} + \max\left(I_{base}^{vis} - mI_{base}^{vis}, 0\right) + \min\left(I_{base}^{vis} - mI_{base}^{vis}, 0\right)
\end{cases},
\tag{9}
$$

where mI_{base}^{inf} and mI_{base}^{vis} are the mean of I_{base}^{inf} and that of I_{base}^{vis}, $\max\left(I_{base}^{inf} - mI_{base}^{inf}, 0\right)$ and $\max\left(I_{base}^{vis} - mI_{base}^{vis}, 0\right)$ are the large-scale bright features of I_{base}^{inf} and that of I_{base}^{vis}, $\min\left(I_{base}^{inf} - mI_{base}^{inf}, 0\right)$ and $\min\left(I_{base}^{vis} - mI_{base}^{vis}, 0\right)$ are the large-scale dark features of I_{base}^{inf} and that of I_{base}^{vis}. Then, we fuse the three parts of I_{base}^{inf} and I_{base}^{vis} as:

$$
\begin{cases}
mI_{base}^{fuse} = \left(mI_{base}^{inf} + mI_{base}^{vis}\right)/2 \\
bI_{base}^{fuse} = \max\left(\max\left(I_{base}^{inf} - mI_{base}^{inf}, 0\right), \max\left(I_{base}^{vis} - mI_{base}^{vis}, 0\right)\right), \\
dI_{base}^{fuse} = \min\left(\min\left(I_{base}^{inf} - mI_{base}^{inf}, 0\right), \min\left(I_{base}^{vis} - mI_{base}^{vis}, 0\right)\right)
\end{cases} \tag{10}
$$

where mI_{base}^{fuse}, bI_{base}^{fuse} and dI_{base}^{fuse} are respectively the fused mean, bright feature map and dark feature map of I_{base}^{inf} and I_{base}^{vis}.

Next, the base images of the infrared image and visual image are fused by merging the above three parts:

$$
I_{base}^{fuse} = mI_{base}^{fuse} + bI_{base}^{fuse} + dI_{base}^{fuse}. \tag{11}
$$

Finally, the fusion image generated by our proposed method can be obtained by integrating the fused low-frequency base image and fused high-frequency bright and dark feature maps:

$$
I^{fuse} = I_{base}^{fuse} + F_b^{fuse} - F_d^{fuse}. \tag{12}
$$

2.3 Parameter Settings

There are two unknown parameters in the proposed method, *i.e.*, the number of scales n and base of the enhancement coefficient ζ. In this study, we have adopted the grid search method to find the optimal pair of n (ranging from 1 to 6 with step equal to 1) and ζ (ranging from 1 to 1.2 with step equal to 0.01) that maximizes the multi-scale structural similarity metric [18]. We obtained that the optimal pair of n and ζ are 6 and 1.05. All the experiments are performed with the same parameter settings (*i.e.*, $n = 6$ and $\zeta = 1.05$), and the experimental results validate the parameter settings here are effective for infrared and visual image fusion.

3 Experimental Results and Discussions

In order to demonstrate the advantages of our proposed infrared and visual image method, we have compared it with five SOTA image fusion methods on a commonly used infrared and visual image dataset. The detailed experimental settings, results and discussions are introduced in the following subsections.

3.1   Experimental Settings

The experimental settings of this study are briefly described follows. First, we have chosen twenty pairs of commonly used infrared and visual images in TNO dataset [19] as our testing image sets, as shown in Fig. 3. Second, we have selected five SOTA infrared and visual image fusion methods as our comparison methods, including the guided-filter based method (GFF) [20], hybrid multi-scale-decomposition based method (HMSD) [14], Laplacian-pyramid and sparse-representation based method (LPSR) [13], GAN based method (FusionGAN) [8], and also the recently proposed deep-learning based method (U2Fusion) [15].

Afterwards, the six methods are respectively evaluated by the qualitative method and quantitative method. Specifically, the qualitative evaluation method is to visually compare the fusion results produced by different image fusion methods. As for the quantitative evaluation method, we have selected six quantitative metrics to quantify the quality of the fusion images achieved by different methods. The six quantitative metrics are entropy (E), spatial frequency (SF) [21], average absolute gradient (AG) [22], standard deviation (STD), visual information fidelity (VIFF) [23] and a new structural similarity (NSSIM) [18]. The larger values of all the six metrics indicate the better performance of the corresponding image fusion method.

Fig. 3. Infrared and visual image dataset used in this study. The images in the first row and third row are the infrared images, and the images in the second row and fourth row are the corresponding visual images.

3.2   Qualitative Evaluation Results

Figure 4 and Fig. 5 show two comparison examples of the six image fusion methods. In Fig. 4, the infrared and visual images were captured under normal-light circumstance. The optimal fusion image should mainly combine the different scales of salient bright features of the infrared image and the rich bright and dark features of the visual image. It can be seen from Fig. 4 that GFF fails to integrate most bright features of the infrared image into its fusion image. HMSD and LPSR do not inject the large-scale bright features of the infrared image into their fusion images (see the building area in the red bounding boxes of Fig. 4(d) and 4(e)). The fusion image of FusionGAN has lost much textures of the visual image and shows the poorest visual effect amongst all the six methods. U2Fusion has well integrated the salient features of the infrared and visual images into its fusion image, but the contrast of its fusion image is relatively low compared to the

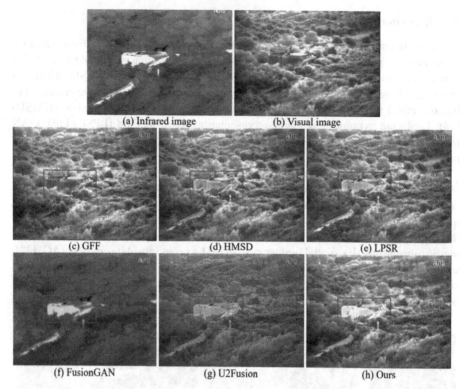

(a) Infrared image   (b) Visual image

(c) GFF   (d) HMSD   (e) LPSR

(f) FusionGAN   (g) U2Fusion   (h) Ours

Fig. 4. First comparison example of different image fusion methods. (Color figure online)

infrared image, visual image and those fusion images of GFF, HMSD, LPSR and ours. Finally, our fusion image has successfully integrated different scales of bright features of the infrared image and the rich details of the visual image, and demonstrated the best visual effect amongst all the fusion images.

In Fig. 5, the infrared and visual images were captured in the daytime and the sky area of the visual image is over-exposed. The ideal fusion image of this pair of infrared and visual images is to integrate the bright features (including those around the sky area) of the infrared image and the visual details of the visual image. It can be seen from Fig. 5 that GFF fails to fuse the bright person regions of the infrared image to its fusion image. HMSD and LPSR have well fused the infrared and visual images in most areas, but failed to inject some bright tree branches of the infrared image (see the area in the red bounding boxes of Fig. 5(d) and 5(e)) into their fusion images. Similar to Fig. 4(f), FusionGAN does not preserve the rich textures of the visual image to its fusion image and the global contrast of its fusion image is relatively low compared to the source images and other methods' results. U2Fusion has integrated most textures of the infrared and visual images into its fusion image, but the contrast of its fusion image is slightly low compared to the source images. Finally, it can be seen from Fig. 5(h) that our fusion image has not only well integrated the bright tree branches of the infrared image, but also obtained good contrast.

(a) Infrared image   (b) Visual image

(c) GFF   (d) HMSD   (e) LPSR

(f) FusionGAN   (g) U2Fusion   (h) Ours

Fig. 5. Second comparison example of different image fusion methods. (Color figure online)

These two comparison examples can validate the fact that our method is able to effectively fuse the salient features of the infrared and visual images into one fusion image and it outperforms the current SOTA image fusion methods. Next, we will further verify the advantages of our method by the quantitative evaluation method.

Table 1. Quantitative evaluation results of different image fusion methods.

Metrics	GFF [20]	HMSD [14]	LPSR [13]	FusionGAN [8]	U2Fusion [15]	Ours
E	6.82	6.91	6.64	6.36	6.75	**6.95**
SF	10.67	11.78	9.57	5.77	11.36	**12.50**
AG	9.13	10.26	9.87	5.05	10.69	**10.94**
STD	37.78	39.93	**43.41**	26.01	31.56	40.33
VIFF	0.25	0.40	0.41	0.18	0.58	**0.61**
NSSIM	0.86	0.93	0.93	0.73	0.92	**0.96**

Note: Value in bold font and value with underline in each row indicate the best and second-best performance, respectively

3.3 Quantitative Evaluation Results

As is known, qualitative evaluation heavily depends on the subjective observation which is inaccurate and laborious, thus six quantitative metrics are used to objectively compare different methods' performance.

The quantitative metric values of all the image fusion methods are first calculated according to their fusion results on the used image dataset, and then the average metric values of all methods are listed in Table 1. It can be seen from Table 1 that our method has got the best performance on all six metrics. Specifically, the largest E, SF and AG values and the second-largest STD value of our method indicate that our fusion images have obtained more salient details than those generated by the other five methods. The largest VIFF and NSSIM values of our method suggest that our generated fusion images have preserved more structural information from the source images than those generated by the other five comparison methods.

Overall, both the qualitative and quantitative evaluation results verify that our proposed method is effective for fusing the infrared and visual images, and outperforms the SOTA image fusion methods in most cases. Moreover, the proposed method takes about 0.50 s to fuse a pair of infrared and visual images, and its efficiency can be further improved by exploiting the parallel computing technique or deploying it on the graphics processing unit.

4 Conclusions

In this study, we propose an effective multi-scale Bézier filter, which is capable of extracting different scales of bright and dark features from the infrared and visual images and producing a smooth base image for each source image. Based on the developed multi-scale Bézier filter, we further propose an infrared and visual image fusion method. The proposed image fusion method can effectively integrate the salient bright and dark features of the infrared and visual images into one informative fusion image. The substantial experiments indicate that the proposed infrared and visual image fusion method outperforms five SOTA image fusion methods (including two deep-learning based methods) from both qualitative and quantitative aspects. Overall, the proposed method exhibits great potential to apply in the civil and military surveillance systems.

Acknowledgments. This work is supported in part by the National Natural Science Foundation of China under Grant No. 62132002, 62171017 and 61976017, and in part by the China Postdoctoral Science Foundation under Grant No. 2021M690297.

References

1. Li, S., Kang, X., Fang, L., Hu, J., Yin, H.: Pixel-level image fusion: a survey of the state of the art. Inf. Fusion **33**, 100–112 (2017)
2. Zhang, Y., Liu, Y., Sun, P., Yan, H., Zhao, X., Zhang, L.: IFCNN: a general image fusion framework based on convolutional neural network. Inf. Fusion **54**, 99–118 (2020)

3. Yin, M., Liu, X., Liu, Y., Chen, X.: Medical image fusion with parameter-adaptive pulse coupled neural network in nonsubsampled shearlet transform domain. IEEE Trans. Instrum. Meas. **68**(1), 49–64 (2018)

4. Liu, Y., Chen, X., Ward, R.K., Wang, Z.J.: Medical image fusion via convolutional sparsity based morphological component analysis. IEEE Sig. Process. Lett. **26**(3), 485–489 (2019)

5. Zhang, Y., Bai, X., Wang, T.: Boundary finding based multi-focus image fusion through multi-scale morphological focus-measure. Inf. Fusion **35**, 81–101 (2017)

6. Liu, Y., Wang, L., Cheng, J., Li, C., Chen, X.: Multi-focus image fusion: a survey of the state of the art. Inf. Fusion **64**, 71–91 (2020)

7. Zhang, Y., Zhang, L., Bai, X., Zhang, L.: Infrared and visual image fusion through infrared feature extraction and visual information preservation. Infrared Phys. Technol. **83**, 227–237 (2017)

8. Ma, J., Yu, W., Liang, P., Li, C., Jiang, J.: FusionGAN: a generative adversarial network for infrared and visible image fusion. Inf. Fusion **48**, 11–26 (2019)

9. Ma, J., Ma, Y., Li, C.: Infrared and visible image fusion methods and applications: a survey. Inf. Fusion **45**, 153–178 (2019)

10. Zhou, Z., Li, S., Wang, B.: Multi-scale weighted gradient-based fusion for multi-focus images. Inf. Fusion **20**, 60–72 (2014)

11. Bai, X., Zhang, Y., Zhou, F., Xue, B.: Quadtree-based multi-focus image fusion using a weighted focus-measure. Inf. Fusion **22**, 105–118 (2015)

12. Burt, P.J.: The Laplacian pyramid as a compact image code. IEEE Trans. Commun. **31**, 532–540 (1983)

13. Liu, Y., Liu, S., Wang, Z.: A general framework for image fusion based on multi-scale transform and sparse representation. Inf. Fusion **24**, 147–164 (2015)

14. Zhou, Z., Wang, B., Li, S., Dong, M.: Perceptual fusion of infrared and visible images through a hybrid multi-scale decomposition with Gaussian and bilateral filters. Inf. Fusion **30**, 15–26 (2016)

15. Xu, H., Ma, J., Jiang, J., Guo, X., Ling, H.: U2Fusion: a unified unsupervised image fusion network. IEEE Trans. Pattern Anal. Mach. Intell. **44**(1), 502–518 (2020)

16. Ren, W., et al.: Gated fusion network for single image dehazing. In: Proceedings of the IEEE Conference on Computer Vision and Pattern Recognition, pp. 3253–3261 (2018)

17. Bai, X., Zhang, Y.: Detail preserved fusion of infrared and visual images by using opening and closing based toggle operator. Opt. Laser Technol. **63**, 105–113 (2014)

18. Ma, K., Zeng, K., Wang, Z.: Perceptual quality assessment for multi-exposure image fusion. IEEE Trans. Image Process. **24**(11), 3345–3356 (2015)

19. Toet: TNO Image Fusion Dataset. Figshare, 26 April 2014. https://figshare.com/articles/TN_Image_Fusion_Dataset/1008029

20. Li, S., Kang, X., Hu, J.: Image fusion with guided filtering. IEEE Trans. Image Process. **22**(7), 2864–2875 (2013)

21. Li, S., Yang, B.: Multifocus image fusion using region segmentation and spatial frequency. Image Vis. Comput. **26**(7), 971–979 (2008)

22. Zhao, W., Wang, D., Lu, H.: Multi-focus image fusion with a natural enhancement via a joint multi-level deeply supervised convolutional neural network. IEEE Trans. Circ. Syst. Video Technol. **29**(4), 1102–1115 (2018)

23. Han, Y., Cai, Y., Cao, Y., Xu, X.: A new image fusion performance metric based on visual information fidelity. Inf. Fusion **14**(2), 127–135 (2013)

Towards Neural Video Compression: A Rate Distortion Modeling Perspective

Chuanmin Jia[1]([✉]), Weimin Zhang[2], Kai Lin[1], and Siwei Ma[1]

[1] Institute of Digital Media, School of Computer Science, Peking University, Beijing 100871, China
{cmjia,kailin,swma}@pku.edu.cn
[2] AVS Industry Alliance, Beijing, China
zwm@aitisa.org.cn

Abstract. A novel trend in video compression is to use end-to-end optimized neural techniques. However, the rate-distortion (R-D) behavior of such scheme remains unexplored. In this paper, we for the first time study the essential characteristics of neural video compression (NVC) by comparatively modeling the R-D behavior of conventional codec and NVC. We give the observation that the proportion of required coding bits for motion field and residual are essentially different between the two kinds of codecs. We also show that improving the efficiency of inter prediction module would be the key factor to shorten the performance gap between NVC and conventional codec. Given such observation, we propose the rate-distortion modeling inspired neural video compression (RD-NVC) framework to increase prediction accuracy and reduce residual coding bits. For the former part, a novel prediction refinement network is proposed to improve predictive coding efficiency. Regarding the latter aspect, coarse-to-fine (C2F) residual modeling and in-loop restoration are proposed to save the residual coding bits. The proposed framework substantially promotes the R-D performance of NVC in a comprehensive manner. The experiment demonstrates that our method outperforms the state-of-the-art single reference frame NVC approaches. To the best of our knowledge, the proposed method is the first NVC that shows comparable R-D performance with H.266/VVC in terms of MS-SSIM under same prediction structure.

Keywords: Neural network · Video coding · End-to-end optimization · Rate-distortion analysis

1 Introduction

Lossy video compression receives increasing attention from both industry and academic society in the past decades because it plays a fundamental role in bridging the image

This work was supported in part by the National Natural Science Foundation of China under grant 62101007, in part by the National Postdoctoral Program for Innovative Talents under grant BX2021009, which are gratefully acknowledged.

capturing as well as the visual understanding. The demand and use cases of video compression have changed when moving into the ultra-high definition plus artificial intelligence era. New types of video format and content also drive the video coding research into a new stage.

Dating back to 1970s, the classical hybrid video compression scheme (predictive plus transform based compression) was established. As shown in Fig. 1(a), the diagram of conventional hybrid coding contains several major modules such as prediction, transform and entropy coding etc. The major objective is to optimize the compression efficiency for each coding module individually. The local optimization of each module extensively promoted the rate-distortion (RD) performances of video codecs, resulting in different family of video compression standards, such as MPEG [34], H.26x [10, 26, 30, 31, 35], AVS [23, 24, 41] and AOM [8] series standards. Basically, these frameworks rely on fine-grained tuning of the hand-crafted statistical models for marginal coding efficiency improvement. On one hand, the coding efficiency of such frameworks is continuously improved by incorporating plenty of crafted coding tools and expanding their candidate lists in the rate-distortion search space. On the other hand, the hybrid coding framework is facing the performance-improving bottleneck because it becomes more difficult to acquire higher coding gain within reasonable computational complexity.

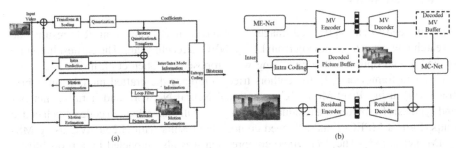

Fig. 1. The block diagrams of two representative video compression paradigms, (a) conventional block-based hybrid compression framework; (b) end-to-end optimized neural video compression.

In recent years, deep learning has made the research on neural network (NN) re-surge, not only for the task of intelligent-oriented analysis but also broadening the horizon of video coding. It has been demonstrated that end-to-end (E2E) optimized image compression has even better coding performance than H.266/VVC intra while neural video compression (NVC) also has enormous potentials to realize better R-D quality than existing video coding standards although lacking sufficient evidences currently. It is not hard to figure out that the next battleground of video coding research should be located in the learning based ones. Regarding NVC, a representative framework is shown in Fig. 1(b) where MV denotes motion vector, ME/MC abbreviate motion estimation and motion compensation respectively. The NVC framework achieve two aspects of fundamental breakthrough.

Existing NVCs tend to increase the coding performance via designing rich spatial temporal contextual information networks [17, 20, 36, 38, 40] and adaptive mode decision to determine the granularity of motion field coding [1, 13, 15]. In addition, several works treated adjacent video frames as volumetric data and adopted three-dimensional convolutions [9, 11]. However, the major drawback of existing solutions is that the essential analysis and understanding of the NVC's R-D behavior is missing, resulting in learned codec a black-box. Given the fact that the R-D behavior analysis has been extensively studied during the development of conventional codecs [27, 32]. This leads to our major motivation: do we understand the R-D characteristics of NVC? In this paper, we try to answer this question, then contribute a novel framework to promote the performance accordingly. The contributions are summarized as follows.

- We provide extensive comparative analysis of NVC and standard codecs. We observe that NVC has different R-D behaviors with conventional codecs.
- We propose RD-NVC to reduce the bit-rate and increase the quality of the reconstructed videos. The proposed RD-NVC outperforms the state-of-the-art single reference frame NVC approaches.
- To the best of our knowledge, our approach is the first learned video codec which achieves comparable R-D performances with H.266/VVC in terms of MS-SSIM metric under lowdelay-P configuration on low resolution sequences.

2   Related Work

Since the end-to-end optimized image codec has realized convincing R-D results, the research interest is now moving from LIC to NVC in recent years. The earliest literature on end-to-end optimized video coding was proposed by Chen et al. in 2017 [7]. In a subsequent framework [9], the authors tried to replace the crafted modules in hybrid framework using Pixel-Motion Convolutional Neural Network and iterative analysis and synthesis for prediction residual, resulting in a fully neural video codec. Such codec outperformed MPEG-2 and achieved comparable results with H.264/AVC using MS-SSIM metric [33]. The deep video compression was also modeled by a probabilistic model for sequential data coding [12].

Currently, representative research schemes on NVC basically adopt the image codec plus learned inter-frame coding paradigm, in which the motion-aware networks are proposed to capture the translational and non-translational displacement between adjacent frames. An explicit motion field (optical flow) is also utilized to obtain the predictive frame by using such network for warp-based motion estimation and motion compensation [19, 22, 29]. Once the prediction frame is obtained, the prediction residual is subsequently encoded using existing learned image coding (LIC) solution. The compression efficiency continuously increases by introducing richer reference information [17], motion field prediction [20] and quality enhancement [38].

In general, the scope and depth of NVC research is far from being comprehensive enough as that in conventional video codec. Both of the compression efficiency and the RD behavior modeling of NVC should be extensively studied in future works. Currently, increasing attention is allocated to the former aspect and the latter receives less interest. The major motivation of this paper is to explore the R-D characteristics of prior codecs such that more explainable behavior and understanding of NVC are investigated.

3 R-D Analysis

The R-D behavior of both conventional codec and NVC is comparatively studied. The main methodology of our analysis is to visualize the components of bitstream to quantitatively interpret what information has been encoded by different codecs. Motivated by the analysis results, we propose a novel NVC scheme accordingly.

3.1 R-D Statistics of Conventional Codec

We denote all of the high-level syntax as header info (R_{header}). The coding bits for residual are defined as residual bits (R_{resi}) while the R_{motion} is used to encapsulate the motion bits. In video compression, the R_{motion} contains essential information for decodability and other side information such as coding tool control flags. They can be regarded as the indication of predictive coding overhead. Meanwhile, the residual bits are the overhead for compressing the quantized coefficients. We should note that the proportion of R_{header} is relatively small and they are considered as part of R_{motion} during our analysis. The total bitstream could be formulated as Eq. 1.

$$R_{all} = R_{header} + R_{motion} + R_{resi}. \tag{1}$$

Observation 1. In conventional codecs, at most half of the bit-rate (20% to 50%) are utilized for coding the prediction related information. More bits are required for residual coding if one would like to achieve higher quality when the bit-budget is sufficient enough.

3.2 R-D Behavior of NVC

Similarly, the proportion of motion and residual bits in NVC is collected and analyzed. We adopted DVC [22] in our NVC R-D analysis. We find out that NVCs tend to utilize smaller amount of bits to encode the residual at low bit-rate than that in high bit-rate. In addition, the bit-rate range of $R resi$ is between 15% and 45%. Third, high resolution videos tend to have larger $R resi$ for residual coding.

Observation 2. In NVC, the ratio of $R resi$ is relatively small than that in conventional codec. Even under high bit-rate scenario, the residual accounts less than half of the total bit-rate. This is the major difference between conventional codec and NVC.

3.3 Comparative Analysis and R-D Modeling

We then comprehensively analyze and model the R-D characteristics of two kinds of codecs. For the similarity part between them, the logarithm regressed curves for both codecs have a generalized form expressed as follows.

$$P_{R_{resi}} = \alpha * \ln R_{all} + \beta, \tag{2}$$

where α and β are the resolution and content dependent parameters. Obviously, the R_{resi} grows higher when the bit-rate increases and it also has positive correlation with the resolution of video sequence. This point shows that residual coding affects the compression efficiency significantly. Observation could also be made that the ratio of R_{resi} tends to saturate for both codecs after the bit-rate reaches certain threshold (around 0.2 BPP).

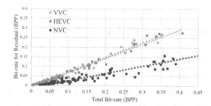

Fig. 2. Bit-rate relationship between R_{resi} and R_{all} in different codecs. Each data point corresponds to a bit-rate info encoded by different codecs.

Regarding the difference, we could observe that the ratio of R_{resi} varies a lot between the two codecs. A more straightforward bit-rate comparison is subsequently shown in Fig. 2, which depicts the relationship between R_{resi} and R_{all}. Obviously, the slope of NVC's curve is relatively smaller than that of HEVC and VVC codec, indicating that the predictive coding efficiency of NVC is inferior to that in HEVC [31] and VVC [6], resulting in more bits for the motion field coding. This phenomenon shows that the dominant factor for promoting coding performance is to increase the efficiency of predictive coding. As such, the R-D optimization objective of NVC could be formulated as an optimization problem. We accordingly provide the motivation of our proposed method.

Motivation. Given the analysis above and the fact that there still exists performance gap between the NVC and VVC, we argue that the next step towards NVC research lies in improving the inter prediction efficiency. Specifically, we propose to achieve this objective from two different directions. We propose to *improve NVC's prediction efficiency* and *reduce residual bits* of the encoded videos.

4   Proposed RD-NVC

In this section, we elaborate the proposed RD-NVC based on the aforementioned R-D analysis. Our proposed scheme contains three novel coding tools on the top of Fig. 1(b). Specifically, we first propose to promote the predictive coding efficiency by introducing Prediction Refinement Network and the in-loop restoration network. They are designed to improve the quality of predicted and compressed pictures respectively. Such that the inter prediction efficiency is significantly improved by suppressing the prediction error and enhancing the reference frame quality. Then, we propose a multi-layer residual modeling module in a coarse-to-fine (C2F) manner, with the help of which the fine-grained textural information could be finely reconstructed in a scalable residual coding fashion.

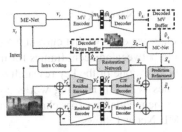

Fig. 3. The flowchart of our proposed RD-NVC framework. The prediction refinement network and in-loop restoration network provide higher prediction and reconstruction quality respectively. The C2F residual modeling scheme is implemented by simply and effectively re-using the residual coding module.

The overall framework of RD-NVC is illustrated in Fig. 3. Given the frame x_t to be encoded, if x_t is the key frame of the group of pictures (GOP), we deploy the intra codec following the solutions in [17, 22] and place the intra coded image into the decoded picture buffer (DPB) as reference frame. Otherwise, motion estimation is conducted from x_t to the most recent reference frame $(\hat{x}_{t-1})$ in DPB to obtain the MV (v_t). Note that the pixel-wise dense MV v_t is obtained from a pre-trained optical flow network then compressed by MV codec. The MV codec is realized by [3]. Subsequently, the motion compensation based inter prediction $(\overline{x}_t)$ is obtained by the MC-Net using $\hat{v}_t$ and $\hat{x}_t$. The proposed prediction refinement network directly enhances the quality of predicted frames and generates $\overline{x}_t$. Once the prediction signal $\overline{x}_t$ is obtained, the normal residual is calculated by Eq. 3.

$$r_t = x_t - \overline{x}_t. \tag{3}$$

We then propose the C2F residual modeling module by cascading a second stage of residual compression. Similar to Eq. 3, the C2F residual could be natural obtained by Eq. 5.

$$r_t = x_t - (\overline{x}_t + \hat{r}_t). \tag{4}$$

After two stages of residual compression, the compressed frame is finally reconstructed as follows.

$$\tilde{x}_t = \overline{x}_t + \hat{r}_t + \hat{r}'_t. \tag{5}$$

To obtain the final reconstruction image, we propose to introduce a novel in-loop restoration network to promote the quality of restore image $\tilde{x}_t$.

$$\hat{x}_t = F_{LF}(\tilde{x}_t | \Theta), \tag{6}$$

where F_{LF} indicates the loop filter network and Θ encapsulates all of the learnable parameters in such network. We elaborate the detailed description in the following sections.

4.1 Inter Predictive Refinement Network

Based on the analysis in Sect. 3, we observe that current NVC framework tends to use more bits to model the motion between adjacent frames for inter prediction. To realize higher predictive coding efficiency, one of the key research direction is to promote the quality of the reference frames [17, 43]. Existing works concentrate on using more reference frames and treating them equally across channels in the networks. We obtain the prediction frame using ME-Net as follows.

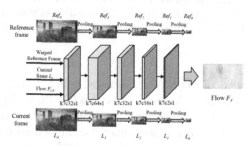

Fig. 4. The diagram of ME-Net in our scheme. The multi-scale optical flow pyramid network has four different pyramids, each of which is represented by the subscript in this figure. The notation "k7c32s1" denotes this convolution layer has 64 channels with 7×7 kernel and the stride is 1 pixel. Note that the reference frame here indicates $\hat{x}_{t-1}$ while current frame corresponds to x_t.

Regarding each inter-coded frame x_t, we propose to utilize the most recent compressed image $\hat{x}_{t-1}$ from the DPB as the reference frame. The ME process is subsequently realized from $\hat{x}_{t-1}$ to x_t by ME-Net using multi-scale optical flow pyramid network. Shown in Fig. 4, the ME-Net could model the translational displacement between adjacent pictures via the pixel-wise motion vector (MV). Specifically, the motions between the reference frame and current pristine image is calculated. We down-sample the picture using 2×2 global average pooling to realize a 5-layered multi-scale motion pyramid and learn the optical flow in a coarse-to-fine fashion. For each layer, the MV is defined as follows.

$$F_i = R(Warp(Ref_{i-1}, F_{i-1}), L_i, F_{i-1}), \tag{7}$$

where F_i is the optical flow of each layer i, Ref_{i-1} is the reference frame, $Warp()$ represents the bilinear warp operation and L_i indicates the current frame in the motion pyramid. encapsulates the learnable parameters in Fig. 4. Thus the loss function can be formulated.

$$L = \Sigma_i \| Warp(Ref_i, \ F_i) - L_i \|_2, \tag{8}$$

Note that F_5 is initiated as *zero* MV and F_0 is our target MV. In our implementation, the ME-Net is separately trained first and the converged weights are used as initializer of ME-Net in end-to-end training. Since F_0 denotes the motion field from compressed image $\hat{x}_{t-1}$ to uncompressed current frame x_t, it should be encoded and transmitted to ensure the consistency between encoder and decoder.

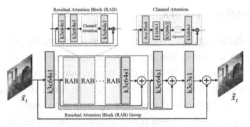

Fig. 5. The proposed prediction refinement network. The convolution kernel size, number of channel and stride are shown. We utilized 5 RABs in our Prediction Refinement Net.

We then establish our proposed prediction refinement network by leveraging the residual channel attention [42] mechanism. Such attention structure could benefit the translational and non-translational motion modeling and obtain better prediction quality. The detailed structure of prediction refinement network is shown in Fig. 5. Different from the original residual attention net, we utilized the direct input-output shortcut connection for residual learning. During training, we added the prediction refinement loss $L_{pred}(x_t, \bar{x}_t) = D(x_t, \bar{x}_t)$ as part of the distortion to the training objective, where $\bar{x}_t = F_{pred}(\bar{x}_t)$ and F_{pred} denotes the prediction refinement net. With the help of prediction refinement, better prediction quality could be obtained. And if the prediction frame has less difference with the original frame, the energy of prediction residual as well as its corresponding bit-rate will be smaller. More ablations will be studied to illustrate the effectiveness in later sections.

4.2 C2F Residual Modeling

Given the R-D behavior analysis in Fig. 2, we have already found that the required bits for residual coding in NVC is much smaller than that in conventional codec. To improve compression efficiency, we propose a simple but effective module to model the prediction residual coding in a C2F manner. Specifically, existing NVC solutions usually reconstruct the final frame ($\hat{x}^{dvc}$) by adding the prediction and codec residual.

$$\hat{x}^{final} = \bar{x}_t + \hat{r}_t. \tag{9}$$

However, such method is directly inherited from conventional codec. In NVC, the residual compression is based on LIC. Such that detailed textures might high be captured in a fundamentally different way with that in conventional codec. Here we propose a C2F residual modeling method by cascading another residual codec after the existing one. As such, the final reconstruction for each coded image could be realized by adding prediction and two stages of residuals together using Eq. 5. We employed the image codec in [3] to realize the second stage C2F residual coding. Noted that the number of channels we used in C2F residual is half of that in normal residual because the overhead of C2F residual is relatively small. The successive encoding of residual helps fine-grained visual reconstruction because the scalable coded residuals restore the image in a fine-granular fashion.

4.3 In-Loop Restoration Network

From the aspect of reducing compression noise, we additionally propose a novel coding tool, in-loop restoration network. Similar approaches have been proven to be effective in conventional framework [18, 25]. In this paper, we for the first time propose an efficient in-loop restoration network to directly reduce the distortion introduced by the codec. Shown in Fig. 6, the proposed in-loop restoration network is fully convolutional and has variable kernel size plus global residual connection. Following existing in-loop restoration network structure in deep network based conventional codecs [14], such design is a reasonable trade-off between performance and complexity. The input of the in-loop restoration network is the reconstruction image calculated by Eq. 5 and this network generates the final restored image. We finally place it into DPB for subsequent motion compensation prediction. The advantage of the proposed restoration network are two folds. It firstly increases the reference frames quality such that better inter-prediction efficiency is guaranteed. It also suppresses compression error by reducing signal level fidelity. We could easily observe that these benefits correspond to our R-D analysis results.

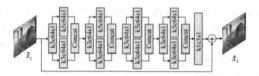

Fig. 6. The proposed in-loop restoration network structure of RD-NVC. Variable convolution kernels and skip shortcut are utilized in the basic building blocks. In addition, the global input-output direction residual is used to learning the minor difference between uncompressed image and the RD-NVC coded image. Similar notations are used with Fig. 5.

4.4 Train for RD-NVC

The loss function of the proposed RD-NVC scheme is designed in Eq. 10. In particular, the distortion is measured by the reconstructed frames and pristine frames and the bit-rate is measured by BPP.

$$J_{RD-NVC} = \lambda * D + R_{RD-NVC}, \tag{10}$$

where λ controls the trade-off between rate (R_{RD-NVC}) and distortion (D), which could be either mean-square-error (MSE) or MS-SSIM [33]. As mentioned above, the prediction error is utilized as partial distortion, yielding the final formulation of D as follows.

$$D = 1/2 * (L_{pred} + L_{recon}), \tag{11}$$

where $L_{recon} = D(x_t, \hat{x}_t)$. Note that the distortion is calculated on RGB color space. The R_{RD-NVC} encapsulates all the required coding bits, including MV, normal residual and C2F residual. Following [22, 38], we employ the progressive training strategy of different modules in our RD-NVC. The detailed set-up information is given in experiments.

5   Experimental Results

Experiment Configurations. Our experiment configurations were based on the training protocol defined in [22, 39]. Specifically, the videos in vimeo-90k dataset [37] were used and randomly cropped into 256 × 256 clips for training coded as I frame while the remaining as P frames. We also kept the same setting as [38, 39] to utilize H.265/HEVC based codec [4] to compress I frame when the distortion metric is MSE and utilize the image codec in [16] when that is MS-SSIM. We initialized the motion estimation network using a pre-trained network [28]. Different from [17], we did not resize the test videos and adopted single reference frame for fair comparison. We trained four models with different lambda values, {256, 512, 1024, 2048} for MSE and {8, 16, 32, 64} for MS-SSIM to different bit-rate. The Adam optimizer was deployed for optimization with a mini-batch of 4. We trained the whole system by 2 Million iterations. The HEVC datasets were adopted for performance comparison. Following [13, 21, 22], we encoded the first 100 frames and set the GOP to be 10. Our proposed model was trained/tested on Tensorflow library using a single NVIDIA RTX 2080 GPU.

5.1   RD Performance

Objective Quality. To illustrate the effectiveness of the proposed framework, we compared R-D performance with conventional video codecs H.264 [35] and H.265 [31] and representative NVC schemes [13, 21, 22]. We averaged the results among each dataset and plotted the R-D curves of different methods in Fig. 7. The notation is summarized as Lu CVPR2019 [22], Hu ECCV2020 [13], Lu ECCV2020 [21], H.264 [35] and H.265 [31] for each curve. It should be noted that we do not compare with [17] because of the fact that multiple references would cause unbalanced comparison since more parameters are used in [17]. All the learning-based solutions in Fig. 7 are based on single reference frame and the comparisons are balanced and persuasive. We should also note that the H.264 and H.265 are based on the ×264 and ×265 codec in ffmepg. We utilized Bjontegaard's method [5] to calculate the BD-rate reduction. Obviously, significant coding gain could be obtained against existing research especially under high bit-rate.

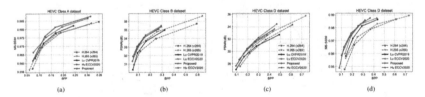

Fig. 7. The R-D curves of proposed method against both conventional codecs [31, 35] and learned codecs [13, 21, 22]. The green curve indicates the R-D performances of the proposed method. Other representative conventional codecs [31, 35] and learned codecs [13, 21, 22] are also compared. Zoom-in for better visualization.

Subjective Quality. We additionally provided the decoded images of different codecs for subjective comparison in Fig. 8. Both of the representative conventional and learned codecs were comparatively illustrated and analyzed. The 12th frame of the test sequence *BlowingBubbles* was chosen for visual quality comparison. It could be easily observed that the proposed method has better perceptual quality and is more visual pleasant in texture areas against conventional and learned codecs, such as [22, 31, 35]. The overall BD-rate reduction of this sequence is more than 20% over existing learned codecs.

(a) x264   (b) x265   (c) DVC   (d) VTM   (e) Proposed

Fig. 8. Subjective evaluations of the 12th frame of BlowingBubbles sequence. (a) H.264/AVC [35] (0.06564/24.9914/0.9075). (b) H.265/HEVC [31] (0.08861/27.0204/0.9413). (c) Lu CVPR2019 [22] (0.9542/26.9265/0.02525). (d) H.266/VVC [6] (0.06066/29.6949/0.9766). (e) Proposed method (0.02035/28.6100/0.9557). The statistics are bpp/PSNR (dB)/MS-SSIM. Zoom-in for better visualization

5.2 Comparison with H.266/VVC

We further compared our method against the latest H.266/VCC standard [6] in Table 1 and Fig. 9. We deployed the lowdelay-P configuration in the CTC of H.266/VVC reference software VTM-10.2 for testing. The pristine YUV-420 sequences were converted to RGB color space for encoding for fair comparison. It should be particularly noted that we restricted the VTM-10.2 to use only one reference frame such that the test conditions were aligned (by setting the number of active reference frames to be 1). Both of the PSNR and MS-SSIM metrics were evaluated. The encoding and distortion evaluation were based on RGB color space. It could be learned that the performance gap between our method and VVC is obvious, although our method has com- parable performances with H.266/VVC under MS-SSIM metric with 8.83% loss. Regarding BD-rate (PSNR), it's observed that our method is still inferior to the H.266/VVC.

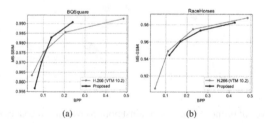

(a)   (b)

Fig. 9. R-D performance comparison between our scheme and H.266/VVC [6] using PSNR and MS-SSIM metrics. (a) BQSquare. (b) RaceHorses.

Analysis. The performance comparisons in the above table and Figs. 8 and 9 are informative and inspiring. In general, the major advantage of NN-based end-to-end video coding is not in compression, but in reconstructing video scenes in a semantic information preserved way. Even with clear signal-level degradation against VTM, the visual quality could be preserved when using the proposed RD-NVC. We also envision that the learned video codecs have great potentials to outperform VVC/H.266 if further optimization and model designation are conducted.

Table 1. R-D performance gap between the proposed method and VTM-10.2. Anchor is the proposed RD-NVC.

	BD-rate (MS-SSIM)	BD-rate (PSNR)
RaceHorses	−15.86%	−48.77%s
BQSquare	−1.81%	−33.06%
Average	**−8.83%**	**−40.91%**

5.3 Ablation Study and Analysis

This subsection provides ablation study of the proposed methods based on HEVC Class D. As depicted in Fig. 9, we quantitatively explored the coding gain of each tool by comparing the tool-off performances and analyzed the encoded bitstream to show the bit-rate distribution. It should be noted that all test conditions were kept the same in the ablation study and we turned off the three tools respectively.

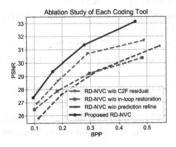

Fig. 10. Ablation study of our scheme.

Prediction Refinement. The blue curve of Fig. 10 indicates the tool off performance of our prediction refinement network. In our analysis, we turned it off together with the MC-Net since they were optimized from scratch together. Note that 2.42 dB BD-PSNR gain could be realized by the proposed prediction refinement. The prediction refinement is essentially necessary for better predictive coding.

In-Loop Restoration. The ablation study on the in-loop restoration network shows that this tools provides 2.49 dB BD-PSNR gain. Based on the purple dash line we learn that the coding gain is larger in high bit-rate that that in low bit-rate scenario. The in-loop restoration directly promotes the quality of compressed frames.

C2F Residual. The dash line in green of Fig. 10 corresponds to the tool off performance of C2F residual modeling, obtaining 1.13 dB BD-PSNR gain at similar bit-rate point respectively. Although the coding gain of C2F residual seems relatively small when comparing with the other two tools, it brings better subjective results.

6 Conclusion

In this paper, we provide comprehensive R-D analysis of different codecs. Our novelty lies in finding that inter prediction efficiency could be enhanced to narrow the performance gap between NVC and conventional codec. Based on the analysis, we propose RD-NVC and compare our scheme with H.266/VVC to show the status. The proposed coding tools for learned codec are generalizable, which are able to significantly reduce the coding bits and improve the predictive coding efficiency.

References

1. Agustsson, E., Minnen, D., Johnston, N., Balle, J., Hwang, S.J., Toderici, G.: Scale-space flow for end-to-end optimized video compression. In: Proceedings of the IEEE/CVF Conference on Computer Vision and Pattern Recognition, pp. 8503–8512 (2020)
2. Agustsson, E., Tschannen, M., Mentzer, F., Timofte, R., Van Gool, L.: Generative adversarial networks for extreme learned image compression. In: Proceedings of the IEEE International Conference on Computer Vision, pp. 221–231 (2019)
3. Balle, J., Laparra, V., Simoncelli, E.P.: End-to-end optimized image compression. arXiv preprint arXiv:1611.01704 (2016)
4. Bellard, F.: Bpg image format. https://bellard.org/bpg. Accessed 11 Oct 2020
5. Bjontegaard, G.: Calculation of average psnr differences between rd-curves. VCEG-M33 (2001)
6. Bross, B., et al.: Overview of the versatile video coding (vvc) standard and its applications (2021)
7. Chen, T., Liu, H., Shen, Q., Yue, T., Cao, X., Ma, Z.: Deepcoder: a deep neural network based video compression. In: 2017 IEEE Visual Communications and Image Processing (VCIP), pp. 1–4. IEEE (2017)
8. Chen, Y., et al.: An overview of core coding tools in the av1 video codec. In: 2018 Picture Coding Symposium (PCS), pp. 41–45. IEEE (2018)
9. Chen, Z., He, T., Jin, X., Feng, W.: Learning for video compression. IEEE Trans. Circuits Syst. Video Technol. **30**(2), 566–576 (2019)
10. Girod, B., Steinbach, E., Farber, N.: Performance of the h. 263 video compression standard. J. VLSI Signal Process. Syst. Signal Image Video Technol. **17**(2–3), 101–111 (1997)
11. Habibian, A., van Rozendaal, T., Tomczak, J.M., Cohen, T.S.: Video compression with rate-distortion autoencoders. In: Proceedings of the IEEE International Conference on Computer Vision, pp. 7033–7042 (2019)
12. Han, J., Lombardo, S., Schroers, C., Mandt, S.: Deep probabilistic video compression. arXiv preprint arXiv:1810.02845 (2018)

13. Hu, Z., Chen, Z., Xu, D., Lu, G., Ouyang, W., Gu, S.: Improving deep video compression by resolution-adaptive flow coding. arXiv preprint arXiv:2009.05982 (2020)
14. Jia, C., et al.: Content-aware convolutional neural network for in-loop filtering in high efficiency video coding. IEEE Trans. Image Process. **28**(7), 3343–3356 (2019)
15. Ladune, T., Philippe, P., Hamidouche, W., Zhang, L., Deforges, O.: ModeNet: mode selection network for learned video coding. In: 2020 IEEE 30th International Workshop on Machine Learning for Signal Processing (MLSP), pp. 1–6. IEEE (2020)
16. Lee, J., Cho, S., Beack, S.-K.: Context-adaptive entropy model for end-to-end optimized image compression. arXiv preprint arXiv:1809.10452 (2018)
17. Lin, J., Liu, D., Li, H., Wu, F.: M-LVC: multiple frames prediction for learned video compression. In: Proceedings of the IEEE/CVF Conference on Computer Vision and Pattern Recognition, pp. 3546–3554 (2020)
18. Liu, D., Li, Y., Lin, J., Li, H., Feng, W.: Deep learning-based video coding: a review and a case study. ACM Comput. Surv. (CSUR) **53**(1), 1–35 (2020)
19. Liu, H., et al.: Learned video compression via joint spatial-temporal correlation exploration. arXiv preprint arXiv:1912.06348 (2019)
20. Liu, H., et al.: Neural video coding using multiscale motion compensation and spatiotemporal context model. arXiv preprint arXiv:2007.04574 (2020)
21. Lu, G., et al.: Content adaptive and error propagation aware deep video compression. In: Vedaldi, A., Bischof, H., Brox, T., Frahm, J.M. (eds.) Computer Vision – ECCV 2020. LNCS, vol. 12347, pp. 456–472. Springer, Cham (2020). https://doi.org/10.1007/978-3-030-58536-5_27
22. Lu, G., et al.: DVC: an end-to-end deep video compression framework. In: Proceedings of the IEEE Conference on Computer Vision and Pattern Recognition, pp. 11006–11015 (2019)
23. Ma, S., Huang, T., Reader, C., Gao, W.: AVS2? making video coding smarter [standards in a nutshell]. IEEE Signal Process. Mag. **32**(2), 172–183 (2015)
24. Ma, S., Wang, S., Gao, W.: Overview of IEEE 1857 video coding standard. In: 2013 IEEE International Conference on Image Processing, pp 1500–1504. IEEE (2013)
25. Ma, S., Zhang, X., Jia, C., Zhao, Z., Wang, S., Wanga, S.: Image and video compression with neural networks: a review. IEEE Trans. Circuits Syst. Video Technol. **30**, 1683–1698 (2019)
26. Oka, S., Misawa, Y.: Multipoint teleconference architecture for CCITT standard video conference terminals. In: Visual Communications and Image Processing 1992, vol. 1818, pp. 1502–1511. International Society for Optics and Photonics (1992)
27. Ortega, A., Ramchandran, K.: Rate-distortion methods for image and video compression. IEEE Signal process. Mag. **15**(6), 23–50 (1998)
28. Ranjan, A., Black, M.J.: Optical flow estimation using a spatial pyramid network. In Proceedings of the IEEE Conference on Computer Vision and Pattern Recognition, pp. 4161–4170 (2017)
29. Rippel, O., Nair, S., Lew, C., Branson, S., Anderson, A.G., Bourdev, L.: Learned video compression. In: Proceedings of the IEEE International Conference on Computer Vision, pp. 3454–3463 (2019)
30. Sidaty, N., Hamidouche, W., Deforges, O., Philippe, P., Fournier, J.: Compression performance of the versatile video coding: Hd and UHD visual quality monitoring. In: 2019 Picture Coding Symposium (PCS), pp. 1–5. IEEE (2019)
31. Sullivan, G.J., Ohm, J.-R., Han, W.-J., Wiegand, T.: Overview of the high efficiency video coding (hevc) standard. IEEE Trans. Circuits Syst. Video Technol. **22**(12), 1649–1668 (2012)
32. Sullivan, G.J., Wiegand, T.: Rate-distortion optimization for video compression. IEEE Signal Process. Mag. **15**(6), 74–90 (1998)
33. Wang, Z., Simoncelli, E.P., Bovik, A.C.: Multi-scale structural similarity for image quality assessment. In: The Thrity-Seventh Asilomar Conference on Signals, Systems and Computers 2003, vol. 2, pp. 1398–1402. IEEE (2003)

34. Watkinson, J.: The MPEG Handbook: MPEG-1, MPEG- 2, MPEG-4. Taylor & Francis, Milton Park (2004)
35. Wiegand, T., Sullivan, G.J., Bjontegaard, G., Luthra, A.: Overview of the h. 264/AVC video coding standard. IEEE Trans. Circuits Syst. Video Technol. **13**(7), 560–576 (2003)
36. Wu, C.-Y., Singhal, N., Krähenbühl, P.: Video compression through image interpolation. In: Ferrari, V., Hebert, M., Sminchisescu, C., Weiss, Y. (eds.) Computer Vision – ECCV 2018. LNCS, vol. 11212, pp. 425–440. Springer, Cham (2018). https://doi.org/10.1007/978-3-030-01237-3_26
37. Xue, T., Chen, B., Wu, J., Wei, D., Freeman, W.T.: Video enhancement with task-oriented flow. Int. J. Comput. Vision **127**(8), 1106–1125 (2019). https://doi.org/10.1007/s11263-018-01144-2
38. Yang, R., Mentzer, F., Van Gool, L., Timofte, R.: Learning for video compression with hierarchical quality and recurrent enhancement. In: Proceedings of the IEEE/CVF Conference on Computer Vision and Pattern Recognition, pp. 6628–6637 (2020)
39. Yang, R., Van Gool, L., Timofte, R.: OpenDVC: an open source implementation of the dvc video compression method. arXiv preprint arXiv:2006.15862 (2020)
40. Yilmaz, M.A., Tekalp, A.M.: End-to-end rate- distortion optimization for bi-directional learned video compression. In: 2020 IEEE International Conference on Image Processing (ICIP), pp. 1311–1315. IEEE (2020)
41. Zhang, J., Jia, C., Lei, M., Wang, S., Ma, S., Gao, W.: Recent development of AVS video coding standard: AVS3. In: 2019 Picture Coding Symposium (PCS), pp. 1–5. IEEE (2019)
42. Zhang, Y., Li, K., Li, K., Wang, L., Zhong, B., Fu, Y.: Image super-resolution using very deep residual channel attention networks. In: Ferrari, V., Hebert, M., Sminchisescu, C., Weiss, Y. (eds.) Computer Vision – ECCV 2018. LNCS, vol. 11211, pp. 294–310. Springer, Cham (2018). https://doi.org/10.1007/978-3-030-01234-2_18

A Fast Line and Ellipse Detection on High Resolution Images

Limin Liu[1]([⊠])(iD), Dingzhe Li[2](iD), Zhaoxi Li[2](iD), and Cai Meng[2,3](iD)

[1] The Cyberspace Institute of Advanced Technology, Guangzhou University,
Guangzhou 510006, China
`2112006139@e.gzhu.edu.cn`
[2] Image Processing Center, Beijing University of Aeronautics and Astronautics,
Beijing 100191, China
`{sy2015208,lizhaoxi}@buaa.edu.cn`
[3] Beijing Advanced Innovation Center for Biomedical Engineering, Beihang University,
Beijing 100083, China

Abstract. Line and ellipse are important image features in pattern recognition and computer vision. Many methods have been developed to extract line or ellipse in images separately but few try to detect them simultaneously. In this paper, a novel fast line and ellipse detection (FLED) method is proposed to detect line and ellipse simultaneously, even in high resolution images. At first, a detection framework (Pre-SGV) for high detection speed is proposed, which explicitly decomposes the detection into precalculate, segment, grouping, validation phases. Secondly, a simple but efficient algorithm is designed to segment the edges into line or arc candidates. Thirdly, the grouping constraints and fitting methods are further improved. Finally, validation are conducted to exclude erroneous detection. Experiments on synthetic images and real image dataset show that the proposed method, FLED, can robustly detect lines and ellipses fast and efficiently, especially for high resolution image (e.g. remote sensing image, the scanning image).

Keywords: Line and ellipse detection · Arc grouping · High resolution images

1 Introduction

Line and ellipse detection is one of the classical tasks in computer vision, and play an important part in vision measuring. Line detection is applied to railway detection [16], building line extraction [3], and ellipse detection is applied to robot guidance [24,31], pupil/eye tracking [34], cell segment [17] and industrial applications [30]. Recent years, there are some great algorithms have been proposed. However, most state of the art detections still can only detect lines or ellipses, and can hardly be used in the real-time applications. In case of lines and ellipses required simultaneously, such as Meng et al. [22], the lines and ellipses only can be detected step by step. A line and ellipse detection has great potential to be used in a pretreatment process which need to have low execution time and high detection accuracy.

This work is supported by the Beijing Natural Science Foundation under Grant 7202103.

A large number of algorithms have beed studied for the line or ellipse detection currently, and these methods are illustrated as follows:

- **Line Detection Methods.** Line detection methods have been utilized for many years. The methods based on Hough [12], is first used to detect the lines. When the slope of the line tends to infinity, there is a problem with this method. The methods based on edge linking, mainly use the straightness criterion [6] to segment lines. Brian Burn [1] proposed a new method based on the consistency of the gradient direction. This method is divided into two processes, link and grouping. This method is improved by Kahn et al. [13]. Apart from these, there are some methods based on PCA, Gurn [10] proposed a method based on the minimal eigenvalue, but this method might detect the smoothing curve as lines and is sensitive to noise, and was improved by Yun-Seok Lee [15]. LSD [9] is a linear-time line segment detector giving subpixel accurate results and has high anto-noise capability, but it is easy to divide arcs to some lines.

- **Ellipse Detection Methods.** Hough transform [4] can detect the ellipse effectively, having high detection accuracy, but it requires massive computation and memory. Xu et al. [33] proposed random hough transform(RHT), this method mainly utilize the random sampling and dynamic list storage to reduce the execution time and memory requirements, but its non-sampling will introduce a large number of invalid accumulation, so RHT has been improved by [18,28]. RTED [23] uses lines to approach the edge contours and proposed many conditions to group some arcs which belong to the same ellipse. The difficulty(include accuracy and real-time performance) of ellipse detection is far greater than that of line detection. Prasad [26] proposed a method basd on edge curvature and convexify and has beed improved by Fornaciari [8].

However, in the application of the monocular Position-Pose measurement [22], line and ellipse features are required simultaneously. The traditional method is to detect lines and ellipses respectively, so the speed and efficiency is affected. Aim at the detection of line and ellipse simultaneously, There are Etemadi's detector [5], UpWrite [20], ELSD [27] methods have been realized. Etemadi's detector [5] realized the line and circle arcs detection simultaneous, and is accurate in reporting the correct detections (line and circle arcs), but has no ability in eliminating false positives, reported on parasite contours. Equally, its precision at reduced scale is poor. UpWrite [20] method can detect the line, circle and ellipse features, and first use 'The Spot Algorithm' to compute local models for every edge pixel at a resolution r. All pixels are linked based on the estimated curvature and predicted location. The GMM method is used to judge which feature type the linking pixels belong to. This method is robust with respect to noise in an image, but it has difficulties in detecting overlapping features. Furthermore, it is low efficient, and it is sensitive to the resolution radius. ELSD [27] method can classify the image edge as line and curve arc, but the algorithm stays on the basic of line and curve classification, and doesn't give the fitting information of line and curve, and the local information cann't guarantee the accurate global information. The UpWrite and ELSD methods will be compared with our method.

According to the synchronous detection requirement of the line and ellipse features, we proposed a fast line and ellipse detection method (FLED) with an improved detection framework Precalculate-Segment-Grouping-Validation**Pre-SGV** in this paper.

The framework Pre-SGV with the new fast calculate nodes (FC-nodes) has lower execution time than other compared methods, the Pre-SGV and FC-node will be illustrate in Sect. 2. In the part of the Segment, a fast segment arcs (FSA) matrix is proposed based on curvature and convexity to get line and ellipse ars candidates. Then, candidate arcs which may belong to the same ellipse are merged based on geometric constraint and improved fitting methods in the grouping process. Finally, each candidate ellipse is verified by the location and tangent constrint. Three mainly contributions of this paper are listed as follows:

- A fast framework **Pre-SGV** with FC-Nodes is designed to get low execution detection time.
- Our effective arc grouping and feature parameter estimation are proposed to get candidate combinations faster and effectively.
- A weighted verification equation and two verification constraints are proposed to make the ellipse fitting more accurately.

The rest of the paper is organized as follows: Sect. 2 introduces the Pre-SGV framework, Sect. 3 provide the FSA matrix, Sect. 4 improve the grouping constraints and Sect. 5 introduce a new validation method. Section 6 performs a number of comparative experiments and comments on the implementation of Pre-SGV. Section 7 gives the conclusion and discussion.

2 Precalculate-Segment-Group-Validate

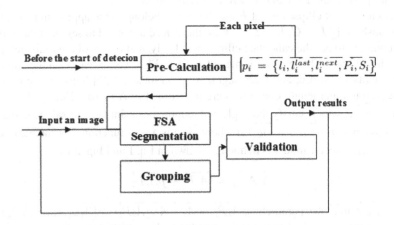

Fig. 1. The block diagram of the Pre-SGV framework

Pre-SGV is a framework designed for long-term detection of line and ellipse in a video stream or a set of images with different sizes. Its block diagram is shown in Fig. 1. The components of the framework are characterized as follows: *Pre-Calculate* allocates a given number $N^{data} = N^{data}_{row} \times N^{data}_{col}$ of nodes to get higher speed, where $N^{data}_{row}(N^{data}_{col})$ are largest than all used images' row(col) number, these nodes are named

FC-Nodes, which are defined as $P_i^{FC} = \{Add_i, Add_i^{last}, Add_i^{next}, F_i, F_i^{sum}\}, i = 1, .., N^{data}$. Add_i stores the pixel location (x_m, y_m) which $i = x_m \cdot N_{col}^{data} + y_m$, $Add_i^{last}(Add_i^{next})$ stores the last (next) location of Add_i. F_i, F_i^{sum} are real 6-by-6 symmetric matrix, we define $m_i = [x_m^2, 2x_m y_m, y_m^2, 2x_m, 2y_m, 1]$, so $F_i = m_i^T m_i$. $Add_i^{last}, Add_i^{next}, F_i^{sum}$ will be used in Sect. 3. *Segment-Group-Validate* are used based on the initialized FC-Nodes, and will be illustrated as follow sections.

3 Segmentation of Arcs

For line and ellipse feature detection, the approximate polygonal contours of the image edges are acquired. Then these contours are segmented into elliptic arc or line candidates based on the curvature and convexity. A new criterion is given for simple and efficient segmentation here. Inspired by the curvature and convexity of line and ellipse [23, 26], we introduce a segment matrix based on the edge approximate contours, i.e. fast segment of arc (FSA) matrix, for efficiently and fast extracting the candidate line and ellipse arc of an image.

To get edge approximate contours, an edge image can be get by using Canny [2]. We provide two search template shown in Fig. 2(a) to get non-branched connected edge contours based on Kovesi's method [14] in an edge image. The search order is from index 1 to index 8. For example, $(x_m, y_m), m = 1, ..., M$ are pixel locations which belong to the same contours by using templates. idx_m is defined $idx_m = x_m \cdot N^{data} + y_m$. So $Add_{idx_m}^{last}, Add_{idx_m}^{next}$ will be updated by their definitions, and $F_{idx_m}^{sum} = F_{idx_{m-1}}^{sum} + F_{idx_m}, F_{idx_1}^{sum} = F_{idx_1}$. Next, Edge approximate contours are approximated by RDP algorithm [25]. Then, FSA-matrix will be get as follows.

It is known that ellipse arc set E and line set L belong to the approximate contours C, obviously, $E \bigcup L \subset C, E \bigcup L = \varnothing$. So there need a method to segment the approximate contours to get the candidate ellipse arcs fastly, and others of contours belong to the candidate lines. This method is named as FSA. FSA mainly bases on the curvature and convexity of ellipse, and three segment constraints [23, 26] (curvature constraint, angle constraint and length constraint) are used to get FSA-matrix. Firstly, three basic points $\widehat{A_1 A_2 A_3}$ which satisfy the angle and length constraint need to calculate the curvature $L_{dir} = sign(\overrightarrow{A_2 A_1} \times \overrightarrow{A_2 A_3})$ where $sign$ is a sign function. For the next points $\widehat{A_{i-1} A_i A_{i+1}}$, a vector model is defined as shown in Eq. 1 and Fig. 2(b).

$$\overrightarrow{A_i A_{i+1}} = t\overrightarrow{A_i P_1} + p\overrightarrow{A_i P_2} \tag{1}$$

where t, p are unknown parameters, $\overrightarrow{A_i P_1} = \overrightarrow{A_{i-1} A_i}, |\overrightarrow{A_i P_2}| = |\overrightarrow{A_{i-1} A_i}|, \angle P_1 A_i P_2 = \theta_T$, θ_T is a threshold used in the angle constraint. FSA matrix is defined as shown in Eq. 2.

$$FSA_i^{L_{dir}} = \frac{1}{|A_{i-1} A_i|^2} \left[\begin{array}{c} \overrightarrow{A_{i-1} A_i} \cdot \overrightarrow{A_i A_{i+1}} \\ L_{dir} \overrightarrow{A_{i-1} A_i} \times \overrightarrow{A_i A_{i+1}} \end{array} \right] \tag{2}$$

A const matrix is defined as $K_{FSA} = \begin{bmatrix} 1 & -cot\theta_T \\ 0 & csc\theta_T \end{bmatrix}$, and t_i, p_i can be calculate by $K_{FSA} FSA_i^{L_{dir}}$. So when $t_i > 0, p_i > 0, R_{min} < |FSA_i^{L_{dir}}| < R_{max}(R_{min}, R_{max}$

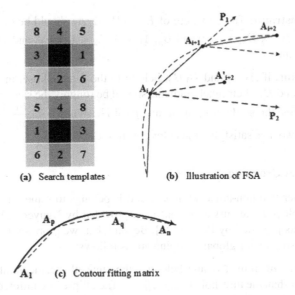

(a) Search templates   (b) Illustration of FSA

(c) Contour fitting matrix

Fig. 2. (a) Shows the clockwise and anticlockwise direction template. (b) Shows the geometric meaning of FSA. (c) Shows how to get the fitting matrix of an edge contour directly.

are used in the length constraint), the point A_{i+1} and $A_{i-1}A_i$ belong to the same candidate ellipse. For some arcs that don't belong to the candidate ellipses, they will be placed in the candidate lines.

4 Arc Grouping and Feature Fitting

After arc segmentation, each elliptic arc is one part of an ellipse. But some elliptic arcs may be from same ellipse which are isolated by overlap, occlusion, or noise. For accurate detection, they should be linked or grouped into one candidate. The following method is used for grouping the edge contours that possibly belong to the same ellipse. This step is conducted in two level: local vicinity and global range. Firstly, the neighboring candidate arcs are judged whether they are from same ellipse. Secondly, the non-adjacent candidate arcs are testified whether they may be from same ellipse. Before the grouping process, all arcs are changed into the same direction.

4.1 Neighborhood Grouping

Suppose arcs A and B meet condition: $|A_nB_1| < T$, then they will be judged whether they need to be merged. Three constraints are employed for the judgement:

FSA Constraint: We get a point O_1 as the midpoint of A_nB_1. So $A_{n-1}O_1B_1$ should meet the three constraints in Sect. 3, we make $A_n = O_1, A_{n+1} = B_1$, and get the fsa matrix FSA_n^{-1}. If FSA_n^{-1} meet the constraints in Sect. 3, arc A and arc B satisfy the FSA constraint.

Curvature Constraint: The curvature of $\widehat{B_{m-1}B_m A_1 A_2}$ should be of the same sign, i.e. when $\overrightarrow{B_{m-1}B_m} \times \overrightarrow{B_m A_1} < 0$ and $\overrightarrow{B_m A_1} \times \overrightarrow{A_1 A_2} < 0$, arc A and arc B satisfy the curvature constraint.

Color Constraint: if $\widehat{A_1 A_n}$ and $\widehat{B_1 B_m}$ belong to the same ellipse, in a small neighborhood of A_n and B_1, their pixel gradients should be roughly the same by using Sobel method. We define the gradient p_1 at A_n and p_2 at B_1. When $0 < \dfrac{p_1 \cdot p_2}{|p_1||p_2|} < T_{eps}$, we consider these two arcs satisfying the color constraint.

4.2   Arc Global Grouping

To judge whether two non-adjacent arcs A and B belongs to same ellipse, three constraints are employed: the curvature constraint provided by Nguyen [23], angular and fitting constraints provided by Prasad [26]. Beyond that, we propose the distance constraint. The constraints for global grouping are as follows:

Distance Constraint: If the two arcs belong to the same ellipse, the number of two arcs should be bigger than the threshold $C_{min-ellipse}$. The ellipse circumference can be calculate by $C_{ellipse} = T(\dfrac{r}{R}) \cdot (R+r)$. R is semi-major axis, r is semi-minor axis, $T(x)$ is elliptic coefficient. According to the experiment, we use the distance $l_{A_n B_m}$ between the end points of the arcs as the semi-major axis, so the min semi-minor axis is $R_{min} l_{A_n B_m}$, R_{min} is the minimum of the l_{major}/l_{minor}. So we get the minimum estimated circumference as shown in Eq. 3.

$$C_{min-ellipse} = (1 + R_{min}) T (R_{min}) l_{A_n B_m} \tag{3}$$

Curvature Constraint: For arc A and arc B, this constraint have the same defination at Sect. 3. So $\widehat{A_1 A_n}, \widehat{B_1 B_m}$ should satisfy $\overrightarrow{A_{n-1}A_n} \times \overrightarrow{A_n B_1} \leqslant 0, \overrightarrow{A_n B_1} \times \overrightarrow{B_1 B_2} \leqslant 0, \overrightarrow{B_{m-1}B_m} \times \overrightarrow{B_m A_1} \leqslant 0, \overrightarrow{B_m A_1} \times \overrightarrow{A_1 A_2} \leqslant 0$.

Fitting Constraint: Arc A and Arc B are fitted with DLS method, the error of DLS must be lower than a chosen threshold. The ellipse semi-minor and the ratio of semi-minor/semi-major must be higher than chosen thresholds.

$$\begin{cases} ERR_{ellipse} < T_{err} \\ l_{short} \geqslant T_{min\_short}, \dfrac{l_{minor}}{l_{major}} \geqslant R_{ratio} \end{cases} \tag{4}$$

Angular Constraint: The angle θ_i of the arc_i on the fitting ellipse should be higher than a threshold θ_{min} after ellipse fitting. If $\theta_1 + \theta_2 \geqslant \theta_{max}$, we think these two arcs belong to the same ellipse, and don't require validation. There is an arc $\widehat{A_1 A_n}$, and O is fitting center. $\overrightarrow{n_1}, \overrightarrow{n_2}$ are defined as the vectors of $\overrightarrow{OA_1}, \overrightarrow{OA_n}$. $\theta_{\widehat{A_1 A_n}}$ can be calculated as follows.

$$\theta_{\widehat{A_1 A_n}} = \pi - sign\left(\overrightarrow{n_1} \times \overrightarrow{n_2}\right) \left[\pi - arccos\left(\dfrac{\overrightarrow{n_1} \cdot \overrightarrow{n_2}}{|\overrightarrow{n_1}||\overrightarrow{n_2}|}\right)\right] \tag{5}$$

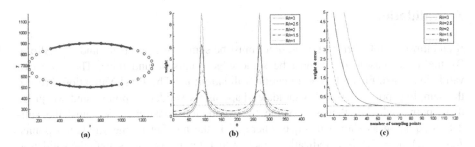

Fig. 3. Validation: (a) the location of validation points; (b) the value of W_i; (c) the discrete error of W_i.

4.3 Feature Parameter Estimation

The least squares methods is used to judge whether the error condition is satisfied for candidate lines and ellipses. The fitting matrix can be got by using FC-nodes. For example, there a arc $\widehat{A_1 A_n}$, idx_{A_i}, idx_{A_n} are defined as the index of the FC-nodes. The fitting matrix $F_{A_1 A_n} = F^{sum}_{idx_{A_n}} - F^{sum}_{idx_{A_1}}$.

- **Fast Line Fitting Algorithm.** The linear equation is $a_1 x + a_2 y + a_3 = 0$ with $a_1^2 + a_2^2 = 1$, $d_i = |a_1 x_i + a_2 y_i + a_3|$ is the distance from (x_i, y_i) to line. The fitting of a general line can be approached by minimizing the sum of d_i^2. S_l is defined as a contour fitting matrix which can be calculated with FC-nodes. So, the data number is $N = S_{6,6}$, the average point is $(\overline{X}, \overline{Y}) = (\frac{S_{4,6}}{N}, \frac{S_{5,6}}{N})$ which can be proved on the line, the linear direction angle is $\theta = arctan\left(\frac{2S^*_{1,2}}{S^*_{1,1} - S^*_{2,2}}\right)$. Finally, $a_1 = cos\theta, a_2 = sin\theta, a_3 = -a_1 \overline{X} - a_2 \overline{Y}$, the fitting error: $e = sin^2\theta S_{4,4} + cos^2\theta S_{5,5} - sin2\theta S_{4,5} - N(sin\theta \overline{X} - cos\theta \overline{Y})^2$.

- **Fast Ellipse Fitting.** The ellipse general equation is $a_1 x^2 + 2a_2 xy + a_3 y^2 + 2a_4 x + 2a_5 y + a_6 = 0$, and the fitting matrix can be calculated with FC-nodes. DLS is a great developed by Fitzgibbon [7] because of its performing fit and non-iterative manner. However, DLS suffers from matrix singularity constraints and non-optimal solution will be find when all data points lie on the ideal ellipse curve [32]. Halir et al. [11] addressed this problem using an alternative formulation of the original task based on the block decomposition of matrix. In order to improve the accuracy of numerical solution, we have scaled down the data in pretreatment. Given a contour $\widehat{A_p A_q}$, the fitting result is calculated by Halir's methods [11]. A transformation from fitting result to ellipse parameter is given as follows: the ellipse center (x_0, y_0), $x_0 = (a_2 a_5 - a_3 a_4) \cdot SCALE$, $y_0 = (a_2 a_4 - a_1 a_5) \cdot SCALE$, angle of rotation is $\theta = \frac{arctan(2a_2/(a_1 - a_3))}{2}$. We define $a_{1p} = cos\theta a_4 + sin\theta a_5$, $a_{2p} = -sin\theta a_4 + cos\theta a_5$, $a_{11p} = a_1 + tan\theta a_2$, $a_{22p} = a_3 - tan\theta a_2$. $C_2 = a_{1p}^2/a_{11p} + a_{2p}^2/a_{22p} - a_6$, so semi-major and semi-minor axis are $l_{major} = C_2/a_{11p}$, $l_{minor} = C_2/a_{22p}$.

5 Validation

If an ellipse is got after grouping, there must be some edge points around this ellipse. By the same reason, there must be some edge points around lines. There are two validation constraints: (1) The Location Validation; (2) The Pixel Validation. We use the sampling points for each candidate shape as its validation points, and we judge these points whether they satisfy the two validation constraints. We give the validation equation as shown in Eq. 6 where N is the number of the validation points, $I_m(x_i, y_i), m = 1, 2$ is an indication function that if points (x_i, y_i) satisfy the validation m, $I_m(x_i, y_i) = 1, m = 1, 2$. If $R_v > R_{min}$, we consider this fitting ellipse is a real one.

$$R_v = \sum_{i=1}^{N} \frac{W_i I_1(x_i, y_i) I_2(x_i, y_i)}{N} \tag{6}$$

For the candidate lines, we take the validation points uniformly. $W_i = 1, i = 1, 2, ..., N$.

For the candidate ellipse, we define semi-major axis as R, semi-minor axis as r, the center as (x_e, y_e), the angle as θ_e. So, the validation point $[x_i, y_i] = [R\cos\theta_i, r\sin\theta_i] R(\theta_e) + [x_e, y_e]$. As shown in Fig. 3(a), the more concentrated to the end points of the semi-major axis the validation points are, the closer they are. We take the rate of slope change as its weight [21], so $W_i = \dfrac{rR}{R^2 cos(\theta_i)^2 + r^2 sin(\theta_i)^2}$. W_i is shown in Fig. 3(b), and shown that dispersing points have bigger weight. W_i is easy to certify $\sum_{i=1}^{N} \dfrac{rR\delta\theta}{R^2 cos(\theta_i)^2 + r^2 sin(\theta_i)^2} \approx \int_0^{2\pi} \dfrac{rR}{R^2 cos(\theta)^2 + r^2 sin(\theta)^2} d\theta = 2\pi$. Because of $N = \dfrac{2\pi}{\delta\theta}$, we can get $\sum_{i=1}^{N} W_i = N$. It is shown that when N is big enough, W_i does not need to be normalized. As shown in Fig. 3(c), when N is bigger than 80, $|N - \sum_{i=1}^{N} W_i|$ is very close to 0. So N must satisfy $N > 80$.

(1) **The Location Validation.** For each validation point $V_i = [x_i, y_i]$, if there exists a edge point on the V_i 8 neighborhood edge points, V_i pass the location validation. Mark $I_1(x_i, y_i) = 1$.

(2) **The Grad Validation.** For each validation point $V_i = [x_i, y_i]$, the point $V_i^{next_N}, V_i^{last_N}$ is the V_i next and last Nth point. Mark $l_i = \overrightarrow{V_i^{last_N} V_i^{next_N}}$. The gradient g_i at V_i is $(-R\sin\theta_i, r\cos\theta_i)$ for ellipse, and $(cos\theta_l, sin\theta_l)$ for line where θ_l is the line slope. GV_i is the score of the slope similarity and can be calculated by $GV_i = \dfrac{g_i \cdot l_i}{|g_i||l_i|}$, if GV_i is larger than the threshold T_{GV}. The point V_i is considered that it pass the grad validation, and mark $I_2(x_i, y_i) = 1$.

Finally, the validation score R_v can be got by the Eq. 6. If the R_v is larger than the threshold T_{RV}. This ellipse (line) can be place the real ellipse (line).

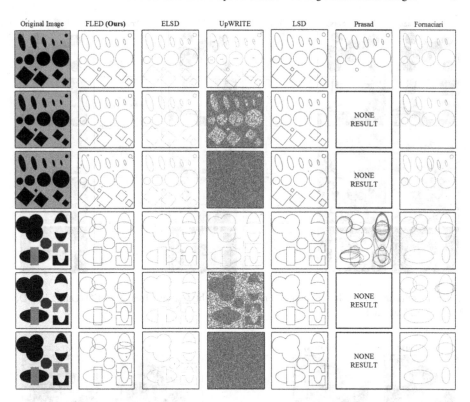

Fig. 4. Results on simulation images (1000 × 1000) of geometric shapes (square, ellipse) for different noise types and different scales. From left to right: Original Image, FLED (Ours), ELSD, UpWRITE, LSD, Prasad, Michele. From top to bottom: noise-free image, 0.05-Gaussian noise, 0.1-Gaussian noise, overlapping shapes, 0.05-Gaussian noise, 0.1-Gaussian noise

Table 1. Comparison of execution time on low resolution images (msec)

Image name	Size	Execution time (ms)				
		FLED (Ours)	ELSD	LSD	Prased	Fornaciari
//LR//1.png	442 × 640	**5.78781**	270	16.4607	821	7.92355
//LR//2.png	480 × 640	**7.75933**	610	19.3336	NONE	16.3411
//LR//3.png	480 × 640	**13.1629**	2930	27.8511	NONE	12.2071
//LR//4.png	488 × 700	**10.9402**	1380	23.2976	NONE	20.6639
//LR//5.png	375 × 500	**7.7169**	1030	17.5384	NONE	10.9937

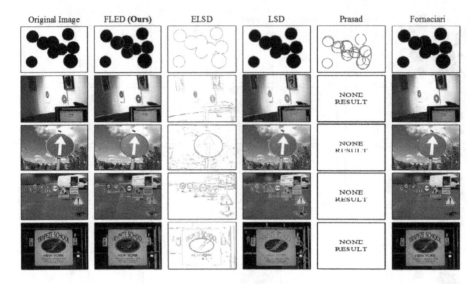

Fig. 5. Results on low resolution images. From left to right: Original Image, FLED (Ours), ELSD, LSD, Prasad, Michele.

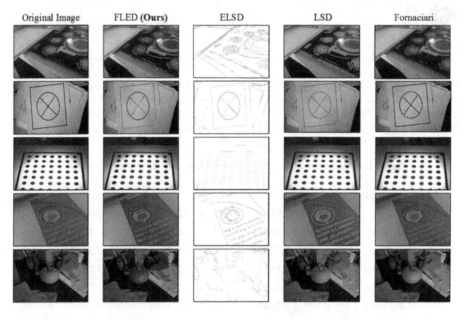

Fig. 6. Results on ordinary resolution images. From left to right: Original Image, FLED (Ours), ELSD, LSD, Prasad, Michele.

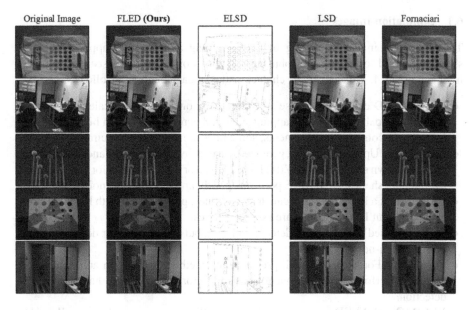

Fig. 7. Results on high resolution images. From left to right: Original Image, FLED (Ours), ELSD, LSD, Prasad, Michele.

Table 2. Comparison of execution time on ordinary and high resolution images (msec)

Size (OR)	Execution Time (ms)				Size (HR)	Execution Time (ms)			
	FLED	ELSD	LSD	Fornaciari		**FLED**	ELSD	LSD	Fornaciari
768 × 1024	**29.6**	3070.0	88.0	72.0	1200 × 1600	**62.1**	4750.0	125.2	1071.0
540 × 960	**10.0**	1180.0	32.6	13.9	1080 × 1920	**142.2**	7350.0	134.9	336.9
1024 × 1280	**15.3**	1890.0	64.8	95.5	1920 × 2560	**76.1**	3970.0	251.5	145.7
768 × 1024	**19.1**	1940.0	46.9	63.5	1200 × 1600	**17.3**	1830.0	92.7	149.2
960 × 1280	**46.0**	4170.0	103.3	129.8	1080 × 1920	**86.3**	2980.0	115.7	168.6

6   Experiments

To verify the proposed method, FLED is tested and compared with other methods. In the comparison, UpWrite [19], ELSD [27], LSD [29], Prasad [26] and Fornaciari [8] are selected, whose codes are available on-line. The experiments can be divided into two parts: With synthetic images and with real images. The synthetic images are simulation images validate methods performance from noise and overlapping. The real images are divided into three categories: (1) The images whose resolution are less than 500 thousand pixels are named Low Resolution Images (LR Image); (2) The images whose resolution are from 500 to 1 500 thousand pixels are named Ordinary Resolution Images (OR Image); (3) The images whose resolution are larger than 1 500 thousand pixels are named High Resolution Images (HR Image). All detectors are tested with their default parameters.

6.1 Simulation Images

The simulation images including both overlapping and non-overlapping geometric shapes, are used to analyse the robustness against noise and shape scales. The result is shown in Fig. 4. We analyze the characteristics of each method as follows.

- **ELSD**: ELSD can detect ellipse arcs effectively on each shape scale and has good anti-noise capability. For overlapping shapes, this method takes on high robustness. But when it comes to line segments, some lines are considered as circles.
- **UpWRITE**: UpWRITE detect geometric shapes by using GMM, and perform well on hand-drawn shape. But UpWRITE has high error detection rate, for flat ellipse and overlapping shapes, UpWRITE performs poorly and has low anti-noise capability.
- **LSD**: LSD is a line detector, it can detect all lines, perform well with high anti-noise capability. But LSD detect an arc as a set of lines.
- **Prased**: Prased's method can detect all ellipse, but have high error detection, while with low anti-noise capability.
- **Fornaciari**: Fornaciari is an ellipse detection method, it has high anti-noise capability and performs well. Fornaciari has low error detection, but has high missed detection.
- **FLED (Ours)**: FLED can detection lines and ellipses at once, performs well and has high anti-noise capability, FLED can detection most all lines and ellipse, for some overlapping shapes, this method might get some error detection.

After evaluating the performance of the method mentioned above, we decide to drop the UpWRITE method in the following real image test section.

6.2 Real Images

In this section, we test our method with other methods in real images. These images are tested in LR Images, OR Images and HR Images respectively, we get results as shown in Fig. 5, Fig. 6 and Fig. 7, the execution time is shown in Tables 1 and 2. The Prased not perform well in LR Images results, so this method won't be used in OR and HR Images.

From the result provided above, ELSD can get lines and ellipses, but its execution time is very high, ELSD can't be used for real-time application. Meanwhile, there are many lines detected as circles in ELSD. LSD can detect all lines in the image, unable to identify that some lines may belong to the same arcs, and Fornaciari's method can detect ellipse, and has low error detection, but has high miss detection. Our method FLED, can detect most lines and ellipse directly, particular, the execution time of FLED is fastest all of these methods. So, no matter in performance or in execution time, our method takes on superior performance.

7   Conclusion

In this paper, we have proposed a fast and robust line segment and elliptical shape detection method. We have made a lot of innovative improvements of the existing methods.

Through a lot of experiments, we adjust and verify the method parameters to achieve the best performance. Experiments show that, compared with the traditional representative methods. Our method (FLED) exhibit absolute advantages such as fast, robust and so on. So it can be widely used in hardware and software of video streamprocessing problems, especially in the processing of high resolution images and video, Our method has a broad application prospect.

Despite its performance, there are some room for improving in our method still has some space for improvement. When elliptic arc segments are divided very small, it is easy to occur false detection and missed detection and miss detection. In the future work, we will continue to improve our method on the basis of FLED from the following aspects: (1) Design a method for grouping muti-arcs to reduce the error detection. (2) Improve the fitting method to get more accurate results. (3) Improve the validation constraints to reduce the error detection. We hope our algorithm will have a better performance in the future.

References

1. Burns, J.B., Hanson, A.R., Riseman, E.M.: Extracting straight lines. Read. Comput. Vis. **8**(4), 180–183 (1987)
2. Canny, J.: A computational approach to edge detection. Read. Comput. Vis. PAMI **8**(6), 184–203 (1986)
3. Ding, W.: Extracting straight lines from building image based on edge orientation image. Acta Optica Sinica **30**(10), 2904–2910 (2010)
4. Duda, R.O., Hart, P.E.: Use of the hough transformation to detect lines and curves in pictures. IPSJ Mag. **13**(1), 512–513 (1975)
5. Etemadi, A.: Robust segmentation of edge data. In: International Conference on Image Processing and Its Applications, pp. 311–314 (1992)
6. Faugeras, O.D., Deriche, R., Mathieu, H., Ayache, N., Randall, G.: The depth and motion analysis machine. Int. J. Pattern Recognit. Artif. Intell. **6**(3), 143–175 (1992)
7. Fitzgibbon, A.W., Pilu, M., Fisher, R.B.: Direct least squares fitting of ellipses. IEEE Trans. Pattern Anal. Mach. Intell. **1**(5), 253–257 (1996)
8. Fornaciari, M., Prati, A., Cucchiara, R.: A fast and effective ellipse detector for embedded vision applications. Pattern Recogn. **47**(11), 3693–3708 (2014)
9. Gioi, R.G.V., Jakubowicz, J., Morel, J.M., Randall, G.: LSD: a fast line segment detector with a false detection control. IEEE Trans. Pattern Anal. Mach. Intell. **32**(4), 722–32 (2010)
10. Guru, D.S., Shekar, B.H., Nagabhushan, P.: A simple and robust line detection algorithm based on small eigenvalue analysis. Pattern Recogn. Lett. **25**(1), 1–13 (2004)
11. Halir, R.: Numerically stable direct least squares fitting of ellipses (1999)
12. Hough, P.V.C.: Method and means for recognizing complex patterns (1962)
13. Kahn, P., Kitchen, L., Riseman, E.M.: A fast line finder for vision-guided robot navigation. IEEE Trans. Pattern Anal. Mach. Intell. **12**(11), 1098–1102 (1990)
14. Kovesi, P.D.: MATLAB and octave functions for computer vision and image processing (2000)
15. Lee, Y.S., Koo, H.S., Jeong, C.S.: A straight line detection using principal component analysis. Pattern Recogn. Lett. **27**(14), 1744–1754 (2006)
16. Li, Q., Shi, J., Li, C.: Fast line detection method for railroad switch machine monitoring system. In: International Conference on Image Analysis and Signal Processing, pp. 61–64 (2009)

17. Li, X., Wang, Y., Deng, Y., Yu, J.: Cell segmentation using ellipse curve segmentation and classification. In: International Conference on Information Science and Engineering, pp. 1187–1190 (2009)

18. Liu, Z.Y., Qiao, H., Xu, L.: Multisets mixture learning-based ellipse detection. Pattern Recogn. **39**(4), 731–735 (2006)

19. Mclaughlin, R.A., Alder, M.: The hough transform versus the upwrite. IEEE Trans. Pattern Anal. Mach. Intell. **20**(4), 396–400 (1997)

20. Mclaughlin, R., Alder, M.: Technical Report - The Hough Transform versus the UpWrite. University of Western Australia (1997)

21. Meng, C., Li, Z., Bai, X., Zhou, F.: Arc adjacency matrix-based fast ellipse detection. IEEE Trans. Image Process. **29**, 4406–4420 (2020). https://doi.org/10.1109/TIP.2020.2967601

22. Meng, C., Xue, J., Hu, Z.: Monocular position-pose measurement based on circular and linear features. In: International Conference on Digital Image Computing: Techniques and Applications (2015)

23. Nguyen, T.M., Ahuja, S., Wu, Q.M.J.: A real-time ellipse detection based on edge grouping, vol. 5, no. 4, pp. 3280–3286 (2009)

24. Park, S., Kim, G.W.: Expanded guide circle-based obstacle avoidance for the remotely operated mobile robot. J. Electr. Eng. Technol. **9**(3), 1034–1042 (2014)

25. Poiker, T., Douglas, D.H.: Algorithms for the reduction of the number of points required to represent a digitized line or its caricature. Cartographica Int. J. Geogr. Inf. Geovisualization **10**(2), 112–122 (1973)

26. Prasad, D.K., Leung, M.K.H., Cho, S.Y.: Edge curvature and convexity based ellipse detection method. Pattern Recogn. **45**(9), 3204–3221 (2012)

27. Pătrăucean, V., Gurdjos, P., von Gioi, R.G.: A parameterless line segment and elliptical arc detector with enhanced ellipse fitting. In: Fitzgibbon, A., Lazebnik, S., Perona, P., Sato, Y., Schmid, C. (eds.) ECCV 2012. LNCS, vol. 7573, pp. 572–585. Springer, Heidelberg (2012). https://doi.org/10.1007/978-3-642-33709-3_41

28. Qiao, Y., Ong, S.H.: Arc-based evaluation and detection of ellipses. Pattern Recogn. **40**(7), 1990–2003 (2007)

29. Rafael, G.V.G., Jérémie, J., Jean-Michel, M., Gregory, R.: LSD: a fast line segment detector with a false detection control. IEEE Trans. Pattern Anal. Mach. Intell. **32**(4), 722–32 (2010)

30. Schleicher, D.C.H., Zagar, B.G.: Image processing to estimate the ellipticity of steel coils using a concentric ellipse fitting algorithm. In: International Conference on Signal Processing, pp. 884–890 (2008)

31. Thamizharasan, S., Baskaran, J., Ramkumar, S.: A new cascaded multilevel inverter topology with voltage sources arranged in matrix structure. J. Electr. Eng. Technol. **10**(4), 1553–1558 (2015)

32. Wong, C.Y., Lin, S.C.F., Ren, T.R., Kwok, N.M.: A survey on ellipse detection methods, pp. 1105–1110 (2012)

33. Xu, L., Oja, E.: Randomized hough transform (RHT): basic mechanisms, algorithms, and computational complexities. Comput. Vis. Image Underst. **57**(2), 131–154 (1993)

34. Yang, Q., Hu, H., Gui, W., Zhou, S., Zhu, C.: 3-parameter hough ellipse detection algorithm for accurate location of human eyes. J. Multimediad **9**(5), 619–626 (2014)

Quality Assurance and Verification of GFDM Satellite Imagery

Jing Yu[1] (✉), Xiaoheng Liang[2], Deyin Liang[1], and Longjiang Yu[1]

[1] Institute of Remote Sensing Satellite, China Academy of Space Technology, Beijing 100094, China
yuj421@sina.com

[2] Beijing Institute of Spacecraft System Engineering, Beijing 100094, China

Abstract. As China's first civilian medium-sized agile satellite, the Gao Fen Duo Mo Satellite (GFDM) has realized a variety of agile imaging modes for the first time, and particularly, the active push-scan imaging mode achieves the satellite's imaging in motion for the first time. Traditional image quality analysis and assurance means in passive push-scan mode are no longer fully applicable. In this paper, the image quality estimation is firstly carried out for the agile satellite GFDM, the key influencing factors are identified, and corresponding measures are taken to ensure the image quality during the engineering design and development process. The resolution of the sub-satellite points is improved to ensure the 0.5 m resolution within a certain maneuvering range. A synchronization monitoring atmosphere corrector is added to solve the influence of the atmosphere on high-resolution images. Integral time is set separately on different CCD chips to solve the problem of the large difference of image movement speed between the center and the edge of the field of view when the satellite is imaging at a large angle. The real-time setting of integral time is used to solve the problem of high dynamic image movement speed on the focal plane under active push-broom. Certain ground process is used to solve the problem of uniformity of indicators such as the resolution in an active push-broom image. Agile imaging is tested and verified on orbit, and the results show that the applied image quality assurance measures are effective. The image quality of the satellite in agile imaging mode meets the expected requirements.

Keywords: GFDM satellite · Image quality · Active imaging

1 Introduction

Agile remote sensing satellites can realize large-angle and rapid maneuvers in a short period of time, and use their fast attitude maneuvering capabilities to quickly change the pointing of the on-board camera to the ground, so as to achieve efficient and flexible observation of ground targets. Many advanced high-resolution remote sensing satellites use this agile imaging system, such as the "IKONOS" and "Worldview" series of the United States, and the "Pleiades" series of France [1–5], including the subsequent

© The Author(s), under exclusive license to Springer Nature Singapore Pte Ltd. 2022
Y. Wang et al. (Eds.): IGTA 2022, CCIS 1611, pp. 55–68, 2022.
https://doi.org/10.1007/978-981-19-5096-4_5

planned launched Worldview Legion series and the Pleiades Neo satellite constellations (of which Pleiades Neo 1, 2 had already been launched).

The Gao Fen Duo Mo (GFDM) high-resolution satellite is an agile optical imaging satellite operating in a sun-synchronous orbit at an altitude of 643.8 km. It was successfully launched from the Taiyuan Satellite Launch Center on July 3, 2020, with a high-resolution camera and an atmospheric detecting instrument used for synchronous correction. The high-resolution camera has three characteristics: high-resolution, nine-spectrums, and the ability of adapting agile imaging. Its sub-satellite point resolution reaches 0.42 m for panchromatic spectrum and 1.68 m for multispectral spectrum, which can be used for more accurate ground object detection. The camera achieves nine-spectrum imaging, covering the spectrum ranges from visible to near-infrared, which can achieve a better acquisition of earth surface properties. The camera is designed to adapt agile imaging modes such as satellite co-orbit multi-point imaging, multi-strip frame imaging, multi-angle imaging, stereo imaging, and off-track active imaging, which greatly improves satellite imaging efficiency and can accurately provides image data of user-required area.

The agile imaging capability of GFDM satellite has greatly improved its imaging efficiency, but it has also put forward new requirements for the assurance of satellite imaging quality, especially how to ensure imaging quality in agile imaging mode. There is no comprehensive and complete image quality analysis of agile imaging modes up to now, and no research on related image quality assurance. This paper not only discusses the image quality analysis, assurance, but also gives the on-orbit performance of the image quality of GFDM satellite. The in-orbit performance of GFDM satellite demonstrates the effectiveness of image quality assurance means.

2   Image Quality Analysis and Assurance

The analysis and evaluation parameters of image quality of remote sensing satellite can be divided into two categories: radiation quality evaluation parameters and geometric quality evaluation parameters [6]. Radiation quality is a quality evaluation linked to energy-related information represented by an image; geometric quality is a quality evaluation linked to image-related location information. Radiation quality parameters mainly include: dynamic transfer function, signal-to-noise ratio, dynamic range, radiation calibration accuracy, etc.; geometric quality mainly includes spatial resolution/width, positioning accuracy, registration accuracy, etc. The parameters of radiation quality and geometric quality are not completely independent, and there is a certain relationship between them. At the same time, from the perspective of remote sensing applications, the quality of the final product depends on the result of the combined effect of the two. While in the satellite argumentation stage, the two types of evaluation indicators are generally disassembled for analysis, so as to facilitate the analysis, assurance and verification of the indicators affecting the image quality. The image quality analysis later in this paper also adopts this idea.

GFDM satellite can carry out 6 types of agile imaging tasks: co-orbit multi-point imaging, co-orbit multi-strip imaging [7], co-orbit multi-angle imaging, co-orbit stereo imaging, along-track active imaging and off-track active imaging. Among them: during the execution of four types of agile imaging tasks: co-orbit multi-point imaging, co-orbit multi-strip imaging [7], and co-orbit multi-angle imaging, the satellite usually completes the attitude maneuver first, and then performs imaging after the satellite attitude is stabilized. While during the execution of the other two agile imaging tasks, along-track and off-track active imaging, the satellite performs attitude maneuvers while imaging. Agile remote sensing satellites can realize various agile imaging work modes through the combination of different maneuvering processes and imaging processes.

Compared with non-agile imaging satellites, the agile imaging process of GFDM satellite mainly has two major features: large-angle (including roll and pitch angle) imaging and active push-broom imaging. Under large-angle imaging situation, the resolution of the satellite image is lower than that of the sub-satellite point imaging, the atmospheric influence path is increased, and the imaging integration time of the center and edge of the camera focal plane is of great difference. Under active push-broom imaging situation, the satellite maneuvers during the imaging process, the attitude stability has a greater impact on the clarity of the image than non-active push-broom imaging situations, and the imaging integration time changes in a large range and changes fast. In the development process of GFDM satellite, the image quality in agile imaging mode is estimated mainly based on the above characteristics, and corresponding measures are taken in the engineering development procedure to ensure the image quality.

2.1 Large-Angle Imaging

2.1.1 Difference Between Image Resolution of Large-Angle Imaging and Sub-satellite Imaging

Considering the influence of the curvature of the earth, the ground sampling distance (GSD) of the camera under different roll and pitch angles of the satellite is calculated, and the results are shown in Fig. 1. It can be seen from Fig. 1 that with the increase of the satellite maneuvering angle, the GSD of the image increases. To ensure the ground resolution of 0.5 m within a certain maneuvering angle of the satellite, it is necessary to appropriately increase the resolution of the satellite sub-satellite point.

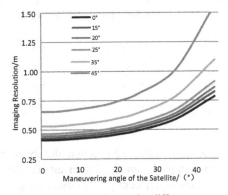

Fig. 1. Imaging ground resolution under different maneuver angles

The high-resolution camera adopts an aspherical coaxial three-mirror optical system and a TDICCD detector to achieve the high-resolution goal. The three-reflector-mirrors partial field coaxial optical system with a focal length of 10.8 m is selected, and the technical means of folded optical path, weight reducing of the reflector and small relative aperture are adopted to ensure the field of view (FOV), resolution and imaging quality, and also realize the light weight of the camera. The focal plane of the camera uses three 7 μm/28 μm 5-band TDICCDs and three 28 μm 4-band TDICCDs. The sub-satellite point resolution is 0.42 m, and 0.5 m resolution of is guaranteed within the angle of 20° pitch and 20° roll (corresponding to the cone angle of 28°).

2.1.2   Increase of the Atmospheric Influence Path

With the increase of the imaging angle, the atmospheric path that the satellite needs to pass to image the surface increases. In this situation, the atmosphere will have a greater impact on the radiation quality of the acquired image, which is mainly manifested as the influence on the image radiated energy parameters, such as Image Modulation Transfer Function (MTF). The influence of the atmosphere on the image MTF when imaging at different imaging angles is simulated. The imaging observation conditions assume that the sun altitude angle is 30°, the atmospheric visibility is 23 km, the target reflectivity is 0.3, and the background reflectivity is 0.05. The atmospheric radiative transfer model adopts 6SV for the simulation. We calculate the radiance of the target object and the background object reaching the entrance pupil of the camera under different imaging angles, and then obtain the decrease of the MTF value of the image caused by the atmosphere. The simulation results are shown in Table 1. We can see from Table 1 that: when the satellite imaging angle increases, the atmosphere transmission path increases, and the atmosphere will have a greater impact on the satellite image MTF.

Table 1. Atmospheric transfer function under different maneuver angles

Satellite imaging angle/(°)	Target radiance/($W \cdot m^{-2} \cdot sr^{-1} \cdot mic^{-1}$) (in the case of reflectivity $\rho = 0.3$)	Background radiance /($W \cdot m^{-2} \cdot sr^{-1} \cdot mic^{-1}$) (in the case of reflectivity $\rho = 0.05$)	Actual contrast of the scene	Camera entrance pupil radiance contrast	Atmospheric influence transfer function
0	61.391	20.108	0.6	0.507	0.844
20	63.445	22.498	0.6	0.476	0.794
40	67.795	28.106	0.6	0.414	0.690
60	76.683	40.443	0.6	0.309	0.516

When satellites image at large angle, in addition to the above-mentioned effects due to the atmospheric transmission path, compared with sub-satellite point imaging, there is also the directionality effects of adjacent pixels influence. When observing the sub-satellite point, the influence of the adjacent pixel is only related to the distance between it and the target imaging pixel, but when observing the ground target from a large angle, the influence of the adjacent pixel is not only related to the distance, but also to the azimuth of the observation azimuth. The adjacent pixels in the observation azimuth have the greatest influence on the remote sensing observation [8].

In order to obtain remote sensing image data with high radiation accuracy, GFDM satellite is equipped with an atmospheric synchronization correct instrument called SMAC to meet the needs of high-precision atmospheric correction, and the following means are adopted: ① The installation of SMAC on the satellite platform ensures that its optical axis direction is strictly consistent with the optical axis direction of the high-resolution camera. Thus the atmospheric parameters of the imaging area of the high-resolution camera can be achieved; ② The data of SMAC and the high-resolution camera are downloaded to ground in one data packet, and this will be convenient for the subsequent atmospheric parameter inversion and image atmospheric correction ground processes.

2.1.3 Difference of Integral Time Between the Center and Edge Field of the Camera Focal Plane

The focal plane of GFDM satellite is composed of three CCDs. When imaging at a large angle, the integration time of the center and edge of the focal plane is different. Figure 2 shows the simulation results of the integration time of the center and edge position of TDICCD under different satellite view angle.

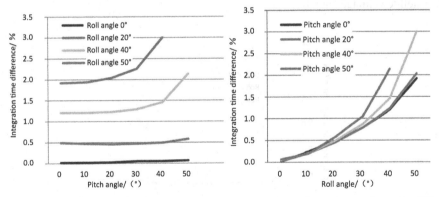

Fig. 2. Difference of integration time between center and edge position of TDICCD under different satellite viewing angles (a) The variety of the integral time difference of the center and edge of the focal plane (variety with pitch angle at different roll angles) (b) The variety of the integral time difference of the center and edge of the focal plane (variety with roll angle at different pitch angles)

It can be seen from the simulation results in Fig. 2 that the larger the satellite viewing angle is, a greater difference of the integration time between the center and edge field of the camera focal plane. When the roll angle increases, the integration time difference increases faster than when the pitch angle increases. According to the simulation results, when the satellite's pitch angle and roll are both 30°, if the integration time of the central field of the camera focal plane is used for the all fields of focal planes, the integration time setting error of edge field is 0.81%, the impact on the image MTF of the image edge field is 0.939; when the satellite pitch and roll angles are both 45°, This unified integration time setup will result in an error of 2.4%. The impact on the image MTF of the image edge field is 0.537. If the integration time is uniformly set, the larger of the satellite imaging angle, the greater of the drop of the MTF value at edge field of view of the image.

GFDM satellite adopts an non-uniformly integration time setting method to solve the problem of large difference of integration time between the center and edge field when the satellite is imaged at a large angle. Each CCD on the focal plane of the high-resolution camera is set according to the theoretical integration time of its central position. After this setting method is adopted, the setting error of the integration time is the theoretical integration time difference between the center and the edge of each CCD.

Figure 3 shows the difference between the theoretical integration times at the center and edge field of one CCD. When the satellite pitch and roll angle are both 30°, the difference of integration time is reduced from 0.81% in the uniform setting method to 0.26% in the non-uniformly setting method. The impact on the image MTF of the image edge field is only 0.994. When the satellite pitch and roll angle are both 45°, the difference of integration time is reduced from 2.4% in the uniform setting method to 0.82% in the non-uniformly setting method. The impact on the image MTF of the image edge field is 0.938. It can be seen that the overall MTF of the image is greatly improved by using the non-uniformly integration time setting method, especially when the satellite is imaged at a large angle.

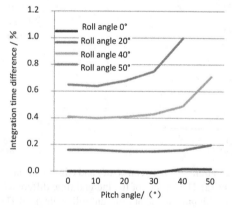

Fig. 3. Difference of integration time between edge and center position of one CCD when the integration time is non-uniformly set

2.2 Active Imaging Mode

In the active imaging mode, the camera of GFDM satellite uses the synthetic motion of camera pointing caused by attitude maneuver and orbital flight to perform push-broom imaging. Use "active" to distinguish it from traditional passive push-broom imaging that only relies on satellite orbital flight motion. Active imaging has great advantages in observing narrow and long strip targets (such as coastal zones, boundary lines, highways, and railways) along non-track direction, and can greatly improve the observation efficiency of this kind of object.

The influence of the active imaging method on image quality mainly include: firstly, real-time maneuvering during the imaging process will cause a worse attitude stability than that of the passive push-broom imaging mode, which will lead the image MTF value to drop; secondly, the moving speed of the projection of the imaging objects (which Determining the integration time) on the camera focal plane change during the imaging process, so the image resolution and other indicators change during the active imaging process.

(1) The satellite attitude stability is worse in the active imaging mode than that of passive push-broom imaging mode. During the active imaging mode, the attitude of the satellite changes in real time during the imaging process. During this process, the attitude stability can reach an accuracy level of 2×10^{-3} ($^\circ$/s), compared with 5×10^{-3} ($^\circ$/s) under passive push-broom imaging. The influence on the image MTF due to the 2×10^{-3} ($^\circ$/s) attitude stability would be 0.9897, and in the 5×10^{-3} ($^\circ$/s) situation would be 0.9994. It can be seen that the influence is small.

(2) Different from passive push-broom imaging, during active imaging, the satellite adjusts its attitude while imaging, and can scan along the target direction of the strip (it may not follow the trajectory of the sub-satellite point). This results in rapid changes in the projection speed of the imaging target on the focal plane of the camera. A typical active push-broom imaging process is simulated and analyzed below.

In the typical scenarios simulation, a relatively extreme active imaging process is considered. In this scenario, the trajectory of the satellite's imaging point (scanning strip of the camera) and the trajectory of the satellite's sub-satellite point are perpendicular to each other, and it is necessary to adjust the larger drift angle to ensure that the imaging point shift direction on the TDICCD focal plane is perpendicular to its line array direction. The target strip length is 170 km and the uniform ground speed is 7 km/s, and a C++ program programm is used to simulate this scenario. The simulation results are shown in Fig. 4. Figure 4(a) shows the trajectory of the satellite's imaging point and the sub-satellite point trajectory, which are perpendicular to each other; Fig. 4(b) shows the real-time changes of the satellite's roll angle, pitch angle, and yaw angle during this scanning process. It can be seen that in this imaging mode, the yaw angle of the satellite is relatively large, and can reach to -78°.

During the active imaging process of the satellite, since the projection speed of the imaging target on the focal plane of the camera changes in real time, the integration time setting of the camera and resolution of the achieved image would both change in real time.

T is assumed to be the integration time of the camera, and $\dot{T}/T$ is defined as the relative rate of change of the integration time, that is, the ratio of the rate of change of the integration time $\dot{T} = \Delta T / \Delta t$ (t is the time) to the current integration time T. This quantity is defined to facilitate following analysis of the effect of the integration time

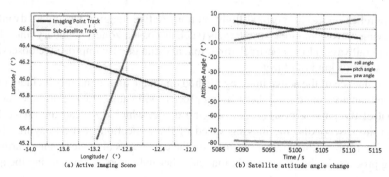

Fig. 4. Typical imaging scene of active imaging process

setting frequency on the satellite image MTF. Figure 5 is the time-dependent curve of the satellite integration time and the relative rate of change of the integration time during the active imaging process in Fig. 4. The rapid change of the projection motion speed of the imaging target on the focal plane requires a faster adjustment of the imaging integration time of the camera. In Fig. 5 imaging process, the maximum relative rate of change of integration time $\dot{T}/T$ is about 3.8×10^{-3}.

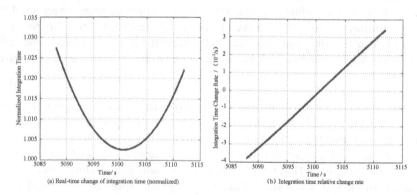

Fig. 5. Integration time change during the active-scan imaging process of Fig. 4.

The real-time interpolation setting of integration time of the camera is adopted to solve this problem of fast change of image movement speed on the focal plane under active imaging. If the traditional integration time setting method is still used, the MTF value of the satellite image would be greatly reduced during the active imaging mode, resulting in reduced image quality or even unusable. GFDM satellite uses the real-time fast setting of the integration time to solve this problem. To obtains the setting frequency requirements of the real-time setting, the impact on the image quality is simulated.

It is required that the image MTF value drop caused by the real-time change of the integration time is less than 0.99, so the image shift due to the setting frequency of the integration time is required to be controlled within 0.02 pixels. Under this restriction, the drop of the image MTF value is 0.9984. This restriction requires that:

$$\frac{\Delta d}{d} = N \cdot (\frac{\Delta T}{\Delta t}/T) \cdot \Delta t = N \cdot \frac{\dot{T}}{T} \cdot \frac{1}{f} < 0.02 \tag{1}$$

where: d is the pixel size of the CCD of the focal plane of the camera; Δd is the image shift value caused by the setting frequency of the integration time; N is the integration level of the camera; T is the integration time of the camera; t is time; f is the setting frequency of the integration time.

Considering more extreme situations, that is the relative change rate of integration time $\dot{T}/T$ reaches 8×10^{-3}. When the number of camera integration stages is 48, it requires that the satellite integration time setting frequency greater than 20 Hz, which can ensure the image shift within 0.02 detector element size due to the real-time change of integration time. When the number of camera integration stages is 24 and 92, the required integration time setting frequency would be greater than 10 Hz and 40 Hz, respectively. We choose the integration time setting frequency to be 48 Hz on GFDM satellite.

In order to engineer the integration time design in real time during the active push-scan imaging process, a cooperation of all the subsystems of the satellite is required. Because the integration time of the satellite changes rapidly under active imaging mode, the integration time calculation and setting need to be carried out in advance of the imaging process. The digital management subsystem of GFDM satellite uses the orbit extrapolation data and attitude extrapolation data to calculate the camera integration time series with a time stamp at a certain time frequency and send it to the camera subsystem, which interpolates the received integration time series to 48 Hz and executes. Figure 6 shows this specific implementation process of this integration time setting method.

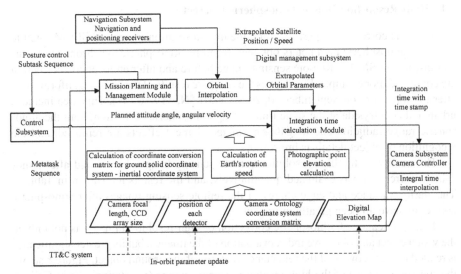

Fig. 6. Realization process of real-time setting of integral time on satellite

The integration time setting range for active imaging mode also has higher requirements, considering the integration time for fast active imaging (generally applied in the case of high imaging efficiency requirements) and slow active imaging of 45° satellite maneuver angle (generally applied in the case of high signal-to-noise ratio requirements of the image) as the minimum (lower limit) and maximum (upper limit) of the integration time setting, respectively. Simulation results show that the GFDM satellite camera needs to adapt to the integration time range of 42 to 250 µs. In order to adapt to the range and accuracy requirements of the integration time setting under active imaging mode, the camera CCD electronics design adopts high-speed, large dynamic range design technology, and can choose two operating modes of integration time (including interpolation and non-interpolation mode) to meet the needs of wide range and fast frequency requirements.

(3) The imaging resolution and other indicators change in real time during the imaging process. In the process of active imaging, the satellite imaging slant distance changes in a wide range and fast, and this will cause the resolution and other indicators in the acquired image changes in real time. For this kind of images, the ground processing system adopts the steady-state re-imaging technology based on sensor correction, carrying out line integration time normalization, CCD object stitching, and sensor correction based on virtual CCD steady-state re-imaging to obtain continuous, complete and consistent resolution images and corresponding rational polynomial coefficients (RPC) parameters, so as to provide high-precision standard image products for subsequent processing and applications.

3 Image Quality Verification of GFDM Satellite

3.1 High-Resolution Image Atmospheric Correction

Atmospheric correction is performed on the high-resolution images of GFDM satellite using the atmospheric parameters obtained from the atmospheric synchronization correct instrument SMAC. Remote sensing image before and after atmospheric correction are compared. For example, Fig. 7 gives the compare results of the smoky California area after the forest fire on September 30, 2020 (39.01 °N, 119.80 °W). This area includes urban and countryside at the same time. Using atmospheric correction, both the atmospheric range radiation and neighboring image element effects are removed, and the recognition of object details is improved.

The quality of the high-resolution remote sensing images before and after atmospheric correction was evaluated quantitatively, and the results are shown in Table 2. The clarity, variance and edge energy of the remote sensing images after atmospheric correction have all been greatly improved.

The significance of atmospheric correction of high-resolution images is not only in the visual effect and objective index evaluation of the images, but its greater significance is related to the recovery of the reflectance features of the ground object. Figure 8 shows the spectral recovery of the high-resolution camera image (vegetation area in California region) using SMAC, giving the surface reflectance before and after atmospheric

(a)   (b)

Fig. 7. Image of GFDM-1 satellite before and after atmospheric correction (a) Images of the California region before atmospheric correction (b) after atmospheric correction

Table 2. Evaluation of GFDM-1 satellite image before and after atmospheric correction

Image evaluation metrics	California	
	Before atmospheric correction	After atmospheric correction
Clarity [9]	7.53	14.81
Image variance	1255	3215
Image edge energy [10]	1.58×10^5	4.46×10^5

correction, and the reference reflectance spectral curve (from the Johns Hopkins University (JHU) Spectrum Library). The ground surface reflectance curve after atmospheric correction is closer to the reference reflectance curve. Therefore, the atmospheric correction can better get the characteristic spectra of ground object and helps quantitative application.

The atmospheric correction has a more obvious correction effect at large angle imaging situation. Figure 9 shows the large-angle (56°) imaging results by GFDM satellite before and after atmospheric correction. In this screen, the atmospheric optical thickness (AOD) is not very large (0.99), but the atmosphere still has a very large effect on the image, and the atmospheric correction effect is obvious.

3.2 Active Imaging Results

The validation of the active imaging was performed by GFDM satellite, as shown in Fig. 10. Figure 10(a) shows the actual ground scan track of the active scanning of the Italian coastline, and Fig. 10(b) shows one of the remote sensing images obtained by active imaging.

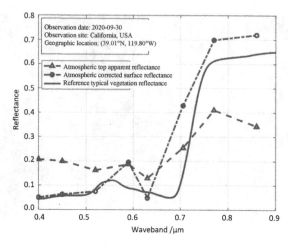

Fig. 8. Observed spectrum of vegetative cover land before and after atmospheric correction

(a)   (b)

Fig. 9. Image acquired with large satellite angle before and after atmospheric correction (a) Image acquired at large-angle before atmospheric correction (b) After atmospheric correction

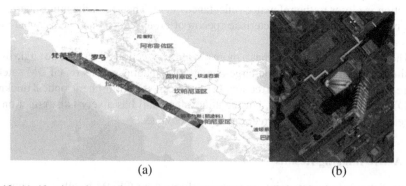

(a)   (b)

Fig. 10. Verification of active imaging process of GFDM-1 satellite (a) Actual ground scan track of a non-along-track active push-scan imaging (b) One of the active imaging images

The Italian active imaging information is shown in Fig. 11. The satellite's subsatellite point trajectory and imaging strip are solved based on the orbit and attitude information in the satellite downlinked auxiliary data and the tight imaging geometry model, as shown in Fig. 11(a); The real-time changes of satellite roll angle, pitch angle and yaw angle during the non-along-track active imaging downlinked is shown in Fig. 11(b), where the horizontal coordinates are the relative star time relative to the start moment of the active imaging, and the same below; The integration time of the satellite is set to change in real time due to the changing of the projection velocity of the imaging target point on the focal plane, as shown in Fig. 11(c); The changing of the resolution of the level 0 image data unprocessed by the ground system is shown in Fig. 11(d). This original image is processed by line integration time normalization, CCD object-square stitching, and sensor correction based on virtual CCD steady-state re-imaging to achieve consistency in the internal resolution of the one-view image, as shown in Fig. 10(b).

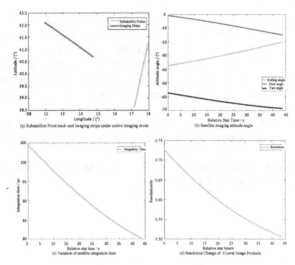

Fig. 11. Verification of active imaging process of GFDM-1 satellite

4   Conclusion

GFDM satellite as the first medium-sized agile remote sensing satellite in China, various agile imaging modes have been realized. This paper is also the first time to systematically analyze and study the image quality for agile imaging modes. As During the development stage of the satellite, a special study was conducted on the image quality assurance of the satellite, and the two main imaging characteristics of agile imaging process, namely, large-angle imaging and active imaging, were analyzed, and corresponding image assurance measures were adopted during the satellite development process. The in-orbit validation results of GFDM satellite show that the image quality assurance measures during the development process are effective, and the image quality of the satellite under various agile imaging modes meets the expected requirements.

References

1. Dial, G., Bowen, H., Gerlach, F., et al.: IKONOS satellite, imagery, and products. Remote Sens. Environ. **88**(1/2), 23–36 (2003)
2. AIRBUS: Pleiades user guide [EB/OL], 11 April 2021. https://www.intelligence-airbusds.com/en/8718-user-guides#pleiades
3. Maxar Technologies: Satellite access [EB/OL], 11 April 2021. https://www.maxar.com/products/satellite-access
4. Satellite Imaging Corporation: IKONOS satellite sensor [EB/OL], 11 April 2021. https://www.satimagingcorp.com/satellite-sensors/ikonos/
5. ESA: Worldview series [EB/OL], 11 April 2021. https://earth.esa.int/eogateway/missions/worldview
6. 刘兆军，周峰，满益云：等.光学遥感器像质评估与评价技术研究. 红外与激光工程 **35**(z1), 222–226 (2006). Liu, Z., Zhou, F., Man, Y., et al.: Prediction and evaluation technology of optical sensor's image quality. Infrared Laser Eng. **35**(z1), 222–226 (2006). (in Chinese)
7. 余婧，喜进军，于龙江：等.敏捷卫星同轨多条带拼幅成像模式研究. 航天器工程 **24**(2), 27–34 (2015). Yu, J., Xi, J., Yu, L., et al.: Study of one-orbit multi-stripes splicing imaging for agile satellite. Spacecraft Eng. **24**(2), 27–34 (2015). (in Chinese)
8. 胡宝新，李小文，朱重光：等.大倾角光学遥感中大气点扩散函数的近似模型. 中国图像图形学报 **1**(1), 19–29 (1996). Hu, B., Li, X., Zhu, C., et al.: Deriving the anisotropic atmospheric point-spread function of off-nadir remote sensing. J. Image Greph. **1**(1), 19–29 (1996). (in Chinese)
9. Jin, H.Y., Wang, Y.Y.: A fusion method for visible and infrared images based on contrast pyramid with teaching learning based optimization. Infrared Phys. Technol. **64**, 134–142 (2014)
10. Gupta, S., Gupta, C., Chakarvarti, S.K.: Image edge detection: a review. Int. J. Adv. Res. Comput. Eng. Technol. (IJARCET) **2**(7) (2013)

Machine Vision and 3D Reconstruction (Visual Information Acquisition, Camera Calibration, Stereo Vision, 3D Reconstruction, and Applications of Machine Vision In Industrial Inspection, etc.)

BSIHKS of Three-Dimensional Point Cloud Model and Model Matching: Bi-temporal Scaling Invariant Heat Kernel Signature

Dan Zhang[1,2]($\boxtimes$), Xiujuan Ma[1,2], Na Liu[3], Pu Ren[4], Zhuome Renqing[1,2], and Yuhuan Yan[1,2]

[1] State Key Lab of Tibetan Intelligent Informntion Processing and Application (Co-established by Province and Ministry), Xining, China
danz@mail.bnu.edu.cn
[2] Academy of Plateau Science and Sustainability, Xining 81017, People's Republic of China
[3] School of Artificial Intelligence of Beijing Normal University, Beijing, China
lna@mail.bnu.edu.cn
[4] Beijing Institute of Graphic Communication, Beijing 102600, China
renpu@bigc.edu.cn

Abstract. Recently, researchers drew widespread attention to three-dimensional point cloud processing, and the essential research work of three-dimensional point cloud processing is the three-dimensional model matching. Model matching of three-dimensional point cloud models is usually calculated by shape descriptors, which can describe the most discriminative features of three-dimensional point cloud models. However, most of the existing feature extraction methods only focus on local features, and do not discuss the global features of the three-dimensional point cloud models. In this paper, a new three-dimensional point cloud feature is proposed to represent the intrinsic characteristics of three-dimensional point cloud models: bi-temporal scaling invariant heat kernel signature (BSIHKS). BSIHKS is a shape descriptor involving in PCD-Laplace-Beltrami (point cloud data) operator. It does not need to triangulate the three-dimensional point cloud model, and can effectively represent the geometric and topological information of the three-dimensional point cloud model. Based on BSIHKS, the model similarity measure between BSIHKS values of a pair of three-dimensional point cloud models is defined as the model matching result, which provides an effective method for three-dimensional point cloud model analysis. Finally, experimental results on public three-dimensional shape databases show the rationality and effectiveness of BSIHKS.

Keywords: Three-dimensional point cloud models · Shape feature · Laplace-Beltrami operator · Shape similarity

Y. Wang et al. (Eds.): IGTA 2022, CCIS 1611, pp. 71–85, 2022.
https://doi.org/10.1007/978-981-19-5096-4_6

1 Introduction

In recent years, with the rapid development of three-dimensional shape generation technology, three-dimensional point cloud model analysis has been widely used in computer graphics, pattern recognition, biocomputing, and other engineering fields. The most basic and important research work of three-dimensional point cloud model analysis is three-dimensional model matching, that is, model similarity measurement. Similarity measurements of three-dimensional point cloud models are usually calculated from shape signatures, which capture the most unique features of a three-dimensional point cloud model. And the shape signature is a compact numerical representation of shapes that computers can understand and recognize.

When choosing a shape descriptor, two issues must be considered: what is the invariance or robustness of the shape descriptor under different transformations, and what shape features the shape descriptor should capture. An ideal shape signature should have the following characteristics: 1. It has the ability to describe the high discrimination of different types of models and the similarity of similar models; 2. It has invariance under different deformations and is robust to noise; 3. The expression is compact and easy to retrieve and store. Because the PCD Laplace-Beltrami operator has good performance and invariance for feature extraction of three-dimensional point cloud models.

In this paper, we define a shape descriptor based on PCD Laplace-Beltrami operator to describe the internal structure of a three-dimensional point cloud model: bi-temporal scaling invariant heat kernel signature (BSIHKS), and present a three-dimensional point cloud models similarity measurement framework based on BSIHKS. By calculating the modified Hausdorff distance between the BSIHKS of the model, we present some experimental results demonstrating that the BSIHKS is robust and stable enough to be transferred across the different non-rigid three-dimensional shape benchmarks.

1.1 Related Works

Compared with the triangular mesh model, the three-dimensional point cloud model is usually obtained directly by scanning equipment, which lacks effective point-to-point topology connection information. Therefore, there are relatively few researches on feature extraction of the three-dimensional point cloud models. The existing feature extraction methods suitable for three-dimensional point cloud model include four types:

(1) The first method is based on direct representation of geometric information of three-dimensional point cloud models, such as principal curvature [13,14], normal vector or [15–17] principal direction [18], to extract geometric discontinuities to extract the features of the three-dimensional point cloud models.

(2) The second kind is to regard the three-dimensional point cloud model as a matrix, and extract the statistical characteristics of the model based on statistical information. For example, based on statistical shape model (SSM)

[19] and principal component analysis (PCA) [20, 21]. Neither of the above two types of methods can guarantee that the features of three-dimensional point cloud models remain invariant under different deformations.

(3) The third kind is based on deep learning, which directly trains the three-dimensional point cloud in the network and implicitly obtains the characteristics of the point cloud [22–24]. PointNet [22] is the most representative research work and extracts a global feature from all point cloud data. Obviously, this is different from the current popular CNN method of extracting local features layer by layer. Inspired by CNN, the author proposes Point-Net++ [22], which can extract local features at different scales and obtain deep features through multi-layer network structure.

(4) The last is to convert the point cloud model into a triangular mesh and extract the features on the triangular mesh. The commonly used feature extraction methods include four types: based-on shape surface features [1–3], based-on shape statistical features [4–6], based-on shape topology informations [7–9], based-on spectral analysis [10–12]. In the above four descriptors, only the descriptor based on spectral analysis can maintain isometric invariance and topological robustness.

Overall, the first method relies heavily on the accuracy of point clouds, which can affect the estimation of geometric information, resulting in low accuracy of features. The second method mostly considers the rigid deformation of three-dimensional point cloud, but seldom considers the non-rigid deformation. The third method requires a large number of training samples and is time-consuming. The last method requires conversion of the storage format, which can easily lose the original information. Therefore, this paper proposes a method based on the spectral analysis method to directly calculate the feature of the three-dimensional point cloud model, which avoids the shortcomings of the above methods.

1.2   Contribution

Spectral shape descriptors attempt to utilize the geometric structure generated by the eigenvalues λ_i and eigenvectors φ_i of the LBO [25]. The global point signature (GPS) is a spectral shape descriptor that maps three-dimensional models in an infinite-dimensional space [26]. Sun et al. [27] proposed the heat kernel signature (HKS) based on the diffusion methods to describe the multiscale features. The wave kernel signature (WKS) [28] is proposed to clearer details by using a bandpass filter to clearly separate different bands of frequencies on the shape surface. However, the above shape descriptors are sensitive to shape scaling changes even if they have the advantages of equidistant non-deformation and topological robustness. By introducing Fourier transform to HKS, Brosten proposed a scale-invariant thermonuclear signature (SIHKS) [29], which eliminated the sensitivity of HKS to scale change.

The effect of SIHKS depends largely on the choice of time parameters. In previous work, researchers usually choose SIHKS sequences with single time parameter or multiple time parameters. The first method can only describe the local or global properties of a shape. The second parameter selection method extends a single signature into a signature vector by introducing a parameter sequence. Compared with the first method, the description ability of the shape feature is expanded. However, the time complexity of this method is higher, especially when the parameter sequence is too long, the time complexity of shape matching will increase exponentially.

Generally, LBO is computed on triangular meshes. To describe three-dimensional point clouds using the above features, format conversion is necessary. To avoid format conversion, we want to find a method that can directly define spectral analysis on three-dimensional point clouds. Mikhail Belkin et al. [30] constructed PCD LBO to calculate PCL LBO on three-dimensional point clouds, which is very convenient. Therefore, this paper selects two different effective time parameters to define a new three-dimensional point cloud descriptor: BSIHKS, which not only inherits the advantages of SIHKS, but also describes the topological and geometric characteristics of the three-dimensional point cloud model. Our research contribution is as follows:

- We directly calculate the PCL LBO of point cloud models and propose a shape descriptor BSIHKS based on the PCL LBO, it well integrates the multi-scale characteristics of SIHKS, and describes the local and global characteristics of three-dimensional point cloud model by selecting different bi-temporal parameters;
- We propose a framework that can directly measure the similarity of three-dimensional point cloud model without triangulation and point cloud registration, including calculating the modified hausdorff distance between BSIHKs of a pair of three-dimensional point cloud models.

The arrangement of this article is shown below. In Sect. 2, we introduce the definition and calculation of PCL LBO and the basic process of the similarity calculation framework. In the Sect. 3, we introduce the definition and calculation of BSIHKS, discuss the invariance of BSIHKS, and calculate the similarity based on the BSIHKS. In Sect. 4, we show the experimental results and analysis of this paper. Finally, we give the conclusion in Sect. 5.

2   Fundamentals and Framework

In this section, we first introduce the definition and discrete computation of PCL LBO, which is the LBO operator defined on the three-dimensional point cloud. Then the framework of similarity measurement of three-dimensional point cloud model based on BSIHKS is introduced.

2.1   Three-Dimensional PCL Laplace-Beltrami Operator

In order to effectively represent the intrinsic information and geometric characteristics of the shape, we regard the three-dimensional non-rigid shape as a Riemannian manifold M. For M, we give the definition of PCL LBO.

PCL LBO is a generalization of laplace operator on three-dimensional point clouds. The Laplace operator is a second-order differential operator defined by the real-valued function f in Euclidean space:

$$\Delta f = \nabla \cdot \nabla f = \nabla^2 f = \frac{\partial^2 f}{\partial x^2} + \frac{\partial^2 f}{\partial y^2} + \frac{\partial^2 f}{\partial z^2} \tag{1}$$

LBO can be obtained by introducing Riemannian manifold metric into Laplace operator. According to the definition of gradient and divergence on Riemannian manifold, LBO can be expressed as [31]:

$$\Delta f = \nabla \cdot \nabla f = \frac{1}{\sqrt{G}} \sum_{i,j=1}^{n} g^{ij} \frac{\partial}{\partial x^i} (\sqrt{G} g^{ij} \frac{\partial f}{\partial x^j}) \tag{2}$$

where g is the metric tensor on M, G is the determinant of the matrix g_{ij}. Since LBO is a self-adjoint operator, it can be decomposed into matrix products of eigenvalues and eigenfunctions by spectral decomposition:

$$\Delta_M \phi_i = \lambda_i \phi_i \tag{3}$$

where λ_i is the $i-th$ eigenvalue and ϕ_i is the corresponding eigenfunction. When Neumann boundary condition is used in the closed region, the first eigenvalue is 0, and the smallest non-zero eigenvalue is λ_2.

For numerical computations, the finite-dimensional discrete LBO is usually represented as discrete LB matrices. The real-valued function f is defined on a three-dimensional point cloud model with n vertices, then the discrete PCL LBO of the function defined on p_i vertices is represented as [30,32]:

$$L(i,j) = \frac{1}{nt(4\pi t)^{3/2}} \begin{cases} \exp(-\frac{\|p_i - p_j\|_2}{4t}), i \neq j \\ -\sum_{k \neq i} \exp(-\frac{\|p_i - p_k\|_2}{4t}), i = j \end{cases} \tag{4}$$

In order to ensure the sparsity of Laplacian matrix, for each point p_i, we only consider the items $L(i,j)$ related to the points $p_j = \{p_j, j \in N_{pi}\}$ that are closest to p_i with respect to the Euclidean distance. Researchers usually use K-nearest neighbors or points belonging to a sphere centered on p_i with radius r to generate neighborhoods of point clouds. In this paper, we use K-nearest neighbor algorithm [33] to get the neighbor point set of point cloud.

2.2   Framework

We construct a three-dimensional point cloud model similarity metric framework. As shown in Fig. 1, the detailed procedures are as follows:

A. Input three-dimensional point cloud models: In the first step, some three-dimensional point cloud models are input. The point cloud model is manifold, and point cloud registration and other preprocessing are not required for the point cloud model.

B. Calculate the PCL LBO of point cloud models: For a pair of three-dimensional point cloud models, the discrete PCL LBO of the three-dimensional point cloud model is calculated, and the spectral decomposition is carried out to obtain the eigenvalues and eigenvectors, please refer to (1) and (3).

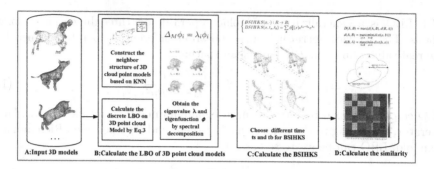

Fig. 1. The three-dimensional point cloud models similarity based on the BSIHKS

C. Calculate the BSIHKS: Based on the eigenvalues and eigenvectors, we can calculate the BSIHKS of three-dimensional point cloud models by choosing two efficient time parameters, please refer to (11) and (12).

D. Output the 3D point cloud models similarity: We calculate the modified Hausdorff distance between the BSIHKS values of a pair of point cloud models as model matching result, please refer to (14).

3   Bi-temporal Scaling Invariant Heat Kernel Signature

In this section, we define the scaling invariant heat kernel signature and propose a way to construct a bi-temporal scaling invariant heat kernel signature describing the feature of three-dimensional point cloud models.

3.1   Scale Invariance Heat Kernel Signature

The HKS is sensitive to shape scaling deformations. To overcome the shortcomings, Bronstein et al. proposed scale invariance heat kernel signature (SIHKS), they removed the dependence of $h_t(x, x)$ from the scale factor β. They used logarithmic sampling and Fourier transform to eliminate the scaling factor β, and added the scaling invariant to the original HKS. The specific process is:

1. For the shape M, the scaled shape is $M' = M$. According to the definition of HKS, the eigenvalues and eigenvectors of the scaled shape satisfy: $\lambda' = \beta^2\lambda$, $\varphi' = \beta\varphi$. Then, the spectral decomposition form of HKS at a point x on the shape M' after scaling can be written as:

$$h_t'(x, x) = \sum_{i=0}^{\infty} e^{-\lambda_i t\beta^2} \varphi_i(x)^2 \beta^2 \tag{5}$$

2. Under scaling changes, $h_t'(x, x) = \beta^2 h_{t\beta^2}(x, x)$, the HKS was sampled logarithmically in the time domain $(t = \alpha^\tau)$ and was formed as:

$h_\tau(x,x) = h_t(x,\alpha^\tau)$. At this time, the effect of β^2 caused by the scaling transformation is converted into time shifting $s = \alpha \log_a \beta$:

$$h_\tau{}' = \beta^2 h_{\tau+s} \tag{6}$$

3. The multiplicative constant β^2 was removed by taking the logarithm of h: $\dot{h}_\tau{}' = \dot{h}_{\tau+s}$ (here, $\dot{h}_\tau = \log h_{\tau+1} - \log h_\tau$). Then, the discrete-time Fourier transform of $\dot{h}_\tau$ was taked to turn this shift in time domain into complex phase:

$$H'(\omega) = H'(\omega)e^{2\pi\omega s}, \quad \omega \in [0, 2\pi] \tag{7}$$

4. Finally, the phase $H'(\omega)$ was in turn eliminated by taking the Fourier transform modulus:

$$\left| H'(\omega) \right| = |H(\omega)| \tag{8}$$

It is theoretically proved that the HKS values after the scaling change only has the offset on the time axis, and SIHKS has the scale invariance.

The discrete heat kernel signature is approximated by:

$$SIHKS(p_i, \tau) \approx \sum_{i=0}^{k} e^{-\lambda_i \alpha^\tau} \phi_i{}^2(x) \tag{9}$$

where p_i is the point of three-dimensional point cloud M. α^τ is the time sampling logarithmically of the heat signature at each shape point p_i.

3.2   Bi Scaling Invariant Heat Kernel Signature

From Eq. 9, we can see that the SIHKS has multi-scale characteristics. It is a descriptor sequence of the time sampling of heat kernel. The SIHKS has multi-scale characteristics by selecting time levels. If the interval of logarithm sampling of time is set to ω, the time parameter sequence of SIHKS can be written as:

$$\{t_i \in T | t_i = t_1 + \frac{\alpha^\tau}{(\omega+1)}(i-1)\}, i > 1, \omega \in Z^+ \tag{10}$$

Equation 11 shows the SIHKS of M at all time levels, t_N is the time parameter, $SIHKS_m(t_N)$ represents the SIHKS of the vertices $m(m \in M)$ at the time t_N, and each column represents the SIHKS of each point at different time levels.

$$SIHKS_M = \begin{bmatrix} SIHKS_1(t_1), SIHKS_1(t_2), ..., SIHKS_1(t_N) \\ SIHKS_2(t_1), SIHKS_2(t_2), ..., SIHKS_2(t_N) \\ ...... \\ SIHKS_m(t_1), SIHKS_m(t_2), ..., SIHKS_m(t_N) \end{bmatrix} \tag{11}$$

For SIHKS, when the time parameter is small, the heat diffuses to the local area of the model, reflecting the local characteristics of the model; on the contrary, when the time parameter is large, the heat diffuses to the global region, and SIHKS describes the global characteristics of the model. Figure 2 shows the

SIHKS(t1)   SIHKS(t3)   SIHKS(t5)   SIHKS(t7)   SIHKS(t9)   SIHKS(t11)

Fig. 2. Choosing the values of the time parameters for SIHKS

SIHKS results based on different time parameters. We hope that shape descriptors can describe the geometric information of 3D point cloud model as much as possible to facilitate model similarity calculation.

In this paper, we want to construct a shape descriptor that can reflect the global and local features of three-dimensional point cloud models at the same time. At the same time, based on the feature fusion method in machine learning, we introduce the concept of feature quotient to define the bi-temporal scaling heat kernel signature (BSIHKS), which can simultaneously simulate the process of small time and big time oscillating in the three-dimensional point cloud models:

$$
\begin{cases}
BSIHKS(x, \cdot) : R \to R; \\
BSIHKS(x, t_s, t_b) = \sum_k \phi_k^2(x) e^{t_s - t_b} e^{\lambda_i}
\end{cases} \tag{12}
$$

where t_l and t_h stand for the small time and big time levels. Then we give the choosing process of t_l and t_h. From Eq. 10, we can obtain the following:

$$
\begin{aligned}
t_l - t_h &= (t_1 + \tfrac{\alpha^\tau}{(\omega+1)}(l-1)) - (t_1 + \tfrac{\alpha^\tau}{(\omega+1)}(h-1)) \\
&= \tfrac{\alpha^\tau}{(\omega+1)}(l-1) - \tfrac{\alpha^\tau}{(\omega+1)}(h-1) \\
&= \tfrac{\alpha^\tau}{(\omega+1)}(l-h)
\end{aligned} \tag{13}
$$

When the values of α, τ and ω are known the value of $\frac{\alpha^\tau}{(\omega+1)}$ is a constant. To better integrate the global and local features of the 3D point cloud model and describe the local differences of the 3D point cloud model as much as possible, we choose the smaller the time h is, the larger the difference $(l - h)$ is, and the better the effect is. In addition, to maintain the local attributes of the shape, the value of h should not be too large. For the values of l and h, we give the experimental values.

3.3   Robutness of BSIHKS

As a point cloud shape descriptor, BSIHK inherits the intrinsic characteristics of SIHKS and has the following characteristics:

Isometric Invariance: The BSIHKS is defined by PCL LBO, so it maintains the intrinsic property of the three-dimensional point cloud models. $I : M \to N$ is an isometric deformation of, $BSIHKS(I(x), t_l, t_h) = BSIHKS(x, t_l, t_h b)$ for all $x \in M$;

Scaling Invariance: The another advantages of BSIHKS is scaling invariance. If we calculate the BSIHKS before and after the scaling deformation of models, theoretically, the BSIHKS value will remain unchanged. $S : X \rightarrow Y$ is an scaling deformation, $BSIHKS(S(x), t_l, t_h) = BSIHKS(x, t_l, t_h)$ for all $x \in M$;

Topological Robustness: In applications, the three-dimensional point cloud model changes more topologically. Because PCL LBO operator is highly robust to topology changes, BSIHKS has topology robustness.

Sampling Robustness: If the vertices on the surface of 3D point cloud model M are resampled, including up-sampling and down-sampling, the BSIHKS value of the resampled model is very close to that of the unsampled model.

3.4 Three-Dimensional Point Cloud Models Similarity Measurement

In this section, based on the modified Hausdorff distance (MHD) [34], we propose a point cloud similarity measurement method without pre-registration. The $MHD(M, N)$ between two discrete point sets M and N can be calculated as:

$$
\begin{aligned}
MHD(M, N) &= \max(d(M, N), d(N, M)) \\
d(M, N) &= \frac{1}{N_M} \sum_{a \in M} \min_{b \in N} \|a - b\| \\
d(N, M) &= \frac{1}{N_N} \sum_{b \in N} \min_{a \in M} \|b - a\|
\end{aligned}
\tag{14}
$$

Compared with Hausdorff distance in calculating $d(M, N)$, MHD uses the average of the minimum distance between each point to replace a single maximum and minimum distance, which not only eliminates the influence of abnormal points on distance calculation, but also improves the accuracy of distance calculation. When calculating the $MHD(M, N)$ in two non-empty point sets, it is not necessary to have the same number of points in the two point sets, nor to perform point cloud registration or find corresponding points in advance. The $D_{BSIHKS}(M, N)$ between a pair of 3D point cloud models $BSIHKS$ can be defined as:

$$
\begin{aligned}
D_{BSIHKS}(M, N) &= \max(d_{BSIHKS}(M, N), d_{BSIHKS}(N, M)) \\
d_{BSIHKS}(M, N) &= \max_{a \in A}(\min_{b \in B}(\|d(BSIHKS(M) - BSIHKS(N)\|)) \\
d_{BSIHKS}(N, M) &= \max_{b \in B}(\min_{a \in A}(\|d(BSIHKS(N) - BSIHKS(M)\|))
\end{aligned}
\tag{15}
$$

If $D_{BSIHKS}(M, N)$ is equal to zero, the three-dimensional point cloud model M and N are completely matched. If the value of $DBSIHKS(M, N)$ is large, the three-dimensional point cloud model M and N do not match, and vice versa.

4 Experiments

We perform several experiments on 64-bit 32G memory, Win10 system Matlab2015. We use the TOSCA high-resolution database [35], a subset of SHREC

2010 database [36]. The TOSCA high-resolution database provides a large number of three-dimensional shapes for non-rigid deformation shape analysis and contains a total of 80 objects with a variety of poses, including 11 cats, 9 dogs, 3 wolves, 8 horses, 4 gorillas, 12 females, and 2 different male images. The query sets of SHREC 2010 include 13 shape classes. For each shape, transformations are split into 12 classes (isometric, topology, scaling, noise, and so on).

4.1 Effectiveness and Parameter Selection of the BSIHKS

Figure 3 shows the eigenvalue λ by spectral decomposition, it shows that the eigenvalues λ of PCL LBO can well describe the intrinsic geometric properties of point cloud model. After repeated experiments, the time parameters of BSIHKS are obtained. As can be seen from Fig. 4, when the value of big time is too large, the description of the global attributes of the shape is more than the local attributes, when the small time parameter is about $l = (1/5) * t_{max} = 3$ and the big time parameter is about $h = (1/2) * t_{max} = 8$. The BSIHKS can simultaneously describe the local and global properties of the cat models, which can be seen from Fig. 4.

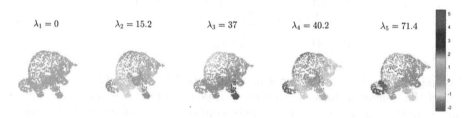

$\lambda_1 = 0$ $\lambda_2 = 15.2$ $\lambda_3 = 37$ $\lambda_4 = 40.2$ $\lambda_5 = 71.4$

Fig. 3. Show the eigenvalue λ by spectral decomposition

4.2 Robutness of the BSIHKS

This section compares the robustness of BSIHKS descriptors through several experiments. First of all, the TOSCA database containing isometric transformation of different shapes is selected to show the isometric invariance of BSIHKS in detail in Fig. 5 and Table 1. Then, the SHREC2010 query database is selected to compare the isometric invariance, topology robustness, scaling invariance and sampling robustness of BSIHKS in Fig. 6. It can be seen from the Fig. 5, Table 1 and Fig. 6 that the BSIHKS inherits the good characteristics of SIHKS, which has isometric invariance, topology robustness, scale invariance and sampling robustness, and it can describe more details of the point cloud model.

After obtaining the empirical values of the time parameters of BSIHKS, we use the existing four spectral shape descriptors: GPS, HKS, WKS, SIHKS and our proposed BSIHKS for comparison (as shown in the Fig. 7) to describe the characteristics of the point cloud model. Compared with the other four spectral

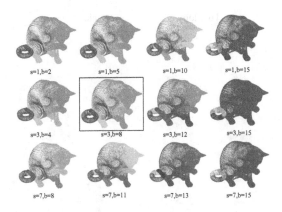

Fig. 4. Choosing the values of the time parameters for BSIHKS

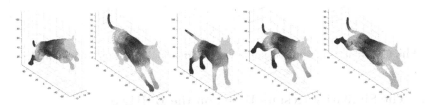

Fig. 5. Visual diagram of the different isometric deformation models of dog by using BSIHKS

descriptors, BSIHKS can clearly characterize the local differences of point cloud models. It has superior feature positioning ability and can distinguish different regions of three-dimensional point cloud.

Table 1. Isometric invariance with different isometric deformation models of BSIHKS on TOSCA database

Model	Cat	Dog	Michael	Centaur	Horse	David
Deformation1	0.2989	0.1531	0.2504	0.0947	0.2925	0.1522
Deformation2	0.0021	0.1966	0.2084	0.7915	0.1398	0.0099
Deformation3	0.0947	0.0945	0.3061	0.0250	0.0753	0.2240
Deformation4	0.0018	0.0234	0.0146	0.1316	0.3418	0.0756
Deformation5	0.2681	0.0644	0.1985	0.7583	0.4591	0.4978
Average	0.1331	0.1064	0.1956	0.3602	0.2617	0.1919

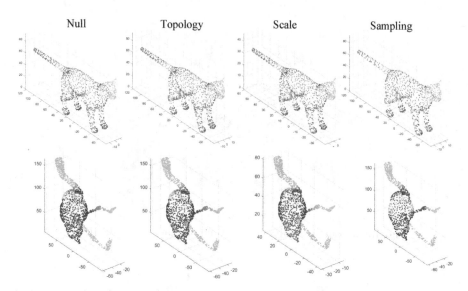

Fig. 6. Visual diagram of the different deformation model by using BSIHKS

4.3   The Similarity Results Based on the BSIHKS

To compare the sampling robustness and scale invariance of different BSIHKS and rapid calculation, this section compares the robustness and efficiency of BSIHKS through the SHREC2010 database. We select 24 models from

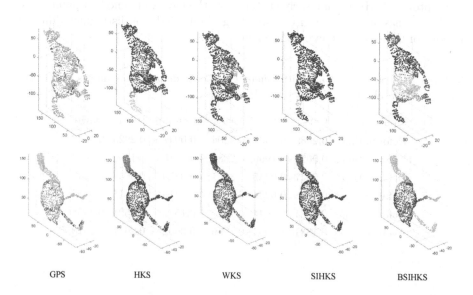

Fig. 7. The models describing by using GPS, HKS, WKS, SIHKS and BSIHKS

SHREC2010 database (There are four models in each category, including the original model and its three models with scaling, topology and sampling transformation). Figure 8 shows the modified Hausdorff distance based on SIHKS(t_3), SIHKS(t_8) and BSIHKS. It can be seen from Fig. 8 that BSIHKS has good performance and invariance compared with SIHKS with single time parameter. Therefore, BSIHKS can be applied to different shape analysis tasks based on the similarity results.

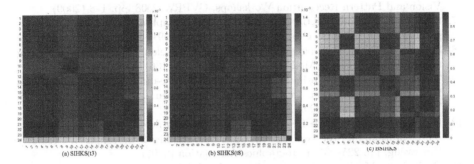

Fig. 8. Visual thermodynamic diagram of the model similarity results using SIHKS(t_3), SIHKS(t_8) and BSIHKS based on the SHREC2010

5   Conclusion

In this paper, we propose a 3D point cloud descriptor named BSIHKS based on PCL LBO, which optimizes the feature extraction and representation of SIHKS. Secondly, based on BSIHKS, we propose a three-dimensional point cloud model matching framework, which is flexible and does not require pre-processing such as point cloud registration or feature matching. The experimental results also show the validity of our framework.

Acknowledgements. This work was supported in part by the National Natural Science Foundation of China (Grant Nos. 62102213 and Nos. 62007019); Key R & D and achievement transformation projects in Qinghai Province (Nos. 2021-GX-111); Young and middle-aged scientific research fund of Qinghai Normal University (Grant Nos. kjqn2021004); Independent project fund of State Key lab of Tibetan Intelligent Information Processing and Application (Co-established by province and ministry) (Grant Nos. 2022-SKL-014) and Beijing Natural Science Foundation (Grant Nos. 4214064).

References

1. Lowe, D.G.: Object recognition from local scale-invariant features. In: IEEE International Conference on Computer Vision, p. 1150 (1999)
2. Castellani, U., Cristani, M., Fantoni, S., Murino, V.: Sparse points matching by combining three-dimensional mesh saliency with statistical descriptors. In: Computer Graphics Forum, vol. 27, no. 2, pp. 643–652 (2010)

3. Belongie, S., Malik, J., Puzicha, J.: Shape matching and object recognition using shape contexts. In: IEEE International Conference on Computer Science and Information Technology, pp. 483–507 (2010)
4. Osada, R., Funkhouser, T., Chazelle, B., Dobkin, D.: Shape distributions. ACM Trans. Graph. **21**(4), 807–832 (2002)
5. Mahmoudi, M., Sapiro, G.: Three-dimensional point cloud recognition via distributions of geometric distances. Graph. Models **71**(1), 22–31 (2009)
6. Ion, A., Artner, N.M., Peyre, G., Marmol, S.B.L.: Three-dimensional shape matching by geodesic eccentricity. In: IEEE Computer Society Conference on Computer Vision and Pattern Recognition Workshops, CVPRW 2008, pp. 1–8 (2009)
7. Shinagawa, Y., Kunii, T.L.: Constructing a Reeb graph automatically from cross sections. IEEE Comput. Graphics Appl. **6**, 44–51 (1991)
8. Sundar, H., Silver, D., Gagvani, N., Dickinson, S.: Skeleton based shape matching and retrieval. In: Shape Modeling International, pp. 130–139. IEEE (2003)
9. Tierny, J., Vandeborre, J.-P., Daoudi, M.: Partial three-dimensional shape retrieval by Reeb pattern unfolding. In: Computer Graphics Forum, vol. 28, no. 1, pp. 41–55. Wiley Online Library (2009)
10. Rustamov, R.M.: Laplace-Beltrami eigenfunctions for deformation invariant shape representation. In: Proceedings of the Fifth Eurographics Symposium on Geometry Processing, pp. 225–233. Eurographics Association (2007)
11. Ovsjanikov, M., Sun, J., Guibas, L.: Global intrinsic symmetries of shapes. In: Computer Graphics Forum, vol. 27, no. 5, pp. 1341–1348. Wiley Online Library (2008)
12. Sun, J., Ovsjanikov, M., Guibas, L.: A concise and provably informative multi-scale signature based on heat diffusion. In: Computer Graphics Forum, vol. 28, no. 5, pp. 1383–1392. Wiley Online Library (2009)
13. Deng, H., Zhang, W., Mortensen, E., Dietterich, T., Shapiro, L.: Principal curvature-based region detector for object recognition. In: 2007 IEEE Computer Society Conference on Computer Vision and Pattern Recognition (CVPR 2007), 18–23 June 2007, Minneapolis, Minnesota, USA. IEEE (2007)
14. Das, S., Bhandarkar, S.M.: Principal curvature guided surface geometry aware global shape representation. In: 2018 IEEE/CVF Conference on Computer Vision and Pattern Recognition Workshops (CVPRW). IEEE (2018)
15. Sanchez, J., Denis, F., Coeurjolly, D., et al.: Robust normal vector estimation in three-dimensional point clouds through iterative principal component analysis. ISPRS J. Photogramm. Remote. Sens. **163**, 18–35 (2020)
16. Huangfu, Z., Yan, L., Zhang, S.: A new method for estimation of normal vector and curvature based on scattered point cloud. J. Comput. Inf. Syst. **8**(19), 7937–7945 (2012)
17. Liang, L., Cao, X., Jie, S.: Three-dimensional point cloud registration based on normal vector angle. J. Indian Soc. Remote Sens. **47**(4), 585–593 (2019)
18. Ke, Y.L., Li, A.: Rotational surface extraction based on principal direction Gaussian image from point cloud. J. Zhejiang Univ. (Eng. Sci.) **40**(6), 942–946 (2006)
19. Srivastava, A., Joshi, S.H., Mio, W., et al.: Statistical shape analysis: clustering, learning, and testing. IEEE Trans. Pattern Anal. Mach. Intell. **27**(4), 590 (2005)
20. Bezerra, M.A., Bruns, R.E., Ferreira, S.: Statistical design-principal component analysis optimization of a multiple response procedure using cloud point extraction and simultaneous determination of metals by ICP OES. Anal. Chim. Acta **580**(2), 251–257 (2006)

21. Chi, Y., Yu, X., Luo, Z.: Three-dimensional point cloud matching based on principal component analysis and iterative closest point algorithm. In: 2016 International Conference on Audio, Language and Image Processing (ICALIP). IEEE (2017)

22. Qi, C.R., Hao, S., Mo, K., et al.: PointNet: Deep Learning on Point Sets for three-dimensional Classification and Segmentation (2016)

23. Qi, C.R., Yi, L., Su, H., et al.: PointNet++: Deep Hierarchical Feature Learning on Point Sets in a Metric Space (2017)

24. Zhou, W., Jiang, X., Liu, Y.H.: MVPointNet: multi-view network for three-dimensional object based on point cloud. IEEE Sens. J. 19(24), 12145–12152 (2019)

25. Fan, D., Liu, Y., Ying, H.: Recent progress in the Laplace-Beltrami operator and its applications to digital geometry processing. J. Comput.-Aided Des. Comput. Graph. **27**, 559–569 (2015)

26. Ovsjanikov, M., Sun, J., Guibas, L.: Global intrinsic symmetries of shapes. In: Proceedings of the Symposium on Geometry Processing, pp. 1341–1348. Eurographics Association (2008)

27. Sun, J., Ovsjanikov, M., Guibas, L.: A concise and provably informative multi-scale signature based on heat diffusion. In: Computer Graphics Forum, vol. 28, no. 5, pp. 1383–1392 (2010)

28. Aubry, M., Schlickewei, U., Cremers, D.: The wave kernel signature: a quantum 587 mechanical approach to shape analysis. In: IEEE International Conference on Computer 588 Vision Workshops, pp. 1626–1633 (2011)

29. Bronstein, M.M., Kokkinos, I.: Scale-invariant heat kernel signatures for non-rigid shape recognition. In: 2010 IEEE Conference on Computer Vision and Pattern Recognition (CVPR), pp. 1704–1711. IEEE (2010)

30. Belkin, M., Sun, J., Wang, Y.: Constructing Laplace operator from point clouds in R d. In: Proceedings of the Twentieth Annual ACM-SIAM Symposium on Discrete Algorithms, SODA 2009, 4–6 January 2009. ACM, New York (2009)

31. Rustamov, R.M.: Laplace-Beltrami eigenfunctions for deformation invariant shape representation. In: Proceedings of the 5th Eurographics Symposium on Geometry Processing, pp. 225–233 (2007)

32. Patané, G.: STAR Laplacian spectral kernels and distances for geometry processing and shape analysis. In: Proceedings of the Computer Graphics Forum, pp. 599–624 (2016)

33. Zhang, S., Zong, M., Sun, K., Liu, Y., Cheng, D.: Efficient kNN algorithm based on graph sparse reconstruction. In: Luo, X., Yu, J.X., Li, Z. (eds.) ADMA 2014. LNCS (LNAI), vol. 8933, pp. 356–369. Springer, Cham (2014). https://doi.org/10.1007/978-3-319-14717-8_28

34. Dubuisson, M.P., Jain, A.K.: A modified Hausdorff distance for object matching. In: 600 International Conference on Pattern Recognition (2002)

35. Bronstein, A.M., Bronstein, M.M., Kimmel, R.: Numerical Geometry of Non-Rigid Shapes. MCS, Springer, New York (2009). https://doi.org/10.1007/978-0-387-73301-2

36. Bronstein, A.M., et al.: SHREC 2010: robust large-scale shape retrieval benchmark. In: Proceedings of the EUROGRAPHICS Workshop on Three-Dimensional Object Retrieval (three-dimensionalOR) (2010)

A Review of Solutions to Stereo Correspondence Challenges

DingZhe Li[1,2], WeiMin Yuan[1,2], ZhaoXi Li[1,2], Cai Meng[1,2(✉)], and QiongGe Sun[2,3]

[1] School of Astronautics, Beihang University, Beijing 100191, China
Tsai@buaa.edu.cn
[2] VISION-BUAA Joint Laboratory of AI & Computational Optics, Beijing, China
[3] Beijing Holographic Vision Optical Technology Co., Ltd., Beijing, China

Abstract. Stereo correspondence has achieved continuous advances in the past decades. However, radiometric variations, situations of slanted surfaces and texture-less regions are still challenges in stereo correspondence. Due to the importance of those challenges and the lack of review articles about them, a comprehensive review on the solutions of those challenges are provided in this paper. The solutions to radiometric variations are discussed from the perspective of pre-processing and matching cost. The solutions to slanted surfaces are described from three aspects: local algorithms, global algorithms and semi-global algorithms. The solutions to texture-less regions are discussed from texture-less regions localization and filtering. This review will guide researchers to be better study the state-of-the-art of stereo correspondence.

Keywords: Stereo correspondence · Radiometric variations · Slanted surfaces · Texture-less regions

1 Introduction

Stereo correspondence is one of the most extensively researched topics in computer vision. In the past decades much progress has been made towards solving the stereo problem. Scharstein proposed an excellent taxonomy of stereo correspondence algorithm in [1]. Stereo correspondence algorithm was categorized as the following four fundamental steps: matching cost computation, support aggregation, disparity optimization and refinement [2]. Figure 1 outlines the pipeline of the algorithm. Stereo correspondence algorithms can be divided into local and global algorithms based on the optimization techniques used.

The goal of stereo correspondence is to determine disparity which is the difference in the horizontal coordinates of the corresponding pixels in stereo images. Accurate disparity map is important in many applications, such as augmented reality and 3D reconstruction [3]. Despite the advances in stereo correspondence, there still exists challenges in this field. The major challenges are as follows:

Y. Wang et al. (Eds.): IGTA 2022, CCIS 1611, pp. 86–102, 2022.
https://doi.org/10.1007/978-981-19-5096-4_7

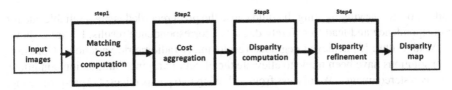

Fig. 1. Generalized block diagram of the stereo correspondence algorithm.

(1) Radiometric variations: Stereo correspondence algorithms are based on the assumption that the intensities or colors of input images have similar values. However, their performance degrades significantly in the presence of the radiometric variations because of the assumption is violated.

(2) Slanted surfaces: Frontal parallel assumption is another assumption in stereo correspondence. It assumes that the disparities within a certain block are the same and objects in the scene are perpendicular to the cameras optical axis. However, frontal parallel assumption is not satisfied in the slanted surfaces (non-frontal parallel surfaces). Disparity map exhibits "staircase effect" in slanted surfaces.

(3) Low-textured regions: The similarity between pixels in this regions is high. Pixels in this regions have large ambiguity and poor distinguishability, which causes the multiple correspondence.

(4) Occlusion: Some pixels in the left image the corresponding pixels does not exist in right image. This is the consequence that some scenes are visible to one camera but occluded to another one due to the obstacles.

In order to solve the above challenges, a significant number of algorithms have been proposed in the past decades. Some review papers [1, 4–10] on stereo correspondence have been presented. Those review articles were mainly focused on summarizing the accuracy level and the execution time of correspondence algorithms, as well as the improvements of algorithms. However, none of these articles provided the detailed discussion about above challenges. An extensive survey of the solutions to handle those challenges would be useful for those engaged to stereo vision, as well as for the newly interested researchers, allowing for a quick introduction to the state-of-the-art. Motivated by these observations, we focus mainly on the solutions of these challenges in this paper. (Occlusion problems, which were discussed in [4], are not within the scope of this paper.)

The rest of the paper is organized as follows: Sect. 2 describes the solutions to handle the radiometric variations. The solutions on slanted surfaces are presented in Sect. 3. The solutions to cope with texture-less regions are presented in Sect. 4. Conclusions are given in Sect. 5.

2 Radiometric Variations

Stereo correspondence is based on the consistency assumption: corresponding pixels have similar intensity or color values. However, there exists real situations in which radiometric variations are inevitable. Radiometric variations include the camera gain and exposure, varying lighting. It could cause the pixel recorded is not a reliable cue for correspondence and lead to severely degraded correspondence results. Figure 2 shows SGM algorithm [3] achieved degraded results under radiometric variations. Considerable solutions have been made to alleviate the effect of varying illumination conditions between stereo images. We discuss from following two perspectives: (1) pre-processing, (2) matching cost.

Fig. 2. (a, b) Stereo images under radiometric variations. (c) Ground truth. (d) Result obtained from SGM.

2.1 Pre-processing

The sensitivity of correspondence algorithm to varying radiometric conditions can be reduced by pre-processing. To eliminate the discrepancy of illumination between the stereo images, many solutions [11–21] have been proposed. Census transform (CT) utilizes the relative ordering of local intensity values, as shown in Eq. (1):

$$\text{Census}(x, y) = Bitstring_{(i,j) \in w}(I(i,j) \geq I(x, y)) \tag{1}$$

Khaleghi [11] proposed a stereo vision system (MESVS-2). CT was employed in pre-processing stage in the system. Same strategy was adopted in [12], stereo images were processed by CT, which make the method more robust against different light sources and camera exposure conditions. However, the defect of CT is that it would perform badly in the texture-less regions.

To eliminate the discrepancy of illumination between stereo images, filter algorithms [13–15] are adopted by researchers. Tophat filter [13] was adopted to mitigate the small parts of optical noises, which is defined as the difference between the original image f and its opening γ. As showed in Eq. (2):

$$\text{Tophat}(f) = f - \gamma(f) \tag{2}$$

Tophat filter is a useful tool for extracting features less the structuring element chosen from the processed image. Vaudrey [14] used residual image, which is the difference between image f and smoothed version of it. To reduce the effect of illumination differences, image were smoothed by mean shift filter. Difference between original images and residual images was calculated. Through mean shift filter, the influence of illumination could be alleviated effectively. Homomorphic filter was employed in [15]. Image f(x, y) is the product of illumination i(x, y) and reflectance r(x, y), as shown in Eq. (3). Illumination is treated as low frequency component while the reflectance is high frequency component. By taking the log of the image and high pass filtering, the illumination variations can be removed.

$$f(x, y) = i(x, y)r(x, y) \qquad (3)$$

There is a class of methods [16–18] adopted histogram. Histogram is widely used in stereo correspondence to address the radiometric variations. In [16] histogram equalization (HE) and binary singleton expansion were employed to eliminate the discrepancy of illumination. Cumulative histogram (CH) describes the orders of relative brightness of pixels, the values of CH at corresponding pixels should be similar regardless of illumination variations. CH was employed in [17, 18]. In [17], Jung used CH values to design a novel matching cost. A consistent stereo correspondence was proposed [18], since correspondence pixels are generally unknown under radiometric variations, the pseudo-disparity was estimated by sorting pixels based on CH in the pre-processing. Another class of methods [19–21] transform RGB color space into Log-RGB color space. Li [19] transformed images into Log-RGB color space and employed NCC measure. This method can reduce the effect of unequal light conditions while produce lowly accurate results on low-intensity region. Intensity in low contrast area was improved to easier detect the difference. HE was used [20] to reduce the effect of imbalanced intensity distribution and CLAHE to improve dim parts of the image. A similar work [21], which generated illumination invariant images used a non-iterative normalization.

2.2 Matching Cost

The consistency assumption includes intensity consistency and color consistency. Correspondingly, the matching cost calculation under radiometric variations is also proposed from these two perspectives.

2.2.1 Matching Costs Based on Intensity

Parametric matching costs, such as AD, SD and their sum versions, are based on the intensity consistent assumption. Those costs are not optimal choices under radiometric variations especially outdoor scenes. Hirschmuller [22] compared performance of 15 matching costs under radiometric variations. Non-parametric costs, which rely on relative ordering of local intensity values, were performed better than parametric ones. CT achieved best performance among non-parametric costs. An extended version CT of sequential vertical consistency constraint was presented in [23]. The result showed qualitatively good disparity map under radiometric variations. But this method was less robustness to noises. Modified census (MC) [24] defined on gradient, which was more stable against changes in illumination. The original census transformation can cope with radiometric variations that not disturb the ordering of the intensity. In MC, the relation between central pixels and its neighbor pixels was more resistant not only in the linear changes, but also against illumination changes. Basaru [25] proposed a modified version called Quantized Census. They generalized Census cost function by incorporating a quantization term, which is defined as follows:

$$C_{QC}(p) = \sum_{q \in N_p} F\{|D_L(q) - D_R(q - d)| > T\} \qquad (4)$$

where T is threshold value. D_L and D_R refer to quantized pixel differences. It was performed better and more robust against different types of radiometric distortions than CT.

Apart from the CT, there are other non-parametric matching costs were presented. Jung [18] proposed a consistent stereo correspondence algorithm. Adaptive color transform found pseudo-corresponding pixels based on rank (Eq. (5)) and transformed the color of each pixel to be consistent. However, this method does not take into account the effects of occluded pixels.

$$RT(x, y, d) = \sum_{(x,y) \in w} \left| Rank_{ref}(x, y) - Rank_{tar}(x - d, y) \right| \tag{5}$$

Dinh [26] applied fuzzy encoding pattern (FEP) as matching cost. FEP can tolerate local nonlinear intensity transformation between images. It is suitable for severe radiometric distortion. Zhang [27] proposed binary stereo correspondence method. BRIEF descriptor was introduced into cost and used to obtain binary strings of each pixel. Shin [28] used transition of pixel values and polynomial curve fitting. The result demonstrated this method had better performance under radiometric variations. LBP [29] as it is robust against outliers. However most LBPs miss the relationship among all of the pixels in the local region. Nguyen established the relationship of a pixel from various directions by introducing SLBP [30], this model performed less sensitivity to illumination changes. Ogale [31] presented a phase-based algorithm based on multiple frequency channels and non-iterative left-right diffusion. The method can handle significant changes between images. Although these approaches are suitable for global illumination change, illumination invariance is not guaranteed for local illumination change. Mouats [32] tackled the problem from a different perspective. Images were transformed to frequency domain and mapped used edges preserving and texture preserving mapping. This representation was invariant to illumination variations. Based on linear local model, method [33] was invariant to illumination variations and performed well in terms of speed and accuracy. Another new matching invariant light transport constancy was introduced by Davis [34], this invariant replaced matching cost and can be used with a variety of existing methods.

Cost function based on gradient information is rarely adopted. In [35], Hermann proved it was a powerful and robust matching cost under radiometric variations. In [36], gradient-based measure was compared with ordering-based measure. The comparison was done using SGM as optimization strategy. Result shown that gradient-based cost could provide a more reliable cost function under varying radiometric variations. All of those similarity measure costs have strengths and weaknesses, so some studies have been devoted to combining the strengths of multiple methods to achieve better performance such as [37, 38]. ELAS is fast and accurate. However, disparity map obtained by ELAS was substantially deteriorated by radiometric variations. Qu proposed an improved version of ELAS [37]. A prior estimation of disparity was conducted based on maximum a-posteriori. DAISY descriptor and CT were combined as matching cost. In method [38] a combination of three similarity measurements (AD + GM + CT) was used to compute the cost with adjustment element, the combination of matching cost can overcome the disadvantage of a single matching cost and more robust against radiometric variations.

2.2.2 Matching Costs Based on Color

Stereo correspondence based on color consistency fails to yield an accurate result due to varying radiometric variations. Algorithms [39–44] are proposed to use color invariant similarity measures in matching cost computation to deal with this challenge. Yong proposed ANCC [39] based on NCC. NCC has invariant property to affine transformation. However, it suffers from errors in object boundary. Yong established log-chromaticity color information model to extract the invariant information. ANCC outperformed other costs under different radiometric conditions. The defect of ANCC was that it fails in case of severe illumination changes. To overcome this limitation, Kim proposed ANCC flow [40]. ANCC was reformulated in a robust and efficient manner and furthered combine it with a cost volume filtering-based optimization. To reduce computational burden, PMF-like random search strategy was adopted. Most of algorithms aim to solve only one specific problem, their performance is degraded significantly when operating with stereo images captured under a variety of scenes. This is the case with ANCC. In [41], Dinh proposed a robust ANCC function that inherited strength of ANCC and can operate robustly for greatly different illuminations of stereo images.

Those approaches do not consider the correlation on cross-color channels, so they showed limited performance under illumination variations. Kim proposed a similarity measure MDCC [42]. It considered the correlation similarity on each color and cross-color channel simultaneously, providing robustness under illumination variations. MDCC estimated more accurate disparity maps than other state-of the-art similarity measures. Mutual information (MI) is a high performance cost as data term in energy function of global correspondence algorithms, which is defined as:

$$E_{data}^{MI}(f) = MI(I_1, I_2, f) = h(I_1) + h(I_2) - h(I_1, I_2, f) \qquad (6)$$

H(I) is the entropy of image I. Method [43] based on MI combined with SIFT as geometric cue to find corresponding pixels. By transforming input images into log-chromaticity color space, MI can establish robust and accurate correspondence. In [44], Heo devised an iterative framework to obtained both disparity map and color-consistent images. Segment-based 3-D plane-fitting constraint was incorporated. The joint pdf between images was computed by disparity maps. Disparity map can be updated by SCHE.

3 Slanted Surfaces

Most of stereo correspondence algorithms exploit the frontal parallel assumption, which assumes the scenes consisted of frontally viewed planes are perpendicular to camera optical axis. However, this assumption does not hold for slanted surfaces (non-frontal parallel surface). A lot of research has been presented to tackle this shortcoming. The solutions of dealing with slanted surfaces are presented from three aspects: local algorithms, global algorithms and semi-global algorithms.

3.1 Local Algorithms

Local algorithms assume that the disparities within a certain block are constant and the objects in the scene are perpendicular to camera optical axis. The drawback is that it is more error prone on slanted surfaces. Frontal-parallel assumption is often violated in real-world scenes. A lot of researches have been proposed to this challenges. Adaptive support weight (ASW) algorithm was presented in [45], which was defined as:

$$W_{BL}(p, q) = e^{(-(\frac{color(p,q)}{\gamma_c} + \frac{spatial(p,q)}{\gamma_s}))} \tag{7}$$

Color (p, q) represents the color dissimilarity, spatial (p, q) computes the Euclidean distance. ASW is a breakthrough of local methods, however the performance of it in slanted surfaces is not satisfactory. In [46, 47] different strategies was adopted to this shortcoming. Based on plane fitting, method [46] computed initial disparity map with ASW. Disparity plane orientation image was extracted from raw disparity map by least squares fitting. 3D adaptive cost aggregation was employed to obtain disparity map at sub-pixel accuracy. In contrast to other existing plane fitting algorithms, the approach is not require a prior image segmentation. Patch-Match [47] was adopted to find support plane for pixel. This method can be used to compute a cost volume for global stereo correspondence methods.

Epipolar constraint makes 2D correspondence search reduce to 1D, greatly reducing computational complexity and likelihood of false matches. But in some cases, one dimensional features of the epipolar line are not significant or cannot be extracted from single epiloar line. The method [48] was designed on the epipolar constraint and considered that information located on epipolar line is sufficient to compute precise disparities. This method was sufficient to provide correct correspondence on slanted surfaces. In [49], Muresan proposed a method by shifting parts from the correspondence windows to solve this problem. Window was shifted left and right with ($\pm 1, \pm 2$) disparity positions to find best position. Best correspondence solutions were fused into a correlation cost along with penalties for each shifting. To improve the correlations between stereo images, Einecke proposed a variant of block-correspondence algorithm [50]. Correspondence for disparities were computed for each pixel, those best pixel-level matches were combined to final values. Mureasan [51] proposed slanted block correspondence (SBM) to improve the matching quality on slanted surfaces by using oriented correspondence blocks. Result showed that SBM outperformed than most of other methods on the slanted surfaces.

3.2 Global Algorithms

Compared with fronto-parallel surfaces, slanted surfaces (non fronto-parallel surfaces) pose a problem for correspondence methods because of the significantly increased number of possibilities. To handle this question, global matching [52–57] algorithms were proposed. Birchfield [52] proposed to minimize energy functional that allows not just constant disparities but rather affine warpings. Stereo images were segmented into a number of non-overlapping regions by multiway-cut. Then find the affine parameters of the displacement function for each region. This method reduced the match sensitivity to slanted surfaces. Li [53] combined first-order with zero-order disparity information.

Contextual information was expressed geometrically by transporting surface normal. However, there are several limitations of the proposed method: first, it needs texture or shading variations to get a reliable local estimation. Second, occlusion is out of consideration in this method. Another work of Li [54] introduced the priors, encouraging the second and third derivatives of depth to be zero. He introduced surface differential geometric constraints to BP, result showed that improved BP can perform well on slanted surfaces.

Based on piecewise linear surface model, method [55] consisted of four modules: initial matching, cross checking, disparity filling and surface modeling. The former three modules were based on fronto-parallel model, while last module called piecewise linear surface model was designed to cope with slanted surfaces. Result showed that this model outperformed piecewise constant surface model. Miao [56] proposed a global method based on image smoothing. The strategy was to develop a sparse gradients counting model of disparity map, coupled with priors of intensity edges. The disparity optimization problem was formulated as a constrained optimization objective function and solved by half-quadratic splitting. Tree-based methods, hindered by the greediness of minimum spanning tree, perform badly on slanted surfaces. This drawback motivated Bai [57] to introduce loop-erased random walk into tree construction to improve the support weighted window near slanted surfaces. The new support windows is closer to ideal one because it can deal with both slanted surfaces and ambiguous regions.

3.3 Semi-global Algorithms

SGM based on mutual information presented in [3], which is one of the most renowned algorithms. It is a widely used efficient method in real-world applications because of a good compromise between accuracy and efficiency. Although SGM works well for textured scenes, it also fails on texture-less slanted surfaces. To compensate for this shortcoming, many researchers have proposed corresponding improvement measures [58–60]. An effective SGM extension SGM-P [58], utilizes pre-computed surface orientation priors. Such priors favor different surfaces. SGM-P performance well on slanted surfaces. SGM-P act as a soft constraint during correspondence and only add a minor computational compared to SGM. Spangenberg presented weighted SGM [59], which weights the cost of each path according to its compliance with surface normal. Histograms of LBPs can provide reliable features in correspondence processing. Lee proposed a memory-efficient approach [60] based on Gaussian mixture model, whose accuracy is comparable to most of SGM. They proposed an update rule slanted surface to maintain the depth smoothness on the slanted surface.

4 Texture–Less Regions

Unfortunately, real images present large texture-less regions, which hinder the calculation of disparity map. Figure 2 shows a scene filled with texture-less regions, a correspondence algorithm (SGM) is applied. The resulting map contains many errors. Computing disparity maps for stereo images in texture-less regions is a challenging task because of lacking of enough visual features and similar correspondence costs inside those regions.

This problem cannot be solved by increasing the aggregation window size or using global optimization techniques. The performance of stereo correspondence algorithms in texture-less regions would be poor and the mistakes will inevitably occur (Fig. 3).

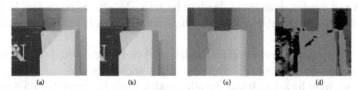

(a)   (b)   (c)   (d)

Fig. 3. Low-textured regions (blue and yellow regions) pose problems to stereo correspondence. (a) and (b) stereo images. (c) Ground truth. (d) Disparity computed from the SGM. (Color figure onlie)

The approach to overcome this challenge consists two steps: Low-textured pixels identified and interpolation performed. The success of obtaining an accuracy disparity map lies in a precise discrimination between texture and texture-less pixels. Delgado [61] built a classifier employed a set of local textures, which can select reliable pixels. This approach was based on selection of a representative set of local features. SVM was trained and used to distinguish pixels as textured and low-textures. Moraves chosen a different window and proposed a modified SSD [62], a robust connect-set filter was adopted to identify low-texture regions. Most of real-time or near real-time algorithms fail in low-texture regions. A plane-fitting algorithm [63] was proposed, which contained multi-view stereo correspondence and stereo fusion. The color segmentation was adopted to segment images, texture-less regions were fitted by locally estimated planes. This method provided a fast and accurate results in the weakly-textured regions. Epipolar distance transform was proposed [64]. The method converted intensity values to a relative location, which made pixels in weakly-textured regions become distinguishable. Epipolar distance transform showed that it works well in low-texture regions. Hu [65] proposed a real-time method, two strategies were adopted to deal with pixels in low-textured regions. Image was divided into low-textured regions and well-texture regions according to different features. MNCC, a method that combines plane priors and pixel dissimilarity was designed, was used to match the pixels in low-textured regions.

The simplest solution to cope with low-texture regions is to use only reliable disparities. However, the total number of disparities may not be sufficient for the practical applications. SACH [66] utilized edge maps to guide cost aggregation process. The method had two advantages, it achieved robustness in low-texture regions and the computational complexity was independent. The characteristics of multi-valued disparity map [67] was used to segregate into texture-less regions, textured regions, and low color variation regions. Disparity in texture-less region was calculated by stable correspondence. The boundary conditions for each region were modified so that accurate discontinuities are preserved. Ma proposed a method [68] based on image segmentation. Pre-processing strategy was employed by modified CT and mean-shift segment. In the modified CT the average of pixel gray values in the window is used to compare with other values instead of the center one in the traditional version of Census Transform.

Propagation-based methods [69, 70] were proposed and achieved relatively satis-factory results. Support pixels selected and propagated along different structures in this method. The algorithm [69] based on pixel-wise line segments and 1D propagation. Reliable pixels were selected and propagated along scan-line. This method only propagated the disparities of the seed pixels along scan-line direction. The propagation process was simple and effective because of the restriction. Based on support point propagation, the method [70] selected highly reliable pixels according to FAST detector and canny edge extraction. The support points selected were propagated along the triangulation and adjacent neighborhood structure.

5 Evaluation

In the previous section we introduced three challenges in stereo matching and the solutions for these challenges. In this section, we selected 7 representative matching algorithms (i.e. SSD [1], the gradient version of SSD(SSD(g)) [4], ASW [45], DP [1], SGM [3], CostFilter [71] and PM [72]), and tested the performance on stereo images with radiometric differences, slanted surfaces and texture-less regions. In the evaluation, we tested those algorithms on Middlebury benchmark [73], Fig. 4 shows the standard Middle-bury benchmark stereo image pairs in the evaluation (a) Baby2, (b) Bowling2, (c) Cloth2, (d) Flowerpots, (e) Plastic. Left images with exposure 1, illumination 1. Right images with exposure 2, illumination2. The slanted surface is marked with ellipse and the texture-less region is marked with rectangle, as showed in the Fig. 4. For all algorithms, the parameters were chosen empirically. The experiments are conducted on a PC equipped with core i3 2.53GHz and 4 GB memories. The algorithms was implemented in python and Matlab programming language.

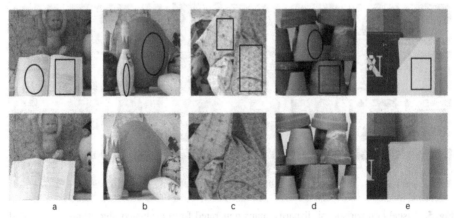

Fig. 4. Middle-bury benchmark stereo image pairs

Table 1 shows that the results of our evaluation. Error rates with threshold 1 pixel, best results are showed in bold. Among the 7 algorithms tested, costFilter [72] achieved the best results, the average error is 12.60. The local (SSD) and global (DP) algorithms of the traditional stereo matching algorithms performed poorly. Figure 5 shows the visual comparison of disparity maps generated from the evaluated algorithms. It can be seen intuitively that the costFilter and SGM algorithm work best, but the performance of SSD and its gradient version is worst. The ASW algorithm that performs well under standard image pairs does not achieve the desired results in this test. Although the error of the disparity map obtained by the DP algorithm is relatively small, there is still a streak phenomenon that needs to be solved.

Table 1. The results of our evaluation (Error Threshold = 1.0)

Method	Average	Error				
	Error	Baby2	Bowling2	Cloth2	Flowerpots	Plastic
SSD [1]	37.87	33.89	38.47	43.81	37.44	35.78
SSD$_{(g)}$ [4]	30.21	30.10	28.90	27.27	31.83	32.94
ASW [45]	26.17	21.37	26.38	26.84	16.25	40.03
DP [1]	24.25	27.09	15.14	21.64	32.46	24.94
SGM [3]	13.51	**13.04**	11.74	17.64	9.56	15.56
CostFilter [72]	**12.60**	21.76	**10.64**	**15.46**	**3.91**	**11.22**
PM [73]	23.43	24.58	28.91	24.15	19.07	20.45

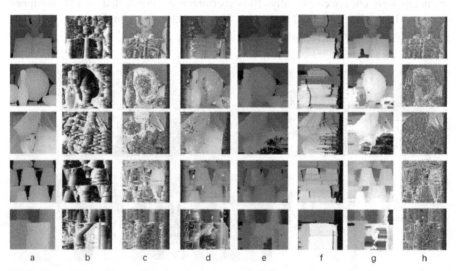

a   b   c   d   e   f   g   h

Fig. 5. Visual comparison of disparity maps generated from evaluated algorithms. (a) Ground Truth. (b) SSD. (c) SSD (g). (d) ASW. (e) SGM. (f) DP. (g) CostFilter. (h) PM.

Table 2. Main features of the discussed algorithms in this paper.

Author	Year	Algorithm	Matching cost	Support aggregation	Disparity optimization	Disparity refinement
Moravec [62]	1998	Local	SSD	Granule W	WTA	–
Ogale [31]	2005	Local	Fast diffusion along scan-lines	FW	WTA	LRC
Li [54]	2006	Global	BT	–	BP	LRC; Surface geometric constraints
Ma [55]	2007	Global	BT	–	GC	LRC; Mean shift; LSE
Xu [23]	2008	Global	CT	–	DP	LRC; Vertical consistency constraint
Zhang [46]	2008	Local	TAD	ASW	WTA	LRC; Hole filling with DPO
Khaleghi [11]	2008	Local	SAD	FW	WTA	LRC
Heo [44]	2009	Global	MI; SIFT	–	GC	LRC; Plane fitting
Simon [35]	2010	Local	Gradient AD	–	BP	LRC
Sach [68]	2010	Local	Modified cosine distance	FW	WTA	LRC
Bleyer [47]	2011	Local	NCC	ASW	WTA	LRC
Sebastien [48]	2011	Local	SSD	FW	WTA	LRC
Perrin [65]	2011	Local	MNCC	FW	WTA	LRC
Dinh [12]	2012	Local	Hamming distance	VW	WTA	LRC; Bilateral filter
Han [13]	2012	Global	SAD	–	BP	LRC
Li [19]	2012	Local	NCC	FW	WTA	LRC
George [21]	2012	Local	NCC	FW	WTA	LRC
Jung [17]	2012	Local	Cost based on CH	ASW	WTA	LRC

(*continued*)

Table 2. (*continued*)

Author	Year	Algorithm	Matching cost	Support aggregation	Disparity optimization	Disparity refinement
Kang [27]	2012	Local	BRIEF descriptor	Binary mask	WTA	LRC; Voting scheme
Jung [18]	2013	Global	Rank	ASW	GC	LRC
Spangenber [59]	2013	Semi-global	CS-LBPs	–	WTA	–
Slabaugh [25]	2014	Local	Quantized CT	FW	WTA	LRC
Nguyen [30]	2014	Global	SLBP	–	BP	LRC
Nguyen [29]	2014	Global	LDE	–	GC	LRC
Kim [42]	2014	Local	MDCC	FW	WTA	LRC
Bai [57]	2014	Local	LERW	ASW	WTA	Reorgnized UST
Einecke [50]	2014	Local	Patch cost	FW	WTA	–
Pramote [20]	2015	Local	NCC	FW	WTA	LRC
Ma [70]	2015	Local	M-cosine distance	FW	WTA	LRC
Shin [28]	2015	Local	Pixel values transition	FW	WTA	LRC
Dinh [26]	2016	Local	FEP	FW	WTA	LRC
Aiswarya [15]	2016	Global	SAD	–	DP	LRC
Hamzah [38]	2017	Local	AD; GM; CT	Iterative GF	WTA	LRC; Weighted BF; Plane fitting
Brown [4]	2017	Local	RANCC	FE	WTA	LRC
Mureasan [51]	2017	Local	TMCST-CT	Shifted W	WTA	Segmentation; Median filter
Yeong [60]	2017	Semi-global	Non-minimum suppression	GMM	WTA	Slanted surface handing
Scharstein [58]	2017	Semi-global	HMI	–	WTA	LRC
San [16]	2017	Local	SAD	FW	WTA	LRC; Mean shifted fiflter

6 Conclusions

In this paper, we have reviewed the solutions to challenges in stereo correspondence. For each challenge, the solutions are discussed from different aspects. For radiometric variations, the solutions are classified by the aspects of pre-processing and matching cost. The solutions to slanted surfaces are discussed from local algorithms, global algorithms and semi-global algorithms. The solutions to texture-less regions are discussed from texture-less regions localization and filter strategy. The main features of the solutions in this paper are summarized in Table 2. An extensive survey of the solutions to handle those challenges would be useful for those engaged to stereo vision, as well as for the newly interested researchers, allowing for a quick introduction to the state-of-the-art. For the future prospect of stereo matching, binocular vision will move closer to multi vision, and optimize each part for different application purposes.

Acknowledgments. This work was supported by the NSFC project (Grant No. 61873010), Beijing NSF Project (Grant No. 7202103), and the National Key R&D Program of China (Grants No. 2019YFB1311703).

References

1. Szeliski, S.R.: A Taxonomy and evaluation of dense two-frame stereo correspondence algorithms. Int. J. Comput. Vis. **47**(1–3), 7–42 (2002)
2. Mattoccia, S., Tombari, F., Di Stefano, L.: Stereo vision enabling precise border localization within a scanline optimization framework. In: Yagi, Y., Kang, S.B., Kweon, I.S., Zha, H. (eds.) ACCV 2007. LNCS, vol. 4844, pp. 517–527. Springer, Heidelberg (2007). https://doi.org/10.1007/978-3-540-76390-1_51
3. Hirschmuller, H.: Accurate and efficient stereo processing by semi-global matching and mutual information. In: CVPR, pp. 807–814. IEEE (2005)
4. Brown, M.Z., Burschka, D., Hager, G.D.: Advances in computational stereo. IEEE Trans. Pattern Anal. Mach. Intell. **25**(8), 993–1008 (2003)
5. Stefano, T.M.: Classification and evaluation of cost aggregation methods for stereo correspondence. In: IEEE Conference on Computer Vision & Pattern Recognition. IEEE (2008)
6. Lazaros, N., Sirakoulis, G.C., Gasteratos, A.: Review of stereo vision algorithms: from software to hardware. Int. J. Optomechatronics **2**(4), 435–462 (2008)
7. Tombari, F., Gori, F.: Evaluation of stereo algorithms for 3D object recognition. In: IEEE International Conference on Computer Vision Workshops. IEEE Computer Society (2012)
8. Tippetts, B., Lee, D.J., Lillywhite, K., et al.: Review of stereo vision algorithms and their suitability for resource-limited systems. J. Real-Time Image Proc. **11**(1), 5–25 (2016)
9. Bleyer, M., Breiteneder, C.: Stereo Matching—State-of-the-Art and Research Challenges (2013)
10. Affendi: Literature survey on stereo vision disparity map algorithms. J. Sens. (2016)
11. Khaleghi, B.: An improved real-time miniaturized embedded stereo vision system (2008)
12. Dinh, V.Q., Nguyen, D.D., Nguyen, V.D., et al.: Local stereo matching using an variable window, census transform and an edge-preserving filter. In: International Conference on Control (2012)

13. Han, Y., Xuan, G., Li, C., et al.: Removing illumination from image pair for stereo matching. In: 2012 International Conference on ICALIP. IEEE (2012)
14. Vaudrey, T., Klette, R.: Residual images remove illumination artifacts. In: Dagm Symposium on Pattern Recognition. Springer (2009)
15. Aiswarya, V.A., Edwin, D.: Efficient disparity map estimation of stereo images under varying radiometric factors. In: International Conference on Next Generation Intelligent Systems (2017)
16. San, T., War, N.: Local stereo matching under radiometric variations. In: IEEE/ACIS International Conference on Software Engineering. IEEE (2017)
17. Kim, J.: Histogram-Based stereo matching under varying illumination conditions (2012)
18. Jung, I.L., Chung, T.Y., Sim, J.Y.: Consistent stereo matching under varying radiometric conditions. IEEE Trans. Multimedia 15(1), 56–69 (2013)
19. Li, G.: Stereo matching using normalized cross-correlation in log-RGB space. In: International Conference on Computer Vision in Remote Sensing. IEEE (2013)
20. Piamsa-Nga, P.: A stereo image matching method on images with varying light conditions. In: 2015 ICSEC. IEEE (2015)
21. Rejimol, G.: A novel stereo matching technique for radiometric changes using Normalized Cross Correlation. In: International Conference on Data Science & Engineering. IEEE (2012)
22. Hirschmuller, H.: Evaluation of stereo matching costs on image with radiometric dierences. IEEE Trans. Pattern Anal. Mach. Intell. 31 (2009)
23. Xu, et al.: Efficient contrast invariant stereo correspondence using dynamic programming with vertical constraint. Vis. Comput. 24(1), 45–55 (2008)
24. Stentoumis, C., Amditis, A., Karras, G.: Census-based cost on gradients for matching under illumination differences. In: International Conference on 3d Vision (2015)
25. Basaru, R.S., Child, C.H.T., et al.: Quantized Census for Stereoscopic Image Matching (2014)
26. Dinh, V.Q., Nguyen, H.V.: Fuzzy Encoding Pattern for Stereo Matching Cost (2015)
27. Li, Y.K.: Binary stereo matching. In: International Conference on Pattern Recognition (2014)
28. Shin, K., Kim, D.: Visual stereo matching combined with intuitive transition of pixel values. Multimedia Tools Appl. 75(23), 15381–15403 (2016)
29. Lee, N.S.J., et al.: Local density encoding for robust stereo matching. IEEE Trans. Circ. Syst. Video Technol. 24(12), 2049–2062 (2014)
30. Nguyen, V.D.: Support local pattern and its application to disparity improvement and texture classification. IEEE Trans. Circ. Syst. Video Technol. 24(2), 263–276 (2014). https://doi.org/10.1109/TCSVT.2013.2254898
31. Aloimonos, O.A.: robust contrast invariant stereo correspondence. In: IEEE International Conference on Robotics & Automation (2003)
32. Mouats, R.: A Novel image representation via local frequency analysis for illumination invariant stereo matching. IEEE Trans. Image Process. 24(9), 2685–2700 (2015)
33. Xu, J., Yang, Q., Tang, J., et al.: Linear time illumination invariant stereo matching. Int. J. Comput. Vision 119(2), 179–193 (2016)
34. Wang, L., Yang, R., Davis, J.E.: BRDF invariant stereo using light transport constancy. IEEE Trans. Pattern Anal. Mach. Intell. 29(9), 1616–1626 (2007)
35. Hermann, S.: The gradient- a powerful and robust cost function for stereo matching. Image & Vision Computing New Zealand. IEEE (2012)
36. Hermann, S., Morales, S., Vaudrey, T., et al.: Illumination invariant cost functions in semi-global matching. Lect. Notes Comput. Sci. 6469, 245–254 (2010)
37. Qu, Y., Jiang, J., Deng, X., et al.: Robust local stereo matching under varying radiometric conditions. IET Comput. Vision 8(4), 263–276 (2013)
38. Abu Hassan, H.: Stereo matching algorithm based on per pixel difference adjustment, iterative guided filter and graph segmentation. JVCIR 42, 145–160 (2017)

39. Yong, et al.: Robust Stereo Matching Using Adaptive Normalized Cross-Correlation (2011)
40. Kim, S., Min, D.: ANCC flow: Adaptive normalized cross-correlation with evolving guidance aggregation for dense correspondence estimation. IEEE ICIP (2016)
41. Dinh, V.Q., Pham, C.C., Jeon, J.W.: Robust adaptive normalized cross-correlation for stereo matching cost computation. IEEE Trans. Circ. Syst. Video Technol. **27**, 1–1 (2016)
42. Kim, S., Ham, B.: Mahalanobis distance cross-correlation for illumination-invariant stereo matching. IEEE Trans. Circuits Syst. Video Technol. **24**(11), 1844–1859 (2014)
43. Lee, S.U.: Mutual information-based stereo matching combined with SIFT descriptor in log-chromaticity color space. CVPR 2009, 20–25 June 2009. IEEE. Miami, Florida, USA. (2009)
44. Heo, Y.S., Lee, S.U.: Simultaneous color consistency and depth map estimation for radiometrically varying stereo images. In: IEEE International Conference on Computer Vision. IEEE (2010)
45. Yoon, K.J., Kweon, I.S.: Adaptive support-weight approach for correspondence search. IEEE Trans Pattern Anal Mach Intell **28**(4), 650–656 (2006)
46. Gong, Z.: Local stereo matching with 3D adaptive cost aggregation for slanted surface modeling and sub-pixel accuracy. In: International Conference on Pattern Recognition (2009)
47. Bleyer, M., Breiteneder, C.: Stereo matching—state-of-the-art and research challenges. Advanced Topics in Computer Vision (2013)
48. Lefebvre, S., Ambellouis, S.,Cabestaing, F.: A 1D approach to correlation-based stereo matching. Image Vis. Comput. **29**(9), 580–593 (2011)
49. Negru, M.: Improving local stereo algorithms using binary shifted windows, fusion and smoothness constraint. In: IEEE ICICCP (2015)
50. Eggert, E.: IEEE Intelligent Vehicles Symposium Proceedings - Block-matching stereo with relaxed fronto-parallel assumption, pp 700–705 (2014)
51. Muresan, M.P., Nedevschi, S., Danescu, R.: Patch warping and local constraints for improved block matching stereo correspondence. In: 2016 ICCP. IEEE (2016)
52. Birchfield, S., Tomasi, C.: Multiway cut for stereo and motion with slanted surfaces. Proceedings of the International Conference on Computer Vision, vol. 1 pp. 489–495 (1999)
53. Li, G., Zucker, S.W.: Stereo for slanted surfaces: first order disparities and normal consistency. In: Rangarajan, A., Vemuri, B., Yuille, A.L. (eds.) EMMCVPR 2005. LNCS, vol. 3757, pp. 617–632. Springer, Heidelberg (2005). https://doi.org/10.1007/11585978_40
54. Li, G., Zucker, S.W.: Surface geometric constraints for stereo in belief propagation. In: IEEE Computer Society Conference on Computer Vision & Pattern Recognition. IEEE (2006)
55. Oh, J.D., Ma, S., Kuo, C.C.J.: Stereo matching via disparity estimation and surface modeling. In: IEEE Conference on Computer Vision & Pattern Recognition. IEEE (2007)
56. Miao, J., Chu, J., Zhang, G.: Disparity map optimization using sparse gradient measurement under intensity-edge constraints. SIViP **10**(1), 161–169 (2016)
57. Bai, X., Luo, X., Li, S., et al.: Adaptive stereo matching via loop-erased random walk. In: IEEE International Conference on Image Processing. IEEE (2015)
58. Taniai, S.: Semi-Global Stereo Matching with Surface Orientation Priors (2017)
59. Spangenberg, R., Langner, T., Rojas, R.: Weighted Semi-Global Matching and Center-Symmetric Census Transform for Robust Driver Assistance. ICCAIP (2013)
60. Yeong, L: Memory-efficient parametric SGM. IEEE Sig. Process. Lett. **25** (2018)
61. Ibarra-Delgado, S., Cozar, J.R., Gonzalez-Linares, J.M., et al.: Low-textured regions detection for improving stereoscopy algorithms. HPCS. IEEE (2014)
62. Moravec, K., Harvey, R.: Scale trees for stereo vision. Vis. Image Sig. Process. IEEE Process. **147**(4), 363–370 (2000)
63. Richarrdt, C., et al. Real-Time Spationtemporal Stereo Matching Using Dual-Cross-Bilateral Grid ICCV (2010)

64. Yang, Q., Ahuja, N.: Stereo matching using epipolar distance transform. IEEE Trans Image Process **21**(10), 4410–4419 (2012)
65. Perrin, J.M.: Letter from the editor strengthening residency education in pediatrics. Ambulatory Pediatrics **5**(5), 261–262 (2005)
66. Sach, L.T., et al.: A Robust Stereo Matching Method for Low Texture Stereo Images. IEEE-RIVF 2009
67. Tytgat, D., Lievens, S.: Stereo Matching Optimization by Means of Texture Analysis. IEEE (2010)
68. Ma, Y., Zhang, Y., Han, J.: A stereo matching handling model in low-texture region. Applied Optics and Photonics China (2015)
69. Sun, X., Mei, X., Jiao, S.: Stereo matching with reliable disparity propagation. In: 2011 International Conference on 3D Imaging, Modeling, Processing, Visualization and Transmission (2011)
70. Wu, H., Song, Z., Yao, J.: Stereo matching based on support points propagation. International Conference on Information Science & Technology. IEEE (2012)

Low Overlapping Plant Point Cloud Registration and Splicing Method Based on FPFH

Shengdong Lin, Yeping Peng$^{(\boxtimes)}$, and Guangzhong Cao

Guangdong Key Laboratory of Electromagnetic Control and Intelligent Robots, College of Mechatronics and Control Engineering, Shenzhen University, Shenzhen 518060, China
pyp8020@163.com

Abstract. Three-dimensional point clouds captured by sensors can quantify plant phenotype, which plays an important role in agricultural intelligence. Many scanned objects in agriculture and forestry are tall and obscured by leaves, so point clouds captured by either terrestrial or airborne methods may be incomplete. In order to obtain a more complete point cloud, this paper proposes a point cloud registration method based on the fast point feature histogram (FPFH), which aligns point clouds collected from different viewpoints. This method calculates the FPFH feature of each point and the Bhattacharyya distance between point pairs. Effective strategies pick out reliable sets of point pairs. Singular value decomposition is used to obtain the transformation relationship between point clouds. Experimental results show that the proposed method has high accuracy for plant point cloud registration in real scenes, and the root-mean-square error is smaller than that of common registration methods of SAC-IA and NDT.

Keywords: Fast point feature histogram · Bhattacharyya distance · Random sample consensus · Point cloud registration

1 Introduction

Plant phenotype is an objective expression of plant growth and plays an important role in plant research and agricultural production. In traditional agricultural and forestry research, plant phenotypic analysis relies on manual observation and measurement of plants. This approach is time-consuming, labor-intensive, and relies heavily on subjective experience. The integration of modern information technology and agriculture has promoted the formation of new production modes such as agricultural information intelligent perception, precise monitoring, and quantitative decision-making, which has promoted the development of precision agriculture [1]. Using modern information technology to obtain the phenotype of plants and crops without damage and quantify the growth state of crops is one of the important steps to achieve precision agriculture [2].

With the wide application of computer vision in the field of agriculture and forestry, plant disease detection [3] and fruit maturity judgment [4] can be achieved by using two-dimensional (2D) images to obtain plant information. Since the three-dimensional (3D) model has more information than the 2D image, it is a potential direction to use

© The Author(s), under exclusive license to Springer Nature Singapore Pte Ltd. 2022
Y. Wang et al. (Eds.): IGTA 2022, CCIS 1611, pp. 103–117, 2022.
https://doi.org/10.1007/978-981-19-5096-4_8

the 3D point cloud model to monitor and manage agricultural production [5]. Wu et al. [6] used point clouds to generate the skeleton of maize plants, and estimated phenotypes such as plant height, leaf length, leaf inclination, and azimuth. Rueda-ayala et al. [7] estimated the plant height, biomass, and volume of sweet wheat grass and ryegrass through the point cloud of grassland. Cabo et al. [8] automatically identified tree stems by analyzing point clouds, and then estimated tree height and trunk diameter. The plant surface morphological information obtained through point clouds has many uses, such as judging the growth state of plants, predicting crop yield, calculating volume, and so on.

At present, most of the methods for the 3D reconstruction of plants are based on optical non-contact sensors. Wang et al. [9] used the terrestrial laser scanning (TLS) method to obtain the point cloud of corn plants, which is fast and simple to operate, but the scanning equipment is expensive. Vázquez-Arellano et al. [10] used a time-of-flight (TOF) camera to sequentially collect point clouds of corn seedlings in the experimental field for registration, and the registration algorithm used iterative closest point (ICP). The point cloud registration method in this paper relies on point clouds whose initial poses are roughly aligned and overlapped, and the price of the capture device is high. Chen et al. [11] used an RGB camera to take multiple photos of kale, wheat, and physalis placed on a turntable, calculated camera internal parameters and pose information according to incremental SFM, used MVSNet to generate a depth map, and finally generated 3D points cloud. The point cloud generated by this method is dense, but the method using the turntable is only suitable for low plants and not suitable for outdoor scenes. Ni et al. [12] used a binocular camera to capture two images of stereo plants, used the efficient large scale stereo matching (ELAS) algorithm to calculate the disparity map, and then obtained the 3D point cloud model of the plant through triangulation. When processing images were taken at close range, the texture of leaves can be clearly displayed, but the reconstruction effect is poor in the case of long-distance. Guan et al. [13] developed an imaging system consisting of an RGB camera and a PMD camera. Using the DBSCAN algorithm, the point cloud of the soybean plant canopy is extracted from the original single-view point cloud, and the point cloud models based on the side view and the top view are generated. But they are not spliced together, so the phenotypic information is not comprehensive enough.

The methods in the above-mentioned articles are almost all applied to obtain 3D point cloud models of low plants. However, for tall plants and trees, due to the limited field of view of the sensor, the above method cannot obtain a high-integrity point cloud model from top, bottom, and side views. To solve this problem, point clouds captured from multiple angles and efficient point cloud registration algorithms are required.

Among the point cloud registration algorithms, the most classic is the iterative closest point (ICP) proposed by Besl et al. [14]. In this method, the point pair with the closest Euclidean distance is used as the matching point, and the transformation matrix between the two point clouds is calculated by the least square method. Then, the matching points are repeatedly selected and calculated iteratively until the error is less than the threshold, and the transformation matrix is regarded as optimal. However, the disadvantage of this method is that it requires an initial value and is sensitive to noise, and it is easy to encounter local optimization [15].

In order to improve the accuracy of registration, many scholars divide the registration into two steps, that is, first use geometric features to obtain rough transformation, and then use ICP for fine registration. Accurately computing transformation matrices relies on accurate descriptions and correct matching of features [16]. At present, representative local feature algorithms include 3D shape context (3DSC) proposed by Frome et al. [17], the signature of histograms of orientations (SHOT) proposed by Salti et al. [18], point feature histogram (PFH) [19], and fast point feature histogram (FPFH) [20] proposed by Rusu et al.

FPFH is a 3D feature descriptor based on PFH. It uses the normal vector to calculate the relationship between the query point and the points in its neighborhood. It represents the features of the point neighborhood in the form of a histogram. Since FPFH has a fast operation speed, only 33 dimensions, and occupies less operation space, this paper proposes a point cloud registration algorithm based on FPFH features. This method is used to register point clouds from different viewpoints to obtain a more complete point cloud model. The method is applied to the multi-source real plant point cloud with a low overlap rate, and a more complete three-dimensional point cloud model of the plant can be obtained, and the error is at the millimeter level. This method is of great significance to agricultural intelligence. The remainder of the paper is organized as follows. The second section will introduce the detailed method and mathematical model. The third section contains experimental verification and a discussion of the results. Finally, the conclusion of this paper is given in the fourth section.

2 Methodology

The purpose of registration is to unify the two point clouds into the same coordinate system. The two point clouds to be registered are marked as a source point cloud and a target point cloud, respectively. This paper proposes a point cloud registration method based on FPFH: (1) Preprocess the two point clouds, including subsampling the point cloud with a voxel grid and statistical filtering to remove outliers; (2) Estimate each point cloud normals of points and compute their FPFH features. Histogram similarity is evaluated according to Bhattacharyya distance. Iteratively compares the FPFH features in the source point cloud and the target point cloud to obtain an initial set of matching point pairs; (3) Improve the accuracy of matching point pairs. For the special case where multiple points match one point, only the corresponding point with the closest distance is selected. Then, sort the remaining matching point pairs and pick the top matching point pairs. At the same time, the distance threshold is used to filter the points that are too concentrated; (4) The random sample consensus (RANSAC) is used to remove the wrong matching point pairs, and the calculation of singular value decomposition (SVD) is performed on the remaining matching point pairs to obtain the rotation matrix and translation vector. The specific implementation of this process is shown in Fig. 1.

2.1 Point Normal Estimation

Since a single point cannot reflect the geometric surface features around it, the features of a point need to be considered by combining the neighboring points within a certain range

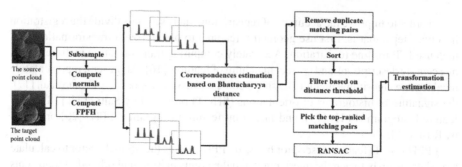

Fig. 1. The pipeline of pairwise point clouds registration.

around it. Typically, geometric surface features are represented based on the normals of points within a neighborhood.

The method of calculating the normal vector of the point cloud surface in this paper is to estimate the normal vector for the points in the neighborhood. Converts the problem of solving the normals of a point on the surface of the point cloud into the problem of estimating the normals of the tangent planes. By minimizing the objective function containing the normal vector, using the idea of the least-squares method, the result of the dot product of the vector formed by the point and each of its neighbors and the normal vector is zero.

First, the plane is represented as a point x and a normal vector $\vec{n}$, as shown in Fig. 2. The points in the neighborhood are represented by $p_i \in P^n$.

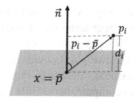

Fig. 2. Estimate the normal vector of a point

Calculate the centroid $\bar{p}$ of the neighborhood points in the given radius r_n and assign it to x, which can be shown as

$$x = \bar{p} = \frac{1}{n} \sum_{i=1}^{n} p_i. \tag{1}$$

The vector from the centroid to the neighborhood point is defined as

$$y_i = p_i - \bar{p}. \tag{2}$$

The distance d_i from the neighboring point p_i to the plane is equal to the projection of $(p_i - x)$ onto the normal vector $\vec{n}$, which is expressed as

$$d_i = (p_i - x) \cdot \vec{n}. \tag{3}$$

The least-square plane estimation problem is constructed. To find a plane passing through the centroid $\bar{p}$ with a normal vector $\vec{n}$, the objective function is

$$\min_{x,\vec{n},\|\vec{n}\|=1} \sum_{i=1}^{n} \left[(p_i - x)^T \vec{n} \right]^2. \tag{4}$$

Substituting the centroid $\bar{p}$ into the above formula can be simplified to

$$\min_{\vec{n},\|\vec{n}\|=1} \vec{n}^T \left(YY^T \right) \vec{n}. \tag{5}$$

where $YY^T = \sum_{i=1}^{n} y_i y_i^T$ is the 3×3 covariance matrix, represented by C. And by the definition of y_i, there are

$$C = YY^T = \sum_{i=1}^{n} y_i y_i^T = \sum_{i=1}^{n} (p_i - \bar{p})(p_i - \bar{p})^T. \tag{6}$$

The relationship between the eigenvalue λ_e and the eigenvector $\vec{v_e}$ of the covariance matrix is

$$C\vec{v_e} = \lambda_e \vec{v_e}, e \in \{0, 1, 2\}. \tag{7}$$

The eigenvalue λ_e and its corresponding eigenvector $\vec{v_e}$ are obtained by singular value decomposition. If $0 \le \lambda_0 \le \lambda_1 \le \lambda_2$, according to the principle of principal component analysis (PCA), the eigenvector $\vec{v_0}$ corresponding to λ_0 is approximately in the direction of the normal vector $\vec{n}$ or $-\vec{n}$.

The ambiguity of normal vector cannot be solved mathematically. Therefore, we set a viewpoint V_p as the judgment basis to make the standard selection of normal direction consistent [21]. All normal directions should conform to the judgment formula, expressed as

$$\vec{n} \cdot (V_p - p_i) > 0. \tag{8}$$

2.2 The Calculation of FPFH

Both PFH and FPFH construct multi-dimensional histograms to describe point feature information. FPFH is the optimization algorithm of PFH. The main differences are the selection method, the calculation of point features, and the dimension of the histogram. The neighborhood influence range of PFH and FPFH is shown in Fig. 3. When calculating PFH, all of p_q's neighbors enclosed in the sphere with a given radius r_p are selected and the relationship between the pairwise is calculated. The calculation of FPFH is to first calculate the relationship between point p_q and its neighborhood points within a given radius r_f. And then compute the relationship between these neighborhood points and their neighborhood points. Therefore, the computational complexity of FPFH is lower than that of PFH [20].

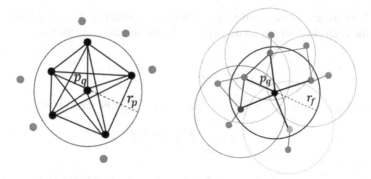

Fig. 3. The influence region of PFH (left) and FPFH (right)

The calculation of FPFH first defines the space within the given radius r_f as the neighborhood of the query point p_q. The query point p_q is then paired with the points in the neighborhood. In order to represent the relationship between each point pair in the local coordinate system, Darboux coordinate frame corresponding to the point pair is established, as shown in Fig. 4.

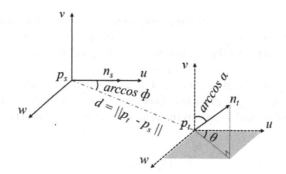

Fig. 4. Darboux coordinate frame

Specifically, Darboux coordinate frame $u - v - w$ is defined as

$$
\begin{cases}
u = n_s \\
v = \dfrac{p_t - p_s}{\|p_t - p_s\|} \times u \\
w = u \times v,
\end{cases}
\tag{9}
$$

where p_s and p_t are the coordinates of source point and target point, and n_s and n_t are their estimated normals respectively; $p_t - p_s$ is the vector between the source point and target point. The direction of the normal n_s is defined as the direction of the u axis. The direction of the v axis is the direction of the cross product of $p_t - p_s$ and u. The w axis is the cross product of the u- and v- axes. Therefore, $u - v - w$ is a cartesian coordinate system with three perpendicular axes.

Four features describing the relationship between two points are defined, which reduces the number of values representing the two points and their normals from 12 to 4. They are expressed as

$$\begin{cases} \alpha = v \cdot n_t \\ \phi = u \cdot \frac{p_t - p_s}{d} \\ \theta = \arctan(w \cdot n_t, u \cdot n_t) \\ d = \|p_t - p_s\|, \end{cases} \tag{10}$$

where α is the dot product of the normal n_t and the v axis, ϕ is the dot product between the u axis and the normalized $p_t - p_s$, θ is the angle between the projection of the target normal n_t on the $u - v$ plane and the u axis, d is the Euclidean distance from p_s to p_t. In some cases, the fourth feature, d, is not very important when the distance between adjacent points increases from the viewpoint. Therefore, d is omitted from the calculation of FPFH [20]. These three angular features, $\{\alpha, \phi, \theta\}$, adopted by FPFH is spread over as much as possible of the available histogram range without exhibiting a bias for certain regions [22].

The calculation of FPFH of query point p_q is divided into the following steps: (1) Calculate the α, ϕ, θ of query point p_q, denoted as $SPFH(p_q)$; (2) Calculate the α, ϕ, θ of K neighborhood points $p_{qi}(i = 1, 2, \cdots, K)$, denoted as $SPFH(p_{qi})$; (3) Each of the three angular features has 11 dimensions, so a histogram with a horizontal coordinate of 33 dimensions can be obtained. The $SPFH(p_q)$ and the $SPFH(p_{qi})$ with weights are counted into the histogram to obtain the $FPFH(p_q)$, which is expressed as

$$FPFH(p_q) = SPFH(p_q) + \frac{1}{K} \sum_{i=1}^{K} \frac{1}{\omega_i} SPFH(p_{qi}). \tag{11}$$

where K is the number of neighborhood points of p_q; ω_i is the weight value inversely proportional to the Euclidean distance between p_q and p_{qi}, which means that the farther the distance between p_{qi} and p_q, the less influence p_{qi} has on the $FPFH(p_q)$.

2.3 Find the Matching Point Pairs

Sample Consensus Initial Alignment (SAC-IA) is a classical and common point cloud registration algorithm that calculates transformation matrix according to local descriptors [20]. The algorithm selects multiple sampling points from the source point cloud, finds one or more similar points in the target point cloud, and then randomly selects a point from the similar points as the corresponding point. According to the different selected point pairs, the transformation matrix is calculated, and an error metric is computed to evaluate the transformation. Finally, a good transformation is found among all the transformations. However, due to the method of selecting matching pairs and the standard of evaluating similarity, the stability of registration is poor in the case of low overlap rate and high noise, and the wrong results may occur. Therefore, the method proposed discards SAC-IA.

In statistics, there are metrics for evaluating the correlation of probability distribution functions, such as Bhattacharyya distance, Hellinger distance, Kullback-Leibler divergence, correlation. Several comparative experiments of these metrics are presented in

Sect. 3. Because of the symmetry and lower computational complexity of Bhattacharyya distance, the method proposed uses Bhattacharyya distance as the metric to evaluate FPFH similarity.

For discrete probability distributions p and q over the same domain X, Bhattacharyya distance $D_B(p, q)$ is defined as

$$D_B(p, q) = -ln(BC(p, q)),\tag{12}$$

where

$$BC(p, q) = \sum_{x \in X} \sqrt{p(x)q(x)}\tag{13}$$

The FPFH histogram is essentially a combination of three 11-dimensional histograms. Therefore, when comparing the similarity of FPFH, the similarity of the three histograms is compared respectively. The three Bhattacharyya distances are calculated separately, and their sum is used to evaluate the similarity between the two FPFH. The FPFH similarity of the two points p_1 and p_2 is calculated as

$$D_{B-FPFH}(p_1, p_2) = D_{B-\alpha}(p_1, p_2) + D_{B-\phi}(p_1, p_2) + D_{B-\theta}(p_1, p_2).\tag{14}$$

Since the range of $BC(p, q)$ is [0, 1], the range of $D_B(p, q)$ is $[0, +\infty)$, and the range of $D_{B-FPFH}(p_1, p_2)$ is also $[0, +\infty)$. The closer the Bhattacharyya distance is to zero, the more similar the histograms of the two points are, which means the more similar the neighborhood features of the two points are.

The points in the source point cloud respectively find the point with the smallest Bhattacharyya distance from the target point cloud as the matching point pair. These match point pairs form the initial set of matched point pairs.

2.4   Strategies to Improve the Accuracy of Matching Pairs

In order to filter some matching point pairs and improve the estimation accuracy of the transformation matrix, some strategies are added to our algorithm, as shown in Algorithm 1.

In the set of matching point pairs, it is inevitable that multiple points will choose the same point as their most similar point. When this happens, the point that has been selected multiple times is reversed to select its most similar point. The reconstituted match pair is then put into the collection, while the remaining point pairs are deleted.

Then, the matching point pairs are sorted according to distance, and the top matching point pairs are selected. At the same time, the distribution range of selected points is enlarged by setting a distance threshold to eliminate the points whose distribution is too concentrated. Finally, RANSAC is used to weed out incorrect matching pairs. The remaining set of matching point pairs is used for subsequent calculations.

Algorithm 1 Iterative selection of correct matching pairs

Input: S_0: the initial matching pair set; N: the number of matching pairs to be selected; t_e: the Euclidean distance threshold;

Output: S_{acc}: the accurate matching pair set;

1: Initialization: $S_0 \leftarrow \emptyset; S_{acc} \leftarrow \emptyset; n = 1$;
2: **for** $i = 1 : size(S_0)$ **do**
3:     **if** the point p_t in the target point cloud is selected multiple times, **then**
4:         point p_t reversely selects its most similar point as the matching pair;
5:         delete other duplicate matching pair(s) of point p_t;
6:     **end if**
7: **end for**
8: Sort the matching pairs in S_0;
9: Put the first matching pair p_1 into S_1;
10: Put the source point of the first matching pair to p_{tc};
11: **for** $j = 1 : size(S_0)$ **do**
12:     **if** $D_{Euclidean}(p_{tc}, p_{tj}) > t_e$ **then**
13:         $S_1 = S_1 \cup p_j$;
14:         $p_{tc} = p_{tj}$;
15:     **end if**
16:     **if** $n = N$ **then**
17:         break;
18:     **end if**
19: **end for**
20: Apply RANSAC to S_1, get the inlier set S_{acc}.

2.5 Calculation of Transformation

According to the matching point pairs, the singular value decomposition method is used to calculate the transformation between the two point clouds. The matching point pair set after filtering is expressed as

$$P = \{p_1, \ldots, p_m\}, P' = \left\{p'_1, \ldots, p'_m\right\}. \tag{15}$$

All point pairs conform to

$$p_k = Rp'_k + t. \tag{16}$$

where R is the rotation matrix and t is the translation vector. The error e_k is constructed as

$$e_k = p_k - \left(Rp'_k + t\right). \tag{17}$$

To obtain R, t, it is necessary to minimize the sum of error squares, which can be expressed as

$$E^2 = \sum_{k=1}^{m} \left\| \left(p_k - (Rp'_k + t)\right) \right\|^2. \tag{18}$$

According to the least-squares fitting of the two point sets P and P', (18) can be simplified as

$$E^2 = \sum_{k=1}^{m} \|q_k - Rq'_k\|^2,$$ (19)

$$t = p - Rp',$$ (20)

where p and p' are the centroids of the two point sets P and P', respectively; q_k and q'_k

$$q_k = p_k - p, q'_k = p'_k - p'.$$ (21)

Singular value decomposition is used to estimate R. Finally, t is solved by substituting R into Eq. (20).

3 Experiment and Analysis

The experimental data include the public point cloud data and the plant point cloud data captured in the real scene. The experiments were implemented on a computer with 8 GB RAM and an Intel Core i5–10500 CPU. The program was developed based on C++ and a third-party open-source library, Point Cloud Library (PCL), which contains many point cloud basic processing functions.

3.1 Registration Experiment of Public Dataset

In order to verify the accuracy and validity of the method using Bhattacharyya distance, the methods using the similarity criteria of Hellinger distance, Kullback-Leibler divergence, and correlation were compared. The registration results of the public point cloud models from different perspectives are shown in Figs. 5, 6 and 7. The initial input point cloud models are selected from the dataset of Stanford 3D scanning repository.

It can be seen that these methods can generally register point clouds from different perspectives. In comparison, the proposed method has better alignment in details without obvious double shadow or offset. In the registration of Bunny 0° and 45° models, except for the proposed method, the alignment at the ear region is poor. In the registration of Bunny 45° and 90° models, the results of the registration method based on correlation show an overall deviation. In the registration of Armadillo 270° and 300° models, the results of the methods based on Hellinger distance, Kullback-Leibler divergence and correlation do not fit well in the claw and head of the model.

The registration error of each method is then quantitatively evaluated by the root mean square error (RMSE) criterion, as shown in Eq. (22).

$$RMSE = \sqrt{\frac{1}{M} \sum_{l=1}^{M} \|Rp_l + t - q_l\|^2}$$ (22)

where R and t are the true values of the rotation matrix and translation vector respectively, p_l and q_l are the points of the initial point cloud and the point cloud transformed by the registration algorithm respectively, and M is the number of points in the point cloud.

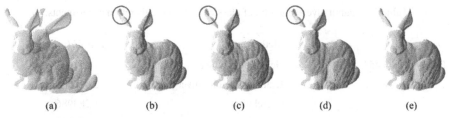

Fig. 5. Initial input of Bunny 0° and 45° and registration results using methods based on different metrics. (a) Bunny 0° and 45°; (b) Hellinger distance; (c) Kullback-Leibler divergence; (d) Correlation; (e) The proposed method.

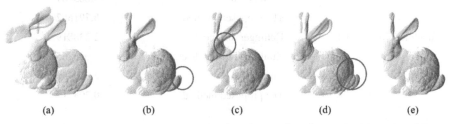

Fig. 6. Initial input of Bunny 45° and 90° and registration results using methods based on different metrics. (a) Bunny 45° and 90°; (b) Hellinger distance; (c) Kullback-Leibler divergence; (d) Correlation; (e) The proposed method.

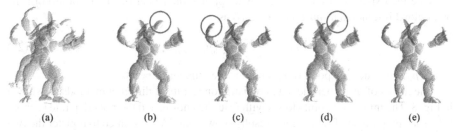

Fig. 7. Initial input of Armadillo 270° and 300° and registration results using methods based on different metrics. (a) Armadillo 270° and 300°; (b) Hellinger distance; (c) Kullback-Leibler divergence; (d) Correlation; (e) The proposed method.

The RMSEs of each experiment are listed in Table 1. It can be seen that the RMSE of the method proposed is lower than that of other methods. The results are consistent with those in Figs. 5, 6 and 7, which illustrates that the proposed method is more accurate and effective when applied to the classic data set.

3.2   Registration Experiment of Noisy Plant Point Cloud

In order to verify the accuracy and anti-noise performance of the proposed method in registering low overlap plant point clouds, the proposed method was compared with typical point cloud registration algorithms SAC-IA and normal distributions transform

Table 1. Quantitative evaluation of classical data set registration experiments.

Data	Method	RMSE (mm)
Bunny 0° and 45°	Hellinger distance	1.051941
	Kullback-Leibler divergence	2.087637
	Correlation	1.283986
	The proposed method	**0.389935**
Bunny 45° and 90°	Hellinger distance	5.387755
	Kullback-Leibler divergence	11.445916
	Correlation	13.663601
	The proposed method	**0.791662**
Armadillo 270° and 300°	Hellinger distance	2.238819
	Kullback-Leibler divergence	2.066865
	Correlation	2.826190
	The proposed method	**0.298217**

(NDT). Experimental data are plant point clouds captured by RGB camera and modeled by COLMAP which is an open-source 3D reconstruction algorithm. At the same time, Gaussian noise with zero mean and variance of $3mr$ was added to the point cloud model to make the experiment closer to the real application scenario. The resolution of the point cloud is denoted as mr and is defined as

$$mr = \frac{1}{n} \sum_{i=1}^{n} \|p_i - p_{in}\|, \tag{23}$$

where p_{in} is the nearest point of p_i, and n is the number of points.

The inputs of the experiment and registration results of different methods are shown in Fig. 8. The inputs are point clouds with Gaussian noise, and their overlap rate is about 8%. The comparison of registration results shows that SAC-IA failed to register the two point clouds, and mistakenly spliced the point cloud of the trunk with that of the crown. Although NDT can roughly identify the transformation of the two point clouds, the registration result of the branch part still appears double shadow. The proposed method can register the two point clouds accurately, and the noise resistance and accuracy are better than the other two methods.

The RMSEs obtained from different methods are shown in Table 2. It can be seen that the RMSE obtained by the proposed method is 0.0168, which is the smallest than that of SAC-IA (1.5362) and NDT (0.0558). This indicates that the proposed method can obtain satisfactory registration of low overlapping plant point clouds, where the noise influence is effectively suppressed.

3.3 Registration Experiment of Multi-source Plant Point Cloud

Multi-source point clouds in real scenes have more noise, and the density between point clouds is diverse, which requires higher discrimination and robustness of registration

Fig. 8. The input of the experiment and the registration results of plant point clouds with different methods. (a) Input; (b) SAC-IA; (c) NDT; (d) The proposed method.

Table 2. Quantitative results of plant point cloud registration experiment with Gaussian noise.

Method	RMSE (m)
SAC-IA	1.5362
NDT	0.0558
The proposed method	**0.0168**

methods. The experiment in this section is to verify the effectiveness of the proposed method in registering plant point clouds captured by different sensors in real application scenes. Experimental data were captured by the RGB camera of unmanned aerial vehicle (UAV) and mobile phone respectively. As inputs, the point cloud captured on the ground by mobile phone and that captured by UAV is shown in Fig. 9. The overlap between the two point clouds is about 25%.

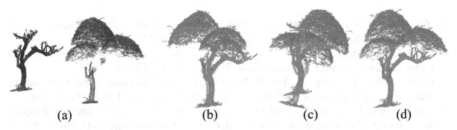

Fig. 9. The input of the experiment and the registration results of plant point clouds with different methods. (a) Input; (b) SAC-IA; (c) NDT; (d) The proposed method.

The proposed method was compared with SAC-IA and NDT, and the results are also shown in Fig. 9. The registration result of SAC-IA is shown in Fig. 9b. The position relation of the two point clouds is roughly correct, but the rotation angle has deviated. As shown in Fig. 9c, NDT gives a wrong transformation when registering the multi-source plant point cloud. The alignment result of the proposed method is more accurate, as shown in Fig. 9d. The branches in the point cloud are fitted without obvious position and angle deviation. After manual measurement, the error at the maximum offset of the results of the proposed method is less than 1 cm, which is within the acceptable range.

According to the experimental results, in real application scenes, the proposed method can effectively register multi-source plant point clouds with a low overlap rate, and the error is within millimeter level. By splicing the point clouds captured by both terrestrial and airborne methods, more complete tree point clouds can be obtained, which lays a foundation for extracting more plant phenotypes.

4   Conclusion

Aiming at the difficulty of obtaining the complete point cloud model of tall plants, a method of point cloud registration in a real scene is proposed. The FPFH features are calculated according to the normal vector of the point cloud, and the similarity of features is evaluated by Bhattacharyya distance to obtain the initial matching pairs. Then, a filtering algorithm based on RANSAC is used to obtain the matching pairs with high accuracy. Finally, the transformation of the point cloud is obtained by singular value decomposition. The experimental results show that the proposed method is more accurate and helps to improve the success rate of point cloud registration for tall plants.

However, when using the proposed method, different application objects need to have different parameters. Therefore, providing the adaptive ability of parameters in the method will be our future research content.

Acknowledgments. This work is supported by the National Natural Science Foundation of China (Grant Nos. 51905351 and U1813212), and the Science and Technology Planning Project of Shenzhen Municipality, China (Grant No. JCYJ20190808113413430).

References

1. Yang, X., et al.: A survey on smart agriculture: Development modes, technologies, and security and privacy challenges. IEEE/CAA J. Automatica Sinica **8**, 273–302 (2021)
2. Costa, C., Schurr, U., Loreto, F., Menesatti, P., Carpentier, S.: Plant phenotyping research trends, a science mapping approach. Front. Plant Sci. **9**, 1933 (2019)
3. Chen, J., Chen, J., Zhang, D., Sun, Y., Nanehkaran, Y.A.: Using deep transfer learning for image-based plant disease identification. Comput. Electron. Agric. **173**, 105393 (2020)
4. Santos Pereira, L.F., Barbon, S., Valous, N.A., Barbin, D.F.: Predicting the ripening of papaya fruit with digital imaging and random forests. Comput. Electron. Agric. **145**, 76–82 (2018)
5. Peng, Y., Yang, M., Zhao, G., Cao, G.: Binocular-vision-based structure from motion for 3-D reconstruction of plants. IEEE Geosci. Remote Sens. Lett. **19**, 1–5 (2022)
6. Wu, S., et al.: MVS-Pheno: a portable and low-cost phenotyping platform for maize shoots using multiview stereo 3D reconstruction. Plant Phenomics. **2020**, 1–17 (2020)
7. Rueda-Ayala, V., Peña, J., Höglind, M., Bengochea-Guevara, J., Andújar, D.: Comparing UAV-based technologies and RGB-D reconstruction methods for plant height and biomass monitoring on grass Ley. Sensors. **19**, 535 (2019)
8. Cabo, C., Ordóñez, C., López-Sánchez, C.A., Armesto, J.: Automatic dendrometry: tree detection, tree height and diameter estimation using terrestrial laser scanning. Int. J. Appl. Earth Obs. Geoinf. **69**, 164–174 (2018)

9. Wang, Y., et al.: Maize plant phenotyping: comparing 3D laser scanning, multi-view stereo reconstruction, and 3D digitizing estimates. Remote Sensing. **11**, 63 (2018)
10. Vázquez-Arellano, M., Reiser, D., Paraforos, D.S., Garrido-Izard, M., Burce, M.E., Griepentrog, H.W.: 3-D reconstruction of maize plants using a time-of-flight camera. Comput. Electron. Agric. **145**, 235–247 (2018)
11. Chen, Z., Lv, H., Lou, L., Doonan, J.H.: Fast and accurate 3D reconstruction of plants using mvsnet and multi-view images. Adv. Intell. Syst. Comput. 390–399 (2021)
12. Ni, Z., Burks, T.: 3D dense reconstruction of plant or tree canopy based on stereo vision. Agric. Eng. Int. CIGR J. **20**, 248–260 (2018)
13. Guan, H., Liu, M., Ma, X., Yu, S.: Three-dimensional reconstruction of soybean canopies using multisource imaging for phenotyping analysis. Remote Sens. **10**, 1206 (2018)
14. Besl, P.J., McKay, N.D.: A method for registration of 3-D shapes. IEEE Trans. Pattern Anal. Mach. Intell. **14**, 239–256 (1992)
15. Zhang, C., Wei, Z., Xu, H., Chen, Y., Wang, G.: Scale variable fast global point cloud registration. Chinese J. Comput. **09**, 1939–1952 (2019). (in Chinese)
16. Tang, M., Zhao, H., Ding, H.: Research on binarized local feature descriptors of point clouds. J. Mech. Eng. **02**, 219–229 (2021). (in Chinese)
17. Xu, G., Pang, Y., Bai, Z., Wang, Y., Lu, Z.: A fast point clouds registration algorithm for Laser Scanners. Appl. Sci. **11**, 3426 (2021)
18. Salti, S., Tombari, F., Di Stefano, L.: Shot: Unique signatures of histograms for surface and texture description. Comput. Vis. Image Underst. **125**, 251–264 (2014)
19. Rusu, R.B., Blodow, N., Marton, Z.C., Beetz, M.: Aligning point cloud views using persistent feature histograms. In: 2008 IEEE/RSJ International Conference on Intelligent Robots and Systems (2008)
20. Rusu, R.B., Blodow, N., Beetz, M.: Fast point feature histograms (FPFH) for 3D registration. In: 2009 IEEE International Conference on Robotics and Automation (2009)
21. Ge, L., Cai, Y., Weng, J., Yuan, J.: Hand PointNet: 3D hand pose estimation using point sets. In: 2018 IEEE/CVF Conference on Computer Vision and Pattern Recognition (2018)
22. Guo, Y., Bennamoun, M., Sohel, F., Lu, M., Wan, J.: 3D object recognition in cluttered scenes with local surface features: a survey. IEEE Trans. Pattern Anal. Mach. Intell. **36**, 2270–2287 (2014)

Integration of Depth Normal Consistency and Depth Map Refinement for MVS Reconstruction

Lifang Yang, Zhengyao Bai$^{(\boxtimes)}$, and Huijie Liu

School of Information Science and Engineering, Yunnan University, Kunming 650500, China
baizhy@ynu.edu.cn

Abstract. To address the problem of incomplete Multi-view Stereo (MVS) reconstruction, the initial depth and loss function of the depth residual iterative network are investigated, and a new multi-view stereo reconstruction network integrating depth normal consistency and depth map thinning is presented. Firstly, downsampling the input image to create an image pyramid and extracting a feature map from the image pyramid; Then, constructing a cost volume from the 2D feature map, adding the depth normal consistency to the initial cost volume to optimize the depth map. On the DTU data set, the network is tested and compared to traditional reconstruction approaches and MVS networks based on deep learning. The experimental results show that the proposed MVS reconstruction network was produced the better results in completeness and increased the quality of MVS reconstruction.

Keywords: Normal-depth consistency · Feature loss · Cost volume · Depth map refinement · MVS

1 Introduction

MVS (Multi-view Stereo) is a popular topic in computer vision, it has been widely employed in virtual reality, automatic driving, digital libraries, and cultural relics restoration [1]. To calculate the correspondence of high-density 3D point clouds and recover 3D point information, traditional MVS algorithms [2, 3] typically use artificially built rules and indicators. Approaches provide satisfactory accuracy, but reconstruction completeness still needs to be improve. Recently, a deep learning method [4, 5] employs a Deep Neural Network to infer the depth map of each view, this approach can extract identifying features and encode the scene's global and local information, allowing it to learn high brightness or reflection information and provide robust feature matching.

MVS reconstruction based on depth learning has yielded satisfactory results. The MVSNet network introduced by Yao et al. [6] is the most well-known. The most important stage is to create a cost volume based on plane scanning, regularize it with a 3D CNN network, and achieve effective depth reasoning accuracy. However, because of the network's high memory comsumption, it is not applicable to in large-scale scenarios. To address this issue, Yao et al. [7] presented R-MVSNet, a cyclic network that employs

Y. Wang et al. (Eds.): IGTA 2022, CCIS 1611, pp. 118–129, 2022.
https://doi.org/10.1007/978-981-19-5096-4_9

Gate Recurrent Unit (GRU) instead of 3D CNN to regularize the cost volume, reducing storage consumption at the cost of the increased average error of estimated depth and running time. Chen et al. [8] proposed the Point-MVSNet network, which iteratively predicts the depth residue as well as visual brightness using edge convolution of the k closest neighbors of each 3D point. The network accuracy improves, but the running time increases linearly as the number of iteration layers increases. A pyramid residual network has recently been utilized to iteratively infer depth reconstruction of multi-view stereo [9, 10] with promising results. The depth residual network tackles the problem of decreasing operating efficiency as the network deepens. The network performance and speed are excellent, but because it uses the coarsest depth as the residual depth to estimate the next level of depth, the depth map generated at the coarsest level is critical to the final reconstruction. The initial depth discontinuity can lead to a loss in the completeness of the entire network since errors at the coarsest level might spread to the final level and cause details to be lost. This research offers a depth reasoning supervision network to tackle the issues by making the estimated depth map continuous.

2 Related Work

Voxels [11], level sets [12], polygonal meshes [13], and depth maps [14] are commonly used in traditional MVS approaches to represent the three-dimensional geometry of objects or scenes. Due to its great accuracy and excellent performance in many settings, the COLMAP algorithm proposed by Schonberger et al. [15] is representative of classic MVS. However, it runs for a long period and is inefficient. Although the classic 3D reconstruction still remains the main part of the research, more and more researchers begin to focus on the MVS method based on volume and depth. Most objects or sceneries can be modeled using volume representation. The volume-based method separates the entire body into small voxels and then applies a photometric consistency measure to determine if the voxel belongs to the surface, given a set volume of an item or scene. These approaches have limitations in modeling scenes. They do not impose constraints on the geometry of objects. The MVS method based on the depth map, on the other hand, allows for more degrees of freedom in scene modeling.

Deep learning-based algorithms are commonly utilized to tackle stereo matching difficulties and obtain good results in three-dimensional vision challenges. These learning-based approaches, on the other hand, are not well suited to multi-view reconstruction challenges. Kar et al. [16] proposed a learnable method for projecting pixel features upwards into three-dimensional objects and classifying whether a voxel is filled by a surface. These networks, however, are incapable of handling large-scale scenarios because the used volume representation requires a lot of memory. MVSNet proposed by Yao et al. [6], was the first multi-view 3D reconstruction using a depth map. MVSNet estimates multi-view depth based on the cost volume generated by differential homography transformation, which is inspired by the binocular stereo matching estimation approach. MVSNet takes a reference image and several source images as inputs, transform the features of several source images into reference images to construct cost volume, regularizes them with 3D CNN to obtain probability, and uses argmax to select the depth with the highest probability as the depth of points. The key to MVSNet is to build low-cost volume using differentiable transformations. Because the network learns the depth map of each view using 3D CNN regularization and derives 3D geometry from many views by fusing the estimated depth map, the network storage capacity will expand, making it harder to utilize the remaining information in high-resolution images. Yao et al. [7] proposed the R-MVSNet circular network for large-scale scene reconstruction to address this problem. The cost volume is first built in the same way as MVSNet [6] and then regularized sequentially using GRUs rather than 3D CNN. This approach requires less memory, but it takes longer to execute. Chen et al. [8] presented Point-MVSNet, a framework for predicting depth from coarse to fine on point clouds that allows information from k nearest neighbors to be obtained in 3D space while repeatedly refining the depth map to greatly minimize running time. It works in the same way as Cascade MVSNet [17], but it minimizes the searching range of cost volume and estimate the high- resolution depth of huge scenes with reduced GPU consumption and improved estimation fidelity.

This study differs from the previously discussed network iterative depth map refinement from coarse to fine. First, these methods ignore the impact of the initial depth map's edge discontinuity on the output, but our network includes a depth normal consistency module after the coarsest depth. Depth normal consistency method [18] that has been formalized because the normal of a surface can represent identical properties on the same plane, it can be used as a constraint to better communicate semantic information, which is similar to using the normal as a depth function and applying a hard constraint to it. Second, typical multi-view stereo reconstruction supervises the learning and training model with a pixel-by-pixel loss function, which produces a big mistake when the same shot moves one pixel or uses various resolutions. Inspired by multi-scale loss functions [18, 19], we use feature loss function to multi-view stereo reconstruction to optimize the training of a deep iterative network, thus improving the reconstruction completeness and robustness.

3   Main Methods

This paper focuses on the study of the depth normal consistency and feature loss function. Depth normal consistency ensures that depth estimation matches geometric prediction results and eliminates the problem of a discontinuous edge at the beginning of the depth measurement. The similarity of object features is taken into account by the feature loss function, which improves the accuracy of the final estimated depth. The main modules of this network are the feature pyramid, cost volume pyramid, depth normal consistency, and loss function, as shown in Fig. 1.

3.1   Feature Pyramid

In this paper, the input source image and reference image are down-sampled to different scales, and an L + 1 level image pyramid $\{I_i^L\}_{i=0}^{N}$, $i \in \{1, 2, ..., N\}$ is constructed. The undersampled original image $I_i^0 = I_i$ is represented by the lowest layer of the image pyramid. After downsampling, the image's resolution gradually decreases. The smaller the image and the lower the resolution, and vice versa. After the acquisition of the image pyramid, the feature extraction network CNN is used to compute features at each

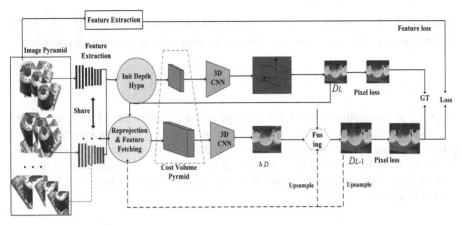

Fig.1. Overall framework of the network in this article

image scale to build the feature pyramid. There are nine convolutional layers in the CNN. LeakyReLU activation layer is inserted after each convolutional layer. The last layer of the feature pyramid is formulized by $\left(f_i^L\right)_{i=0}^N$, $f_i^L \in R^{H/2^L*W/2^L*F}$, F = 16, W and H are length and width of the feature map. With less computing effort, the feature pyramid combines feature maps with strong low-resolution semantic information and weak high-resolution semantic information.

3.2 Cost Volume Pyramid

The cost volume pyramid is mainly composed of the cost volume of rough depth map reasoning and the cost volume of multi-scale depth residual reasoning. A cost volume for the L-level feature map with the lowest resolution is first established. The cost volume of the reference map is created by uniformly sampling M parallel planes in the depth range, assuming that the depth range measured on the reference image of the scene is $d_{min} - d_{max}$. The sampling depth is $d = d_{min} + (d_{maxx} - d_{min})/M$, $m \in \{0, 1, 2, ..., M - 1\}$ represent depth plane, and its normal n_0 is the reference camera's main axis. Given the reference image set I_{ref} and the camera parameter $\{K_i, R_i, t_i\}$, $i = I_{ref} \cup A$, the differentiable homography matric between the first source view and reference view with depth d is defined as

$$H_i(d) = K_i^L R_i \left(I - \frac{(t_0 - t_i)n_0^T}{d}\right) R_0^{-1} \left(K_0^L\right) \tag{1}$$

where K_i^L and K_0^L is K_i and K_0 calibration internal parameter matrix at the L layer, and I is the identity matrix, which K_i, R_i, t_i represents the camera's intrinsic characteristics and external items. This study reconstructs the feature map $\{f_i^L\}_{i=1}^N$ corresponding to the reference view f_0^L using differentiable bilinear interpolation, then produces the cost volume prediction, given the source view and the L-level feature pyramid $\left\{\overline{f}_{i,d}^{L}\right\}_{i=1}^{N}$. The feature variance of N + 1 views is defined as the cost volume of all pixels at depth d.

$$C_d^L = \frac{1}{N+1} \sum_{i=0}^{N} \left\{\overline{f}_{i,d}^{L} - \overline{f}_d^{L}\right\} \tag{2}$$

where $\overline{f}_d^{L}$ is the depth of the reference image and the mean value of all feature maps is d. A multi-scale 3D CNN network is used to regularize the cost volume, and the probability distribution of depth estimation at different depth samples is obtained to eliminate the influence of non-ideal Lambertian volume. The second stage is the cost volume prediction using multi-scale depth residuals, which will be covered in depth normal consistency Sect. 3.3.

3.3 Depth Normal Consistency

Due to interference factors such as the environment, noise, and mutual occlusion between objects, the depth map of the reference image at the coarsest level is discontinuous, affecting the depth map D_0 of the inferred reference view and resulting in low reconstruction completeness. This research suggests employing depth normal consistency to improve the continuity of the predicted depth map D_{L+1} so that multi-scale 3D convolution gives useful context information for depth residual estimate, based on the orthogonality between normal and local surface tangent, as illustrated in Fig. 2.

First step: To get the normal of each central point, one must first figure out where it is neighbor and how much weight it has. In this work, eight nearby sites are chosen to deduce the normal vector of the central point P_i, forming a set of neighborhood coordinates of the central points to. The central point P_i(P is the camera coordinate system coordinate, and P is the pixel coordinate system coordinate) can be identified if the depth Z_i and camera internal parameter matrix K are known. Because $\overline{P_iP_{ix}}$ and $\overline{P_iP_{iy}}$ orthogonality, the central point normal vector N_i may be computed using a cross product as follows:

$$\overline{N}_i = \overline{P_iP_{ix}} \times \overline{P_iP_{iy}} \tag{3}$$

In order to increase the credibility, the normal vector in this paper is averaged over 8 neighborhoods $N_i = \frac{1}{8} \sum_{i=1}^{8} \overline{N}_i$.

Second step: The final optimized depth map can be produced from the normal depth map and the beginning depth map. Each pixel $p_i(x_i, y_i)$ should be refined to the depth of its neighbor pixel points $P_{neighbor}$. Assume that the camera's internal parameter matrix is K, the depth is Z_i, the camera coordinate system's corresponding point is P, the normal vector $\overline{N}_i(n_x, n_y, n_z)$ infers the depth of nearby points P_i, and the calculation algorithm is

$$\left(K^{-1}Z_i - K^{-1}D_{neighbor}P_{neighbor}\right) \begin{bmatrix} n_x \\ n_y \\ n_z \end{bmatrix} = 0 \tag{4}$$

Weights are used to make the depth more consistent with geometry due to the discontinuity of normal vectors on some edges or irregular surfaces. The weight $W_i = e^{-\partial_1}|\nabla I_i|$ are determined by the gradient between P_i and $P_{neighbor}$, with the bigger the gradient, the lower the depth optimization's dependability. Because this study calculates the depth of eight neighborhoods, the weight is determined as $W_i' = W_i / \sum_{i=1}^{8} W_i$. The weighted total of depth in eight distinct directions is the depth $\overline{D}_{neighbor}$ after adding depth normal consistency refinement, and the calculation formula is as follows:

$$\overline{D}_{neighbor} = \sum_{i=1}^{8} W_i' D_{neighbor} \tag{5}$$

This improves the continuity of the initial depth map.

The depth D_0 of the reference image is determined iteratively, starting with the depth estimation of the $L + 1$ layer to obtain the depth map D_L of the preceding layer, and ending with the depth D_0 of the lowest reference image. Firstly, D_{L+1} is up-sampled upper layer by bicubic interpolation, and sample $\uparrow \tilde{D}_{neighbor}$ is obtained. Then the cost volume is constructed and the residual depth chart ΔD_L of D_L is obtained by regression method, and the iteration depth of layer L is $D_L = \uparrow \tilde{D}_{neighbor} + \Delta D_L$. In this fashion, the depth of the following layer is refined iteratively until the final refined depth D_0 is attained.

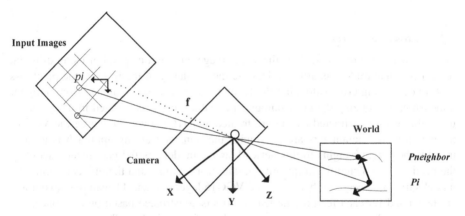

Fig. 2. Normal depth consistency

3.4 Loss Function

The loss function is used to evaluate the difference between predicted value of the model and its actual value, and it is crucial to the model's performance. The loss function is mostly used to restrict the pixel layer information in supervised learning MVS to ensure texture detail matching. Pixel-level constraints, on the other hand, contain several limits, such as illumination and image translation, which will result in pixel alterations.

Supervised learning technique is used to train the loss function in this paper. Because the human visual system perceives a scene through features rather than single pixels, and semantic information can mitigate obstacles in non-ideal areas (such as low texture, etc.) to some extent, this paper uses the weighted sum of pixel loss and feature loss as the loss function, with the following calculation formula.

$$L_{oss} = \beta_1 L_{xsss} + \beta_2 L_{tzss} \tag{6}$$

Feature loss helps stabilize training, improve the network robustness, and improve the reconstruction accuracy.

3.4.1 Pixel Loss

The difference between the predicted image pixel and the actual image pixel is calculated by the pixel loss. The pixel loss in this paper takes into account both the thinned initial depth map and the residual iterative depth map at the same time, and the difference between the true and estimated depths is calculated using the norm. The loss function is defined as the weighted sum of the residual iterative loss for each training sample, and the computation procedure is

$$L_{xsss} = \sum_{i=0}^{L} \sum_{m \in \Omega} \left\| D_{GT}^{L}(p) - D^{L}(p) \right\|_1 \tag{7}$$

3.4.2 Loss of Features

For two identical images, such as the same image moving one pixel or using different resolutions, feature loss is utilized. Despite the similarity of the images, the pixel loss will produce a big error value, but the feature loss can sense the image from a higher dimension, minimizing the error output. The feature loss is calculated in this research using the features extracted by the pre-trained VGG16 network. Because the VGG16 network's model parameters are enormous, the transfer learning approach is used to transfer the taught weights to this network as the model's initial parameters, avoiding the need to train a significant quantity of data from scratch and thereby enhancing the model's training speed. In this paper, the VGG16 layer 4, 8 and 11 feature map outputs are taken and for each feature, the feature loss is constructed based on the concept of crossed multiple views, using the corresponding pixel p_i' in F_{src}. The feature matching expression from the reference image feature F_{ref} to the source image feature F_{src} is estimated. The loss L_F is calculated as

$$F_{src}' = F_{src}\left(p_i'\right)$$
$$L_F = \frac{1}{m} \sum \left(F_{ref} - F_{src}'\right) \times M \tag{8}$$

The final feature loss is the weighted sum of features of different scales, and the features of the 4th, 8th, and 11th layers of the network are taken as the feature loss of this study, where M denotes the total number of masks and M indicates the total number of effective points in each mask.

$$L_{tzss} = \partial_1 L_{F4} + \partial_2 L_{F8} + \partial_3 L_{F11} \tag{9}$$

L_{F4} represents the feature loss of layer 4 in the pre-trained network VGG16, $\partial_1, \partial_2, \partial_3$ is the weight coefficient, the value of the weight coefficient can be adjusted to control the degree of influence of the initial depth map and iterative refinement depth map on the network training, in this paper $\partial_1, \partial_2, \partial_3$ is set to 0.1, 0.5, 0.5.

4   Experiment and Result Analysis

4.1   Datasets and Parameters Setting

The DTU dataset [5] contains 124 different scences, each one was taken at 49 or 64 different angles. The image resolution is 1600×1200, and there are seven different lighting conditions ranging from orientation to diffusion. The network is implemented on a Linux system, with Pytorch 1.4. 0, Python 3.6, and Python 2.7 as deep learning frameworks, a GPU of NVIDIA RTX 3090Ti, and point cloud visualization using OpenCV. There were 27097 ($49 \times 7 \times 49$) images trained and 7546 ($49 \times 7 \times 22$) images evaluated in this study. The depth map is also set to 1600 1152, as is the resolution of the training and testing input images. Each reference image is evenly sampled on these virtual planes with a sampling interval of 1 and batch size of 1 on 192 depth virtual planes that are up-sampled from 425 mm to 935 mm. Using the Adam optimizer, iteratively train 28 epochs. The first epoch's learning rate is set to 0.001, while the sixth, twelveth, eighteenth, and twentieth epochs are multiplied by 0.2. Each training uses one reference image and two source images, for a total of three views each iteration.

4.2   Results and Analysis

The trained network is tested with the DTU test set, and the training process is the same as in CVP-MVSNet [9]. The network reconstruction performance is evaluated using three quantitative indicators provided by the DTU data set: calculation accuracy, completeness, and overall. The lower the value for these three indexes, the better the algorithm reconstruction quality.

This work compares classic approaches like Furu [20], Tola [21], Camp [3], Gipuma [22], Colmap [15] with learning-based SurfaceNet [23] MVSNet [6], P-MVSNet [24], Point-MVSNet [8], and CVP-MVSNet [9]. In terms of completeness and integrity, the approach presented in this work outperforms the old algorithm, as demonstrated in Table 1. The overall improved by 11.4% and the completeness by 19.3% when compared to MVSNet [6], while the overall index climbed by 2.8% and the completeness increased by 7.7% when compared to Point-MVSNE [8]. The overall index increased by 0.3%, while the completeness increased by 7.2% as compared to CVP-MVSNE [9]. Figure 3 depicts a portion of the scene depth map and reconstruction representations. The suggested method not only entirely reconstructs the target object, but also has superior reconstruction fidelity than existing methods, according to experimental results.

Table 1. Comparison of test results of different methods

Method	Overall (mm)	Accuracy (mm)	Completeness (mm)
Furu	0.777	0.613	0.941
Tola	0.766	0.342	1.190
Camp	0.695	0.835	0.554
Gipuma	0.578	*0.283*	0.873
Colmap	0.532	0.400	0.664
SurfaceNet	0.745	0.450	1.040
MVSNet	0.462	0.396	0.527
P-MVSNet	0.420	0.406	0.434
Point-MVSNet	0.376	0.342	0.411
CVP-MVSNet	0.351	0.296	0.406
CVP-MVSNet*	0.389	0.426	0.352
Our	*0.348*	0.362	*0.334*

Note: the lettering indicates the optimal value, CVP-MVSNet* is the experimental result of using CVP-MVSNet's method on our equipment.

Fig. 3. Example of test results (*From left to right*) depth map of scan1; depth map of scan9; reconstruction effect map of scan1; construction effect map of scan9.

4.3 Ablation Test

Ablation tests and qualitative analysis are carried out for the depth normal consistency module and feature loss module suggested in this study in order to prove the usefulness of this network. The depth normal consistency module and feature loss module are introduced to the system foundation of this article based on CVP-MVSNet [9]. To analyze the advantages of these two modules, four groups of ablation tests were conducted. To assess the quality of the reconstruction, accuracy and completeness indicators are used, while completeness indicators are used to assess its overall performance. Memory use, running time, and model parameters are all kept track of. Table 2 shows the results of the experiment. S stands for the unrefined initial depth module in CVP-MVSNet [9], P for the pixel loss function module, F for the initial depth module corrected by depth normal consistency, and T for the feature loss function module in this article.

For cycling an epoch, the running time is the average of the running times of a single model parameter. The depth normal consistency module is added to the original network CVP-MVDNet [9], and the overall is decline by 1.5%, the completeness is improved by 5.9%, the memory is increased by 398M, and the model parameters are increased by 27063, as shown in Table 2. This is because the normal consistency of depth enhances the quality of the estimated initial depth map, allowing the images at the margins and non-ideal locations to be reconstructed as well, resulting in more complete reconstruction results. The completeness of the original network is improved by 4.4%, the memory is increased by 315M, and the model parameters are increased by 11836 by adding the feature loss module, which is attributed to the fact that the feature loss module retains low-level semantic information such as geometry and texture, which is useful for network supervision and training; by adding the normal depth consistency module and feature loss module to the original network, the completeness is improved by 7.2%, the memory is increased by 315M, and the model parameters are increased in this study, combining two modules yields not only clear and high-quality reconstruction results, but also the ability to reconstruct some edges or small sections, as well as a higher reconstruction completeness and efficiency.

Table 2. Comparison of ablation test results

Method	Overall (mm)	Accuracy (mm)	Completeness (mm)	GPU/M	Time/s	Parameters
S + P	0.351	*0.296*	0.406	*3641*	*0.052*	*55185*
S + P + F	0.366	0.385	0.347	4012	0.053	55864
S + P + T	0.370	0.378	0.362	3956	0.064	56436
S + P + F + T	*0.348*	0.362	*0.334*	4275	0.064	56842

Furthermore, this article compares non-ideal images with CVP-MVSNet [9] to demonstrate the superiority of this method. First, as illustrated in Fig. 4, from the DTU data set, this paper picks 13 scenes with uneven texture distribution for comparative studies. The network reconstruction capabilities of this study is superior than the CVP-MVSNet [9] approach, and there are many points reconstructed at the edge in this paper. Finally, for a comparative experiment, scene 24 with repeating texture is picked from the DTU data set. The points reconstructed via the CVP-MVSNet [9] approach are missing in the lower-left corner of the highest chimney. In comparison to this method, the network reconstruction points in this study are dense, allowing for the restoration of more details and a superior overall reconstruction result. The suggested algorithm's reconstruction in the fine structure is cleaner and has less various points, as evidenced by comparison testing of these scenes.

Fig. 4. Comparison of test results of scenes (*From left to right*) The two images on the left is a comparison of scene13 CVP-MVSNet with our results; The two images on the right is a comparison of scene24 CVP-MVSNet with our results.

5   Conclusion

A multi-view stereo reconstruction network with depth normal consistency and depth map refinement is presented based on the depth residual iterative network to alleviate the problem of low reconstruction completeness caused by anomalous and discontinuous initial depth. The normal depth consistency module is used in this paper to improve the quality of the final iterative depth map by refining the initial depth. Simultaneously, the feature loss module is presented to reduce output error ofthe pixel-level loss function and the non-optimal model training owing to image resolution or movement, thereby improving the completeness of multi-view stereo reconstruction. The proposed network has the best completeness according to experimental results on DTU data sets.

The parameters of deep learning neural networks become increasingly complex as the number of layers increases, leading expensive experimental equipments. Future work will focus minimizing running time and memory consumption, and design a lightweight, real-time 3D reconstruction system.

References

1. Liu, J.G.: Three-dimensional reconstruction of multi-view images of movable cultural relics. J. Archeol. **12**, 97–103 (2016)
2. Seitz, S.M., Curless, B., Diebel, J., et al.: A comparison and evaluation of multi-view stereo reconstruction algorithms. In: Proceedings of the 2006 IEEE Computer Society Conference on Computer Vision and Pattern Recognition, pp: 519–528. IEEE Press, New York (2006)
3. Campbell, N.D.F., Vogiatzis, G., Hernández, C., Cipolla, R.: Using multiple hypotheses to improve depth-maps for multi-view stereo. In: Forsyth, D., Torr, P., Zisserman, A. (eds.) ECCV 2008. LNCS, vol. 5302, pp. 766–779. Springer, Heidelberg (2008). https://doi.org/10.1007/978-3-540-88682-2_58
4. Merrell, P., Akbarzadeh, A., Wang, L., Mordohai, P.: Real-time visibility-based fusion of depth maps. In: Proceedings of the 2007 IEEE International Conference on Computer Vision, pp: 1--8. IEEE Press, Brazil (2007)
5. Jensen, R., Dahl, A., Vogiatzis, G., Tola, E.: Large scale multi-view stereopsis evaluation. In: Proceedings of the IEEE Conference on Computer Vision and Pattern Recognition, pp: 406--413. IEEE Press, Columbus (2014)
6. Yao, Y., Luo, Z., Li, S., Fang, T.: MVSNet: depth inference for unstructured multi-view stereo. In: Proceedings of the European Conference on Computer Vision, pp: 767--783. Springer Press, Munich (2018)

7. Yao, Y., Luo, Z., Li, S., et al.: Recurrent MVSNet for high-resolution multi view stereo depth inference. In: Proceedings of the IEEE/CVF Conference on Computer Vision and Pattern Recognition, pp: 5525--5534. IEEE Press, Long Beach (2019)
8. Chen, R., Han, S.F., Xu, J., Su, H.: Point-based multi-view stereo network. In: Proceedings of the IEEE/CVF International Conference on Computer Vision, pp: 1538--1547. IEEE Press, Seou (2019)
9. Yang, J., Mao, W., Alvarez, J. M., Liu, M.: Cost volume pyramid based depth inference for multi-view stereo. In: Proceedings of the IEEE/CVF Conference Computer Vision and Pattern Recognition, pp: 4877--4886. IEEE Press, Seattle (2020)
10. Ye, C.K., Wan, W.G.: Multi-view depth estimation based on feature pyramid network. J. Electr. Measur. Technol. **11**, 91–95 (2020)
11. Kutulakos, K.N., Seitz, S.M.: A theory of shape by space carving. J. Int. J. Comput. Vis. **38**(3), 199–218 (2000)
12. Pons, J.P., Keriven, R., Faugeras, O., Hermosillo, G.: Variational stereovision and 3D scene flow estimation with statistical similarity measures. In: Proceedings Ninth IEEE International Conference on IEEE Computer Vision, p: 597. IEEE Press, Nice (2003)
13. Esteban, C.H., Schmitt, F.: Silhouette and stereo fusion for 3D object modeling. J. Comput. Vis. Image Underst. **96**(3), 367–392 (2004)
14. Kang, S.B., Szeliski, R., Chai, J.: Handling occlusions in dense multi-view stereo. In: Proceeding of the 2001 IEEE Computer Society Conference on Computer Vision and Pattern Recognition, pp:1. IEEE Press, Kauai (2001)
15. Schonberger, J.L., Frahm, J.M.: Structure from motion revisited. In: Proceedings of the IEEE Conference on Computer Vision and Pattern Recognition, pp: 4104--4113. IEEE Press, Las Vegas (2016)
16. Kar, A., Hane, C., Malik, J.: Learning a multi-view stereo machine. J. Adv. Neural Info. Process. Syst. **30**, 365—376 (2017)
17. Gu, X., Fan, Z., Zhu, S., Dai, Z.: Cascade cost volume for high-resolution multi-view stereo and stereo matching. In: Proceedings of the 2020 IEEE/CVF Conference on Computer Vision and Pattern Recognition, pp: 2495--2504. IEEE Press, Seattle (2020)
18. Yang, Z., Wang, P., Xu, W.: Unsupervised learning of geometry with edge-aware depth-normal consistency. J. arXiv preprint arXiv. (2017)
19. Johnson, J., Alahi, A., Li, F.F.: Perceptual losses for real-time style transfer and super-resolution. In: European Conference on Computer Vision, pp:694--711. Springer Press, Amsterdam (2016)
20. Furukawa, Y.,Ponce, J.: Accurate, dense, and robust multi view stereopsis. J. IEEE Trans. Pattern Anal. Mach. Intell.. **32**(8), 1362—1376 (2009)
21. Tola, E., Strecha, C., Fua, P.: Efficient large-scale multi-view stereo for ultra high-resolution image sets. J. Mach. Vis. Appl. **23**(5), 903–920 (2012)
22. Galliani, S., Lasinger, K., Schindler, K.: Massively parallel multi-view stereopsis by surface normal diffusion. In: Proceedings of the IEEE International Conference on Computer Vision, pp: 873--881. IEEE Press, Santiago (2015)
23. Ji, M., Gall, J., Zheng, H., Liu, Y.: Surfacenet: An end-to-end 3D neural network for multi-view stereopsis. In: Proceedings of the IEEE International Conference on Computer Vision, pp: 2307--2315. IEEE Press, Venice (2017)
24. Luo, K., Guan, T., Ju, L., Huang, H.: P-MVSNet: learning patch-wise matching confidence aggregation for multi-view stereo. In: Proceeding of the 2019 IEEE/CVF International Conference on Computer Vision, pp: 10452--10461. IEEE Press, Long Beach (2019)

Image/Video Big Data Analysis and Understanding (Object Detection and Recognition, Image/Video Retrieval, Image Segmentation, Matching, Analysis and Understanding.)

Adaptive Registration for Multi-type Remote Sensing Images via Dynamic Feature Selection

Fei Song[1,2,3], Qiang Chen[1,3], Tao Lei[1,3(✉)], and Zhenming Peng[2(✉)]

[1] Institute of Optics and Electronics, Chinese Academy of Sciences, Chendu 610209, China
taoleiyan@ioe.ac.cn
[2] School of Information and Communication Engineering, University of Electronic Science and Technology of China, Chendu 610209, China
zmpeng@uestc.edu.cn
[3] School of Electronic, Electrical and Communication Engineering, University of Chinese Academy of Sciences, Beijing 100049, China

Abstract. Remote sensing image registration (RSIR) has been performed in various RS applications for decades. However, how to adaptively register multi-type (multi-view, multi-temporal, and multi-sensor) RS images remains a challenging problem due to different degrees of local nonrigid distortions, rotation angles, and nonlinear intensity differences between such images. This paper presents a general RSIR method for multi-type RS images. The multi-type mixed feature descriptor (MMFD) is first constructed by combining the respective advantages of channel features of orientated gradients (CFOG) descriptor, speeded up robust features (SURF) local distance, and neighbouring structure descriptor. According to prematching of SURF local distance and CFOG descriptor, a dynamic threshold adjusts the feature points number adaptively. Finally, the dynamic feature selection strategy is implemented to adjust weight parameters of MMFD by the thresholding techniques. Extensive experiments on proposed method are performed over satellite and UAV datasets, and results show that the proposed method provides favorable performance (RSME of 1.59761 and 1.0811) with respect to eight state-of-the-art methods.

Keyword: Remote sensing · Multi-type · Image registration · Dynamic threshold

1 Introduction

Remote sensing image registration (RSIR) is a crucial prerequisite to effectively eliminate the geometric error since it can align images that are captured with different viewpoints (multi-view), different times (multi-temporal), or disparate imaging sensors (multi-sensor) [1–3]. Therefore, it has already been used in various remote sensing applications, such as farming, resource census, disaster control, military damage assessment, environment monitoring and ground targets identification, etc. This paper intends to propose a general image registration method that is competent to align adaptively the

Y. Wang et al. (Eds.): IGTA 2022, CCIS 1611, pp. 133–144, 2022.
https://doi.org/10.1007/978-981-19-5096-4_10

Fig. 1. Multi-type (i.e., multi-view, multi-temporal, and multi-sensor) remote sensing images, including satellite remote sensing images and UAV remote sensing images.

multi-type (i.e., multi-view, multi-temporal, and multi-sensor) remote sensing images (see Fig. 1).

Currently, a wide variety of remote sensing systems have undergone rapid development [3, 5, 6], e.g., Landsat, moderate resolution imaging spectroradiometer (MODIS), and small unmanned aerial vehicles (UAVs). But when satellite revolves around the earth in a substantial circle or ellipse, there are significant local geometrical distortions on image acquisition on account of the effect of inaccuracies in the sensor geometry modeling, and the jitter of the instruments platform [1, 6]. Aircraft platforms (e.g., small UAVs) in combination with lightweight and low-cost inertial measurement units (IMUs), global positioning system (GPS) receivers, and scientific imaging sensors can collect images with very fine spatial and temporal resolutions [3, 6]. Nonetheless, images taken from arbitrary perspectives with aircraft platforms generate unavoidably large rotation angles and viewpoints changes relative to the ground target positions in flight practices due to its flight height, wind speed/direction and other human factors. As a result, RSIR becomes an essential stage to effectively eliminate the geometric error of these images. By integrating multiple images, data captured by different imaging systems can be combined into high spatial resolution/ high temporal resolution data at different spatial and temporal scales for further processing and analysis, e.g., fusing high spatial resolution/low temporal resolution Landsat images with low spatial resolution/high temporal resolution MODIS images. All these analyses require accurate RSIR in advance.

In the field of RSIR, numerous algorithms [7–10, 13, 18, 19] have been presented in the past decades for different registration scenarios. For example, the scale invariant feature transform (SIFT) [7], the speeded up robust features (SURF) [8], the coherent point drift (CPD) algorithm [9], the partial intensity invariant feature descriptor based AGM-Reg [10], pixelwise HOG (histogram of oriented gradient) descriptor based the channel features of orientated gradients (CFOG) for multi-modal (or multi-sensor) images [6]. However, most approaches only consider one type of feature to set up the correspondence relationship, which causes insufficient robustness in various registration processes. Therefore, GLMDTPS presented a global and local mixture distance. It applied a flexible method for evaluating correspondences between two point sets by minimizing global or local structural differences using a linear assignment solution [11]. In order to keep global and local structures during feature point matching, PRGLS adopted the estimation of a mixture of densities [12]. Simultaneously, ZGL_CATE was proposed to maintain a high matching ratio on inliers while taking advantages of outliers for varying the warping grids [13]. Although recent studies have shown that mixture features are robust to scale and large rotation angles, these methods often do not achieve satisfactory performance for multi-model (or multi-sensor) remote sensing images. Fundamentally, they primarily rely on extracting highly repeatable common features between image pair, which can limit their ability because of nonlinear intensity differences in multi-model (or multi-sensor) images. In addition, most methods are not sensitive enough to multi-temporal remote sensing images. For these matter, the aforementioned methods cannot effectively cope with different types of remote sensing image pairs.

In this paper, we propose a general remote sensing image registration method for multi-type remote sensing images. The major contributions of our work consist of the following: In order to make the respective strengths of ground target geometry and image intensity information to complement each other, multi-type mixed feature descriptor (MMFD) is first established for multi-type remote sensing image by combining with three different types of features, i.e., CFOG, SURF local distance, neighbouring structure descriptor (NSD). According to prematching of SURF local distance and CFOG descriptor, the dynamic thresholds adjust the feature points number adaptively. Moreover, dynamic feature selection is achieved to adjust weight parameters of MMFD during the registration process by virtue of the thresholding techniques. Extensive experiments on the proposed image registration method are undertaken over different types satellite and small UAVs images. As compared with the eight state-of-the-art methods, the proposed method demonstrates superior registration performance in the majority of scenarios.

2 Methodology

In this section, we first give details about three contributions of the proposed method:

- Dynamic threshold based prematching
- Multi-type Mixed Feature Descriptor (MMFD)
- Dynamic feature selection

Then, the parameter setting is discussed in the latter part of this section. The main process of the proposed remote sensing image registration method includes three steps: (i) feature extraction; (ii) feature point registration (correspondence estimation and transformation updating), and (iii) image transformation. Figure 2 shows the framework of the proposed method. The expectation maximization (EM) algorithm [12, 13] that alternates between correspondence estimation and transformation updating is adopted for estimating the parameters of Gaussian mixture model (GMM). In the image transformation, the backward approach [15] is first adopted to establish a thin-plate spline (TPS) [16] transformation model. Subsequently, the transformed image I_t can be calculated using the model.

In this paper, $R_{M \times 2} = \{r_1, \cdots, r_M\}^T$ and $S_{N \times 2} = \{s_1, \cdots, s_N\}^T$ are considered as two point sets extracted from the reference image I_r and the sensed image I_s, M and N denote the number of points in R and S, respectively.

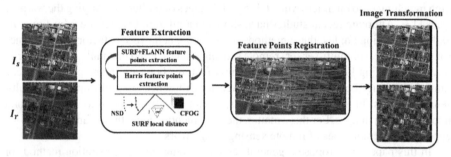

Fig. 2. Flowchart of the proposed image registration method. I_r and I_s denote the reference image and the sensed image, respectively. NSD and CFOG denote the neighbouring structure descriptor and pixelwise HOG (histogram of oriented gradient) descriptor based the channel features of orientated gradients.

2.1 Dynamic Threshold Based Prematching

SURF Local Distance: The speeded up robust features (SURF) algorithm is utilized broadly in image registration to improve image feature extraction accuracy, which is robust against scale, rotation, and illumination variance. Therefore, we first extract enough robust, reliable, and uniformly distributed feature points by SURF algorithm. Base on FLANN algorithm, the discrepancy of two images is detected by mutually matching their descriptors and choosing the one that minimizes the Euclidean distance between them at the feature prematching. Thus, SURF local distance $\tilde{D}$ with each entry

$d(n, m) = \left\| \widetilde{des}_n^s - \widetilde{des}_m^r \right\|^2$, where $\widetilde{des}_n^s$ and $\widetilde{des}_m^r$ are the SURF descriptors of

s_n and r_m, respectively. a row-by-row rescaling process is performed on SURF local distance $\tilde{D}$ making each $\tilde{d}_{mn}$, and the matrix form is as follows

$$\tilde{d}_{mn} = \frac{d(n, m) - \sum_{k=1}^{M} \min\{d(n, k)\}}{\sum_{k=1}^{M} (\max\{d(n, k)\} - \min\{d(n, k)\})} \tag{1}$$

CFOG Descriptor: Compared to the traditional HOG descriptor, CFOG descriptor [6] is computed at each pixel by reducing the stride between adjacent blocks since a gradient magnitude at a pixel contributes to the histograms for all cells (see Fig. 3). A template window is first divided into some overlapping blocks covering 4×4 pixels and a block is further divided into 2×2 cells covering 2×2 pixels. For each cell (i.e., each pixel), the gradient magnitudes and directions are quantized into nine evenly spaced angular bins of an orientation histogram.

$$M(x, y) = abs(\{f_x(x, y), f_y(x, y)\} \cdot \{cos\theta, sin\theta\}) \qquad (2)$$

where θ ranges between $[0, 180^0)$. Subsequently, the orientated gradient channel is convolved with a 3D Gaussian-like kernel of standard deviation σ since traditional HOG consumes much time using trilinear interpolation method. Note that the kernel is not really 3D Gaussian function in the 3D space. In fact, it consists of a 2D Gaussian kernel in the X and Y directions, and a kernel of $[1, 2, 1]^T$ in the gradient orientation direction (i.e., Z direction). The convolution in the Z direction can smoothen the gradients in the orientation direction, thereby reducing the effect of orientation distortions led to by local geometrical distortions and intensity deformations between image pairs.

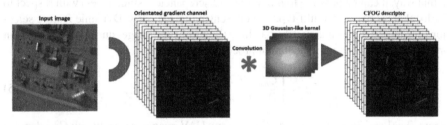

Fig. 3. Construction process of CFOG descriptor.

Insufficient feature points can be problematic during establishing correspondence estimation efficiently, while over abundant feature points suffer from accumulated error and a large computational burden. Therefore, how to acclimate the feature points number adaptively according to the images in different scenes is one of the key issues in improving image registration efficiency Therefore, the dynamic thresholds θ_0 and θ_1 are adopted to filter out mismatch points and select coarsely a large number of feature point pairs because there usually exist some mismatch points in the SURF and CFOG prematching results.

$$\theta_1 = \min\{d(n, m)\} + \frac{1}{\alpha}(\max\{d(n, m)\} - \min\{d(n, m)\}) \qquad (3)$$

$$\theta_0 = \min\left\{\frac{1}{N}\sum_{n=1}^{T_1} \epsilon(n)\right\} + \frac{1}{\beta}(\max\{\frac{1}{N}\sum_{n=1}^{T_1} \epsilon(n)\} - \min\{\frac{1}{N}\sum_{n=1}^{T_1} \epsilon(n)\}) \qquad (4)$$

where ϵ denotes the residual of the corresponding landmarks T and $\overline{S}$ extracted feature points by harris [6], T_1 is the number of S. α and β denote balancing weight parameters.

2.2 Dynamic Feature Selection

Feature matching, which aims to the process of establishing reliable correspondences between two feature sets (especially point features), is a critical prerequisite in feature-based image registration. However, the various types of feature descriptors have their own advantages and limitations in different scenes. For example, HOG can be resistant to nonlinear intensity differences between multi-modal (or multi-sensor) image pairs, but it's performance is limited by time-consuming and computational efficiency since it has to compute the weights of each pixel for both the spatial and orientation bin. The performance of NSD [3] is limited on the assumption that the corresponding points have similar local geometric structures, while the SURF feature descriptors contain no spatial information. Therefore, we can make their respective advantages, which adaptively adjust the feature descriptors according to the images in different registration scenarios.

The Multi-type Mixed Feature Descriptor (MMFD): It integrates three different types of feature descriptors, i,e., CFOG descriptor, SURF local distance, NSD. Only in that way, it can be possible to measure the discrepancies (similarities) with respect to the local areas between multi-type remote sensing image pairs. Dynamic feature selection is proposed to simultaneously matching the multi-type images during the registration process. The specific implementation process is as follows:

$$C_{mmfd} = \begin{cases} C_{nsd}, \text{ if } Type1 \text{ or } N \leq N_\theta \\ \tilde{D} \odot C_{nsd}, \text{ if } Type2 \text{ or } N > N_\theta \end{cases} \tag{5}$$

where $Type1$ and $Type2$ belong satellite data and UAV images, respectively; C_{nsd} denotes a cost matrix of NSD; $\odot$ denotes Hadamard product. When the extracted feature points by SURF-FLann algorithm are more than the threshold N_θ, $\tilde{D}$ and C_{nsd} are used to select confident inliers satisfy. Otherwise, Harris and CFOG descriptor will be automatically switched to extract more feature points, and C_{nsd} is applied to select confident inliers satisfy. To calculate the prior probability matrix $\mathfrak{R}$, the cost matrix C_{mmfd} is solved as the linear assignment problem.

$$C_{mmfd}(\mathfrak{R}) = \sum_{m=1}^{M} \sum_{n=1}^{N} \mathfrak{R}_{mn} c_{mn} \tag{6}$$

The permutation matrix $\sum_{n=1}^{N} \mathfrak{R}_{mn} = 1$, where $\mathfrak{R}_{mn} \in [0, 1]$. The $m \times n$ prior probability matrix $\mathfrak{R}$ is then taken by GMM based transformation solver.

2.3 Parameter Setting

In this paper, there are five sets of experimental parameters, as follows: balancing weight parameters α and β are set to 7.5 and 0.5, respectively. Threshold N_θ is set to 25. Outlier balancing weight parameter with an initial 0.5 is applied to the mixed model NSD. Gaussian radial basis variance is set as 2. Transformation coefficient matrix is initialized to all zeros.

3   Experiments and Results

3.1   Experimental Datasets

In order to perform adequate analysis and experiments, datasets consist of (I) 24 pairs multi-temporal and multi-sensor satellite images acquired from Google Earth, geospatial data cloud website (http://www.gscloud.cn), USGS (http://www.usgs.cn), and test dataset provided by [14]; (II) 30 pairs multi-view and multi-temporal UAV images captured from the DJI Phantom 4 Pro (DJI, Shenzhen, China) with a CMOS camera, and from a small UAV panoramic photography website (http://www.gscloud.cn). The size of the images range from 505 × 324 to 1460 × 1381 pixels. Table 1 gives a detailed description of our experimental datasets.

Table 1. The experimental datasets description.

Category	Datasets			
	Sensors	Image type	Image size (pixels)	Number (pair)
(I)	LinDAR, TerraSAR-X, Landsat, Airborne optical, China's GF satellite	Multi-sensor	505 × 324−1460 × 1381	8
	Landsat, China's GF satellite	Multi-temporal, Multi-view	600 × 400−900 × 600	16
(II)	Small UAV	Multi-view	780 × 439−1153 × 865	15
		Multi-temporal	752 × 416−900 × 600	15

3.2   Evaluation Metrics and Implementation Details

We adopt the root of square mean error (RSME) to quantify the registration error. Meanwhile, we use the precision ratio (PR) to measure the accuracy of feature matching [11, 12]. The experiments are implemented in MATLAB 2018 on a computer with a 2.60 GHz Intel(R) Core (TM) CPU and a 16 GB RAM.d Evaluation Metrics.

4   Results and Discussion

In this section, we first test the performance of proposed method on image registration as well as compare with four state-of-the-art methods (CPD [9], GLMDTPS [11], PRGLS [12] and ZGL_CATE [13]). Quantitative comparison using the mean RMSE are completely given in Table 2. Typical registration examples Multi-view, multi-temporal UAV images are shown in Fig. 4. Typical registration examples multi-temporal, multi-sensor

UAV images are shown in Fig. 5. Note that, FP denotes feature points extracted by proposed method. In general, one can see that proposed method has reached the superior performance (RMSE = 1.59761, 1.0811) when appearance difference in the multi-type (i.e., multi-view, multi-temporal, and multi-sensor) image pair is larger. ZGL_CATE can obtain a better performance (RMSE = 4.3256, 3.8621) but larger error on visible light and LiDAR images. Moreover, it is susceptible to outlier extracted from multi-temporal or multi-sensor image pairs. The performance of CPD is seriously degraded in UAV images due to only consider a type feature to establish the correspondence relationship. In contrast, GLMDTPS and PRGLS can get better performance since they both utilized global and local mixture features to establish correspondence. However, the features employed are susceptible to abnormal value and similar neighboring structure.

In addition, Fig. 6 demonstrates quantitative results and two representative feature matching examples for proposed method and four different feature matching methods. SURF-Flann [8] and EOH (Edge Oriented Histogram)-SIFT [17] register image pairs with no failure on UAV images. However, they gives a relatively lower performance on satellite images (with large intensity difference) than UAV images. CFOG [6] has the second best performance on satellite images and UAV images, but it cannot deal with the images with large rotation angle, especially UAV images with large viewpoint change. The proposed method implemented with Surf-Flann and dynamic threshold based CFOG gives the best performance on the satellite images and UAV images.

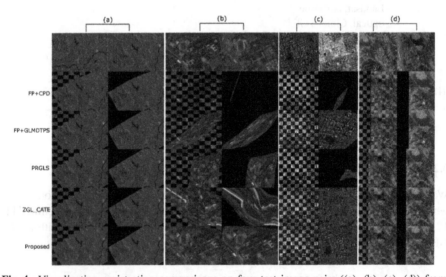

Fig. 4. Visualization registration comparisons on four test image pairs ((a), (b), (c), (d)) from dataset (I). For every entry, the first row is the test images pairs I_s (left) and I_r (right). The registration results of FP+CPD, FP+GLMDTPS, PRGLS, ZGL_CATE and the proposed method (FP denotes feature points extracted by proposed method) are shown from the 2nd row to the last row, respectively. For each method, the registration results are shown in two columns, where the first column shows the transformed image I_t, and the second column shows 10×10 checkboards.

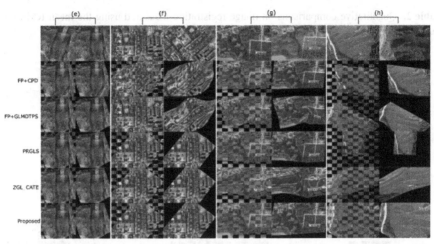

Fig. 5. Visualization registration comparisons on four test image pairs ((e), (f), (g), (h)) from dataset (II). For every entry, the first row is the test images pairs I_s (left) and I_r (right). The registration results of FP+CPD, FP+GLMDTPS, PRGLS, ZGL_CATE and the proposed method (FP denotes feature points extracted by proposed method) are shown from the 2nd row to the last row, respectively. For each method, the registration results are shown in two columns, where the first column shows the transformed image I_t, and the second column shows 10×10 checkboards.

Finally, we compute computational efficiency of the proposed method. In this framework, the feature matching step consumes different time because they are based on different feature descriptors. The run time mainly depends on the time of extracting feature points and feature matching. Figure 7 gives the calculation time of proposed and four methods. PRGLS takes the least time for feature matching, followed by the proposed method, ZGL_CATE, FP + GLMDTPS and FP + CPD consumes approximately similar time span under same condition. Although PRGLS takes the least run time among these similarity measures in the matching processing, it cannot register image pairs with large intensity difference. All of the above results illustrate the effectiveness of the proposed remote sensing image registration framework for multi-type remote sensing images, and the proposed method achieves the favorable registration performance and computational efficiency.

Table 2. Quantitative comparisons on image registration measured using the mean RMSE are carried out.

Methods	Datasets	
	(I)	(II)
CPD	10.2581	8.4392
GLMDTPS	7.3453	6.0131
PRGLS	6.1572	4.1278
ZGL_CATE	4.3256	3.8621
Proposed	**1.59761**	**1.0811**

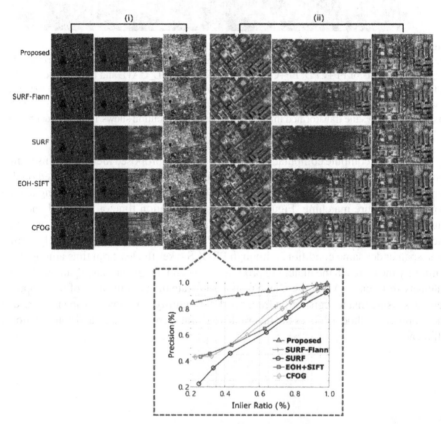

Fig. 6. Comparison of the proposed method against four state-of-the-art methods (SURF-Flann, SURF, EOH-SIFT and CFOG) on feature matching. (i) and (ii) are two representative feature matching examples for proposed method and four different feature matching methods.

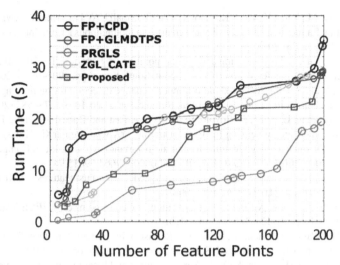

Fig. 7. Run times of the proposed method with different numbers of feature points under a computer with a 2.60 GHz Intel(R) Core (TM) CPU and a 16 GB RAM.

5   Conclusions

Remote sensing image registration is a crucial step for many photogrammetric and remote sensing applications. However, how to adaptively align the multi-type (i.e., multi-view, multi-temporal, and multi-sensor) remote sensing images remains a challenging problem owing to local nonrigid distortions, large rotation angles, low overlap ratios, and intensity difference among such images. In this paper, we present a general remote sensing image registration framework for multi-type remote sensing images. The key idea of the proposed method is to maintain a dynamic feature selection method which adjusts MMFD that is constructed by combining the advantages of CFOG descriptor, SURF-Flann distance and NSD. Furthermore, a dynamic threshold is applied to adaptively adjust the number of feature points according to prematching of CFOG descriptor. Extensive experiments on the proposed image registration framework are undertaken over different types satellite and small UAVS images. As compared with the eight state-of-the-art methods, the proposed method demonstrates superior registration performance in the majority of scenarios. In future work, we will integrate thematic applications (e.g., land cover change detection in mountainous terrain) of the proposed method considering multi-type remote sensing images will identify more changed area in typical regions.

References

1. Ma, J., Jiang, X., Fan, A., Jiang, J., Yan, J.: Image matching from handcrafted to deep features: a survey. Int. J. Comput. Vis **129**(1), 23–79 (2021). https://doi.org/10.1007/s11263-020-013 59-2
2. Sedaghat, A., Mohammadi, N.: Uniform competency-based local feature extraction for remote sensing images. ISPRS J. Photogramm. Remote Sens. **135**, 142–157 (2018)

3. Song, F., Li, M., Yang, Y., Yang, K., Gao, X., Dan, T.: Small UAV based multi-viewpoint image registration for monitoring cultivated land changes in mountainous terrain. Int. J. Remote Sens **39**(21), 7201–7224 (2018)

4. Zhou, J., et al.: Robust variational Bayesian point set registration. In: 2019 International Conference on Computer Vision (ICCV), Seoul, South Korea, pp. 9905–9914 (2019)

5. Song, F., et al.: Small UAV-based multi-temporal change detection for monitoring cultivated land cover changes in mountainous terrain. Remote Sens. Lett **10**(6), 573–582 (2019)

6. Ye, Y., Bruzzone, L., Shan, J., Bovolo, F., Zhu, Q.: A Fast and Robust Matching Framework for Multimodal Remote Sensing Image Registration. arXiv preprint arXiv (1808)

7. Lowe, D.: Distinctive image features from scale-invariant keypoints. Int. J. Comput. Vis. **60**, 91–110 (2004). https://doi.org/10.1023/B:VISI.0000029664.99615.94

8. Bay, H., Ess, A., Tuytelaars, T., Van Gool, L.: Speeded-up robust features (SURF). Comput. Vis. Image Underst. **110**(3), 346–359 (2008)

9. Myronenko, A., Song, X.: Point set registration: coherent point drift. IEEE Trans. Pattern Anal. Mach. Intell **32**(12), 2262–2275 (2010)

10. Wang, G., Wang, Z., Chen, Y., Zhao, W.: Robust point matching method for multimodal retinal image registration. Biomed. Signal Process. Control **19**, 68–76 (2015)

11. Yang, Y., Ong, S.H., Foong, K.W.C.: A robust global and local mixture distance based non-rigid point set registration. Pattern Recognit. **48**(1), 156–173 (2015)

12. Ma, J., Zhao, J., Yuille, A.L.: Non-rigid point set registration by preserving global and local structures. IEEE Trans, Image Process **25**(1), 53–64 (2016)

13. Zhang, S., Yang, K., Yang, Y., Luo, Y., Wei, Z.: Non-rigid point set registration using dual-feature finite mixture model and global-local structural preservation. Pattern Recognit. **80**, 183–195 (2018)

14. Ma, J., Jiang, X., Jiang, J., Gao, Y.: Feature-guided Gaussian mixture model for image matching. Pattern Recognit. **92**, 231–245 (2019)

15. Ji, S., Peng, S.: Terminal perturbation method for the backward approach to continuous time mean–variance portfolio selection. Stoch. Process. Appl. **118**(6), 952–967 (2008)

16. Bookstein, F.L.: Principal warps: thin-plate splines and the decomposition of deformations. IEEE Trans. Pattern Anal. Mach. Intell. **11**, 567–585 (2002)

17. Aguilera, C., Barrera, F., Sappa, A.D., Toledo, R.: A novel SIFT-like-based approach for FIR-VS images registration. In: Proceedings of the Quantitative InfraRed Thermography Naples, Italy, June, pp. 11–14 (2012)

18. Chen, J., Chen, S., Liu, Y., Chen, X., Yang, Y., Zhang, Y.: Robust local structure visualization for remote sensing image registration. IEEE J. Sel. Top. Appl. Earth Observ. Remote Sens. **14**, 1895–1908 (2021)

19. Chen, J., et al.: IGS-Net: seeking good correspondences via interactive generative structure learning. IEEE Trans. Geosci. Remote Sens. **60**, 1–13 (2021)

Deform-CAM: Self-attention Based on Deformable Convolution for Weakly Supervised Semantic Segmentation

Feihong Huang[1,2], Da-Han Wang[1,2(✉)], Hai-Li Ye[1,2], and Shunzhi Zhu[1,2]

[1] School of Computer and Information Engineering, Xiamen University of Technology,
Xiamen, China
`hfh@stu.xmut.edu.cn`, {`wangdh,szzhu`}`@xmut.edu.cn`,
`yehl@mail.sustech.edu.cn`

[2] Fujian Key Laboratory of Pattern Recognition and Image Understanding, Xiamen, China

Abstract. Weakly-supervised semantic segmentation (WSSS) receives increasing attentions from the community in recent years as it leverages the weakly annotated data to solve the problem of lacking of fully annotated data. Among them, the WSSS method based on image-level annotation is the most direct and effective while the image-level annotation is easy to obtain. Most advanced methods use class activation maps (CAM) as initial pseudo-labels, however, they only identify local regions of the target, while ignoring the context information among local regions. To solve this problem, this paper proposes a deformable convolution based self-attention module (DSAM), which introduces a pixel relationship matrix, to learn the contextual information of the image. A regularization loss is introduced to narrow the distance between the DSAM and the CAM. Compared to the base CAM method, our method can identify more target features and robustly improve the performance of WSSS without training the classifier multiple times. Our proposed method achieves the mIoU of 65.5% and 66.8% on the Pascal VOC 2012 val and test sets, respectively, demonstrating the feasibility of the method.

Keywords: Deformable convolution · Self-attention · Convolutional neural network · Weakly-supervised semantic segmentation

1 Introduction

Recently, the semantic segmentation model [1–3] based on deep learning has achieved significant progress due to the power of feature learning. However, fully supervised learning [4, 5] has the major limitation of relying on pixel-level annotations, which is especially expensive for annotating and organizing pixel-based semantic segmentation. Hence, current research attempt to use some of the more accessible annotations rather than pixel-level annotations, such as bounding-box [6], graffiti [7], dot [8], image-level label [9], etc. These different types of weak labels are used for semantic segmentation. Among them, image-level tags require the least amount of annotation work and have been popularly used. This paper mainly studies weakly-supervised semantic segmentation based on image-level labels.

Weakly-supervised semantic segmentation (WSSS) methods with image-level supervised labels mainly learn visual features to generate pseudo labels of pixels, such as Class Activation Maps (CAM) [10], which adds a global average pooling (GAP) on top of a fully convolutional network to obtain the class localization map. However, this network structure only recognizes the most discriminative object regions and tends to obtain incorrect pixel labels for boundary pixels of objects or different regions. To solve this problem, Alexander Kolesnikov *et al.* [11] improve the CAM through three principles of "seed", "expand" and "constrain". Yunchao Wei *et al.* [12] proposed an adversarial erasing (AE) method, which completes pseudo-pixel-level labels by stitching erased images. Jiwoon Ahn *et al.* [13] proposed the AffinityNet network structure to effectively exploit the semantic similarity between adjacent coordinate pixel pairs in an image. These methods can improve the quality of CAM effectively, but they also mark the background area.

The latest research trend is to add auxiliary tasks such as consistency regularization, sub-category classification, and cross-image semantic mining, and jointly train with the classification network to make the network focus on more pixels [14–16]. Yude Wanget *et al.* [14] adopted the idea of sharing weights in Siamese networks, and proposed a SEAM network framework. Yu-Ting Chang *et al.* [15] clustered image features, generated pseudo-subclass labels for each parent class label. Guolei Sun *et al.* [16] took the cross-image as the starting point, and proposed a co-attention module and an adversarial attention module. Tong Wu *et al.* [17] proposed EDAM, which learns collaborative features for the same set of input images. However, these methods involve a complex training phase or require the introduction of additional information, such as saliency maps.

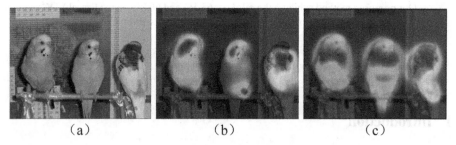

(a)   (b)   (c)

Fig. 1. Visualizations of CAMs. (a) input image. (b) conventional CAMs. (c) the Deform-CAM

To address the above problems, this paper proposes a novel framework called Deform-CAM that introduces a deformable convolution based self-attention module (DSAM) to CAM to learn the contextual information of the image and hence generate more robust pixel classification results, as shown in Fig. 1. The main characteristics of DSAM is to generate an image pixel relationship matrix based on the learned pixel context features using the self-attention mechanism. By minimizing the distance between the pixel relationship matrix and the CAM, the background noise is reduced and the target boundary is refined, leading to higher performance of semantic segmentation. Experiments on public datasets demonstrate the effectiveness of our method.

Our main contributions are as follows:

1. We propose a deformable convolution self-attention module DSAM to explore the context information of image pixels with the self-attention mechanism, which effectively reduces the background noise and refines the target boundary.
2. We propose a novel WSSS framework called Deform-CAM that combines the DSAM and CAM. The proposed Deform-CAM effectively improve the quality of CAM without complex training and the introduction of additional information.

2 Methodology

This section details the proposed Deform-CAM method. Figure 2 shows the network structure of Deform-CAM. Besides the backbone network, our network structure contains two branches: one branch is traditional CAM, and the other branch introduces DSAM to learn the correlation between image pixels. The feature maps of the stage3 and stage4 output by the backbone network, and the original image are concatenated to form the input of DSAM, which ensures that the features are more abundant. Then, DSAM uses deformable convolution to add offsets to reduce the influence of background noise at the target boundary, and applies a self-attention mechanism to explore the synergistic information between feature maps at different stages and the original image, which we call the pixel relationship matrix. Finally, the gap between the pixel relation matrix and the CAM is reduced via minimizing a contrastive loss. Compared to the based CAM, the proposed Deform-CAM method covers more target area and reduces the boundary noise.

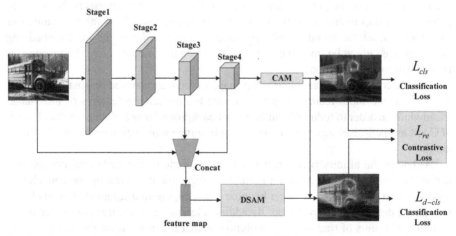

Fig. 2. The network architecture of the proposed Deform-CAM method. *Stage1*-*Stage4* represent the four stages of the backbone network respectively.

2.1 Class Activation Maps

First, we introduce the traditional methods of generating attention maps, CAMs. For the input image $I \in R^{3 \times H \times W}$, the image I is passed to the multi-label classification network. Under the action of the feature extractor, the extracted image feature $F(I) \in R^{C \times H \times W}$ is obtained after passing through the final classifier, a set of CAMs of class activation maps can be obtained. The formula for CAMs is as follows.

$$A_c = W_c * F(I), \tag{1}$$

where $A_c \in R^{N \times H \times W}$ are the resulting CAMs. W_c is the weight of the last fully connected layer in class c.

2.2 Deformable Convolution Based Self-attention Module

In Fig. 3, we introduce the structure of the Deformable Convolution based Self-Attention Module (DSAM). DSAM consists of three parts, deformable convolution, pixel relationship matrix and channel attention module. The pixel relationship branch and the channel relationship branch are two parallel branches to capture the context information of pixels and channels, respectively.

Since the self-attention mechanism can well capture the contextual information of pixels, this paper performs self-attention processing on the underlying features of the backbone network. In addition to building the affinity matrix between pixels, this module can also extract high-level features of the image. The self-attention module formula is as follows:

$$y_i = \frac{1}{C(x_i)} \sum_{\forall j} e^{\theta(x_i)^\mathsf{T} \phi(x_j)} \cdot g\left(\hat{x}_j\right) + x_i, \tag{2}$$

where i, j represent the position index, x is the input feature, y represents the obtained pixel relationship matrix, and $g\left(\hat{x}_j\right)$ gives the representation of the input feature x_j of each location, all the signal are all aggregated to position j, and the three embedding functions θ, ϕ, g can be implemented by a 1×1 convolutional layer. The response is normalized by a factor $C(x_i)$.

To obtain a richer pixel relationship map, we concatenate the original image $I \in R^{3 \times H \times W}$ to the input feature map to integrate the underlying features of the image. Meanwhile, in order to reduce the influence of background noise, we use another branch of CAM as pixel-level supervision to perform training modification on the pixel relation matrix.

Although the affinity between pixels is more obvious, the traditional convolution kernel has limitations that it cannot accurately locate the target during the convolution process and it also makes the target boundary challenging to distinguish. On this basis, we add the deformable convolution. By adding a learnable offset, it is not limited to the regular grid points of traditional convolution so that it can focus on the image texture boundary. The deformable convolution formula is as follows:

$$y(p) = \sum_{k=1}^{K} w_k \cdot x(p + p_k + \Delta p_k) \cdot \Delta m_k, \tag{3}$$

where $x(p)$ and $y(p)$ represent the feature at position p in the input feature x and the output feature y, respectively. K is the convolution kernel of K sampling locations, and w_k and p_k represent the weight and pre-specified offset of the k-th location. Δp_k and Δm_k are the learnable offset and modulation scalar for the k-th position. The range of Δm_k is $[0, 1]$. When computing $p + p_k + \Delta p_k$, we used bilinear interpolation.

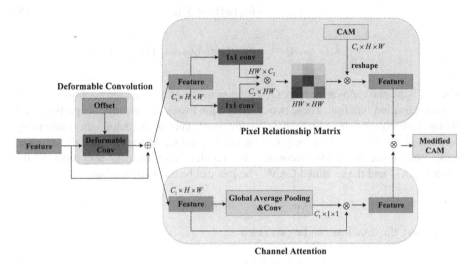

Fig. 3. The structure of DSAM

Since the channel map of each high-level feature can be viewed as the response of a specific class, we exploit the interdependence between channels to emphasize the irrelevant feature maps, thereby reducing the noise effect. Therefore, we introduce the channel attention module, and we directly perform a global average pooling operation on the feature map $I \in R^{C \times H \times W}$ obtained by deformable convolution. By the above operations, we can get the attention vector $I_2 \in R^{C_1 \times 1 \times 1}$ that contains the semantic dependencies between channels. Each vector in I_2 aggregates the contextual information of the image. The channel attention formula is:

$$Y_c = \frac{1}{H \times W} \sum_{i=1}^{H} \sum_{j=1}^{W} X_c(i, j), \tag{4}$$

where i, j represent the position index, H, W represent the size of the feature map, X_c represents the input feature map X of the c-th channel, Y_c represents the channel attention vector of the c-th channel.

Compared with the traditional self-attention module, the DSAM adds deformable convolution and applies the residual structure, so that the edge texture information of different targets can be adaptively learned. In the pixel relationship matrix, we use the ReLU activation function with L1 normalization to mask irrelevant pixels, generating an affinity attention map that is smoother in relevant regions. A channel attention mechanism is also introduced to further subdivide the pixel relationship through the inter-channel interdependence to reduce the interference of background noise.

2.3 Loss Design of Deform-CAM

In this paper, only image-level labels are used in our experiments, as well as in the loss design. We perform the GAP processing at the end of the network, using a multi-label classification loss for classification. The classification loss can be expressed as:

$$L_{cls} = -log(\sigma(G(A_c))), \tag{5}$$

$$L_{deform-cls} = -log\big(\sigma\big(G\big(A_{deform-c}\big)\big)\big), \tag{6}$$

where A is the class activation map, $G(\cdot)$ represents the global average pooling. $\sigma(\cdot)$ represents activation function. These two classification losses can improve the performance of object localization. In order to maintain the consistency of the output, the relationship between pixels needs to be aggregated on the original CAM to minimize the effect of background noise. We added reconstruction regularization to make it correspond the original CAM and the modified CAM. The loss can be easily defined as.

$$L_{re} = \big|A_{cls} - A_{deform-cls}\big|. \tag{7}$$

In short, the final loss can be expressed as:

$$L_{all} = L_{cls} + L_{deform-cls} + \alpha \cdot L_{re}, \tag{8}$$

where α is the balance of weights for different losses. Coarse localization of target is performed using classification losses L_{cls} and $L_{deform-cam}$. The reconstruction loss L_{re} is used to bridge the gap between pixel-level and image-level supervised processes and integrate DSAM with the network. We give details of the network training setup and study the effectiveness of each modules in the experimental section.

3   Experiments

3.1   Implementation Details

In this section, we present the implementation details of our method. In the official *PASCAL VOC 2012* dataset, there are 1464 images for training, 1449 for validation, and 1456 for testing. We set up one background class and 20 foreground classes to evaluate our method. Following the commonly used experimental protocol for semantic segmentation, we extract additional annotations from SBD [18] to construct an augmented training set containing 10582 images. However, during network training we only use image-level labels.

In the experiments, we use ResNet38 with output stride = 8 as the backbone network. During training, we crop all images to 448 × 448 as network input. The model is trained on Tesla V100-PCIE-32 GB. *batch_size* is set to 8, *epoch* is 15, the *learning* rate is 0.01, and the learning rate policy uses $lr_{itr} = lr_{init}(1 - itr / (max - itr))^\gamma$, where $\gamma = 0.9$.

3.2 Ablation Studies

We conducted ablation experiments on DSAM, the main module of Deform-CAM. Here, we still used the mIoU as the evaluation index. As shown in Table 1, the CAM accuracy of the baseline is 48.1%. After the adjustment of the DSAM module, we improved the accuracy to 50.5%. Based on the baseline, we can see that adding the pixel relationship matrix (PRM) can enrich the semantic information between pixels, and the accuracy is improved by 1.2%. By applying the deformable convolution (DC) again to refine the image boundaries and reduce the background noise at the boundaries, the accuracy is further improved by 0.5%. Finally, by adding the channel attention (CA) branch to enhance intra-class features between channels, the generated pseudo-labels achieve 50.5% accuracy on the *PASCAL VOC* validation set.

Table 1. The ablation study for each part of DSAM. **CAM:** Class Activation Maps. **PRM:** pixel relationship matrix. **DC:** deformable convolution. **CA:** channel attention.

CAM	PRM	DC	CA	mIoU
√				48.1%
√	√			49.3%
√	√	√		49.8%
√	√	√	√	50.5%

Table 2 shows the ablation results of the network loss. Baseline accuracy is 48.1%. When applying the classification loss only to the output of the DSAM module, the accuracy instead drops to 47.3%, this is because the DSAM module can acquire more target areas, but it introduces some background noise for some classes, which will affect the quality of the CAM. By reconstructing the regularization loss L_{re}, the network expands the correct local features, increasing the accuracy by 0.5%. When we introduce classification loss and reconstruction loss together, the accuracy rises to 50.5%, not only the noise information is reduced, but the features on the boundary are also more precise.

Table 2. The ablation study of the network loss.

L_{cls}	L_{deform}	L_{re}	mIoU
√			48.1%
√		√	48.6%
√	√		47.3%
√	√	√	50.5%

Table 3. Performance comparisons of our method with other methods on *PASCAL VOC 2012* dataset. *: the segmentation results with post-processing. Indicate: *I*-image-level, *S*-external saliency maps.

Method	Backbone	Sup	val	test
AffinityNet [13]	ResNet-38	*I*	61.7	63.7
SEAM [14]	ResNet-38	*I*	64.5	65.7
RRM [19]	ResNet-38	*I*	62.6	62.9
BES* [20]	ResNet-101	*I*	65.7	66.6
OOA [21]	ResNet-101	*I*	65.2	66.4
IRNet [22]	ResNet-50	*I*	63.5	64.8
CIAN [23]	ResNet-101	*S*	64.1	64.7
CDA [24]	ResNet-38	*I*	64.2	65.8
H-DSRG [25]	ResNet-38	*I*	64.6	65.2
Ours	ResNet-38	*I*	**65.5**	**66.8**

3.3 Comparison with Existing State-of-the-Art Methods

To further improve the accuracy of pseudo-pixel-level annotations, we follow the work of IRNet [22] and add a boundary branch to the modified CAM. According to our generated CAM, the boundary branch is trained, and the semantic segmentation task is completed by generating random seeds and performing a random walk strategy. The final generated pseudo-labels achieve 66.5% accuracy on the *val* set of *PASCAL VOC 2012*.

In Table 3, the *mIoU* comparison between our method and previous methods is shown. We can find that on the validation set, the accuracy of our method is almost the same as that of BES [20] using denseCRF post-processing. And on the test set, we are even higher than that. Compared with other baseline methods, Deform-CAM achieves significant performance improvements on both *val* and *test* sets under the same training settings. Notably, our accuracy gains do not come from large network results, but through an efficient combination of variable convolution, pixel relations, and channel attention. Figure 4 shows qualitative results on the *val* set, we can find that compared to IRNet, our proposed method can identify more accurate regions in columns 1 and 7. In columns 2 and 3, we can better identify the boundary details. And from columns 4 to 6, we can see that our network did not segment the background region. In conclusion, our results are closer to the GT than IRNet, illustrating that the proposed method achieves good results on both large and small objects.

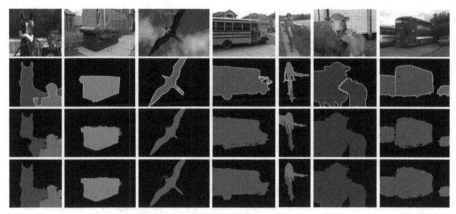

Fig. 4. Qualitative segmentation results on *PASCAL VOC* 2012 *val* set. *From top to bottom*: input images, ground-truths, IRNet [22] and our segmentation results.

4 Conclusion

This paper designs a Deform-CAM network structure to leverage image-level labels to close the supervision gap between FSSS and WSSS. DSAM expands the correct local feature range through deformable convolution and an efficient combination of pixel-to-pixel relationships. Our Deform-CAM is implemented with an efficient reconstruction loss network structure, and the generated CAM not only has less background noise, but also better approximates the shape of GT. According to the generated pixel-level pseudo-labels, combined with the random walk strategy, a good improvement is achieved on the *PASCAL VOC 2012* dataset, proving the effectiveness of Deform-CAM.

Acknowledgments. This work was supported by the Natural Science Foundation of China (No. 61773325 and 61806173), the Industry–University Cooperation Project of Fujian Science and Technology Department (No. 2021H6035), the Natural Science Foundation of Fujian Province (No. 2021J011191), the Joint Funds of the 5th Round of Health and Education Research Program of Fujian Province (No. 2019-WJ-41), the Science and Technology Planning Project of Fujian Province (No. 2020H0023), and the Young Teacher Education Research Project of Fujian Province (No. JT180435).

References

1. Ronneberger, O., Fischer, P., Brox, T.: U-net: convolutional networks for biomedical image segmentation. In: Navab, N., Hornegger, J., Wells, W.M., Frangi, A.F. (eds.) MICCAI 2015. LNCS, vol. 9351, pp. 234–241. Springer, Cham (2015). https://doi.org/10.1007/978-3-319-24574-4_28
2. Long, J., Shelhamer, E., Darrell, T.: Fully convolutional networks for semantic segmentation. In: Proceedings of the IEEE Conference on Computer Vision and Pattern Recognition (2017)
3. Chen, L.C., Papandreou, G., Kokkinos, I., et al.: DeepLab: semantic image segmentation with deep convolutional nets, atrous convolution, and fully connected CRFs. IEEE Trans. Pattern Anal. Mach. Intell. **40**(4), 834–848 (2018)

4. Chen, L.-C., Zhu, Y., Papandreou, G., Schroff, F., Adam, H.: Encoder-decoder with atrous separable convolution for semantic image segmentation. In: Ferrari, V., Hebert, M., Sminchisescu, C., Weiss, Y. (eds.) ECCV 2018. LNCS, vol. 11211, pp. 833–851. Springer, Cham (2018). https://doi.org/10.1007/978-3-030-01234-2_49

5. Fu, J., et al.: Dual attention network for scene segmentation. In: Proceedings of the IEEE/CVF Conference on Computer Vision and Pattern Recognition (2019)

6. Papandreou, G., et al.: Weakly-and semi-supervised learning of a deep convolutional network for semantic image segmentation. In: Proceedings of the IEEE International Conference on Computer Vision (2015)

7. Lin, D., et al.: Scribblesup: Scribble-supervised convolutional networks for semantic segmentation. In: Proceedings of the IEEE Conference on Computer Vision and Pattern Recognition (2016)

8. Bearman, A., Russakovsky, O., Ferrari, V., Fei-Fei, L.: What's the point: semantic segmentation with point supervision. In: Leibe, B., Matas, J., Sebe, N., Welling, M. (eds.) ECCV 2016. LNCS, vol. 9911, pp. 549–565. Springer, Cham (2016). https://doi.org/10.1007/978-3-319-46478-7_34

9. Pathak, D., et al.: Fully convolutional multi-class multiple instance learning. arXiv preprint arXiv:1412.7144 (2014)

10. Zhou, B., et al.: Learning deep features for discriminative localization. In: Proceedings of the IEEE Conference on Computer Vision and Pattern Recognition (2016)

11. Kolesnikov, A., Lampert, C.H.: Seed, expand and constrain: three principles for weakly-supervised image segmentation. In: Leibe, B., Matas, J., Sebe, N., Welling, M. (eds.) ECCV 2016. LNCS, vol. 9908, pp. 695–711. Springer, Cham (2016). https://doi.org/10.1007/978-3-319-46493-0_42

12. Wei, Y., et al.: Object region mining with adversarial erasing: a simple classification to semantic segmentation approach. In: Proceedings of the IEEE Conference on Computer Vision and Pattern Recognition (2017)

13. Ahn, J., Kwak, S.: Learning pixel-level semantic affinity with image-level supervision for weakly supervised semantic segmentation. In: Proceedings of the IEEE Conference on Computer Vision and Pattern Recognition (2018)

14. Wang, Y., et al.: Self-supervised equivariant attention mechanism for weakly supervised semantic segmentation. Proceedings of the IEEE/CVF Conference on Computer Vision and Pattern Recognition (2020)

15. Chang, Y.-T., et al.: Weakly-supervised semantic segmentation via sub-category exploration. In: Proceedings of the IEEE/CVF Conference on Computer Vision and Pattern Recognition (2020)

16. Sun, G., Wang, W., Dai, J., Van Gool, L.: Mining cross-image semantics for weakly supervised semantic segmentation. In: Vedaldi, A., Bischof, H., Brox, T., Frahm, J.-M. (eds.) ECCV 2020. LNCS, vol. 12347, pp. 347–365. Springer, Cham (2020). https://doi.org/10.1007/978-3-030-58536-5_21

17. Wu, T., et al.: Embedded discriminative attention mechanism for weakly supervised semantic segmentation. In: Proceedings of the IEEE/CVF Conference on Computer Vision and Pattern Recognition (2021)

18. Hariharan, B., et al.: Semantic contours from inverse detectors. In: 2011 International Conference on Computer Vision. IEEE (2011)

19. Zhang, B., et al.: Reliability does matter: an end-to-end weakly supervised semantic segmentation approach. In: Proceedings of the AAAI Conference on Artificial Intelligence. vol. 34, issue number 07 (2020)

20. Chen, L., Wu, W., Fu, C., Han, X., Zhang, Y.: Weakly supervised semantic segmentation with boundary exploration. In: Vedaldi, A., Bischof, H., Brox, T., Frahm, J.-M. (eds.) ECCV 2020.

LNCS, vol. 12371, pp. 347–362. Springer, Cham (2020). https://doi.org/10.1007/978-3-030-58574-7_21

21. Jiang, P.-T., et al.: Integral object mining via online attention accumulation. In: Proceedings of the IEEE/CVF International Conference on Computer Vision (2019)

22. Ahn, J., Cho, S., Kwak, S.: Weakly supervised learning of instance segmentation with inter-pixel relations. In: Proceedings of the IEEE/CVF Conference on Computer Vision and Pattern Recognition (2019)

23. Fan, J., et al.: CIAN: cross-image affinity net for weakly supervised semantic segmentation. In: Proceedings of the AAAI Conference on Artificial Intelligence, vol. 34, issue number 07 (2020)

24. Su, Y., et al.: Context decoupling augmentation for weakly supervised semantic segmentation. In: Proceedings of the IEEE/CVF International Conference on Computer Vision (2021)

25. Chong, Y., et al.: Erase then grow: generating correct class activation maps for weakly-supervised semantic segmentation. Neurocomputing **453**, 97–108 (2021)

Density-NMS: Cell Detection
and Classification in Microscopy Images

Minghui Chen, Qiao Pan[(✉)], and Yishu Luo

College of Computer Science and Technology, Donghua University,
Shanghai 201620, China
{panqiao,ysluo}@dhu.edu.cn

Abstract. With the development of digital pathology, the automatic detection and classification of microscopy image cells using artificial intelligence technology has become a research hotspot. However, due to the problems of multi-scale cells, unbalanced foreground and background, and cell adhesion in micro images, the existing artificial intelligence object detection algorithms directly used in microscopic images have poor detection results. Therefore, to solve these problems, this paper proposes a region proposal networks based on sample weighting for cell detection and classification in microscopy images. In particular, on the basis of GA-RPN which combines the guided anchoring (GA) and the region proposal network (RPN), the sample weight learning module is added to the network, so that the network can learn the weight through the sample characteristics, which can significantly improve the detection effect. In addition, we propose a new non-maximal suppression algorithm, Density-NMS, which dynamically adjusts the suppression threshold according to the density of cell instances, allowing the model to have good detection in the case of cell adhesions. We test the proposed approach on two open cell detection challenge, Blood Cell Detection (BCCD) and Malaria. Experimental results show that the region proposal network applying sample weighting achieved superior performance on the cell detection and classification in microscopy images when compared with traditional object detection methods. In conclusion, our method can achieve better performance in object detection domain and provide an auxiliary method for pathologists to diagnose patients' diseases.

Keywords: Cell detection and classification · Density NMS · Deep learning · Digital pathology

1 Introduce

Digital pathology is one of the main developments of modern medicine, that is, to identify diseases such as cancer by examining microscopic images through digital pathology in clinical practice. Pathomorphological examination is the gold standard for the diagnosis of many diseases. In traditional pathological diagnosis, pathologists focus on cell morphology and structural distribution for early diagnosis and prognostic assessment [1]. The main challenge of pathomorphological examination is to detect and accurately analyze each cell, because the identification of cancer disease mainly depends on the data at the cell level. Therefore, the detection and classification of cells is an important task in medical image examination, and it is the key to early diagnosis and prognostic assessment of the disease.

In traditional pathological examinations, microscopic images are mostly evaluated and analyzed manually by pathologists. The diagnosis and analysis of microscopic images rely on trained pathologists. The pathological changes caused by different pathogens are different, which requires the accumulation of professional knowledge as the basis and familiarity with the cytological characteristics of these lesions. Therefore, manual analysis of a large number of microscopic images to diagnose a patient's disease is a very time-consuming and challenging task for pathologists. In recent years, artificial intelligence has been rapidly developing in the field of digital pathology. With the addition of artificial intelligence technology, the detection and classification of microscopic image cells by artificial intelligence help doctors to assist in diagnosis. J Zhao [2] proposed a method based on convolutional neural network and random forest to automatically detect and classify leukocytes from peripheral blood images; PB shanthi [3] used CNN to convolve learning features in input images to classify cervical cells in cytology images; H Kutlu [4] used region-based convolutional neural network R-CNN for leukocyte detection and classification; SM Abas [5] used YOLOv2 method for leukocyte detection and classification in leukemia. Therefore, if the object detection algorithm of deep learning can be applied to detect and classify cells in microscopic images using pathomorphological examination, it can effectively alleviate the scarcity of human resources for pathologists in China and improve the accuracy of medical image diagnosis by avoiding missed detection and false detection.

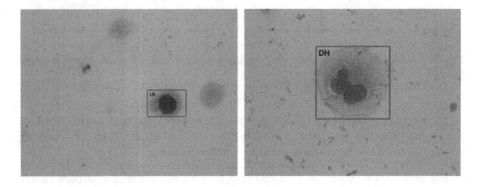

Fig. 1. The problem of multi-scale objects in microscopic images.

In recent years, although deep learning-based object detection algorithms have been widely used in the medical field, they have also achieved quite good results. However, due to some special detection problems in medical images, the detection accuracy still can not meet the application requirements. Firstly, the problem of multi-scale objects with large differences in size and scale exists in microscopy images, as shown in Fig. 1, there are large differences in size between cell instances in the same dataset. Large scale cells with large cell volume and rich features are easily detected, while small scale cells are difficult to be detected due to few available features, leading to the problem of missing objects in the object detection model. Secondly, the problem of unbalanced foreground and background samples in microscopy images is also worth considering, as shown in Fig. 2(a). In microscope images, there are significantly fewer foreground cell instances to detect and identify than background areas, resulting in low accuracy of the object detection model. The problem of cell adhesion and aggregation exists in microscopy images, as shown in Fig. 2(b). For the sample data with dense distribution of instance objects and high overlap, when using the non-maximal suppression algorithm to filter the generated region proposals, those region proposals containing objects may be filtered out together with the region proposals with a high overlap, resulting in not being able to identify all the objects.

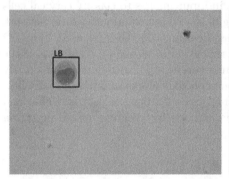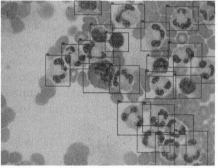

(a) Imbalance between foreground and background in microscopic images   (b) High-density cell adhesion problem in microscopic images

Fig. 2. Imbalance of foreground and background and cell adhesion in microscopic images

In this paper, the Mask RCNN, a two-stage object detection model based on the region proposal approach, is used as the baseline model, and the following improvements have been made to address these issues:

1. For multi-scale problems with different scales and extremes of aspect ratios, this paper uses the Guided Anchoring Region Proposal Network (GA-RPN), which predicts non-uniform anchor points and able to use the different layer feature maps of the FPN to generate proposals that are more adapted to cell instances, allowing the algorithm to perform accurate detection for objects of various scales.

2. In view of the imbalance between the positive and negative samples of foreground and background, we add a feature weight learning module to the region proposal network module, which adopts a nonlinear feature decorrelation method based on Random Fourier Features for each layer of features to reweight the samples of RPN, which can effectively alleviate the foreground and background sample imbalance and improve the accuracy and generalization ability of the model.
3. For the problem that the traditional non-maximum suppression algorithm is easy to miss the detection of high-density cell adhesion scenes, this paper proposes a dynamic suppression strategy, which adaptively adjusts the threshold of NMS according to the aggregation and sparsity of cell instances.

2   Related Word

The current mainstream object detection algorithms are mainly based on deep learning models and can be roughly divided into two main categories. (1) Single-stage object detection algorithms, which do not require a region proposal stage and can generate the category probability and location coordinate values of objects directly through single-stage. The typical algorithms are YOLO [6], SSD [7] and RetinaNet [8]; (2) Two-stage object detection algorithms, these detection algorithms divide the detection problem into two stages. In the first stage, the regional proposal boxes is generated firstly, and then extracts the features of each regional proposal box to generate the final location box and predict its category, typical representatives of this type of algorithms are Fast RCNN [9], Faster RCNN [10] and Mask RCNN [11]. The main performance metrics of the object detection models are detection accuracy and speed, where accuracy is mainly considers the object localization as well as classification accuracy. In general, two-stage algorithms have an advantage in accuracy, while single-stage algorithms have an advantage in speed. However, with the development of research, both types of algorithms have been improved in two aspects, which can achieve better results in accuracy and speed.

2.1   Anchor-Based Methods

The generation of regional proposal boxes plays an important role in the object detection model. It generates a set of rectangular bounding boxes, and then uses these bounding boxes for classification and location. At present, most of the object detection methods use an anchor mechanism. Faster RCNN [10] uses nine different anchor points in a feature map with three scales and three aspect ratios. YOLOv2 [12] uses the anchors of sliding window for classification and spatial location prediction to achieve higher recall than before. MetaAnchor [13] uses additional neural networks to predict dynamic anchors from customized previous boxes, but they are only available for single-stage detectors. Zhong [14] proposed an anchor optimization method that does not change the number of predefined anchors but optimizes the size and ratio of anchors during training to achieve higher detection accuracy. However, these methods need to manual preset anchor parameters and do not reduce the calculation cost of predefined anchor points and are not fully applicable in multi-scale microscopy image scenes.

2.2 Imbalance Between Foreground and Background

In most of the sampling methods, all proposals are detected by random sampling. However, due to random sampling from one image, a large number of negative samples are generated, resulting in extreme imbalance between positive and negative samples. Therefore, Shrivastava [15] proposed the OHEM algorithm for the imbalance of hard and easy samples, where they considered that a small number of hard samples is more effective for accuracy improvement compared to a large number of easy samples. They sort the loss of region of interest for each image, select some samples with large loss as hard samples, and retrain them. However, this process leads to additional memory and speed overheads, which slow down the training process. In addition, OHEM is affected by noise labels, so it cannot work normally in all cases. Focal loss [8] solves the imbalance problem between foreground background in single-stage object detection with a simple loss function. However, it is not effective in two-stage object detection due to different imbalance situations.

2.3 Post-processing Methods

As a common post-processing algorithm in computer vision, NMS is an important part of many detection methods. It is applied to many tasks, such as feature point detection [16], face detection [17], object detection [6], etc. In object detection, because the model uses the anchor mechanism to generate multiple proposal boxes, in which there are many repeated boxes for the same object, the main role of NMS is to extract the detection boxes with high confidence scores and suppress the false detection boxes with low confidence scores. The biggest problem in the NMS algorithm is that it adopts a greedy algorithm to force the detection boxes below the threshold to be removed, but in dense scenes where multiple objects exist for occlusion there will be missed detections. Soft-NMS [18] does not directly discard all proposal boxes with scores below the threshold, but reduces the confidence score of the bounding box by linearly weighting or Gaussian weighting, and then selects the appropriate confidence threshold to remove the bounding box, which greatly reduces false deletions. Adaptive-NMS [19] is applied to the pedestrian detection scene. The method designs a sub-network that can predict NMS thresholds according to the density of the instance objects, which improves the adaptability of the threshold to a certain extent.

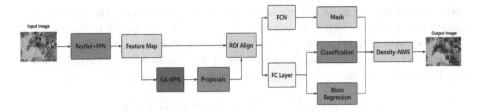

Fig. 3. Overall flow chart of the model.

3   Method

In this section, we will introduce the proposed object detection model based on microscopic images in detail. As shown in Fig. 3, we will use the two-stage object detection model Mask RCNN as the baseline model and use three techniques to make it more suitable for cell detection and classification. Firstly, the Guided Anchoring scheme is used to combine GA and RPN to generate a high-quality scheme of input image. Then we use the feature decorrelation method to obtain the sample weights in each feature layer of RPN, and combine the weights with the loss function of RPN to solve the problem of imbalance between positive and negative samples. Finally, this paper proposes Density-NMS, which can filter proposal boxes to obtain more accurate bounding boxes and classification labels.

3.1   Guided Anchoring in the Regional Proposal Network

Modern deep learning object detection tasks are usually regarded as a problem of classification and regression of a group of region proposals, but the use of multi-scale features and sliding windows to obtain the region proposals appears to be bulky and time-consuming. Therefore, most advanced object detection methods use the anchor mechanism, that is through pre-defined anchor boxes with different proportions, aspect ratios and sizes, they can cover all region proposals of position and scale. However, there will be the following problems. The scale and aspect ratio of the anchor box will be predefined as constants, and a large number of densely distributed and fixed anchor boxes will be generated. Therefore, the anchor mechanism is suitable for object detection with uniform distribution and the same scale. However, in the microscopic image, there is a common sparse distribution of cells and a dense distribution scenario of cell adhesions, and there is a multi-scale problem of large differences in morphology and size between cells. The predefined anchor mechanism will limit the efficiency of the detection method and the detection results. So, we choose a more effective anchor scheme.

In this paper, we take a dynamic approach to predicting non-uniform and arbitrary shape anchor points [20], which abandons the previous way of generating dense and uniform anchors. This method will be more suitable for the task of cell detection and classification in microscopic images. We will introduce the working principle of this method, as shown below. We use (x, y, W, H) to represent the location and shape of the cell instance, where (x, y) represents the spatial coordinate of the object center, W is the width of the object and H is the height of the object. Assuming that we need to draw this cell instance in microscopic image I, its location and shape can be described by the mathematical formula for the conditional distribution probabilities associated with image I, as follows:

$$P(x, y, W, H|I) = P(x, y|I) * P(W, H|x, y, I) \tag{1}$$

According to the conditional probability decomposition of Formula 1, we believe that the cell detection process can be divided into two branches: (1) Assuming a microscopic cell image I, cell instances exist only in a specific region of image I; (2) There is a correlation between the shape (scale and aspect ratio) and location of cell instances.

The implementation of the GA Module is shown in Fig. 4. It mainly consists of two parts: the anchor generation module and the feature adaptation module. The anchor generation module consists of two branches: location prediction and shape prediction. We give a microscopic image I, which is extracted by ResNet101 and FPN network to obtain the feature map P of the image. In the GA module, this feature map P will enter two branches, Anchor generation and Feature adaptation. In the Anchor generation module the location prediction branch generates the probabilistic map of the possible locations of cell instances, while the shape prediction branch predicts the shape associated with the location. Finally, the locations with predicted probability scores above a preset threshold are selected from the output of these two branches and a set of anchors is generated for each location's shape. Due to the diversity of anchor shapes, the features of different positions should obtain receptive fields in different ranges. On this basis, a feature adaptive module is introduced, whose purpose is to use multiple feature maps on different layers. It will change the features by deformation convolution at each location according to the anchor shape of the foundation.

3.2   Sample Weight Learning

The existing object detection models, including single-stage and two-stage, usually use the region-based method to sample the region in the image through the anchor mechanism, and then the detector classifies and localizes its sampled regions. Therefore, the selection of regional samples plays a crucial role in the detection effect of object detection. However, in microscopic images, cell instances survive in a large number of tissue fluid and most of the samples are located in the background area, resulting in the imbalance between positive and negative samples in the detection, which affects the detection results. Therefore, we designed an additional feature sample weight learning module in the region proposal network (RPN). This module solves the problem of sample imbalance through the method of global sample weighting, directly decorrelates all the features of each cell instance in the input image and eliminating the sample features of the tissue fluid background region that are not related to cells. Specifically, we use the properties of Random Fourier

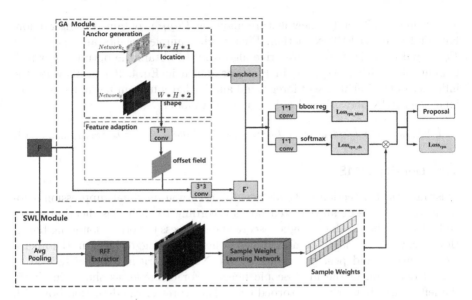

Fig. 4. Detailed structure of the regional proposal network based on sample weighting.

Features (RFF) and sample weighting to resolve the linear and nonlinear dependencies between features and to derive sample weights to alleviate the imbalance between positive and negative samples.

The principle of the feature sample weight learning module is described as follows. The Random Fourier Features method of approximating the kernel function. Its main purpose is to find a low-dimensional mapping function $Z(x)$ that can map the initial data in dimension D to the random feature space in dimension d, that is, $Z:R^D \rightarrow R^d$, the formula of this mapping function Z is as follows:

$$Z(x) = \sqrt{\frac{2}{D}}[\cos(w_1^T + \phi_1), ..., \cos(w_D^T + \phi_D)]^T, w \sim N(0,1), \phi \sim U(0, 2\pi) \quad (2)$$

where w is the sample weight taken from the standard normal distribution and ϕ is taken from the uniform distribution. Then we calculate the sample weights according to the mapping function, as shown in Eq. 3.

$$w = \underset{w \in \triangle n}{\arg\min} \sum_{1 \leq i < j \leq m_z} \left\| Z_{:,i} * Z_{:,j} \right\|^2 \quad (3)$$

where $\triangle n = \{w \in R| \sum_{i=1}^n w_i = n\}$, $Z_{:,i}$ represents the i-th variable in the mapping space Z, and similarly the j-th variable is $Z_{:,j}$ and m_Z is the dimensions of space Z.

The specific implementation of the sample weighting module is shown in Fig. 4. We are given a microscopic image I, and the feature map P of this image I is obtained by ResNet101 and FPN. In this module, we first average pool this feature map P, Then the new feature mapping P_{RFF} is obtained using random Fourier feature (RFF) extraction. Finally, the sample weights are learned for P_{RFF} and optimized by an iterative algorithm to obtain the optimal w, which is multiplied with $Loss_{rpn\_cls}$ in RPN, as shown in Eq. 4. It can alleviate the influence of the imbalance of foreground and background samples in microscopic images on RPN network and object detection model.

$$Loss_{rpn} = w * Loss_{rpn\_cls} + Loss_{rpn\_bbox} + Loss_{rpn\_loc} + Loss_{rpn\_shape} \quad (4)$$

3.3 Density-NMS

Existing object detection methods usually use a non-maximal suppression algorithm (NMS) to sort all detected boxes according to their classification scores and select the box with the highest score and suppress the other bounding boxes. However, there is a large number of cell adhesion and aggregation in the microscopic images, and post-processing by the NMS algorithm can easily lead to missed detection of the microscopic images. For example, as shown in Fig. 5, the left figure shows three adsorbed cells. The scores of the detection box with yellow dotted line and green dotted line in the right figure are 0.75 and 0.62 respectively. If a lower threshold of NMS is applied, these two detection boxes will be suppressed, while the red solid line detection box containing two cells is retained. Due to the dense scene of cell adhesion and aggregation in the microscopic image, filtering the detection boxes below the preset threshold through NMS will increase the possibility of missed detection and false detection.

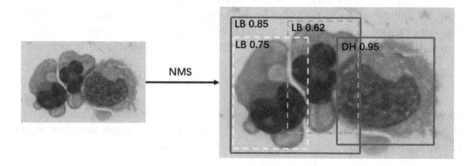

Fig. 5. Detection results of traditional NMS algorithm

In realistic scenarios, the density of instance objects varies widely, and a higher NMS threshold may increase false positives in regions where instance objects are sparse. To address this issue, instead of directly discarding all region proposals below the threshold, many NMS algorithms reduce the detection scores of adjacent bounding boxes by adding a penalty function that overlaps with higher scoring bounding boxes. Soft-NMS [18] uses a linearly weighted or Gaussian weighted function instead of direct discard, as shown in Eq. 5, where bi represents the i-th detection box in the set of detection boxes excluding M, s_i represents the score of that box, N_t is a preset threshold, M is the highest scoring detection box for that instance object, and $f(iou(M, b\_i))$ is an overlapped weighting function.

$$s_i = \begin{cases} s_i & , iou(M, b_i) < N_t \\ s_i * f(iou(M, b_i)) & , iou(M, b_i) \geq N_t \end{cases} \tag{5}$$

In Soft-NMS [18], $f(iou(M, b_i))$ can choose linear weighting $(1 - iou(M, b_i))$ or Gaussian weighting $(e^{-\frac{(iou(M, b_i))^2}{\sigma}})$ as a penalty function overlapping with M to decay the confidence score. Adaptive-NMS [19], optimizes Soft-NMS for the special crowd scene of pedestrian detection. This method presents a prediction for judging the density of instance objects, which can dynamically increase or decrease the NMS threshold according to the density sparsity of instance objects. It defines the density of the i-th instance object as follows:

$$d_i = max(b_i, b_j) \qquad b_j \in G, i \neq j \tag{6}$$

where d_i represents the maximum IoU in the set G of ground truth with other objects. However, this method adds additional subnetworks and uses the maximum IoU value of the overlapping part with the instance object as the density of that object is not very general and not very applicable in microscopic images. Therefore, inspired by Soft-NMS [18] and Adaptive-NMS [19], this paper designs the Density-NMS method, which calculates the values around a cell instance object according to the Euclidean distance, and obtains the density of the instance object through function calculation.

First, we calculate the center point of each bounding box, the density of that bounding box is described by the geometric distance between the points, if one bounding box has a higher density, it means that the center points of many other bounding boxes are closer to the center point. Then we use the following strategy for the suppression step based on the obtained density value $idensity$. We calculate the adaptive threshold $N_{density}$ by similar Gaussian function.

$$N_{density} = \frac{1}{\sqrt{2\pi\sigma}} e^{-\left(\frac{\sum_{j=1}^{k} b_j - idensity}{\sum_{j=1}^{k} b_j}\right)^2} \tag{7}$$

We compare the calculated threshold $N_{density}$ with the pre-defined N_t and obtain the maximum value between them.

$$N_d = max(N_t, N_{density}) \tag{8}$$

Finally, through the comparison of $iou(M, bi)$ and Nd, the detection score of the adjacent boxes that overlap with the M is reduced by the penalty function $f(iou(M, bi))$, that is, the more highly overlapped detection boxes with M, the more severely their scores decrease.

$$s_i = \begin{cases} s_i & , iou(M, b_i) < N_d \\ s_i * f(iou(M, b_i)) & , iou(M, b_i) \geq N_d \end{cases} \tag{9}$$

4   Experiments and Results

4.1   Dataset

In this paper, we use a cerebrospinal fluid microscopic image dataset and two public datasets (BCCD dataset and Malaria dataset) to validate the effectiveness of the proposed method. The details are described below.

CerebroSpinal Fluid Dataset. The cerebrospinal fluid dataset is a total of 1299 microscopic images of cerebrospinal fluid examination provided by a third-class hospital in Shanghai. The size of each picture in this dataset is $2560 * 1920$, and 3905 cell boundary boxes and category information manually marked by pathologists. In each of these images, there are differences between the distribution, size and morphology of the cells. The cerebrospinal fluid dataset contains three major categories: Lymphocytes, Mononuclear, and Neutrophils. We divided the dataset into 929 training sets and 370 test sets according to the way of patient image packaging and the rules of cell category distribution. In this paper, we will use this dataset for comparison and ablation experiments to validate the effectiveness of the proposed method.

BCCD Dataset. The dataset is a publicly available dataset of blood cell microscopy images by Roboflow, with a total of 364 images, classifies cells into three categories: white blood cells (WBCs), red blood cells (RBCs), and platelets. About 4888 cells are labeled with information in the dataset. The size of each image is $416 * 416$, which is a small-scale medical image object detection dataset, so we divide this dataset into 292 training sets and 72 test sets to evaluate the performance of the proposed model. We want to be able to use this dataset to demonstrate the generalization capability of the proposed method.

Malaria Dataset. We used the image collection bbbc041v1, which can obtainS [21] from the Broad Bioimage Benchmark Collection. The dataset contains 1364 images of blood smears (approximately 80,000 cells) stained with Giemsa reagent. The data include two categories of uninfected cells (RBCs and leukocytes) and four types of infected cells (gametocytes, rings, trophozoites, and schizonts), and the dataset allows pathologists to label difficult to distinguish indistinct cells as difficult categories. We preprocessed this dataset with difficult labeling filtering and divided this dataset into 866 training sets and 155 test sets. Similarly, this dataset is usually used to evaluate the performance of cell detection. We will use this dataset to validate the generalization capability and performance of the proposed method.

4.2   Evaluation Metrics

The performance evaluation metrics in object detection mainly include accuracy, recall, average precision (AP) and average precision mean(mAP) [22].

Accuracy rate refers to the percentage of the number of correctly identified samples among the identified positive samples. Recall rate refers to the percentage of all positive samples in the test set that are correctly identified. Average accuracy refers to the area under the accuracy and recall curve, and the points on the curve are generated by moving the IoU threshold from high to low. The mAP means that the average precision is first calculated for each category, and then calculating the average value of each AP. Today, mAP is the mainstream evaluation metric for object detection. The detection results of the experiments in this paper will be evaluated using the COCO dataset metrics, including AP_{50}, AP_{75}, AP_S, AP_M, AP_L and IoU thresholds set at 0.5 to 0.95 for mAP.

4.3   Experimental Result

The experiments were trained and verified on a server equipped with two 12GB Tesla K80 GPUs. We use the Mask RCNN implemented in the MMDetection library as a baseline model and perform the implementation of the methods in this paper. We used ResNet101 and FPN as the backbone network and employed Stochastic Gradient Descent (SGD) during training and optimization for a total of 12 training iterations, setting the learning rate to 0.02 and using a standard Gaussian distribution for the other parameters.

Table 1. Comparative experiment.

Method	mAP	AP_{50}	AP_{75}	AP_S	AP_M	AP_L
SSD [7]	0.623	0.922	0.666	0.226	0.605	0.592
RetinaNet [8]	0.613	0.926	0.652	0.363	0.628	0.587
YOLOv3 [23]	0.620	0.95	0.691	0.404	0.633	0.552
Faster RCNN [10]	0.622	0.935	0.676	0.333	0.640	0.557
Mask RCNN [11]	0.636	0.946	0.728	0.363	0.676	0.587
Cascade RCNN [24]	0.635	0.932	0.690	0.388	0.652	0.566
Ours	0.663	0.943	0.730	0.412	0.677	0.566

In recent years, many mainstream object detection models have been applied to microscopy images for cell detection and classification. Therefore, in order to compare the performance of the proposed method, we conduct comparative experiments on some mainstream models in this paper. As shown in Table 1, we applied some mainstream object detection models to the cerebrospinal fluid dataset and compare them with the proposed method. From the results, the method in this paper has a better performance mAP of 66.3%, AP_{50} of 94.3%, AP_{75} of 73%, AP_S of 41.2%, AP_M of 67.7%, AP_L of 56.6%, compared with other methods, which indicates that the method can better detect cells at different scales and can detect the bounding boxes and classes of cells more accurately.

In order to verify the effectiveness of the different modules in improving detection performance, we conducted ablation experiments on the cerebrospinal fluid dataset and compared the different performance evaluations of the different modules, as shown in Table 2. The baseline model represents the classical Mask RCNN model structure, and then the GA (Guided Anchoring) module, the SWL (Sample Weight Learning) module and Density-NMS are added to the baseline model respectively. It can be seen from the table that after adding the GA module to the baseline model, the performance of the results is higher than that of the baseline model. It also verifies that the GA module can dynamically predict non-uniform and arbitrary shape anchor points, and can solve multi-scale problems. Similarly, after adding the SWL module to the baseline model, the AP_S is higher than the baseline model and the model with the GA module added. It is proved that adding the sample weight learning module can alleviate the problem of unbalanced foreground and background samples, and can better detect small object instances in microscopic images. Finally, after adding Density-NMS to the benchmark model, the mAP is 64% higher than that of the baseline model, which is 62.5%, which also proves that Density-NMS has a better detection effect in dealing with cell adhesion problems.

Table 2. Ablation experiment.

Method	mAP	AP_{50}	AP_{75}	AP_S	AP_M	AP_L
Baseline	0.625	0.934	0.68	0.336	0.642	0.57
Baseline + GA	0.643	0.940	0.705	0.348	0.675	0.581
Baseline + SWL	0.635	0.939	0.694	0.401	0.643	0.553
Baseline + Density-NMS	0.640	0.934	0.700	0.335	0.654	0.546
Ours	0.663	0.943	0.730	0.412	0.677	0.566

In this paper, we consider the application of the object detection model for cell detection and classification in microscopy images, and hope that the method in this paper can achieve better performance in cell detection on different datasets. Therefore, we evaluate the performance of the baseline model and the proposed method on two public datasets to validate the generalization ability of our method. As shown in Tables 3 and 4, the performance of the baseline model and our method are compared on the BCCD dataset and the Malaria dataset, respectively, and it can be seen from the results in the table that our method can obtain better performance in microscope images even on different datasets.

Table 3. Comparative experiment of BCCD dataset.

Method	mAP	AP_{50}	AP_{75}	AP_S	AP_M	AP_L
Baseline	0.670	0.908	0.845	0.663	0.819	0.570
Ours	0.675	0.913	0.846	0.661	0.846	0.566

Table 4. Comparative experiment of Malaria dataset.

Method	mAP	AP_{50}	AP_{75}	AP_S	AP_M	AP_L
Baseline	0.738	0.882	0.856	0.738	0.369	0.327
Ours	0.742	0.892	0.878	0.772	0.406	0.310

5   Conclusion

In this paper, we propose a region proposal networks based on sample weighting. Firstly, we employ a GA-RPN module, which could use multiple feature maps of FPN at different levels to predict non-uniform and arbitrary shape anchors. We also propose a sample weight learning module to alleviate the imbalance between positive and negative samples by calculating the sample weight. Finally, we designed Density-NMS to dynamically adjust the NMS threshold according to the density of cell instances, which can effectively detect cells in high-density cell adhesion scenarios. From the experimental results, it is shown that the method in this paper has better detection performance than existing object detection methods, and is more suitable for the task of cell detection and classification of microscopic images.

Acknowledgements. This work was supported by the National Key RD Program of China under Grant 2019YFE0190500.

References

1. Irshad, H.: Methods for nuclei detection, segmentation, and classification in digital histopathology. IEEE Rev. Biomed. Eng. **7**, 97–114 (2014)
2. Zhao, J., Zhang, M., Zhou, Z., Chu, J., Cao, F.: Automatic detection and classification of leukocytes using convolutional neural networks. Med. Biol. Eng. Comput. **55**, 1287–1301 (2017)
3. Shanthi, P.B.: Deep convolution neural network for malignancy detection and classification in microscopicuterine cervix cell images. Asian Pac. J. Cancer Prevent. APJCP **20**(11), 3447–3456 (2019)
4. Kutlu, H.: White blood cells detection and classification based on regional convolutional neural networks. Med. Hypotheses **135**, 109472 (2020)
5. Abas, S.M.: Detection and classification of Leukocytes in Leukemia using YOLOv2 with CNN. Asian. J. Res. Comput. Sci. **8**, 64–75 (2021)
6. Redmon, J., Divvala, S., Girshick, R., Farhadi, A.: You only look once: Unified, real-time object detection. In: 2016 IEEE Conference on Computer Vision and Pattern Recognition (CVPR), pp. 779–788. IEEE, USA (2016)
7. Liu, W., et al.: SSD: single shot multibox detector. In: Leibe, B., Matas, J., Sebe, N., Welling, M. (eds.) ECCV 2016. LNCS, vol. 9905, pp. 21–37. Springer, Cham (2016). https://doi.org/10.1007/978-3-319-46448-0_2
8. Lin, T.Y.: Focal loss for dense object detection. IEEE Trans. Pattern Anal. Mach. Intell. **42**(2), 318–327 (2020)

9. Girshick, R.: Fast R-CNN. In: 2015 IEEE International Conference on Computer Vision (ICCV), pp. 1440–1448. IEEE, Chile (2015)
10. Ren, S.: Faster R-CNN: Towards real-time object detection with region proposal networks. IEEE Trans. Pattern Anal. Mach. Intell. **39**(6), 1137–1149 (2020)
11. He, K., Gkioxari, G., Dollár, P., Girshick, R.: Mask R-CNN. In: 2017 IEEE International Conference on Computer Vision (ICCV), pp. 2980–2988. IEEE, Italy (2017)
12. Redmon, J., Farhadi, A.: YOLO9000: better, faster, stronger. In: 2017 IEEE Conference on Computer Vision and Pattern Recognition (CVPR), pp. 7263–7271. IEEE, USA (2017)
13. Yang, T., Zhang, X., Li, Z., Zhang, W., Sun, J.: Metaanchor: Learning to detect objects with customized anchors. In: Advances in Neural Information Processing Systems 31. NeurIPS, China (2018)
14. Zhong, Y., Wang, J., Peng, J., Zhang, L.: Anchor box optimization for object detection. In: 2020 IEEE Winter Conference on Applications of Computer Vision (WACV), pp. 1275–1283. IEEE, USA (2020)
15. Shrivastava, A., Gupta, A., Girshick, R.: Training region-based object detectors with online hard example mining. In: 2016 IEEE Conference on Computer Vision and Pattern Recognition (CVPR), pp. 761–769. IEEE, USA (2016)
16. Mikolajczyk, K.: Scale & affine invariant interest point detectors. Int. J. Comput. Vision **60**, 63–86 (2004)
17. Viola, P., Jones, M.: Rapid object detection using a boosted cascade of simple features. In: Proceedings of the 2001 IEEE Computer Society Conference on Computer Vision and Pattern Recognition, pp. I–I. IEEE, USA (2001)
18. Bodla, N., Singh, B., Chellappa, R., Davis, L. S.: Soft-NMS-improving object detection with one line of code. In: 2017 IEEE International Conference on Computer Vision (ICCV), pp. 5562–5570. IEEE, Italy (2017)
19. Liu, S., Huang, D., Wang, Y.: Adaptive NMS: Refining pedestrian detection in a crowd. In: 2019 IEEE/CVF Conference on Computer Vision and Pattern Recognition (CVPR), pp. 6452–6461, IEEE, USA (2019)
20. Wang, J., Chen, K., Yang, S., Loy, C. C., Lin, D.: Region proposal by guided anchoring. In: 2019 IEEE/CVF Conference on Computer Vision and Pattern Recognition (CVPR), pp. 2960–2969. IEEE, USA (2019)
21. Ljosa, V.: Annotated high-throughput microscopy image sets for validation. Nat. Methods **9**(7), 637–637 (2012)
22. Zhao, Y.Q.: Overview of deep learning object detection methods. J. Image Graph. **25**(04), 0629–0654 (2020)
23. Redmon, J.: YOLOV3: an incremental improvement. arXiv preprint arXiv:1804.02767 (2018)
24. Cai, Z., Vasconcelos, N.: Cascade R-CNN: delving into high quality object detection. In: Proceedings of the IEEE conference on computer vision and pattern recognition, pp. 6154–6162. IEEE, USA (2018)

Face Detection in Distorted Images Based on Image Restoration and Meta-learning

Xinru Liu[1], Mingtao Pei[1(✉)], Wei Liang[1,2], and Zhengang Nie[3]

[1] Beijing Laboratory of Intelligent Information Technology,
Beijing Institute of Technology, Beijing, People's Republic of China
peimt@bit.edu.cn
[2] Yangtze Delta Region Academy of Beijing Institute of Technology, Jiaxing, China
[3] School of Information and Electronics Beijing Institute of Technology,
Beijing 100081, People's Republic of China

Abstract. Face detection in distorted images is a challenging task, and a natural idea is to conduct image restoration before face detection. Most of current image restoration techniques focus on improving the perceptual quality of the output image for single type of distortion, without taking the subsequent high-level detection task and unknown distortion into account. In this paper, we propose a restoration-based face detector in which the images are restored based on the detection loss instead of the perceptual quality loss, leading to better performance on subsequent detection task. Furthermore, we employ meta-learning to initialize the model with more appropriate parameters, thus our detector can adapt quickly to unseen distortions only using few examples with the corresponding distortion. Experiments on public datasets show that our proposed method could improve the performance of face detection in distorted images, and have a better generalization ability when applied to images with unseen distortions.

Keywords: Face detection · Distorted images · Image restoration · Meta-learning

1 Introduction

Face detection has a wide range of applications and has attracted many researchers attention. Many face detection methods are proposed and achieve promising detection performance in high-quality images. However, when applied to images of poor quality, the performance of the detection algorithms will be easily degraded. Although advanced cameras have been developed in the past few decades, rain drops, haze, different types of blurs and noises are still inevitable due to the weather condition, pollution and the movement of the cameras. Thus, images captured under these conditions are often of poor quality, which naturally affects the performance of subsequent face detection.

A straightforward way to resolve this problem is to do image restoration before face detection. Most of current image restoration methods are designed to improve

Y. Wang et al. (Eds.): IGTA 2022, CCIS 1611, pp. 171–180, 2022.
https://doi.org/10.1007/978-981-19-5096-4_13

the perceptual quality of the output images [16], ignoring the performance of subsequent computer vision tasks such as face detection. Therefore, we propose to restore the image before face detection based on the detection loss instead of the perceptual quality loss to improve the performance of face detection in distorted images. Specifically, we concatenates an image restoration model and a face detection model together, i.e. a face detection model is attached at the end of an image restoration model, and the whole model is trained by the loss of the detection model. Here, the concatenated models can be regarded as a single model, and can be trained in an end-to-end manner. As a result, the image restoration model is optimized to help the detection model achieve better performance, instead of achieving lower perceptual loss. The difference between the two training scheme is shown in Fig. 1.

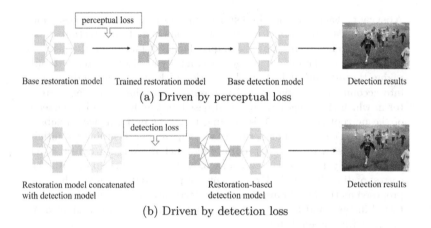

Base restoration model   Trained restoration model   Base detection model   Detection results

(a) Driven by perceptual loss

Restoration model concatenated   Restoration-based   Detection results
with detection model   detection model

(b) Driven by detection loss

Fig. 1. Face detection in distorted images driven by perceptual loss and detection loss.

Besides, the types of distortion involved in images can be diverse, such as noises, blur, raindrops, haze, and low light. Most of current image restoration methods focus on resolving single type of distortion [6,8,13], which means when they meet real-world images where the type of distortion often is unknown, the model usually produces unsatisfactory performance. One possible solution is to retrain the model by the images with corresponding distortion. However, for applications in real world, images with certain distortion are hard to obtain, and only a small number of images can be obtained which is not enough to retrain the model.

We employ meta-learning to solve the above problem. Meta-learning can adapt the model to new task with only a few new training samples based on the knowledge learned from other tasks. Specifically, we regard images with some types of distortion as training tasks, and regard images with other types of distortion as test tasks, and employ MAML [3] to make the restoration-based detection model trained on training tasks adapts rapidly towards the test tasks. During meta-training phase, task-level knowledge are learned through the

MAML, and the model is trained to find the optimal initialization point with the detection loss of the training examples. During meta-test phase, based on the sensitive initial parameters obtained in the previous stage, the model can learn appropriate parameters with only a few available labeled samples of new tasks. Compared with the original model which is initialized with pretrained parameters, the trained meta-learning model can achieve better performance on various detection benchmarks.

Our contributions are summarized as follows: (1) We propose to optimize the image restoration model by detection loss to help the detection model achieve better performance. (2) We employ meta-learning to learn an optimal initial weights of the model, thus leading to a rapid adaptation when facing new task. (3) We achieve promising detection performance on public datasets, which proves the effectiveness of our method.

2 Related Works

2.1 Face Detection in Distorted Images

Traditional methods for face detection in distorted images mainly rely on extracting distortion-invariant visual features. With deep learning applied, carefully designed network architectures and loss functions are proposed to improve the performance, and in some existing methods, image restoration is conducted before detection. Besides, as different types of distortion can be regarded as different domains, domain adaptation has also been adopted to cope with this problem [1,14].

2.2 Deep Learning for Image Restoration

Most of current image restoration methods are oriented to a single image restoration task, including denoising [17], deraining [8], dehazing [13], deblurring [6], light enhancement [4] and super-resolution [9]. A few image restoration techniques are designed to tackle diverse types of distortions. For instance, Suganuma et al. [11] regard the real-world distortions as multiple known distortions combined with unknown mixture ratios, and propose a layer architecture which performs various restoration operations weighted by an attention mechanism. Besides, most of current image restoration methods are committed to improve the perceptual quality of the output images, which may fail to guarantee the performance when the output images are applied to subsequent vision tasks. Only a small part of researches pay attention to the performance of high-level tasks, e.g. Son et al. [10] present a universal and recognition-friendly image enhancement model, which could improve the performance of coupled existing recognition models.

2.3 Meta-learning

Meta-learning mainly aims for such scenarios: while trying to address new task with unknown samples, we would like the model learn new knowledge with only a few new training samples, based on existing knowledge. Different methods have been proposed to achieve this goal, and these methods can be categorized into three groups: (i) metric-based methods, (ii) memory network-based methods, and (iii) optimization-based methods. Currently, several meta-learning methods have been applied to various vision tasks, such as super-resolution [9], tracking [12] and face recognition [5], where promising performance has been achieved.

3   Method

The overall scheme of our proposed framework is shown in Fig. 2. The framework consists of three phases, namely task-level data sampling, meta-training and meta-testing, and the latter two phases are both driven by the result of high-level vision tasks.

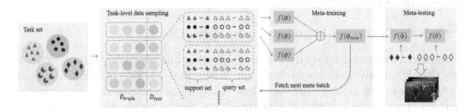

Fig. 2. The overall scheme of our proposed framework. Four detection tasks on different types of distorted images are presented in the figure for a demonstration. Each symbol represents a distorted images. Different shapes and colors of symbols represent different types of distorted images, while solid symbols and hollow symbols represent the support set and query set, respectively.

3.1   Preliminary

We adopt MPRNet [16] as the base image restoration model, and RetinaFace [2] as the base detection model. The detection model is concatenated directly after the restoration model. As it is model-agnostic, the MAML [3] scheme can be easily applied to the entire model.

MPRNet is a multi-stage image restoration model which progressively learns the functions to restore the distorted images. Specifically, it contains three stages, the first two stages are based on encoder-decoder architecture to learn the broad contextual information, while the third stage is designed to operate directly on the original resolution in order to recover the fine-grained information.

RetinaFace is a robust pixel-wise single-stage face detector, which adopts the ideology of extra-supervised and self-supervised multi-task learning.

MAML is oriented to a range of tasks and consists of meta-training and meta-testing. Given a model denoted as f with inputs x and outputs y and a distribution over tasks $p(T)$, the goal of MAML is that the model can adapt to a large number of new tasks through finding an optimal initial parameters.

During meta-training, a set of tasks $\{T_1, T_2, ..., T_i, ...\}$ are sampled from $p(T)$ to build the meta batch, which is divided into support set and query set. Here, support set is used to optimized the base learner, and the initial parameters can be updated based on the loss of query set on base learner. During meta-testing, with the help of meta learner, a new task T_{new} can adapt to the model quickly with only a few training examples.

In our case, the input x and the output y are distorted images and face detection results respectively, and detection on images with diverse types of distortion constitutes the task distribution.

3.2 Task-Level Data Sampling

Suppose there are N tasks, and each of them represents the detection task on a single type of distorted images. We split these N tasks into $N-1$ tasks for meta-training, denoted as D_{train}, and 1 task for meta-testing, denoted as D_{test}. We first generate the task distribution $p(T)$ on D_{train} according to the N tasks. To be specific, we iterate on the N tasks, and for each task, we randomly choose k_1 images as parts of support set, and k_2 images as parts of query set. Both of them form the sub-task, which is the basic component of $p(T)$. This procedure will be repeated for M times for each task, thus the size of $p(T)$ will be $N \times M \times (k_1 + k_2)$.

We further build the meta batch, N sub-tasks are sampled from $p(T)$, and notice that there are one sub-task for each detection tasks. All the $N \times (k_1 + k_2)$ selected images form a meta batch, i.e. the size of our meta batch is $N \times (k_1 + k_2)$. The meta batch is the basic unit for training our model.

3.3 Meta-training

During the meta-training phase, we try to seek a sensitive initial point to replace the pretrained initial point, thus small changes caused by a few training examples can bring notable improvement on detection results.

Here we denote the model parameters as θ, and if the parameters act as initial point, we denote them as ϕ in particular. Following the guiding ideology of MAML, we perform the meta-training procedure on D_{train}, and in our method, adaptation to support set of T_i with respect to the model parameters is one descent updates, which means we assumed that the model can find the optimal initial parameters after only one epoch. The model parameters is updated as:

$$\theta_i' = \phi - \alpha \nabla_\phi L_{T_i}(\phi) \tag{1}$$

where α denotes the task-level learning rate.

Based on the task-specific updates, the model parameters are trained to minimized the loss value of D_{train} across tasks, namely the meta-objective can be summarized as:

$$\arg\min_\theta \sum_{T_i \sim P(T)} L_{T_i}(\theta_i') = \arg\min_\theta \sum_{T_i \sim P(T)} L_{T_i}(\phi - \alpha \nabla_\phi L_{T_i}(\phi)) \tag{2}$$

With stochastic gradient descent(SGD) adopted, the initial parameters are updated across tasks involved in D_{train} as follows:

$$\phi = \phi - \beta \nabla_\phi \sum_{T_i \sim P(T)} L_{T_i}(\theta_i') \qquad (3)$$

where β denotes the meta-learning rate across tasks.

3.4   Meta-testing

The meta-testing phase follows the MAML procedure. Given a new task T_{new}, the model trained in meta-training phase is adapted towards T_{new} based on a few labeled training examples of T_{new}. Here the number of the training example should also be k_1, and a few gradient descent updates are conducted in order to discover the adapted model. Then, the rest of the images in D_{test} are fed into the model to get the detection results.

4   Experiments

4.1   Datasets

We conduct experiments on UFDD [7] and DARKFACE [15] dataset to evaluate our method.

UFDD contains face images with different distortions, such as weather-based distortion, blur, illumination variations and lens impediments. The examples are shown in Fig. 3(a), the image from left to right and from top to bottom represents rain, haze, snow, blur, illumination variations and lens impediments respectively.

DARKFACE contains 10,000 images (6,000 for training and validation, and 4,000 for testing), and all the images are captured in under-exposure environments, as shown in Fig. 3(b).

Learning rate α is set as 0.01 and β is set as 0.0001 in the training phrase. One gradient update is conducted to obtain the adapted parameters in the meta-test phase.

4.2   Evaluations on UFDD Dataset

We divide the UFDD dataset into six tasks ($N = 6$) according to the types of the distortion, that is, each subset contains images captured under rain, snow, haze, lens impediment, blur and illumination variations conditions, respectively. The training-task set contains five tasks for meta-training, while the test-task set contains one task for meta-test. To ensure the validity of the experiment, we select each distorted type as test task and the others act as training tasks, and the detection results of each task and the averaged result are reported.

We conduct experiment under the few-shot setting to illustrate that our meta-learning model is suitable for unknown tasks with only few training examples.

(a) UFDD

(b) DARKFACE

Fig. 3. Images with different distortions in UFDD and DARKFACE datasets.

Specifically, we set (k_1, k_2) as $(5, 10)$, $(10, 20)$, and $(15, 25)$, respectively. That is, we random choose 5, 10 and 15 images from the training task dataset as the training data in the meta-training phase, and all the data in the test task are used for the evaluation.

We build two baselines to prove the effectiveness of using detection loss to train the restoration model and the effectiveness of meta-learning ideology. Baseline1 conducts image restoration by MPRNet before face detection by RetinaFace. Here, the MPRNet is trained with perceptual loss and the RetinaFace is finetuned on D_{test}. In baseline2, the two pretrained models are trained on D_{train} and finetuned on D_{test} as a whole. We also compare with URIE [10] since URIE is an image enhancement model trained with recognition loss, which is similar to our model. We attach the RetinaFace at the end of URIE and finetune the whole model on D_{test} for the comparison.

Table 1 shows the comparison results. The different cases shown from 'Rain' column to 'Lens' column demonstrates using rain, snow, haze, blur, illumination variations and lens impediment as test task respectively. We can see that our meta-learning model achieves the best performance than the compared methods for all the tasks, which demonstrates the effectiveness of meta-learning. The average gain obtained by the meta-learning model over the contrast model is 0.59%, 0.57% and 0.55% for 5-shot. 10-shot and 15-shot settings, respectively.

Table 1. The mAP(%) results on UFDD dataset with different models and data distribution. The best results are highlighted in bold.

k-shot	Model	Rain	Snow	Haze	Blur	Illum	Lens	Average
5-shot	URIE	70.12	70.12	70.15	70.25	70.23	69.98	70.142
	Baseline1	71.08	71.05	71.06	71.18	71.15	70.96	71.08
	Baseline2	71.09	71.03	71.05	71.22	71.17	70.99	71.092
	Ours	71.61	71.66	71.70	71.86	71.79	71.48	71.683
10-shot	URIE	70.19	70.20	70.17	70.35	70.32	70.03	70.21
	Baseline1	71.10	71.09	71.07	71.19	71.15	71.05	71.108
	Baseline2	71.15	71.13	71.09	71.27	71.25	71.05	71.153
	Ours	71.69	71.72	71.69	71.87	**71.86**	71.53	71.726
15-shot	URIE	70.22	70.20	70.23	70.41	70.38	70.01	70.242
	Baseline1	71.16	71.17	71.13	71.23	71.21	71.01	71.152
	Baseline2	71.19	71.21	71.18	71.33	71.29	71.05	71.208
	Ours	**71.71**	**71.76**	**71.73**	**71.88**	71.85	**71.58**	**71.752**

It demonstrates that meta-learning model is suitable for the task with only few training examples.

4.3   Evaluations on DARKFACE Dataset

We also evaluate our method on the training and validation sets of DARKFACE [15], which contains human face images captured under low light condition. These images can be regarded as real-life image with unknown distortions.

Here, we train the URIE, Baseline1, Baseline2 and our model with the data in UFDD dataset. Specifically, all the six tasks in the UFDD are involved in D_{train}, and the procedure of the task-level data sampling is exactly the same as that in Sect. 4.2. The experimental results are shown in Table 2.

Table 2. The mAP(%) results on DARKFACE dataset. The best results are highlighted in bold.

	5-shot	10-shot	15-shot
URIE	39.02	39.10	39.12
Baseline1	40.09	40.15	40.13
Baseline2	40.12	40.15	40.16
Ours	**40.23**	**40.27**	**40.31**

We can see that our meta-learning model achieves the best performance than the baselines and URIE for all the tasks, which further demonstrates the effectiveness of our method.

5   Conclusion

In this paper, we propose a face detection method for distorted images based on image restoration and meta-learning. Specifically, the image restoration model is trained by the detection loss instead of perceptual loss, and can help the face detection model achieve better performance. The meta-learning can help the model adapt quickly to new tasks with only a few training examples.

Our future work include generalizing our method to various vision tasks such as visual tracking, recognition, and 3D reconstruction, and using different vision tasks as multiple meta-learning tasks to train a model which can achieve good performance for various vision tasks in distorted images with just few samples of training data.

References

1. Chen, Y., Li, W., Sakaridis, C., Dai, D., Van Gool, L.: Domain adaptive faster R-CNN for object detection in the wild. In: Proceedings of the IEEE Conference on Computer Vision and Pattern Recognition, pp. 3339–3348 (2018)
2. Deng, J., Guo, J., Zhou, Y., Yu, J., Kotsia, I., Zafeiriou, S.: Retinaface: Single-stage dense face localisation in the wild. arXiv preprint arXiv:1905.00641 (2019)
3. Finn, C., Abbeel, P., Levine, S.: Model-agnostic meta-learning for fast adaptation of deep networks. In: International Conference on Machine Learning, pp. 1126–1135. PMLR (2017)
4. Guo, C., et al.: Zero-reference deep curve estimation for low-light image enhancement. In: Proceedings of the IEEE/CVF Conference on Computer Vision and Pattern Recognition, pp. 1780–1789 (2020)
5. Guo, J., Zhu, X., Zhao, C., Cao, D., Lei, Z., Li, S.Z.: Learning meta face recognition in unseen domains. In: Proceedings of the IEEE/CVF Conference on Computer Vision and Pattern Recognition, pp. 6163–6172 (2020)
6. Kupyn, O., Martyniuk, T., Wu, J., Wang, Z.: Deblurgan-v2: deblurring (orders-of-magnitude) faster and better. In: Proceedings of the IEEE/CVF International Conference on Computer Vision, pp. 8878–8887 (2019)
7. Nada, H., Sindagi, V.A., Zhang, H., Patel, V.M.: Pushing the limits of unconstrained face detection: a challenge dataset and baseline results. In: 2018 IEEE 9th International Conference on Biometrics Theory, Applications and Systems (BTAS), pp. 1–10. IEEE (2018)
8. Quan, R., Yu, X., Liang, Y., Yang, Y.: Removing raindrops and rain streaks in one go. In: Proceedings of the IEEE/CVF Conference on Computer Vision and Pattern Recognition, pp. 9147–9156 (2021)
9. Soh, J.W., Cho, S., Cho, N.I.: Meta-transfer learning for zero-shot super-resolution. In: Proceedings of the IEEE/CVF Conference on Computer Vision and Pattern Recognition, pp. 3516–3525 (2020)
10. Son, T., Kang, J., Kim, N., Cho, S., Kwak, S.: URIE: universal image enhancement for visual recognition in the wild. In: Vedaldi, A., Bischof, H., Brox, T., Frahm, J.-M. (eds.) ECCV 2020. LNCS, vol. 12354, pp. 749–765. Springer, Cham (2020). https://doi.org/10.1007/978-3-030-58545-7_43

11. Suganuma, M., Liu, X., Okatani, T.: Attention-based adaptive selection of operations for image restoration in the presence of unknown combined distortions. In: Proceedings of the IEEE/CVF Conference on Computer Vision and Pattern Recognition, pp. 9039–9048 (2019)

12. Wang, G., Luo, C., Sun, X., Xiong, Z., Zeng, W.: Tracking by instance detection: a meta-learning approach. In: Proceedings of the IEEE/CVF Conference on Computer Vision and Pattern Recognition, pp. 6288–6297 (2020)

13. Wu, H., et al.: Contrastive learning for compact single image dehazing. In: Proceedings of the IEEE/CVF Conference on Computer Vision and Pattern Recognition, pp. 10551–10560 (2021)

14. Wu, Z., Suresh, K., Narayanan, P., Xu, H., Kwon, H., Wang, Z.: Delving into robust object detection from unmanned aerial vehicles: a deep nuisance disentanglement approach. In: Proceedings of the IEEE/CVF International Conference on Computer Vision, pp. 1201–1210 (2019)

15. Yuan, Y., Yang, W., Ren, W., Liu, J., Scheirer, W.J., Wang, Z.: Ug^{2+} track 2: a collective benchmark effort for evaluating and advancing image understanding in poor visibility environments. arXiv preprint arXiv:1904.04474 (2019)

16. Zamir, S.W., et al.: Multi-stage progressive image restoration. In: Proceedings of the IEEE/CVF Conference on Computer Vision and Pattern Recognition, pp. 14821–14831 (2021)

17. Zhang, K., Zuo, W., Chen, Y., Meng, D., Zhang, L.: Beyond a gaussian denoiser: residual learning of deep CNN for image denoising. IEEE Trans. Image Process. **26**(7), 3142–3155 (2017)

Person Re-identification Using Multi-branch Cooperative Network

Yongchao Xu[(⊠)], Fengyuan Zhang, and Yao Hu

College of Information Science and Engineering, Northeastern University, Shenyang 110819, China
1626377654@qq.com

Abstract. Person Re-identification (Re-ID) is to match the images of the given person across multiple non-overlapping cameras. To solve the problems of occlusions and unconstrained poses, we propose a multi-branch cooperative network for person Re-ID. First, attention branch and multi-scale branch are designed respectively. In the attention branch, we design shade module, random erasing module and stepped module, and guide each module to learn discriminative features of different regions through the consistent activation penalty function. In the multi-scale branch, we design a global and a local module to learn deep features to improve the performance of person Re-ID. Finally, the two branches are cascaded to concatenate multi-branch features. Extensive experiments on Market-1501, DukeMTMC-reID and CUHK03 demonstrate that the proposed method outperforms the state-of-the-art methods.

Keywords: Person re-identification · Multi-branch network · Attention branches · Robustness

1 Introduction

Person re-identification (Re-ID) identifying a target person in different scenarios, is an important subject in the field of computer vision [1]. It is widely used in video surveillance and autonomous driving. Early research efforts mainly focus on hand-crafted construction. With the vigorous development of deep learning, convolutional neural networks (CNNs) have become the predominant choices for Re-ID [2], achieving better recognition performances than traditional methods. However, due to various complicated factors, such as body poses and occlusions, learning robust and discriminative features is still a difficult and challenging task.

Re-ID based on CNNs can be summarized into 1) splitting images or feature maps into some horizontal grids. The PCB model [3] implicitly divides images into horizontal grids of multiple scales directly, ignoring the relations between body parts. 2) utilizing a pose estimator to extract a pose map. Wei [4] uses key points positioning to predict and estimate human body poses, which effectively solves the difficulty of person feature alignment, but requires a large amount of additionally labeled data for model training and prediction, and the retrieval accuracy is largely limited by the performance of the

© The Author(s), under exclusive license to Springer Nature Singapore Pte Ltd. 2022
Y. Wang et al. (Eds.): IGTA 2022, CCIS 1611, pp. 181–192, 2022.
https://doi.org/10.1007/978-981-19-5096-4_14

model. 3) leveraging generative adversarial networks (GANs) to generate more images. Zheng [5] uses GAN to generate more simulated data for data enhancement and improve the generalization ability of the model. However, it is easy to generate noisy samples, which significantly affects the accuracy and performance of the model. 4) computing attention maps to focus on a few key parts, but the extracted regions may not contain discriminative body parts, missing some important data.

To solve the above problems, in this paper, we propose a cooperative network based on multi-branch, which can effectively extract more discriminative features. In the shade module, the framework focuses on extracting features from low-response parts. In the stepped module, it focuses on reducing complex and noisy background cutter. Besides, combined with random erasing module, we use consistency activation penalty (CAP) function to ensure that the high activation regions of three networks do not overlap. In the multi-scale branch, We propose a branch to extract different levels of characteristics, which effectively preserves the integrity of pedestrian features. Finally, multiple branches are combined to form a complete multi-branch cooperative network, which can effectively deal with problems such as occlusions, poses changes.

In summary, our contributions can be summarized as follows:

(1) We propose a branch that integrates multiple attention mechanisms. Through erasing high-response regions, we can generate more complex occlusion samples. We also use random erasing module to simulate low-quality samples in the real world. Besides, relations between different parts of pedestrians can be effectively extracted with the help of stepped module. We effectively combine the three modules through the consistent activation penalty function, so as to improve the model's feature extraction ability for samples with less information and solve the problem of low model accuracy.
(2) We use a multi-scale branch to extract local features of persons, and combine them with global features to learn the relation between person parts and mine non-significant information. Consequently, the recognition ability and accuracy of the algorithm are improved significantly.
(3) Experimental results on three large-scale person Re-ID datasets including Market-1501, DukeMTMC-reID, and CUHK03 prove that the proposed methods exceeds state-of-the-art methods.

2   Multi-branch Cooperative Network

We propose a person Re-ID method based on multiple attention mechanisms and multi-scale branches. The multiple attention mechanisms are used to improve the adaptability of the model to occlusions, pose changes, illumination, low resolution and other factors, while the multi-scale branch is used to improve the ability to fuse and extract global and local features. The complete multi-branch cooperative network structure is shown in Fig. 1.

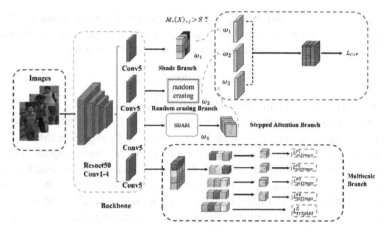

Fig. 1. The proposed network structure

2.1 Shade Module

In the actual application of the algorithm, it is inevitable to encounter the phenomenon of occlusions in pedestrian pictures. Occlusions will cause partial loss of pedestrian features and affect the integrity of features. When distinguishing features are lost, the recognition performance of the model will decline significantly. In order to extract more discriminative pedestrian features, we block the areas with high spatial attention response and retain the feature maps with low response, so as to generate more difficult samples.

The spatial attention model used in this paper is calculated as follows:

$$N_s(Y) = BN\left\{C_2^{2\times1}\left(C_1^{3\times3}\left(C_0^{1\times1}(Y)\right)\right)\right\}. \tag{1}$$

where BN is the data normalization operation, C is the convolution operation, the upper right corner is the size of the convolution kernel, and $Ns(Y)$ is the spatial attention map.

After the spatial attention response map is obtained, the high response region is set to 0 and the low response region remains unchanged, so as to obtain the mask $\tilde{N}(Y)$, which is calculated as follows:

$$\tilde{N}(Y) = \begin{cases} 0, N_s(Y)i,j > S \\ N_s(Y)i, j, \text{others} \end{cases}. \tag{2}$$

where $N_s(Y)_{i,j}$ represents the value of the spatial attention map at positions i and j, and S represents the threshold, that is, when the response value is greater than S, it is set to 0, otherwise it remains unchanged.

By setting the high response region to 0, the effect of forcing the model to learn distinctive features from the low response region is realized, and the recognition performance of the model is improved.

2.2 Random Erasing Module

We set the original image as M, the image size as W and H, the image area as U, the erasure probability P, the random initialization erasure area as Us, the value range of

Us/U is set as *(U1, U2)*, the erasure aspect ratio is *Qs*, the value range of *Qs* is set as *(q1,1/q1)*, *Ms* is the random erasure rectangular box, and the random initialization P1*(Xs, Ys)* is the coordinate point randomly selected in the image *M*.

$$O(x,y) = random(x, y). \tag{3}$$

where *random()* is the random number generation function.

The random erasing algorithm can be described as follows: Input the pedestrian image, and the random initialization probability is P_1, if P_1 is greater than the erasure probability P, the original image is directly output. Otherwise, the erasing area and aspect ratio are randomly initialized according to the erasing area and image length and width range. The coordinate point P(Xs, Ys) is initialized randomly. When the erasing area is set to be smaller than the image size, the random erasing area is randomly selected *(0,255)* for assignment to achieve the effect of random erasing. The specific process is shown in the following pseudocode (Table 1):

Table 1. The process of random erasing algorithm

Algorithm: Random Erasing Algorithm
Input: $M, W, H, P, U, U_1, U_2, q$
Output: I'
1: Initialize $P_1 = O(0,1)$
2: **if** $P_1 \leq P$ **then**
3:      $U_s = O(U_1, U_2) \times U$
4:      $Q_s = O(q_1, 1/q_1)$
5:      $H_s = \sqrt{U_s} \times Q_s$
6:      $W_s = \sqrt{U_s} \div Q_s$
7:      $X_s = O(0, W)$
8:      $Y_s = O(0, H)$
9: **end if**
10: **while** $X_s + Y_s \leq W, Y_s + H_s \leq H$ **do**
11:      $I_s = (X_s, Y_s, X_s + W_s, Y_s + H_s)$
12:      $I(I_s) = O(0,255)$
13: **end while**
14:      $I' = I$

2.3 Stepped Module

The traditional feature segmentation method adopts horizontal segmentation, which pays more attention to different regions of pedestrians, but it is easy to ignore the local relations between pedestrians and the information that may exist at the edge of the block.

As shown in Fig. 2, the PCB algorithm divides each row into six horizontal slices, the handbag and umbrella of pedestrians are separated into different blocks between different blocks, which will cause the loss of important information such as edge information and local relation of the blocks, making it impossible to obtain the ideal effect when analyzing each block individually.

We use the method of dividing 8 slices in a stepped manner, as shown in Fig. 2, starting from the first block, every four blocks are taken as a relatively complete local area, which moves down continuously, and finally five block areas are obtained, as shown in the following figure a, b, c, d, e. We observed that the blocks d and e retain the complete information of handbag and umbrella. At the same time, because the cut is smaller than the original feature map, the noise and background cutter are reduced, so the recognition accuracy and performance are significantly improved.

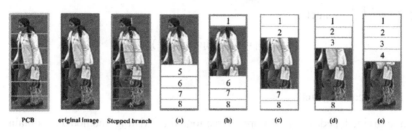

Fig. 2. Ladder block method

In the previous methods based on feature space segmentation, each horizontal slice enjoys the same weight, and the details such as umbrella and handbag can not be highlighted effectively. In this paper, we assign relatively larger weights to the blocks containing more important information, so that the model can focus on the parts with strong resolution. For this branch, an image is input through conv5_x to get the feature map $F \in R^{C \times H \times W}$, and then the feature map F is input into SBAM module at branch 2 and branch 3. In the SBAM module, firstly, step block is carried out, and F is divided into 8 horizontal parts. Every four parts are grouped to obtain a local region. The starting block of the local region moves downward in step 1 from the first block, and finally five local regions are extracted, of which each feature region is $F_i \in R^{C \times \left(\frac{H}{2}\right) \times W}$ $(i = 1, 2, 3, 4, 5)$, Then focusing on each F_i, first it is compressed in the spatial dimension, and the calculation method is as follows:

$$F_i' = FC_2(FC_1\left(avg_s(F_i)\right) + FC_2(FC_1(max_s(F_i))). \tag{4}$$

where avg_s and max_s are the average pooling and maximum pooling of the input data in the spatial dimension respectively, and two one-dimensional vectors are obtained after compression.

FC1 and FC2 are used as shared parts to compress and restore the two vectors on the channel. Finally, they are added and fused to get $F_i' \in R^{C \times 1 \times 1}$. In order to give weight to each local region, F_i' is compressed in the channel dimension and expressed as

$$s_i = Sum_c(F_i'). \tag{5}$$

$$m_i = Max_c(F_i'). \tag{6}$$

where Sum_c and Max_c are respectively the sum and maximum value of the input data in the channel dimension. Eventually, we can get $s_i \in R^{C \times 1 \times 1}$ and $m_i \in R^{C \times 1 \times 1}$.

According to the calculation of s_i and m_i of each local area, the proportion can be calculated. The calculation formula is:

$$V_i = \lambda(F_{sum}(s_i) + F_{max}(m_i)). \tag{7}$$

where λ is set to 6 according to the calculation, and finally the proportion value is adjusted between 0 and 1 through the sigmoid function. The original local area F_i is multiplied by the adjusted proportion value to obtain the update result of the local area $S_i \in R^{C \times \left(\frac{H}{2}\right) \times W}$, namely:

$$S_i = F_i \times sigmoid(V_i). \tag{8}$$

2.4 Multi-scale Branch

For fine-grained pedestrian feature extraction, the existing method can obtain fine pedestrian features by horizontally segmenting the features. However, due to the local misalignment and occlusion of pedestrian images, it is easy to produce wrong matching.

At the same time, due to the separate existence of each segment, complete pedestrian characteristics cannot be perceived. In contrast, in the multi-scale branch, fine-grained global module and local module are designed to refine the representation of pedestrian features, and achieve the effective feature extraction of "global + local" (Fig. 3).

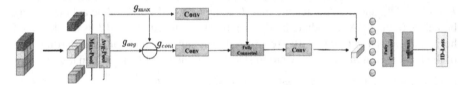

Fig. 3. Multiscale local branch

For the fine-grained global module, the size of the feature map obtained in the convolutional neural networks (CNNs) is $R^{C \times H \times W}$ (C represents the number of channels, H represents the height, and W represents the width). In the H dimension, we divide the feature map into N parts, and perform maximum pooling and average pooling operations on each part respectively to obtain feature vectors $g_{maxi}(i = 1, 2, 3 \cdots n)$ and $g_{avgi}(i = 1, 2, 3 \cdots n)$. Afterwards, the max-pooling and average-pooling results of different parts are concatenated respectively to obtain the description vectors G_{max} and G_{avg} of the fine-grained global branch. In this paper, triplet loss is used to train G_{max} and G_{avg}, which can realize the integrity of information while considering local correlation, and achieve effective identification of similar parts of different persons.

For fine-grained local modules, different local blocks are considered separately. Global average pooling is easy to introduce background or local noise information, while global maximum pooling can overcome noise interference, but cannot consider all information in the same layer.

Therefore, it is possible to better extract the information between the same layers by performing the difference operation for the two. The specific calculation is as follows:

$$g_{cont} = g_{aug} - g_{max}. \quad (9)$$

After that, we perform convolution dimension reduction for g_{max} and g_{cont} respectively to obtain g'_{max} and g'_{cont}, and then we perform cascade and convolution dimension reduction to obtain g_{inter}. Finally, the global max pooling result g'_{max} and g'_{cont} are recombined as the layer feature $\tilde{L}_1$ of the same layer, which is calculated as follows:

$$\tilde{L}_1 = g'_{max} + g'_{inter}. \quad (10)$$

Finally, we connect through the full connection layer and conduct joint training through softmax and ID-Loss. By analyzing the correlation between non-adjacent parts, more significant potential information can be mined. In addition, through the analysis of discarded local information, the actual situation of local occlusion is effectively simulated, which enhances the robustness and discrimination of the model.

2.5 CAP Network

For the cascade of three branches of different attention mechanisms, in order to make different branches focus on different regions of the image and enhance the diversity and comprehensiveness of local feature extraction, CAP network is introduced in this paper to coordinate different attention branches and make each branch focus on different regions with different characteristics. Different weights are assigned to different branches through LAN, and Hellinger distance [7] is used to measure the consistency of output weights of different branches:

$$H(\omega_i, \omega_j) = \frac{1}{\sqrt{2}} \| \sqrt{\omega_i} - \sqrt{\omega_j} \|_2. \quad (11)$$

where the sum of the elements of ω_i and ω_j is 1, then the square of the above formula can be obtained:

$$H^2(\omega_i, \omega_j) = 1 - \sum \sqrt{\omega_i \omega_j}. \quad (12)$$

In order to ensure that the high activation regions of different attention models do not overlap, it is necessary to maximize the distance between ω_i and ω_j, that is, to minimize the value of $\sum \sqrt{\omega_i \omega_j}$, then the CAP loss can be defined as follows:

$$L_{CAP} = \sum \sqrt{\omega_i \omega_j}. \quad (13)$$

Through the above formula, it can be optimized to diversify the local feature extraction and enhance the representation ability of the model.

3 Experiments

3.1 Datasets

Experiments are conducted on three commonly-used large-scale person Re-ID datasets. The Market-1501 (Zheng et al., 2015) [8] dataset contains 32,668 images of 1,501 persons captured by 6 cameras. In the experiment, a total of 12,936 images of 751 persons are used as the training set, and a total of 19,732 images of 750 persons are used as the test set. The DukeMTMC-reID (Ristani et al., 2016) [9] dataset contains 36,411 images of 1,404 persons captured by 8 cameras. In the experiment, a total of 16,522 images of 702 persons are used as the training set, and a total of 17,661 images of 702 persons are used as the test set. The CUHK03 (Li et al., 2014) [10] dataset contains 14,097 images of 1,467 persons captured by 10 cameras. The experiment uses 767 persons samples as the training set and 700 persons samples as the test set.

3.2 Implementation Details

We use the Pytorch framework based on deep learning, and use the GPU RTX2080Ti server for training. During the training process, the input image size is adjusted to 384 * 128, and data enhancement methods such as random flipping and random cropping are used. In the experiment, the training batch is 32, where P is 8 and K is 4. ResNet50 pre-trained on ImageNet is used as the backbone network. In this paper, SGD is used as the optimizer, and the learning rate is set to 8e-4. The weight decay is 5e-4, the momentum is set to 0.9, and the number of training iterations (epoches) of the whole network is set to 300. This paper uses the cumulative matching characteristic curve (CMC) and the mean average precision (mAP) to analyze and evaluate the performance of the algorithm. Among them, Rank-1 represents the ratio of finding the person to be queried in the first search results. mAP is the average of the area under the accuracy-recall curve of all query samples, which reflects the overall performance of person Re-ID methods.

3.3 Experimental Results

In order to verify the effectiveness of the method proposed in this paper, the method proposed in this paper is compared with existing pedestrian re-identification methods, including PCB [3], MGN [11], PCB + RPP [3], Harmonized Attention Convolutional Neural Network (HA-CNN) [12], Second-Order Non-Local Attention (SONA) [13], AlignedReID [14], HONet [15], GCP [16], CDNet [17], PAT [18]. Table 2 shows the comparison of experimental results on the three datasets.

Table 2. Comparison of experimental results of different algorithms on data sets

Methods	CUHK03-Labeled		CUHK03-Deteced		Market1501		DukeMTMC-reID	
	mAP	Rank-1	mAP	Rank-1	mAP	Rank-1	mAP	Rank-1
PCB(ECCV2018)	-	-	54.2	61.3	77.3	92.4	63.5	81.9
MGN(MM2018)	67.4	68.0	66.0	66.8	86.9	95.7	78.4	88.7
PCB + RPP(ECCV2018)	-	-	57.5	63.7	81.0	93.1	68.5	82.9
HA-CNN(CVPR2018)	41.0	44.4	38.6	41.7	75.7	95.6	63.8	80.5
SONA(ICCV2019)	79.2	81.9	76.4	79.1	88.7	95.7	78.1	89.3
AlignedReID(PR2019)	-	-	59.6	61.5	79.1	91.8	69.7	82.1
HONet(CVPR2020)	-	-	-	-	84.9	94.2	75.6	86.9
GCP(AAAI2020)	75.6	77.9	69.6	74.4	88.9	95.2	78.6	89.7
CDNet(CVPR2021)	-	-	-	-	86.0	95.1	76.8	88.6
PAT(CVPR2021)	-	-	-	-	88.0	95.4	78.2	88.8
Ours	**82.4**	**84.6**	**81.5**	**82.7**	**90.1**	**96.2**	**81.1**	**90.2**

As shown in Table 2, compared with the PCB + RPP method, our method has significant improvements on Market-1501, DukeMTMC-reID and CUHK03 datasets. The Rank-1 indicators increased by 3.8%, 8.3%, and 21.4% respectively. And the mAP indicators increased by 12.8%, 17.6%, and 27.3% respectively. The reason is that the multi-branch method considers the relationship between different parts of the human body, better characterizing person information through the joint collaboration of multiple branches, so the experimental results are significantly improved. Compared with the GCP method, we achieve significant improvements on all three datasets. The main reason is that although the GCP method adopts the relation analysis module, it does not pay enough attention to the global features. In this paper, the global and local training are combined on the multi-scale branch, and the extracted features are more discriminative. Thereby a better effect is achieved. Compared with the MGN method, the branch set in this paper is more reasonable. Compared with the current SONA with the highest accuracy, all indicators in this paper have been significantly improved on the three datasets. The model in this paper has achieved best results compared with the existing algorithms with better effects, which verifies the robustness of the model and effectively improves the accuracy of the pedestrian re-identification algorithm.

3.4   Ablation Experiments

In order to further verify the effectiveness of the multi-branch proposed in this paper, we analyze the model from both qualitative and quantitative aspects. First, we test the experimental effect of the baseline network of ResNet50 pre-trained on ImageNet. After that, the experiments of multiple branches and mutual combination methods are added respectively. The specific comparison results are shown in the following table.

Table 3. Ablation study on three datasets

Methods	CUHK03-Labeled		CUHK03-Detected		Market1501		DukeMTMC-reID	
	mAP	Rank-1	mAP	Rank-1	mAP	Rank-1	mAP	Rank-1
Baseline	60.2	63.3	54.7	60.1	81.1	92.7	71.0	82.3
Baseline+SB	67.1	68.4	66.4	66.8	83.3	93.4	74.4	83.4
Baseline+RE	66.3	70.5	62.3	63.5	82.5	93.1	73.9	82.8
Baseline+SBAM	72.5	74.1	71.5	74.4	86.4	95.4	77.8	88.2
Baseline+SB+RE	73.4	76.9	70.6	72.3	84.8	94.1	76.5	85.5
Baseline+SB+SBAM	76.7	78.2	74.4	76.0	87.5	95.8	79.2	89.1
Baseline+RE+SBAM	75.6	77.3	73.8	75.5	86.8	95.5	78.6	88.4
Baseline+SB+RE+SBAM	78.8	78.6	77.1	78.7	89.1	95.9	80.1	89.3
Baseline+SB+RE+SBAM+CAP	80.1	81.5	80.2	81.5	89.9	96.1	80.7	89.9
Baseline+MB	79.9	80.1	78.4	77.2	88.3	94.4	77.4	84.4
Baseline+SB+RE+SBAM+CAP+MB	**82.4**	**84.6**	**81.5**	**82.7**	**90.1**	**96.2**	**81.1**	**90.2**

The construction of the multi-branch cooperative network is to extract the features of pedestrians more effectively, improving the recognition performance of the model and achieving good recognition results in more complex environments and conditions. Table 3 shows the comparison between the baseline method and the model proposed in this paper. It can be seen from the table that the recognition accuracy of the baseline method is the lowest, and multiple branches are better than the baseline method whether used alone or in combination. For the attention branch, the introduction of the CAP network can significantly improve the results, which verifies the rationality of the network structure. At the same time, the results of the network including all branches are better than that of each branch working alone, and Rank-1 and mAP are significantly improved. It shows that there is a complementary and cooperative relationship between different branches, and person features with different levels of discrimination can be extracted respectively, which verifies the effectiveness of the model design in this paper.

3.5 Query Results Display

As can be seen from the Fig. 4, the recognition accuracy of the proposed baseline method is not high, and the error rate in top10 recognition results is high. However, the features learned by the attention branch and the multi-scale branch can complement each other, which significantly improves the recognition accuracy.

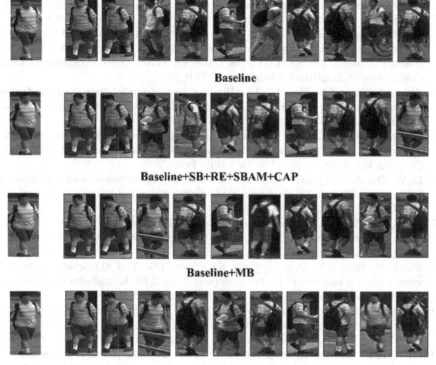

Fig. 4. Market1501 dataset recognition examples

4   Conclusions

Designing multi-branch networks to learn rich feature representation is one of the important directions in person re-identification (Re-ID). However, when extracting pedestrian features, the regions and non-significant regions where the model has significant recognition ability should be extracted as much as possible to enhance the robustness and recognition performance of the model. Therefore, this paper proposes a joint network based on multi-branch cooperation. Through the occlusion module, the random erasing module and the stepped module, strong person features are jointly extracted, and the CAP network is used to ensure the diversity of local feature extraction. It exploits the potential connections of non-adjacent parts through multi-scale branching, and combines global features to construct a high-precision person Re-ID network. The experimental results on three public person Re-ID datasets show that the multi-branch cooperative network proposed in this paper extract more discriminative and robust pedestrian features.

References

1. Luo, H., Jiang, W., Fan, X., Zhang, S.P.: A survey on deep learning based person re-identification. Acta Automatica Sinica **45**(11), 2032–2049 (2019)

2. Zhu, F.Q., Kong, X.W., Fu, H.Y., Tian, Q.: two-stream complementary symmetrical CNN architecture for person re-identification. J. Image Graph. **23**(7), 1052–1060 (2018)

3. Sun, Y., Zheng, L., Yang, Y., Tian, Q., Wang, S.: Beyond part models: person retrieval with refined part pooling (and a strong convolutional baseline). In: Ferrari, V., Hebert, M., Sminchisescu, C., Weiss, Y. (eds.) ECCV 2018. LNCS, vol. 11208, pp. 501–518. Springer, Cham (2018). https://doi.org/10.1007/978-3-030-01225-0_30

4. Wei, L.H., Zhang, S.L., Yao, H.T.: GLAD: global-local-alignment descriptor for pedestrian retrieval. In: Proceedings of the 25th ACM International Conference on Multimedia, Mountain View, CA, USA, pp. 420–428 (2017)

5. Zheng, Z.D., Zheng, L., Yang, Y.: Unlabeled samples generated by GAN improve the person re-identification baseline in vitro. In: Proceedings of 2017 IEEE International Conference on Computer Vision, Venice, pp. 3774–3782. IEEE Press (2017)

6. Li, W., Zhu, X., Gong, S.G.: Harmonious attention network for person re-identification. In: Proceedings of 2018 IEEE Conference on Computer Vision and Pattern Recognition, Salt Lake City, pp. 2285–2294. IEEE Press (2018)

7. Li, S., Bak, S., Carr, P.: Diversity regularized spatiotemporal attention for video-based person re-identification. In: 2018 IEEE/CVF Conference on Computer Vision and Pattern Recognition, Salt Lake City, pp. 369–378. IEEE Press (2018)

8. Zheng, L., Shen, L.Y., Tian, L., Wang, S.J., Wang, J.D., Tian, Q.: Scalable person re-identification: a benchmark. In: Proceedings of 2015 IEEE International Conference or Computer Vision, Santiago, pp. 1116–1124. IEEE Press (2015)

9. Ristani, E., Solera, F., Zou, R., Cucchiara, R., Tomasi, C.: Performance measures and a data set for multi-target, multi-camera tracking. In: Hua, G., Jégou, H. (eds.) ECCV 2016. LNCS, vol. 9914, pp. 17–35. Springer, Cham (2016). https://doi.org/10.1007/978-3-319-48881-3_2

10. Li, W., Zhao, R., Xiao, T., Wang, X.G.: DeepRe ID: deep fliter pairing neural network for person eidinition. In: Proceedings of 2014 IEEE Conference on Computer Vision and Pattern Recognition, Columbus, pp. 152–159. IEEE Press (2014)

11. Wang, G.S., Yuan, Y.F., Chen, X., Li, J.W., Zhou, X.: Learning discriminative features with multiple granularities for person re-identification. In: Proceedings of the 26th ACM International Conference on Multimedia, New York, pp. 274–282. IEEE Press (2018)

12. Fu, Y., et al.: Horizontal Pyramid Matching for Person Re-identification (2018)

13. Xia, B., Gong, Y., Zhang, Y.Z., Poellabauer, C.: Second-order non-local attention networks for person re-identification. In: Proceedings of 2019 IEEE/CVF International Conference on Computer Vision, Washington, pp. 3759–3768. IEEE Press (2019)

14. Luo, H., Jiang, W., Zhang, X., Fang, X., Qian, J.J., Zhang, C.: AlignedReID++: dynamically matching local information for person re-identification. Pattern Recogn. **94**, 53–61 (2019)

15. Wang, G.A., et al.: High-order information matters: learning relation and topology for occluded person re-identification. In: Proceedings of 2020 IEEE/CVF International Conference on Computer Vision, Seattle, pp. 3759–3768. IEEE Press (2020)

16. Park, H., Ham, B.: Relation Network for Person Re-identification (2020)

17. Li, H.J., Wu, G.J., Zheng, W.S.: Combined depth space based architecture search for person re-identification. In: Proceedings of 2021 IEEE/CVF International Conference on Computer Vision. IEEE Press (2021)

18. Li, Y.L., He, J.F., Zhang, T.Z., Liu, X., Zhang, Y.D., Wu, F.: Diverse part discovery: occluded person re-identification with part-aware transformer. In: Proceedings of 2021 IEEE/CVF International Conference on Computer Vision. IEEE Press (2021)

Cross-Domain Object Detection Through Image-Category Features Joint Alignment

Yijie Zhou[1], Qiao Pan[1(✉)], Li Shen[2], and Dehua Chen[1]

[1] School Computer Science and Technology, Donghua University,
Shanghai 201620, China
`zhouyijie_happy@126.com`, {`panqiao,chendehua`}`@dhu.edu.cn`
[2] A-star, Singapore, Singapore
`lshen@i2r.a-star.edu.sg`

Abstract. The object detection task in general assumes that the training and test data come from a same distribution. However, in real situations, the model often does not work as well as expected due to the domain shift problem. In this paper, a domain adaptive model based on image and category features is proposed to solve the cross-domain object detection task. The proposed model for domain adaption is based on the one-stage object detection model RetinaNet. Image-level features are used for adversarial learning so that feature distributions can be aligned. Besides, category-level features for contrastive learning enables foreground features with the same category but from different domains to be mapped more closely. Comprehensive experiments are conducted with existing domain adaptive models on three public available road object detection datasets. The experiments show that the domain shift problem is well solved by our method. Besides, compared with two-stage domain adaptive models, the method in this paper performs better and detects more efficiently.

Keywords: Object detection · Domain shift · RetinaNet · Domain adaption

1 Introduction

In recent years, convolutional neural networks (CNN) have achieved remarkable performance in various task scenarios, such as image classification [1], image segmentation [2] and object detection [3]. However, these performances are all achieved on the basis of massive amounts of labeled data. In real-world scenarios, the performance of a well-trained model drops dramatically in scenarios it has not encountered before [4]. For example, in the autonomous driving task, the training data is obtained in normal weather, but the data characteristics in the actual scene will be affected by different weather conditions and cameras, resulting in the model unable to detect the target. This is because the data distribution in the new scene is different from the data distribution in the training set, which is also known as the domain shift problem [5]. In this problem, the dataset used for model training is called the source domain, and the new dataset used for validation is called the target domain.

The most direct solution to the domain shift problem is to obtain a large number of labels on the target domain, and add the labeled data to the model training. However, in the task of object detection, acquiring new labels always consumes a lot of time and cost. In recent years, methods have emerged to address the domain shift problem when the target domain dataset has no labels. Since the domain shift problem is caused by the difference in data distribution between the two datasets, unsupervised domain adaptation methods [6–8] are often implemented by minimizing the domain discrepancy of the source domain and the target domain through a deep neural network (Fig. 1).

(a) Normal Weather   (b) Foggy Weather   (c) Video Games

Fig. 1. Illustration of different datasets in different scenarios: left image is from Cityscapes [9], middle one from FoggyCityscapes [10] and right one from SIM 10k [11]. These three images are from three different datasets while we can find obvious feature discrepancy among them.

The first work to solve the domain shift problem in the object detection task is Domain adaptive Faster R-CNN [8]. Its basic idea is to use image-level features and instance-level features to align the source and target domains. Meanwhile, it maintains the consistency between two domains. However, as a two-stage target detection network, Faster R-CNN generates regional proposal boxes at first, and then finds foreground categories from the proposal boxes, which requires a long inference time to detect targets. In real-world scenarios, such as autonomous driving tasks, we hope that the inference speed of the model is as fast as possible, so that it can perform real-time operations for subsequent processing. Many following UDA (unsupervised domain adaptation) methods emerge based on Faster R-CNN [12]. Although the accuracy of object detection is improved, it still does not solve the problem of operation speed in actual scenes. Compared with the two-stage object detection network, the one-stage object detection network simultaneously completes the object positioning and classification tasks in one stage. Multiscale domain adaptive YOLO [13] is proposed to use the one-stage object detection network Yolo [14] as the benchmark network. It obtains feature maps of different scales in the feature extraction layer, and use multi-scale feature information for adversarial learning. However, in the object detection task, instance-level features also contain rich semantic information. In cross-domain scenarios, instance features with the same category should also be similar, so we can also perform feature alignment at the category-level. In previous tasks, category-level information was not considered when training one-stage cross-domain object detection models, which waste rich instance features.

In this paper, we propose a novel RetinaNet-based [15] framework for cross-domain adaptive object detection. First, we use image-level features for adversarial learning. This global feature contains feature information mapped from two different domains. Since features' scales from feature extraction network are different, the multi-scale image-level features have richer feature representations. Instead of image-level classification of feature maps, we assign domain class labels to each pixel in the feature map for adversarial learning, which fully captures semantic information. Second, we extract instance-level features for contrastive learning. Since there is no RPN(region proposal network) in the one-stage network, instance-level features cannot be directly obtained. We propose a new classification subnet to meet the needs. In the process of training, the category center of each domain is continuously updated, by measuring the feature distance from each instance in the mini-batch to the center of each category. At the same time, we can also take the relationship between the features of the same category and different categories into account. By narrowing feature distances of the same category across domains and widening feature distances of different categories, domain alignment is achieved on instance-level features. Through the role of the image-level and category-level adaptive modules, the cross-domain generalization effect of the model is improved. We verify the performance and efficiency of the model on the Cityscapes [9] dataset, the FoggyCityscapes [10] dataset and the SIM 10k [11] dataset.

Therefore, the main contributions can be summarized as follows:

- We propose a new domain adaptation network Image-Category DARetinaNet, which solves the unsupervised domain adaptation problem of object detection task and greatly improves the detection efficiency.
- We modify the classification subnet in RetinaNet to achieve instance-level features from a one-stage object detection model.
- RetinaNet is optimized, and reduce the discrepancy between cross-domain features by adding the adversarial learning module of global features and the contrastive learning module of local features.

2   Related Work

Object Detection. Domain-specific image object detectors that exist at this stage can usually be divided into two categories, one is two-stage detectors [3,16], and the other is one-stage detectors [14,15,17]. RetinaNet [15] adopts the FPN (feature pyramid structure) as the neck, and proposes Focal Loss to compute the classification loss, aiming to solve the single-stage object detection scene with extreme imbalance between foreground and background categories during training. However, methods mentioned above do not address the domain shift problem.

Domain Adaption. Several domain-adaptive methods have been proposed to solve tasks such as classification [6], semantic segmentation [7], and object detection [8,18–20]. In the object detection task, [8] is the first work that applies domain adaptation in this task scenario. When judging the input image which domain belongs to, it not only pays attention to the global picture features, and also uses the instance-level features predicted by the object detection network, and finally adds a loss constraint of consistency between global features and local features. [13] extracts the features after the last three layers of downsampling in the feature extraction network Resnet-50 [1] for domain discrimination. This is the first work to improve the performance of one-stage detectors. It does not take category information into account because one-stage detectors is hard to obtain instance-level information.

3   Methods

3.1   Image-Category DARetinaNet

Based on RetinaNet [15], we design a network containing a dual-domain adaptive module to address the domain shift problem in the UDA object detection task. The model not only pays attention to the multi-scale features of the image level, but also pays attention to the category features of the instance level. Through the joint function of the two adaptive modules of global and local features, the feature distributions of the two domains are mapped as close as possible. The network architecture of Image-Category DARetinaNet is shown in the Fig. 2. The yellow part in the middle is the initial object detection network; another component of the model is the domain adaptation module, and the green and blue parts below represent the image-level adaptation module and the category-level adaptation module, respectively. The image-level adaptive module computes the domain discriminative loss through global image features, while the category-level adaptive module computes the contrastive loss through feature distances between local instances. These three modules work together to reduce the discrepancy between the source domain and target domain features and improve the generalization effect of the model on the target domain.

3.2   Image-Level Adaptive Module

According to [21], the generative adversarial network (GAN) consists of a generator and a discriminator. The principle is to make the discriminator unable to judge whether the input image is true or false through the confrontation between the original image and the generated image. In domain adaptation, the features extracted from the data set from the target domain through the feature extraction network can be directly regarded as the generated samples. The features from the source domain are handed over to the discriminator for judgment together with features from the target domain. During the training process, the discriminator is continuously optimized to distinguish whether the features are

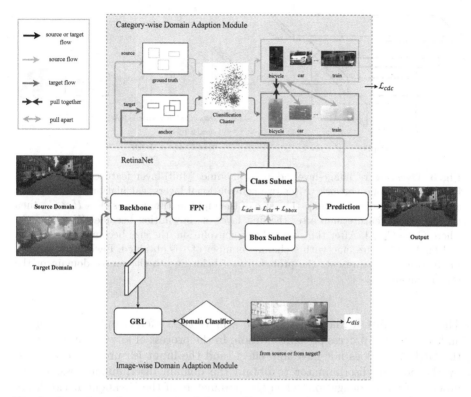

Fig. 2. Overview of our proposed Image-Category DARetinaNet. We address the domain shift problem through image-wise and category-wise domain adaption module. During training, the labeled source domain and unlabeled target domain images are input simultaneously. The black arrows represent the modules that both the source and target domain images need to go through, the green arrows represent the modules that the source domain images need to go through, and the red arrows represent the training process of the target domain images. (Color figure online)

from the source domain or the target domain, and the feature extraction network is continuously optimized to confuse the discriminator. After the constant game between the two, the discriminator improves the discrimination ability, and the feature extraction network maps the features of the two different domains closer. As a result, the object detection model trained with the data of the source domain can achieve better results on data of the target domain.

The input image is processed by convolution and residual structure to extract high-dimensional features, and then the extracted features are used to input the neck network to further extract features. In this module, we borrow the input of the neck network, and take the last three layers of features in the backone as image-level global features, and then we use multiple-layer features to achieve adversarial-based domain adaptation. As shown in the Fig. 3, the input features of each layer first go through a gradient reversal layer (GRL).

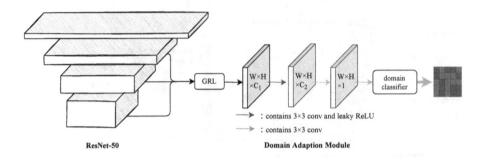

Fig. 3. Overview of image-level adaptive module. Multi-layer features are extracted from the backbone network. After two convolutional layers' calculation, the output is a pixel-level classification map. The size of the input feature map is $W \times H \times C_1$, then the size of the feature map after the first layer of convolution becomes $W \times H \times C_2$, where $C_2 = C_1//4$. After the second-layer convolution, the size becomes $W \times H \times 1$, and finally a feature map with a channel number of 1 is obtained. Each pixel value in the feature map represents the probability of belonging to the source domain or the target domain.

The purpose of GRL layer design is to achieve two different optimization goals and simplify the process of confrontation. In the process of forward propagation, the GRL layer does not have any effect, and the input features are calculated by the domain discriminator to obtain the domain discriminant loss. In the process of backpropagation, when the parameters of the backbone network are propagated, the gradient calculated by the domain discrimination loss will be reversed, thereby reducing the error rate of domain classification and reacting to the feature extraction network.

$$\max_{D} \min_{G} \mathcal{L}\left(f_s, f_t\right) \tag{1}$$

$$\mathcal{L}_{dis} = \sum_{l} \mathcal{L}_{dls}^i \tag{2}$$

The finally goal is to minimize the loss of the object detection network G while maximizing the classification loss of the domain discriminator D. The classification loss $\mathcal{L}_{dis}$ is accumulated by multi-layer features sent to this module.

3.3   Category-Level Adaptive Module

In the UDA task, the source and target domains share the same labels $C = \{1, 2, \ldots, N\}$, and each category will have its own unique features. Although the overall feature distribution of the dataset in the source and target domains is different, we assume that instance features of the same category have similar characteristics. Therefore, we try to mine the relationship between instance features between different categories in the object detection scenario. In the contrastive learning strategy of unsupervised learning [22], for an input sample, a positive sample with the same class label and N − 1 negative samples with different category labels are obtained. After combining, these N pairs of samples are used to calculate N-pair loss. With such effort, we expect that features with the same category label are drawn closer, and features with different category labels are pushed farther, which has become the mainstream method in unsupervised tasks.

$$\mathcal{L} = -\log \frac{\exp\left(f^T f^+\right)}{\exp\left(f^T f^+\right) + \sum_{i=1}^{L-1} \exp\left(f^T f\right)} \tag{3}$$

Inspired by the contrastive learning method, we compare the category-level instance features in the target domain with the category-level instance features from the source domain, so as to learn cross-domain domain-independent foreground features. For the input target domain features, we treat the features with the same category label in the source domain as positive samples, and vice versa as negative samples (Fig. 4).

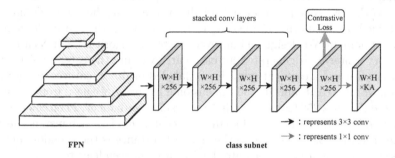

Fig. 4. Overview of modified class subnet for category-level adaption. An additional convolutional layer is added to obtain feature of anchors for contrastive learning.

In order to obtain category-level features for contrastive learning, we need to make changes to the classification subnet in RetinaNet. In the classification subnet of RetinaNet, each pixel is used as an anchor point, and anchor are generated according to 9 pre-defined scales, so as to obtain instance-level features through the anchor. Since the feature map after convolution cannot reflect the features of each anchor, we simplify the problem and use the 256-dimensional features of $W \times H$ anchor points as instance-level features. Therefore, we modified the network structure of the classification subnet, adding a 3×3 convolutional layer after stacking the convolutional groups, and obtained the required 256-dimensional features corresponding to each anchor point. The final convolutional layer plays the same role as the FC layers after ROI Pooling layer in the two-stage object detection network.

$$\theta_i = \alpha\theta_i + (1 - \alpha)\theta_{i-\text{new}} \tag{4}$$

For the image x_s^i in the source domain, we need to obtain the instance-level feature f_s to cluster the source domain features. Since the image in the source domain has the label y_s^i, the corresponding anchor point coordinates (w, h) can be obtained after the coordinate transformation of y_i^{loc}. Then the feature (f_s, y_s^{cls}) is obtained, and we are able to update the cluster to ensure the reliability of the category center θ_i. As the training continues, the number of features in the cluster continues to grow, and how to balance the weight of the original center and the new center during update becomes a problem. We use the EMA [23] strategy to update the cluster center θ_i with Eq. (4). Where α should be set as large as possible, so that $(1 - \alpha)$ will become as small as possible. This is because in each iteration, the new center θ_{i-new} of each category will be calculated according to the input data, and the samples of the input data will be much smaller than the original category center θ_i as the training progresses. If $(1 - \alpha)$ is set too large, it will cause the category center to continuously shift and oscillate, which cannot reflect the real center position, resulting in unstable learning.

For the image x_t^i in the target domain, since there is no instance-level class label y_t^i, we need to obtain the category pseudo-label y_t^i. However, due to the function of the image-level adaptive module, the feature gap between two domains becomes closer, so the category pseudo-labels of the instances in the target domain can be obtained by calculating the feature distance between the source domain and the target domain. We design an improved clustering algorithm. For N categories, a category center θ_n is generated for each category, and the category center can reflect the feature of each category. For unlabeled instance features in the target domain, we need to obtain the 256-dimensional feature f_t we need from our newly generated $W \times H \times 256$ feature map in the classification subnet. Then calculate the distance d_i from f_t to all source domain class centers θ_n. For each instance feature f_t^i, the category corresponding to the smallest distance is the pseudo-label $\hat{y}_i^{cls}$. We use cosine similarity to calculate the distance between features.

$$\cos \theta = \frac{f_t \cdot f_s}{|f_t| \times |f_s|} \tag{5}$$

$$d_i = \cos \left(f_t^i, \theta_n \right), n \in N \tag{6}$$

$$\hat{y}_i^{cls} = \max \left(d_i \right) \tag{7}$$

Since a feature map often contains thousands or even tens of thousands of anchors, the obtained pseudo-labels are not necessarily credible. Therefore, for the instance features with pseudo-labels in the target domain, the experimental settings for prediction in RetinaNet are used for reference, and only the top 1000 anchors with the highest similarity are selected for subsequent contrastive learning.

We calculate the contrastive loss not only in the target domain, but also in the source domain. During the training process of the model, we keep the updates of both the source domain center θ_{source} and target domain center θ_{target}. When the input is the target domain image, the contrastive loss is calculated by comparing the target domain instance feature in a mini-batch with the category center in θ_{source}; on the contrary, when the input comes from source domain, the loss is calculated with the target domain cluster θ_{target}.

3.4 Network Optimization

The training procedure of our proposed framework integrates three major components.

Supervised Learning. The loss function for object detection in RetinaNet [15] is calculated as follows:

$$\mathcal{L}_{det} = \mathcal{L}_{cls} + \mathcal{L}_{bbox} \tag{8}$$

where $\mathcal{L}_{cls}$ represents the classification loss, which is calculated using Focal Loss in RetinaNet. The formula is as follows:

$$\mathcal{L}_{cls} = -\alpha_t \left(1 - p_t\right)^\gamma \log\left(p_t\right) \tag{9}$$

$\mathcal{L}_{bbox}$ represents the coordinate offset regression loss of the anchor box generated from the anchor point, which is calculated using the Smooth L1 loss:

$$\mathcal{L}_{bbox} = \begin{cases} 0.5x^2, & |x| < 1 \\ |x| - 0.5, & \text{otherwise} \end{cases} \tag{10}$$

Image-Level Adaption. Suppose the domain discriminator D, the feature extraction network f, and the features obtained through feature mapping are represented as $f(x_i)$. Then the specific loss of the domain discriminator is calculated by binary cross entropy as follows:

$$\mathcal{L}_{dis} = -\sum_{x_i \in \mathbb{P}} \left[(1 - y_i) \log\left(1 - D\left(f\left(x_i\right)\right)\right) + y_i \log\left(D\left(f\left(x_i\right)\right)\right)\right] \tag{11}$$

Here y_i is the domain label of the i-th training image. When $y_i = 1$, it means that the image comes from the source domain, and when $y_i = 0$, it means that the image comes from the target domain. $D(f(x_i))$ represents the probability that the discriminator determines whether the feature belongs to the source domain or the target domain.

Category-Level Adaption. $\mathcal{L}_{cdc}$ can be calculated by substituting the obtained relative distance D and label matrix Y into the softmax function and the cross entropy loss function. For the data in the source domain, the input sample is the regularized feature f_s, $\mathcal{L}_{cdc-s}$ can be expressed as:

$$\mathcal{L}_{cdc-s} = -\sum_{i=1}^{n} y_i \log \frac{\exp\left(f_i^s f^+\right)}{\sum_{j=1}^{N} \exp\left(f_i^s f_j\right)} \tag{12}$$

Likewise, for input samples f_t from the target domain, $\mathcal{L}_{cdc-t}$ can be expressed as:

$$\mathcal{L}_{cdc-t} = -\sum_{i=1}^{n} y_i \log \frac{\exp\left(f_i^t f^+\right)}{\sum_{j=1}^{N} \exp\left(f_i^t f_j\right)} \tag{13}$$

Finally, the total loss function of the final network population is calculated as follows:

$$\mathcal{L}_{sum} = \mathcal{L}_{det} + \alpha\mathcal{L}_{dis} + \beta\mathcal{L}_{cdc-s} + \gamma\mathcal{L}_{cdc-t} \tag{14}$$

The weight values of these loss values need to be determined through experiments, so that the model can achieve the best results.

4 Experiments

4.1 Datasets

We use three public datasets for experiments. (1) The Cityscapes [9] dataset is a benchmark dataset for semantic segmentation of urban roads, which can be used for object detection tasks after data processing. The dataset contains 2975 labeled training images and 500 validation images. (2) The FoggyCityscapes [10] dataset is a foggy dataset synthesized in real scenes, evolved from the Cityscapes dataset. The data labels are shared with the Cityscapes dataset, and the training set and validation set are divided in the same way. (3) SIM 10k [11] dataset, which is sampled from the computer game GTA5 (Grand Theft Auto V) and contains virtual images generated by the game engine. It contains 10,000 labeled images in two categories: car and motorbike.

4.2 Implementation Details

In the experiments, all training data and test data are scaled with a shorter side of 600 pixels. The backbone network is ResNet-50 [1] pre-trained on ImageNet [24]. During the training process, the parameter settings of the object detection model refer to the settings in RetinaNet. We used the SGD optimizer to train the model with an initial learning rate of 0.001, momentum set to 0.9, and weight decay to 0.0005. At the same time, we adopt a warm-up strategy [1] in the first 500 iterations of training. During model validation, we use the mean average precisions (mAP) with a threshold of 0.5.

In our experiments, the GPU used is an NVIDIA GeForce 2080 Ti. The batch size is set to 2 when training DARetinaNet, one from the labeled source domain dataset and the other from the unlabeled target domain dataset. Our method is implemented through the PyTorch deep learning framework.

4.3 Results

Cityscapes→FoggyCityscapes. In this experiment, we take Cityscapes [9] dataset under normal weather as the source domain and the FoggyCityscapes dataset as the target domain. Following the experimental settings of the previous papers on these two datasets, the semantic-level labels of each image are formatted to obtain the bounding boxes and categories of the corresponding objects. We selects images with the highest degree 0.02 of fog for training and validation in FoggyCityscapes [10].

Table 1. Experimental results of cross-domain object detection tasks from normal weather to foggy weather (%).

Methods	Person	Rider	Car	Truck	Bus	Train	Motor	Bicycle	mAP
Faster-RCNN [16]	26.9	38.2	35.6	18.3	32.4	9.6	25.8	28.6	26.9
DA-Faster [8]	29.2	40.4	43.4	19.7	38.3	28.5	23.7	32.7	32.0
DivMatch [18]	31.8	40.5	51.0	20.9	41.8	34.3	26.6	32.4	34.9
MTOR [19]	30.6	41.4	44.0	21.9	38.6	40.6	28.3	35.6	35.1
SW-DA [20]	31.8	44.3	48.9	21.0	43.8	28.0	28.9	35.8	35.3
RetinaNet [15]	29.0	30.7	35.5	14.7	22.8	5.2	18.4	30.8	23.4
Ours*	35.8	38.6	52.9	25.5	34.7	20.3	25.7	39.5	34.1
Ours	36.9	39.6	51.7	24.8	38.9	22.9	29.9	38.3	35.4

Our method is experimentally verified by adding global adaptive and local adaptive modules to the basic RetinaNet ($\alpha = 0.1$, $\beta = \gamma = 0.01$). The previous methods we compared are DA-Faster [8], DivMatch [18], MTOR [19], SW-DA [20], and the feature extraction backbone are all ResNet-50 [1]. These methods are improved on the basis of Faster-RCNN, so the method they compare without adaptation is Faster-RCNN. While comparing our method with above, we also compare with the benchmark RetinaNet [15] and Ours*.Ours* represents the model with image-level adaption module alone. As shown from Table 1, when only using source-only method for the cross-domain target detection task in this scenario, the mAP is 23.4%, which is −3.5% behind the experiment using only the Faster-RCNN [16] model. However, after adding the two adaptive modules we propose, +12% improvement can be achieved, which can achieve 35.4% mAP. Compared with the two-stage adaptive model mentioned above, our method improves by +3.4%, +0.5%, +0.4%, and +0.1%, respectively. In ablation study, 1.3% performance gain is achieved due to the implementation of the category-level adaption module. In the specific categories of subdivision, after we use the category feature information for local adaptive alignment, they have also been improved to varying degrees.

Table 2. Comparison of detection efficiency of different domain adaptive models.

Methods	Images	Speed (task/s)	Time cost (s)
Faster-RCNN*	492	14.4	34
RetinaNet*	492	15.2	32

Since DARetinaNet is improved on the basis of RetinaNet [15], the detection efficiency is also improved while the accuracy is higher than the above-mentioned methods. As shown in Table 2, Faster-RCNN* represents the adaptive network model proposed by the two-stage object detection model as the benchmark, while RetinaNet* represents our method. Tested on a total of 492 images in the validation set, the detection efficiency of RetinaNet* is higher than that of Faster-RCNN*, and as the amount of data expands, the advantage of detection efficiency will be more obvious (Fig. 5).

(a) Ground Truth   (b) Source-only   (c) DA RetinaNet

Fig. 5. The detection results on the task Cityscapes→FoggyCityscapes, in which Ground Truth, Source-only and our method are evaluated.

SIM 10k→Cityscapes. The common data category of the SIM 10k [11] dataset and the Cityscapes [9] dataset is car, so label files need to be processed. After data processing, 8,895 and 2,832 images were selected from the source and target domains for training, and 478 images were selected from the validation set of the target domain for verification. As can be seen from Table 3, with the basic RetinaNet model trained on the source domain, the validation set on the target domain obtains 29.9% mAP. The effect of the model trained by our method can be improved by +11.2% and can finally achieve 41.1%.

Table 3. Experimental results of cross-domain object detection tasks from simulated scenes to real scenes (%).

Methods	Car AP
Source-only	29.9
Ours	41.1

4.4   Ablation Study

For the adversarial adaptive module based on global image-level features and the contrastive learning adaptive module based on local category-level features proposed in our method, we conduct ablation experiments to explore the effects of different features and parameters on the model performance. We conduct experiments in cross-domain scenarios of urban roads from normal weather to foggy weather.

Table 4. Experiment results of global adaptive module feature selection (%).

	F1	F2	F3	Person	Rider	Car	Truck	Bus	Train	Motor	Bicycle	mAP
Adversarial module	✓			33.3	8.6	47.7	20.7	30.0	12.0	24.3	38.6	30.7
		✓		32.8	40.4	43.4	19.7	38.3	28.5	23.7	32.7	32.0
			✓	35.9	38.2	47.4	24.0	30.2	27.7	18.1	36.5	32.2
	✓	✓		34.3	39.5	48.6	26.1	32.9	14.9	22.0	38.9	32.2
	✓		✓	36.4	40.7	49.7	19.5	34.0	22.4	22.4	38.8	33.0
		✓	✓	35.9	39.9	49.5	21.0	31.5	23.7	24.5	37.3	32.9
	✓	✓	✓	35.8	38.6	52.9	25.5	34.7	20.3	25.7	39.5	34.1

In the introduction of the global adaptive module above, it is proposed to use the last three layers of features output in the feature extraction backbone network ResNet-50 for adversarial learning, and we also conduct ablation experiments for the selection of feature layers. As shown in Table 4, F1, F2, and F3 respectively represent three-layer feature maps of different scales with channel numbers of 512, 1024, and 2048. Selecting the features of different layers as the input of the adaptive module will result in different results. For example, when only single-layer features are selected, the categories of truck, train, and motor have different degrees of interest, resulting in huge differences in the detection effect on a single category. After all three layers of features are selected, the model can fully learn the features at different scales, which can achieve 34.1% mAP.

In the second category-level local adaptation module, pseudo-labels need to be acquired for unlabeled images of the target domain for comparative learning. Due to the lack of labels, in the introduction of the above modules, we use the method of calculating cosine similarity to obtain pseudo labels. Then it is difficult for us to ensure that the obtained pseudo-labels must be correct. Referring to the settings in the classification subnet in RetinaNet, top 1000 predicted anchors with the highest classification scores are used for subsequent calculations. Therefore, we first follow this experimental setting. For the unlabeled features in the target domain, we take the top 1000 anchor boxes with the highest cosine similarity to the source domain category center, and then update the target domain category center and compare the loss calculation after obtaining the pseudo-label. In the experiments in this scenario, the module achieves the best performance when we choose top 1500 anchors.

5 Conclusion

In this paper, we propose a Image-Category DARetinaNet model for solving the cross-domain object detection task. In this framework, the first module is the global image feature adaptation module, which uses multi-scale features for adversarial learning, so that the image features of the two domains are mapped closer in the feature extraction layer. The second module is a local category-level feature adaptation module, which uses category information to perform comparative learning, so that the intra-class features are closer and the outer-class features are pushed farther. In two-scenario experiments, our proposed method not only performs better than the two-stage adaptive algorithm, but also has advantages in detection efficiency.

Acknowledgment. This work was supported by the National Key RD Program of China under Grant 2019YFE0190500.

References

1. He, K., Zhang, X., Ren, S., Sun, J.: Deep residual learning for image recognition. In: 2016 IEEE Conference on Computer Vision and Pattern Recognition (CVPR), Las Vegas, pp. 770–778. IEEE (2016)
2. Long, J., Shelhamer, E., Darrall, T.: Fully convolutional networks for semantic segmentation. In: 2015 IEEE Conference on Computer Vision and Pattern Recognition (CVPR), Boston, pp. 3431–3440. IEEE (2015)
3. Girshick, R.: Fast R-CNN. In: 2015 IEEE International Conference on Computer Vision (ICCV), Santiago, pp. 1440–1448. IEEE (2015)
4. Gopalan, R., Li, R., Chellappa, R.: Domain adaptation for object recognition: an unsupervised approach. In: 2011 International Conference on Computer Vision, Barcelona, pp. 999–1006. IEEE (2011)
5. Torralba, A., Efros, A.: Unbiased look at dataset bias. In: 2011 IEEE Conference on Computer Vision and Pattern Recognition (CVPR), Colorado Springs, pp. 1521–1528. IEEE (2011)
6. Long, M., Wang, J., Ding, G., Sun, J., Yu, P.: Transfer feature learning with joint distribution adaptation. In: 2013 IEEE International Conference on Computer Vision, Sydney, pp. 2200–2207. IEEE (2014)
7. Tsai, Y., Hung, W., Schulter, S., Sohn, K., Yang, M., Chandraker, M.: Learning to adapt structured output space for semantic segmentation. In: 2018 IEEE/CVF Conference on Computer Vision and Pattern Recognition, Salt Lake City, pp. 7472–7481. IEEE (2018)
8. Chen, Y., Li, W., Sakaridis, C., Dai, D., Van Gool, L.: Domain adaptive Faster R-CNN for object detection in the wild. In: 2018 IEEE/CVF Conference on Computer Vision and Pattern Recognition, Salt Lake City, pp. 3339–3348. IEEE (2018)
9. Cordts, M., et al.: The cityscapes dataset for semantic urban scene understanding. In: 2016 IEEE Conference on Computer Vision and Pattern Recognition (CVPR), Las Vegas, pp. 3213–3223. IEEE (2016)
10. Hahner, M., Dai, D., Sakaridis, C., Zaech, J., Van Gool, L.: Semantic understanding of foggy scenes with purely synthetic data. In: 2019 IEEE Intelligent Transportation Systems Conference (ITSC), Auckland, pp. 3675–3681. IEEE (2018)

11. Johnson-Roberson, M., Barto, C., Mehta, R., Sridhar, S.N., Rosaen, K., Vasudevan, R.: Driving in the matrix: can virtual worlds replace human-generated annotations for real world tasks? In: 2017 IEEE International Conference on Robotics and Automation (ICRA), Singapore, pp. 746–753. IEEE (2017)

12. Girshick, R., Donahue, J., Darrell, T., Malik, J.: Rich feature hierarchies for accurate object detection and semantic segmentation. In: 2014 IEEE Conference on Computer Vision and Pattern Recognition, Columbus, pp. 580–587. IEEE (2014)

13. Hnewa, M., Radha, H.: Multiscale domain adaptive YOLO for cross-domain object detection. In: 2021 IEEE International Conference on Image Processing (ICIP), Anchorage, pp. 3323–3327. IEEE (2021)

14. Redmon, J., Divvala, S., Girshick, R., Farhadi, A.: You only look once: unified, real-time object detection. In: 2016 IEEE Conference on Computer Vision and Pattern Recognition (CVPR), Las Vegas, pp. 779–788. IEEE (2016)

15. Lin, T., Goyal, P., Girshick, R., He, K., Dollar, P.: Focal loss for dense object detection. IEEE Trans. Pattern Anal. Mach. Intell. **42**, 318–327 (2018)

16. Ren, S., He, K., Girshick, R., Sun, J.: Faster R-CNN: towards real-time object detection with region proposal networks. IEEE Trans. Pattern Anal. Mach. Intell. **39**, 1137–1149 (2017)

17. Liu, W., et al.: SSD: single shot multibox detector. In: Leibe, B., Matas, J., Sebe, N., Welling, M. (eds.) ECCV 2016. LNCS, vol. 9905, pp. 21–37. Springer, Cham (2016). https://doi.org/10.1007/978-3-319-46448-0_2

18. Kim, T., Jeong, M., Dim, S., Choi, S., Kim, C.: Diversify and match: a domain adaptive representation learning paradigm for object detection. In: 2019 IEEE/CVF Conference on Computer Vision and Pattern Recognition (CVPR), Long Beach, pp. 12448–12457. IEEE (2019)

19. Cai, Q., Pan, Y., Ngo, C., Tian, X., Duan, L., Yao, T.: Exploring object relation in mean teacher for cross-domain detection. In: 2019 IEEE/CVF Conference on Computer Vision and Pattern Recognition (CVPR), Long Beach, pp. 11449–11458. IEEE (2019)

20. Saito, K., Ushiku, Y., Harada, T., Saenko, K.: Strong-weak distribution alignment for adaptive object detection. In: 2019 IEEE/CVF Conference on Computer Vision and Pattern Recognition (CVPR), Long Beach, pp. 6949–6958. IEEE (2019)

21. Goodfellow, I.: Generative adversarial nets. In: Advances in Neural Information Processing Systems, vol. 27 (2014)

22. Chen, T., Kornblith, S., Norouzi, M., Hinton, G.: A simple framework for contrastive learning of visual representations. In: Proceedings of the 37th International Conference on Machine Learning, pp. 1597–1607 (2020)

23. Laine, S., Aila, T.: Temporal ensembling for semi-supervised learning. In: International Conference on Learning Representations (2017)

24. Russakovsky, O., Deng, J., Su, H., Krause, J.: ImageNet large scale visual recognition challenge. Int. J. Comput. Vis. **115**, 211–252 (2015). https://doi.org/10.1007/s11263-015-0816-y

Detection of Abnormal Crowd Behavior Based on ViBE and Optical Flow Methods

Xinqian Zhao, Jian Chen[✉], Hongwei Lin, Yibo Zhao, and Changchuan Wei

School of Mechanical Engineering, Yangzhou University, Huayang Weststr. 196,
Yangzhou 225000, People's Republic of China
chenjian.tud@hotmail.com

Abstract. With the rapid development of computer vision and image processing technology, the detection of abnormal behavior in video has gradually attracted more and more scholars' attention. This paper proposes a fast method to detect abnormal behavior in surveillance videos. Firstly, the Visual Background Extraction (ViBE) method was used to extract the foreground object. Then, the image speed was separated according to the optical flow method. Finally, the Otsu method was used to binarize the image, the detection effect was evaluated by defining the density of moving pixels in a single frame of image relative to all pixels. In this paper, an experiment with the sudden scattering of concentrated crowds was conducted to simulate crowd abnormal behavior, the results show that the experimental effect is in line with expectations. Compared with other commonly used machine learning methods, the proposed method can be quickly used to detect crowd abnormal behavior in a surveillance video, the detection results can also be quickly evaluated, which has the advantages of low cost and convenience.

Keywords: Abnormal behavior detection · ViBE method · Foreground object extraction · Optical flow method · Otsu method

1 Introduction

Abnormal crowd behavior usually refers to the occurrence of illegal and criminal incidents in public places, the sudden dispersal of the crowd that had gathered together, or the sudden appearance of people who violate the rules of crowd movement in the regular movement of the crowd [1, 2]. With the continuous increase of urban population and the number of densely populated areas, there are more and more security risks, the occurrence probability of illegal and criminal behaviors also increases correspondingly, such as fighting and robbery, which greatly endangers public security. If these abnormal events can be detected in time, the harm of abnormal events to public security may be reduced.

The main work of abnormal behavior detection is to extract target features from a video and classify detection results. There are many ways to extract character features and classify the detection results. Xu et al. [3] used the Principle Component Analysis (PCA) for feature selection and the Support Vector Machine (SVM) for classification

© The Author(s), under exclusive license to Springer Nature Singapore Pte Ltd. 2022
Y. Wang et al. (Eds.): IGTA 2022, CCIS 1611, pp. 208–219, 2022.
https://doi.org/10.1007/978-981-19-5096-4_16

of human behaviors. Nady et al. [4] employ space-time auto-correlation of gradients (STACOG) descriptor to extract spatio-temporal motion features from video sequence, the K-medoids clustering algorithm was used to partition the STACOG descriptors of training frames into a set of clusters. With considering the significance of the temporal comparison of motion states for detecting changes in crowds, a method based on the temporal context of motion was presented, to measure changes in the distribution of the physical characteristic descriptors of crowd motion [5]. Rodriguez et al. [6] proposed to leverage information on the global structure of the scene and to resolve all detection jointly, especially for some particularly challenging detection tasks, such as: heavy occlusions, high person densities and significant variation in people's appearance. In the paper of Wang et al. [7], pedestrian features were extracted by the multi-feature fusion method, the similar features in current frame of all candidate objects were matched with the characteristic information of pedestrians in the previous frame. This method has good robustness in complex traffic, but at the same time, the calculation is relatively large.

In order to improve the efficiency of video analysis, this paper proposes to extract the target foreground of the image firstly, then, carry out motion feature detection. The development of foreground object extraction technology has been relatively mature so far, most of them apply different processing algorithms, such as inter-frame difference method [8], the principle is simple, easy to be implemented, it also has good robustness, but is limited by the principle of inter-frame difference between adjacent frames, it has poor speed recognition effect on moving objects and is prone to produce cavitation phenomenon. Another example is the mixed Gaussian model method [9], although it has the adaptability of real-time update and better extraction effect compared with the former, it is difficult to obtain better results in the case of more noise in the image. In the year 2011, Barnich et al. [10] proposed Vibe method, experimental results show that compared with the mixed gaussian model method, the ViBe method has the advantages of higher speed and accuracy. Van Droogenbroeck [11] and Biao et al. [12] put forward their own improvement suggestions based on ViBe method respectively in 2012 and 2016, which made ViBe method more efficient and reduced the degree of "ghost phenomenon" in foreground images.

In addition, the optical flow method [13–17] can accurately identify the optical flow velocity of pixels. For the problem studied in this paper, the abnormal event detection of sudden crowd scattering or irregular behavior in public places, speed characteristic is the key to determine abnormal or not. Therefore, the concept of optical flow velocity separation was proposed in this paper, the optical flow method was used to filter the velocity, so as to filter out the low-speed information in the optical flow field and retain the high-speed information.

In the presented work, the abnormal behavior detection based on the improved ViBe algorithm as well as optical flow method was conducted. In order to detect the occurrence of abnormal events more easily, an abnormal event scoring mechanism was proposed, the mean score of high-speed part of optical flow field was calculated, the occurrence of abnormal events was detected according to the mean score.

2 Foreground Object Extraction

Background subtraction approach is one of the relatively common algorithms used in foreground detection. By which the foreground target was judged according to the changes of gray scale and other features. In other words, the current image and the background are differentiated. When the difference value is greater than a certain threshold, the target is considered to be detected [8]. The principle flow is shown in Fig. 1.

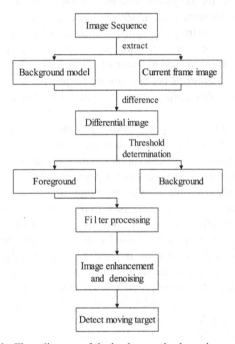

Fig. 1. Flow diagram of the background subtraction method

For the background subtraction method, the accuracy of the final foreground target detection was directly affected by the selected background model. Therefore, it is particularly important to select an appropriate algorithm to solve the background model. This paper mainly refers to the current advanced and efficient ViBe algorithm [10–12] for solving the problem.

2.1 ViBE Algorithm

ViBE algorithm uses neighborhood pixels to create a background model, and detects the foreground by comparing the background model with the current input pixel value, which can be subdivided into three steps:

Step1: Initialize the background model for each pixel in a single frame of image
It is assumed that the pixel values of each pixel and its neighbor pixel have similar distribution in the spatial domain. Based on this assumption, each pixel model can be

represented by its neighborhood pixels. In order to ensure that the background model conforms to statistical law, the range of neighborhood should be large enough. When the first frame of the image is entered, that is, when $T = 0$, the background model of pixels can be expressed as follows:

$$BK_M^0 = f^0(x^i, y^i) | (x^i, y^i) \in N_G(x, y) \tag{1}$$

in which, $N_G(x, y)$ represents the adjacent pixel values in the airspace, $f^0(x, y)$ represents the pixel value of the current point. In the process of N initialization, the possible times of pixel (x^i, y^i) in $N_G(x, y)$ being selected are $L = 1, 2, 3, ..., N$.

Step2: Foreground object segmentation for the subsequent image sequence
When $t = k$, the background model of pixel point (x, y) is $BK_M^{k-1}(x, y)$, the pixel value is $f^k(x, y)$, then, the following formula is used to determine whether the pixel value is a foreground.

$$f^k(x, y) = \begin{cases} BK_M^{k-1}(x^r, y^r) > T & \text{foregound} \\ BK_M^{k-1}(x^r, y^r) \leq T & \text{background} \end{cases} \tag{2}$$

in this case, the superscript r is chosen at random, T is the preset threshold. If $f^k(x, y)$ meets the background N times, the pixels $f^k(x, y)$ can be regarded as the background, otherwise are the foreground.

Step3: Update method of background model
The update of Vibe algorithm is random in both time and space.

Randomness in time: Among N background models, one is randomly selected and set as image P_G, Table 1 represents the image of P_G position x and its eight pixels in the neighborhood. When a new frame of image P_t is obtained, if the pixel $P_t(x)$ corresponding to the x position in the image P_t is judged to be the background, P_G needs to be updated. This extraction process reflects the randomness of time.

Table 1. Selecting PG randomly from N frame background

$P_G(1)$	$P_G(2)$	$P_G(3)$
$P_G(4)$	$P_G(x)$	$P_G(5)$
$P_G(6)$	$P_G(7)$	$P_G(8)$

Randomness in space: A pixel $P_G(r)$ is randomly selected in the eight neighborhood of $P_G(x)$, and $P_G(r)$ is replaced by $P_t(x)$, which reflects the randomness of model update space.

2.2 Improved Vibe Algorithm

(1) Median filtering

In order to further improve the quality of the image obtained, the correlation method of morphological processing was adopted in this paper, to conduct secondary processing on the foreground target image extracted by Vibe algorithm, and filter out the relevant noise in the image.

As a signal processing method, median filtering [18] technology can effectively filter out noise. In this paper, the median filtering technology was used to replace the element points in the extracted foreground target image with the median of each element point in the specified field. The pixels in the foreground object in the image are closer to the real value, and the noise in the image was further eliminated. In two-dimensional images, the output formula of median filtering is as follows:

$$g(x, y) = \text{med}\{f(x - k, y - l)|k, l \in W\} \tag{3}$$

in which, $f(x, y)$ represents the original image, $g(x, y)$ represents the processed image, W is the used two-dimensional template.

(2) Corrosion expansion treatment

Supposing there are two images A and B, where A is the image to be processed and B is the corresponding template image of corroding or expanding. Usually, B is called the structural element. For the corrosion or expansion of A by B, it is manifested as the translation of B in the plane of A in any way. For corrosion, only when B is included in A, the black pixels in A are left, and the remaining pixels that do not meet the requirements are turned to white. For expansion, if the intersection of A and B is not empty, the corresponding white pixels in A are turned into black pixel, and the pixel that does not meet this condition are still white. This indicates that corrosion can reduce the boundary of the original image and eliminate the isolated noise points, while expansion can expand the boundary of the image and connect the isolated points.

By using the processing method in morphology [19], the target image is now corroded, the boundary points of the object are eliminated in a relevant way, so that the area of the processed image is reduced by one pixel along its periphery compared with that before corrosion. Then, the image is expanded, and all background pixels in contact with the object are integrated into the object, so that the object increases the area of the corresponding number of points.

The mathematical definition of corrosion is similar to expansion, A is corroded by B can be recorded as: $A \ominus B$, which is defined as:

$$A \ominus B = \left\{z|(B)_z \cap A^c \neq \varnothing\right\} \tag{4}$$

In other words, A corroded by B is the set of origin positions of all structural elements, where the translation of B does not stack with the background of A, in which, $\varnothing$ is an empty set, and B is a structural element. Inflation is defined as a set operation. A is expanded by B, denoted as $A \oplus B$, and defined as:

$$A \oplus B = \left\{z\middle|(\hat{B})_z \cap A \neq \varnothing\right\} \tag{5}$$

(3) **Opening operation**

In this paper, the method of open operation was adopted to eliminate and separate the pixels representing noise in the original image without significantly changing the area of the original image. The morphological opening operation of A by B can be written as $A \bigcirc B$, which is the result of expansion and corrosion of B after A is corroded by B.

Based on the original Vibe algorithm, the background difference method was used to obtain the extraction results of foreground objects, then, the median filter was used to remove the noise, and the corrosion and expansion algorithms in morphology were used to optimize the results. Finally, after a series of improved and optimized, the Vibe algorithm was obtained.

$$A \circ B = (A \ominus B) \oplus B \tag{6}$$

2.3 Foreground Extraction

The improved Vibe algorithm was used to extract the foreground target in the video, and the result is shown in Fig. 2.

(a) Original image   (b) Image extracted by ViBe algorithm

Fig. 2. Frame 412 in the video

3 Target Feature Extraction Based on Optical Flow Method

According to the movement information of the crowd in the video image, the occurrence of abnormal events can be judged. In order to highlight the influence of motion information on abnormal event detection, the speed separation of the processed image was carried out, the low-speed part of the image was filtered out while the high-speed part was retained. The high-speed part of the optical flow image reflects the high-speed moving region in the video, which is often the place where people are most interested, it is also the key region used to judge whether abnormal events occur or not. However, in the high-speed images extracted from optical flow images, high-speed regions are scattered, and some regions even have a few tiny points. These tiny high-speed regions do not contribute to abnormal behavior detection, and even affect the normal abnormal behavior detection results. In order to eliminate these effects, morphological processing of high-speed images can eliminate these small regions, while preserving large high-speed regions.

3.1 Optical Flow and Its Estimation Method

Optical flow is a motion mode, which is the movement of the target between the observer and the background. To be exact, optical flow is the projection of the target velocity to the wall in the three-dimensional space on the two-dimensional plane. Such projection on a two-dimensional plane can accurately reflect the movement information of the target.

Let I (x, y, t) be the illumination intensity at the position of the image (x, y) at the moment I, $w(x, y)$ and $v(x, y)$ are the optical flow components of the point in the horizontal and vertical directions respectively:

$$I(x, y, t) = I(x + u\Delta t, y + v\Delta t, t + \Delta t) \tag{7}$$

There are two unknowns u and v in the above equation, and the equation cannot be solved. To solve this equation, some new assumptions need to be added. Assuming that the velocity of the target sports field is continuous and smooth in the horizontal and vertical directions, we can perform first-order Taylor series expansion on it and obtain:

$$I(x, y, t) \approx I(x, y, t) + \frac{\partial I}{\partial x}\Delta x + \frac{\partial I}{\partial y}\Delta y + \frac{\partial I}{\partial t}\Delta t + \varepsilon \tag{8}$$

At this point, the second-order infinitesimal ε is ignored, the basic equation of optical flow method is as follows:

$$\frac{\partial I}{\partial x}\Delta x + \frac{\partial I}{\partial y}\Delta y + \frac{\partial I}{\partial t}\Delta t = 0 \tag{9}$$

The following set of equations can be obtained from pixels:

$$\begin{cases} I_{x_1}u + I_{y_1}v = -I_{t_1} \\ I_{x_2}u + I_{y_2}v = -I_{t_2} \\ \cdots \\ I_{x_n}u + I_{y_n}v = -I_{t_n} \end{cases} \tag{10}$$

The equation set has only three unknowns, but there are more than three equations, which means there is redundancy in the set. But it is clear that this equation set can be solved, and the system can also be expressed as:

$$\begin{bmatrix} I_{x_1} & I_{y_1} \\ I_{x_2} & I_{y_2} \\ \cdot & \cdot \\ \cdot & \cdot \\ \cdot & \cdot \\ I_{x_n} & I_{y_n} \end{bmatrix} \begin{bmatrix} u \\ v \end{bmatrix} = \begin{bmatrix} -I_{t_1} \\ -I_{t_2} \\ \cdot \\ \cdot \\ \cdot \\ -I_{t_n} \end{bmatrix} \tag{11}$$

3.2 Normalization of Optical Flow Images

The optical flow field calculated by the above optical flow method can be divided into horizontal direction and vertical direction. The optical flow field images represent the velocity components in horizontal and vertical directions respectively. However, in the study of abnormal behavior detection, we do not care about the direction of velocity, but only its magnitude. To facilitate the study, the two directions of the optical flow image can be fused, as shown in the formula:

$$I = \sqrt{u^2 + v^2} \tag{12}$$

In order to display the optical flow field intuitively, some additional display methods need to be defined. Since the gray level range of general images is [0,255], the size of optical flow is normalized to this range for display:

$$I' = \frac{I}{\text{Max}(I)} \cdot L \tag{13}$$

where, I' is the image after normalization, I is the image to be normalized, $Max(I)$ is the maximum number of pixels in the image. I' represents the gray level range, where the optical flow image of [0,255] can be normally displayed on the computer after it is normalized to the range of [0,1].

3.3 Separation of Optical Flow Velocity

Optical flow reflects the motion information of video images. In abnormal event detection, the occurrence of abnormal events can be easily judged by the motion information of images. According to the motion state of the crowd in the image, the human eye can easily distinguish the occurrence of abnormal events: when abnormal events occur, they are usually accompanied by large speed changes, which can be well reflected by the optical flow field image. By observing the optical flow field image of the abnormal event video, it can be found that when the abnormal event occurs, the gray image block in the image gradually becomes brighter due to the sharp increase of velocity, and the bright block spreads around. This paper determines the occurrence of abnormal events by analyzing the change characteristics of bright blocks in the optical flow field. In this paper, the concept of optical flow velocity separation was proposed: the optical flow image was divided into high-speed part and low-speed part, and the low-speed part of the optical flow field was filtered out and the high-speed part of the image was analyzed, which can reflect the occurrence of abnormal events more intuitively. The rules of optical flow image speed separation are shown in the formula:

$$\begin{cases} I_H = I_{x,y} \ I'_{x,y} > thresh \\ I_L = 0 \ \ I_{x,y} \leq thresh \end{cases} \tag{14}$$

here, the threshold is a constant value.

The high-speed part of optical flow image can directly reflect the occurrence state of abnormal events, and the selection of threshold value is very important, which is related to the effect of separation. If the method of fixed threshold value is used, there is no way to apply to all scenarios, so this paper adopts dynamic threshold method. Generally, it is most appropriate to set the threshold as the median value of the optical flow field image. Considering the efficiency of the algorithm, a fast threshold calculation method is needed. Here, multiple of the maximum value of the image was taken as the threshold value, namely:

$$thresh = a\text{Max}(I) \tag{15}$$

in which, $Max(I)$ is the maximum number of pixels in the image. $thresh$ is a constant value, generally between 0.25 and 0.5. According to this strategy, the high-speed part and the low-speed part in the optical flow field can be clearly separated.

After separation, there will be many scattered gray areas in the high-speed part of the optical flow field image. These areas are not helpful for abnormal detection, but will affect the normal detection results. In order to eliminate the influence of these scattered areas, the corrosion operation in morphological filtering was used to filter out the separated high-speed images, many noise information affecting abnormal detection results were removed.

| (a) Original image | (b) Image extracted by ViBe algorithm | (c) Image obtained by the optical flow method |

Fig. 3. The processing result of frame 482 of the video, frame 482 was chosen because this is the middle segment where the abnormal behavior occurs

By comparing Fig. 3(b) and (c), it can be found that the image processed by optical flow method only contains the high-speed part, and the low-speed part of the foreground extraction part (such as the residual image of the car in the image) was completely filtered, which makes it easier to find the occurrence of abnormal events in the video.

4 Evaluation of Detection Effect

Before the occurrence of abnormal events, the distribution of abnormal event scores is gentle. According to the distribution characteristics of abnormal event score, this paper proposes to use the mean value of high-speed partial optical flow image to judge the changing process, so as to ensure the high accuracy of abnormal event detection.

As can be seen from the high-speed optical flow image, when the crowd is moving at a relatively low speed, the high-speed part of the image appears dark, and only a small part of the image has a non-zero pixel value. However, when the crowd is moving at high speed, the high-speed part of the optical flow image appears bright, and the pixels in the large area are not zero anymore. The process from dimming to brightening of high-speed partial optical flow images can determine the occurrence of abnormal events. According to this characteristic, the mean value of high-speed partial optical flow image was used to judge the changing process.

$$S_M = \frac{\sum I_{x,y}}{N} \tag{16}$$

In Eq. (16), S_M is the mean score of the image, also known as optical flow density, $\sum I_{x,y}$ represents the sum of all white pixels in the image, the Otsu method was used to binarize the image, N represents the number of pixels. This mean score can well reflect the overall motion speed of the video area, so as to distinguish whether abnormal events occur.

Otsu's method, named after its inventor Nobuyuki Otsu [20], is one of the most popular binarization algorithms. In computer vision and image processing, Otsu's method is used to automatically perform clustering-based image thresholding or reduction of a gray level image to a binary image.

In order to visualize the detection effect of optical flow method on abnormal behaviors, the changing trend of video score before and after optical flow method filtering was plotted in a certain video, as shown in Fig. 4. Black curve for the extraction of vision after this video grading, whole presents the score higher status, the score only said the white pixels of the change of situation, no practical significance, although in the beginning and end stage, had a tendency of lifting, but small change is not obvious, is impossible to judge whether there are abnormal event occurs. The blue curve is the score of the video processed by optical flow method. Compared with the black curve, the score of the blue curve decreases overall. Blue curve for the optical flow method after processing the segment ratings on video, compared to the black curve.

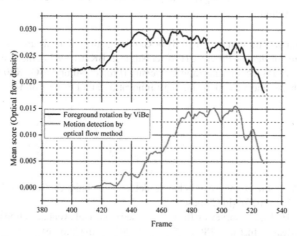

Fig. 4. Proportion of white pixels in a single frame image (Color figure online)

The abnormal behavior (high-speed part) is directly reflected as the white area in the binary image filtered by the optical flow method. Since the target with abnormal behavior moves faster, the white area should be larger in the optical flow image. However, because the optical flow image filters out the low-speed part and noise in the whole image, the proportion of the number of white pixels to the total pixels in the corresponding single frame image will be significantly reduced, but we can still judge whether abnormal events occur by the change trend of the proportion of white pixels after filtering (high-speed moving part), that is, the change of score.

It can be found that between frames 420 and 480, the score has a large continuous upward trend, which indicates that the number of high-speed moving pixels in the video begins to increase, and abnormal events occur at this time. Between frames 510 and 520, the score drops significantly, which indicates the end of abnormal events. This is consistent with the time point of abnormal behavior in the video, so it can be considered that the detection effect is good. Therefore, it can be concluded that the optical flow method can effectively identify the occurrence of abnormal events. When the abnormal time starts to occur, the scoring trend is large, but the overall score is in a low state.

5   Conclusions

In this paper, the ViBe background modeling method was used to extract the foreground, then, the optical flow method was used to extract the features of abnormal behaviors, so as to obtain a single frame binary image containing only the abnormal behaviors of the crowd. From these binary images, the abnormal behaviors of the crowd could be clearly identified.

The method proposed in this paper can be used to evaluate the detection effect quickly and accurately. However, for some other scenes, such as ghost probe, building collapse, explosion, etc., the detection result will still have deviation, especially under the situation of the video light changes strongly. The generality of this model in different scenarios will be further studied.

Acknowledgements. The authors gratefully acknowledge the financial support from the Natural Science Foundation of Jiangsu Province (Project Number: BK20190873), the Graduate Education Reform and Practice Project of Yangzhou University (Project Number: JGLX2021_002), as well as the Undergraduate Science and Technology Innovation Fund Project of Yangzhou University (X20210324).

References

1. Zhang, Z.: A review of abnormal behavior detection techniques. Comput. Knowl. Technol. **16**(06), 199–201 (2020). (in Chinese)
2. Wu, X., Guo, H., Li, N.: Survey on the video-based abnormal event detection in crowd scenes. J. Electron. Meas. Instrum. **28**(06), 575–584 (2014). (in Chinese)
3. Wu, X., Ou, Y., Qian, H.: A detection system for human abnormal behavior. In: IEEE/RSJ International Conference on Intelligent Robots and Systems. IEEE (2005)

4. Nady, A., Atia, A., Abutabl, A.E.: Real-time abnormal event detection in crowded scenes. J. Theor. Appl. Inf. Technol. **96**(18), 6064–6075 (2018)
5. Chen, X., Lai, J.: Detecting abnormal crowd behaviors based on the div-curl characteristics of flow fields. Pattern Recogn. **88**, 342–355 (2019)
6. Rodriguez, M., Laptev, I., Sivic, J.: Density-aware person detection and tracking in crowds. In: IEEE International Conference on Computer Vision, ICCV 2011, Barcelona, Spain, 6–13 November 2011 (2011)
7. Wang, X., Song, H., Cui, H.: Pedestrian abnormal event detection based on mmulti-feature fusion in traffic video. J. Light Electronoptic **154**, 22–32 (2018)
8. Wang, Z., Zeng, H.: A new algorithm of moving vehicle detection and tracking based on combining frame difference method with optical flow technique. Comput. Appl. Softw. **29**(05), 117–120+129 (2012)
9. A, X.: Hybrid Gaussian Representation Model and its Application in Machine Industry Vision Inspection. Master's thesis, Kunming University of Science and Technology, Kunming, China (2021). (in Chinese)
10. Barnich, O., Van Droogenbroeck, M.: ViBE: A powerful random technique to estimate the background in video sequences. In: IEEE International Conference on Acoustics (2009)
11. Von Droogenbroeck, M., Paquot, O.: Background subtraction: experiments and improvements for ViBe. In: IEEE International Conference on Acoustics (2012)
12. Biao, W., Zheng, L.: Improvements on vibe algorithm for detecting foreground objects. In: International Conference on Computer Science and Network Technology (2017)
13. Gutchess, D., Trajkovics, M., Cohen-Solal, E.: A background model initialization algorithm for video surveillance. In: Proceedings IEEE International Conference on Computer Vision (2001)
14. Pless, R., John, L., Siebers, S.: Evaluation of local models of dynamic backgrounds. In: IEEE Computer Society Conference on Computer Vision and Pattern Recognition (2003)
15. Barron, J.L., Fleet, D.J., Beauchemin, S.S.: Performance of optical flow techniques. In: Proceedings Computer Vision and Pattern Recognition (1992)
16. Negahdaripour, S.: Revised definition of optical flow: integration of radiometric and geometric cues for dynamic. IEEE Trans. Pattern Anal. Mach. Intell. **20**(9), 961–979 (1998)
17. Beauchemin, S.S., Barron, J.L.: The computation of optical flow. ACM Comput. Surv. **27**(3), 433–466 (1995)
18. Liu, D.: Research of image denoising method based on wavelet transform. Mod. Electron. Technol. **36**(14), 93–95 (2013). (in Chinese)
19. Gao, X., Hu, Y., Du, W.: Application of decreasing noise of gray image by corrosion and expansion algorithm. J. Beijing Institute Graphic Commun. **22**(04), 63–65 (2014). (in Chinese)
20. Otsu, N.: A threshold selection method from gray-level histograms. Automatica **11**, 23–27 (1979)

Generating Lymphoma Ultrasound Image Description with Transformer Model

Dehua Chen[1]([✉]), Chunlin Zhang[1], and Yijie Dong[2]

[1] School of Computer Science and Engineering, Donghua University,
Shanghai 201620, China
chendehua@dhu.edu.cn
[2] Department of Ultrasound, Ruijin Hospital,
Shanghai Jiaotong University School of Medicine, Shanghai 200025, China

Abstract. Lymphoma is a malignant tumor originating from lymphatic hematopoietic system and is the most common type of hematologic tumor. High-resolution ultrasound can display the size, morphology, internal echo structure and its changes of lymphoma, providing rich diagnostic information, clinicians can rely on its microscopic ultrasound performance to screen out suspected tumors and then obtain a definite pathological diagnosis through puncture biopsy. The ultrasonographic manifestations of lymphoma are complex and varied, which affects the accurate judgment of the nature of lymphoma by the sonographer. To solver these problems, this paper proposes a lymphoma ultrasound image description generation model based on Transformer [11] to provide auxiliary advice for ultrasound doctors in screening. In this paper, deep stable learning [8] was integrated into the model, and the dependence between features was removed by learning and training sample weights to make the model more focused on lymphoma. In order to make ultrasound doctors better understand the reason of the model description, the mapping of the prediction sequence to the input image in the cross attention layer was visualized to show the ultrasonic image basis of each prediction word in the model. The experimental results on the ultrasonic diagnosis dataset of lymphoma in 696 patients from Shanghai Ruijin Hospital show that the prediction effect of the proposed model is superior to that of the relevant methods mentioned in the literature.

Keywords: Lymphoma · Image captioning · Deep stable learning · Transformer

1 Introduction

Lymphoma is a malignant tumor originating from the lymphatic hematopoietic system with a high incidence and various clinical manifestations worldwide. In recent years, the incidence of lymphoma in China has gradually increased, and has reached 6.68 cases per 100,000 people. Lymphoma is often misdiagnosed as other diseases, such as influenza, tuberculosis or fatigue, because the symptoms

Y. Wang et al. (Eds.): IGTA 2022, CCIS 1611, pp. 220–232, 2022.
https://doi.org/10.1007/978-981-19-5096-4_17

are not obvious. The high misdiagnosis rate leads to delayed treatment timing and increased risk of death. There are many screening methods for suspected malignant lymphoma. The clinical application of advanced ultrasound examination technology has provided more convenient conditions for the diagnosis of lymphoma. High resolution ultrasound can display the size, morphology, internal echo structure and its changes of lymphoma, providing rich diagnostic information. Clinicians can screen out suspected tumors by virtue of their microscopic ultrasonic manifestations and obtain a definite pathological diagnosis by needle biopsy. The ultrasonographic manifestations of lymphoma are complex and varied, which affects the accurate judgment of the nature of lymphoma by the sonographer. In addition, in the imaging diagnosis of many diseases, especially the pathological microscopic imaging, the diagnostic consistency between ultrasound doctors is very low. Therefore, in clinical practice, ultrasound doctors usually need to obtain supplementary opinions as a reference.

In recent years, a great deal of work has been devoted to image subtitle task, which is a comprehensive problem integrating computer vision, natural language processing and machine learning, aiming at producing natural language statements that can describe the image content according to the image. With the development of machine learning and deep learning technology, more and more scholars began to explore how to automatically generate image description for clinical medical images. Automated generation of medical image descriptions can greatly speed up workflow, improve quality and promote standardization of healthcare. Radiological and pathological imaging, such as pneumonia and pneumothorax, has been widely used in hospital diagnosis and treatment. The clinician only needs to upload the final medical image result of the patient's pathological examination or X-ray examination to the auxiliary diagnosis and treatment system, and the image description can be used as auxiliary reference. For ultrasound screening, the ultrasound doctor moves a microscope over and over to check the tumors in the area for signs of lymphoma. The clinician needs a real-time, dynamic description of what is seen under the current microscope as a reference. This is no longer a results-to-conclusion process. Instead, our system is required to generate the corresponding visual description dynamically and in real time for every frame of images seen by ultrasound doctors under the microscope during the screening process of clinicians, so as to provide help for the screening of lymphoma.

The task of image description generation is easy for humans, but challenging for machines. It requires not only the use of models to understand the content of images but also the use of natural language to express their relationships. In addition, the model needs to be able to capture the semantic information of the image and generate human-readable sentences. Lymphoma ultrasound image description is characterized by multiple long sentences. This usually includes the patient's medical observations, a description of normal and abnormal features, and an impression or conclusion of the most significant observations. Therefore, the traditional image subtitle method [3,11,13] may not be enough to generate meaningful medical image descriptions. This method aims to describe the main objects in a visual scene in short sentences and involves little detail. In addition, unlike radiology and other medical imaging, the identification of soft tissue background and lymphoma in ultrasound is more difficult. The performance of traditional medical image generation [5,16] in ultrasound image is also unsatisfactory. In addition to generating meaningful medical image description, the interpretability of model prediction results is also an important reason limiting the wide application of model in clinical diagnosis. Ultrasound doctors need to understand the reasons for the prediction of the model to believe the correctness of the model generated description and to assist clinical diagnosis according to the image description generated by the model.

Aiming at the above problems and shortcomings, a model structure for ultrasonic image description generation is proposed in this paper. The main contributions of our work are:

- A Transformer model based on lymphoma ultrasound image description generation model is proposed. An image description of the incoming lymphoma ultrasound image is generated based on sequence structure. In addition, the model visualizes the attention diagram of the cross-attention layer in the decoder to provide visual interpretation for each word in the prediction, so that users can clearly understand the ultrasonic image basis of the model prediction.
- Deep stable learning [8] is integrated into traditional Transformer framework. The model focuses more on the object (lymphoma) than on the context (soft tissue background) by learning the dependency between weight removal features from training samples. Specifically, the model adopts the nonlinear feature de-correlation method based on the stochastic Fourier feature of linear computational complexity. In the process of model iteration, the feature and weight of the model are saved and reloaded to globally perceive and remove the correlation.

2   Model

As shown in the Fig. 1, this model is based on the Transformer framework [11] of the chain rule to generate the image description of lymphoma ultrasound image. The model consists of four structures: vision extractor, encoder, decoder and deep stable learning network. First, we used the patient's lymphoma ultrasound image Img as the original input of the model. For the input image Img, the model extracted its pixel features $X = \{x_1, x_2, \ldots, x_n\}$ through a visual extractor and input them into the deep stable learning network to modify the model loss function. Secondly, we obtain the hidden state sequence $H = \{h_1, h_2, \ldots, h_n\}$ of the encoder as the output result of the encoder by encoding the pixel feature X extracted from the visual extractor. Finally, the target sequence $Y = \{y_1, y_2, \ldots, y_n\}$ of the model is obtained through the decoder structure.

As mentioned above, the whole process of model report generation follows the chain rule, which is expressed as follows:

$$P\left(Y|Img\right) = \prod_{t=1}^{T} P\left(y_t|y_1, \ldots, y_{t-1},\ Img\right) \tag{1}$$

Model's goal is through the negative condition of logarithmic likelihood function maximization raise$P(Y|Img)$, in the case of a given ultrasonic image Img:

$$\theta^* = \underset{\theta}{argmax} \sum_{t=1}^{T} log\, p\,(y_t|y_1, \dots, y_{t-1},\, Img; \theta) \tag{2}$$

where θ is the parameter of the model. In the following sections, the visual extractor, encoder, decoder, deep stable learning structure and model prediction process are described in detail.

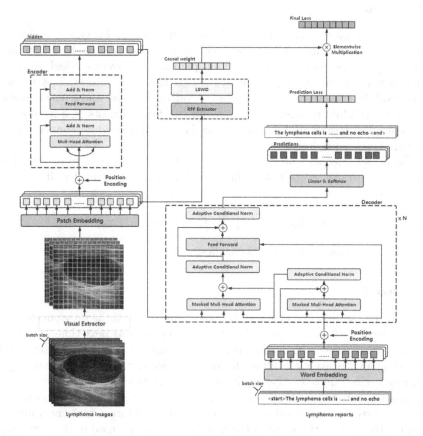

Fig. 1. The complete framwork for our lymphoma diagnostic report generation model

2.1 Visual Extractor

For the lymphoma ultrasound image Img that was input into the model, the model extracted its pixel feature X by pre-training Deep residual network ResNest101 [14]. Compared with previous work, ResNest borrowed the ideas of multi-path and feature-map Attention and innovatively introduced split-attention mechanism to improve module extraction effect. The model will be combined and connected with the pixel feature vectors extracted by Resnest101, and the encoded final sequence will be taken as the output of the structure of our visual extractor. The formula for this process is stated as follows:

$$\{x_1,\ x_2,\ \ldots,\ x_n\} = f_{ve}(Img) \tag{3}$$

where $f_{ve}(\Delta)$ stands for model visual extractor.

2.2 Encoder

Encoders are used to extract features from input and provide effective semantic information for decoding. The encoder consists of a linear layer based on input embedding and position coding and multiple encoder layers stacked on top of each other. Each encoder layer consists of two sub-layer connection structures: the first sub-layer consists of a multihead self-attention layer and a normalization layer and a residual connection; the second sub-layer consists of a feedforward full connection layer and a normalization layer and a residual connection. Its structure is shown in Fig. 1.

The model encoder encodes the pixel feature sequence X from the visual extractor, and outputs its hidden layer content H as the encoder. Its formula can be expressed as:

$$\{h_1,\ h_2,\ \ldots,\ h_n\} = f_{en}(x_1,\ x_2,\ \ldots,\ x_n) \tag{4}$$

where $f_{en}(\cdot)$ represents the model encoder.

2.3 Decoder

Based on the result of encoder and the prediction result of the previous decoder, the decoder features the predicted value that may appear next time. Similar to the encoder structure, the decoder consists of a linear layer based on target text embedding and location encoding and multiple decoder layers stacked on top of each other. Each decoder layer contains three sub-layer connection structures: The first layer includes a long since the attention the child layer and normalization, and a residual connection since the attention of target text encoding, the second is the layer is the same as the first layer structure used in the text image map coding, the third is the layer consists of a feedforward totally connection layer and normalization, and a residual connection to enhance model to accelerate convergence. Its structure is shown in Fig. 1, the decoder structure formula is expressed as follows:

$$y_t = f_{de}(h_1,\ \ldots,\ h_S,\ (y_1,\ \ldots,\ y_{t-1}) \tag{5}$$

2.4   Deep Stable Learning Network

Existing deep learning models try to make use of the correlation between all observable features and the target task for learning and prediction. However, tag-related features in training data are not necessarily essential features of their corresponding categories [15]. Different from X-ray and pathological images, the soft tissue background surrounding lymphocytes in ultrasound images has an important influence on the judgment of the model. The deep stable learning network is introduced to solve the problem of distribution offset by globally weighted samples, and all the features of each input sample are directly removed to eliminate the statistical correlation between related and unrelated features. By using the Random Fourier feature (RFF) feature and sample weighting feature, the linear and nonlinear dependence between features is eliminated.

In the following description of deep stable learning principle, the symbols represent the following meanings: $X \subset R^{m_X}$ represents the original pixel space, $Y \subset R^{m_Y}$ represents the result space, and $H \subset R^{m_H}$ represents the representation space. Where m_X, m_Y, m_H represents the spatial dimension of X, Y and H. $f : X \to H$ represents the representation function and $g : Z \to Y$ represents the prediction function. The model contains n groups of sample pixel feature $X \subset R^{n \times m_X}$ and report statement sequence $Y \subset R^{n \times m_Y}$, and we use X_i, Y_i to represent the i-th group of sample. The $H \subset R^{n \times m_H}$ represents the representation learned by Transformer and the $Z_{:,i}$ represents the i-th variable in the space. We use $w \subset R_n$ to represent the sample weight, and u and v to represent the random Fourier eigenmapping function.

Independent Test Statistics We introduce hypothesis testing statistics to measure the independence between random variables to eliminate the dependence between any pair of features ($Z_{:,i}$ and $Z_{:,j}$) in the representation space. We use two one-dimensional random variables A, B to simplify to represent $Z_{:,i}$ and $Z_{:,j}$, and take samples (A_1, A_2, ..., A_n) and (B_1, B_2, ..., B_n) from the distribution of A and B accordingly. We express the correlation between the two variables in the following way: k_A represents the positive definite kernel in the domain of random variable A, H_A represents the corresponding RKHS, and the same is true for variables k_B and H_B. The cross covariance $\sum AB$ of H_A and H_B is expressed as follows:

$$<h_A, h_B \sum AB> = E_{AB}[h_A(A)h_B(B)] - E_A[h_A(A)]E_B[h_B(B)] \tag{6}$$
$$where \quad h_A \in H_A, \quad h_B \in H_B$$

Independence, then, can be determined by the following statement [1]: if flight $K_A K_B$ is typical, and $E[K_A(A, A)] < \infty$ and $E[K_B(B, B)] < \infty$, then there exists:

$$\sum AB = 0 \Leftrightarrow A \perp B \tag{7}$$

When the Hilbert-Schmidt independence criterion (HSIC) [1] is used as the de-correlation criterion for features, the squared Hilbert-Schmidt norm of $\sum AB$ should be zero. However, HSIC requires high computational cost and grows with the increase of data set size, so it is difficult to train depth models on large data sets. However, HSIC requires high computational cost and grows with the increase of data set size, so it is difficult to train depth models on large data sets. Since HilbertSchmidt norm in Euclidean space can be corresponding to Frobenius norm, independent test statistics can be based on Frobenius norm [10]. Let the covariance matrix be:

$$\hat{\Sigma}_{AB} = \frac{1}{n-1} \sum_{i=1}^{n} [(u(A_i) - \frac{1}{n} \sum_{j=1}^{n} u(A_j))^T \cdot (v(B_i) - \frac{1}{n} \sum_{j=1}^{n} v(B_j))],$$
$$where \quad (8)$$

$$u(A) = (u_1(A), u_2(A), \ldots, u_{n_A}(A)), u_j(A) \in H_{RFF}, \forall j,$$
$$u(B) = (v_1(B), v_2(B), \ldots, v_{n_B}(B)), v_j(B) \in H_{RFF}, \forall j,$$

The corresponding sampling functions n_A and n_B, H_{RFF} in H_{RFF} represent the function space of random Fourier features, and their expressions are as follows:

$$H_{RFF} = h : x \to \sqrt{2} \cos(\omega x + \phi) \mid \omega \sim N(0, 1), \phi \sim Uniform(0, 2\pi) \quad (9)$$

where, ω is sampled from the standard normal distribution, and ϕ is sampled from the uniform distribution. Finally, the independence test statistic I_{AB} is defined as the Frobenius norm $I_{AB} = \left\| \hat{\Sigma}_{AB} \right\|_F^2$ of the partial cross covariance matrix.

Since I_{AB} is always non-negative, when I_{AB} falls to 0, the variables A and B tend to be independent. Therefore, this method can effectively calculate the independence between random variables. The accuracy of the independence test also increases with n_A and n_B. When both n_A and n_B are set to 5, it is sufficient to ensure the independence of the random variables.

Sample Weight Study for De-correlation. In this paper, we try to eliminate the correlation dependence between specialties in the representation space by sample weights, and use RFF to measure their independence. The sample weight is defined as $W \in R_+^n$, where $n = \sum_{i=1}^{n} w_i$. With the help of defined sample weights, the covariance matrix of random variables A and B in Formula 8 can be redefined as follows:

$$\hat{\Sigma}_{AB}; w = \frac{1}{n-1} \sum_{i=1}^{n} [(w_i u(A_i) - \frac{1}{n} \sum_{j=1}^{n} u w_j(A_j))^T \cdot$$
$$(w_i v(B_i) - \frac{1}{n} \sum_{j=1}^{n} w_j v(B_j))] \quad (10)$$

Stable learning attempts to eliminate the correlation dependence between arbitrary features to ensure the independence of features. For features $Z_{:,i}$ and $Z_{:,j}$, the partial covariance matrix is $\left\|\sum \hat{Z}_{:,i} Z_{:,j}; w\right\|_F^2$, relative to 10. In addition, we optimized the sample weight W to w^*:

$$w^* = arg \max_{w \in \Delta_n} \sum_{1 \leq i < j \leq m_Z} \left\|\sum \hat{Z}_{:,i} Z_{:,j}; w\right\|_F^2 \tag{11}$$

where $\Delta_n = \{w \in R_+^n \mid \sum_{i=1}^n w_i = n\}$. When the model uses the optimal weight w^* to weight the training samples, the correlation between features can be greatly reduced. In the process of iteration, the time step t representation function, prediction function and sample weight are shown as follows:

$$f^{(t+1)}, g^{(t+1)} = arg \max_{f, g} \sum_{t=1}^n w_{i=1}^{(t)} L(g(f(X_i)), y_i),$$

$$w^{(t+1)} = arg \max_{w \in \Delta_n} \sum_{1 \leq i < j \leq m_Z} \left\|\sum \hat{Z}_{:,i}^{(t+1)} Z_{:,j}^{(t+1)}; w\right\|_F^2 \tag{12}$$

where $Z^{(t+1)} = f^{(t+1)(X}, L(\cdot, \cdot)$ is the cross entropy loss function. At the beginning, $w^{(0)}$ is initialized to: $(1, 1, \ldots, 1)^T$.

3   Experiment and Result

3.1   Experiment Settings

Experimental Data Set. The data used in this study were from the Lymphoma ultrasound Detection program of Ruijin Hospital affiliated to Shanghai Jiao Tong University Hospital. The program collects lymphoma ultrasound images, CFI data, puncture information, pathology reports and biomarkers from patients for lymphoma disease studies. This study used data from 696 ultrasound images of patients with lymphoma and related diagnostic reports collected from Shanghai Ruijin Hospital between 2019 and April 2020. For the experimental data set, we excluded cases with missing descriptions of non-lymphoma conditions. The model input data were divided into training set, validation set and test set in a ratio of 7:2:1.

Evaluation Indicators and Baseline Setting
Evaluation Indicators. In this paper, the evaluation method of Jing et al. [5] was extended to measure the model performance through BLEU, Rouge-L and METEOR in NLG indicators.

Baseline Setting. For a detailed analysis of the effects of our model, we used the original Transformer framework with three layers, eight attention headers, and 512 hidden unit configurations as the Base model. In addition, we also compared our model with previous traditional image caption generation models, including ST [11], ATT2IN [7] and ADAATT [6]. Meanwhile, it is also compared with the previous classical medical image description generation models COATT [5].

3.2 Analysis of Experimental Results

In order to evaluate the performance of the ultrasonic image description generation model proposed in this paper, we designed and tested the influence of different modules on the image description generation effect, that is, the method proposed by each module is compared with the existing basic method, highlighting the advantages and significance of the improved method; Secondly, the proposed image description generation model is compared with the methods proposed in other literatures, which further verifies the practicability and validity of the proposed model. Unfortunately, compared with IU X-ray, mimy-CXR and other text reports, the similarity between lymphoma ultrasound reports was relatively low and the description target was relatively single, resulting in high NLP indexes in specific experiments. The results were analyzed as follows:

Effect Study of Each Module

Deep Residual Network Module. This article reports improvements to the generation model over the original Vision Transformer. The original Deep residual network Resnet was replaced by Resnest as a visual extractor. The improved model integrates the idea of feature-map Attention and mulit-patch mechanism in pixel extraction, which effectively improves the Feature extraction ability of the model. In addition, the improved model is compared with commonly used Deep residual networks (Resnet [2], SE-Resnet [4], Resnext [12]), and the comparison results are shown in Table 1. Table 1 shows that using Resnest as a Deep residual network in the model has a better effect than Resnet, SE-Resnet and Resnext, achieving better experimental results.

Table 1. The performance of our full model with different Deep residual networks on the test sets of lymphoma dataset width respect to NLG metric.

Model	BL-1	BL-2	BL-3	BL-4	MTR	RG-L
Base+Resnet	0.831	0.761	0.703	0.655	0.460	0.820
Base+Resnext	0.838	0.773	0.724	0.684	0.482	0.826
Base+SE-Resnet	0.841	0.785	0.745	0.712	0.482	0.830
Base+Resnest	0.846	0.789	0.748	0.713	0.487	0.850

Deep Stable Learning Module. In order to better distinguish lymphoma from soft tissue background, we incorporated deep stable learning module into the model. As shown in Table 2: Stable deep stable learning modules were added into Transformer, Transformer+Resnest, and the model indexes were improved to a certain extent. The validity of the method is proved. In addition, to further verify whether stable module can improve the model's ability to distinguish lymphoma and soft tissue background, SoomthGrad proposed by Smilkov et al. [9] is used to visualize the gradient score of the function on the input image pixels. The result of significance graph is shown in Fig. 2, which is a feature graph generated by the parameters learned from the model rather than the Deep residual network junction. As shown in the Figure, the model can be more focused on lymphoma after stable module is added.

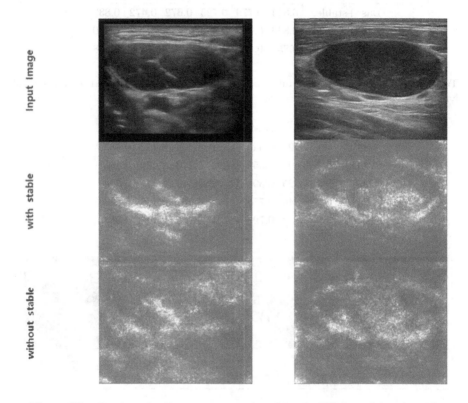

Fig. 2. Visualization of saliency maps produced by the VGG model and stable.

Comparison of Previous Experiments On lymphoma data sets, we compared our model with previous work on image subtitle description tasks, and the results are shown in Table 3. As can be seen from the NLP index results in the table, compared with the traditional image caption model ST, the Transform model based on attentional sequence structure can effectively model the semantic information in lymphoma image description, and has a significant advantage in lymphoma image description generation. In addition, compared with the traditional Transformer model ADATT, our model has a considerable improvement. Because the traditional attention-based subtitle model aims to generate short sentences describing things with prominent features in the graph, it is not suitable for the task of medical image description generation. Compared with

Table 2. The performance of all baselines and our full model on the test of lymphoma dataset with respect to NLG metric.

model	BL-1	BL-2	BL-3	BL-4	MTR	RG-L
Base	0.831	0.751	0.693	0.623	0.450	0.820
Base+stable	0.844	0.779	0.725	0.672	0.472	0.833
Base+Resnest	0.846	0.789	0.748	0.713	0.487	0.850
Ours	0.853	0.795	0.741	0.705	0.496	0.858

Table 3. Comparisons of our full model with previous studies on the test sets of lymphoma dataset.

Model	BL-1	BL-2	BL-3	BL-4	MTR	RG-L
ST	0.594	0.545	0.502	0.464	0.332	0.585
ADAATT	0.605	0.552	0.508	0.470	0.330	0.560
ATT2IN	0.625	0.590	0.552	0.519	0.341	0.609
COATT	0.846	0.773	0.712	0.663	0.466	0.832
Ours	0.853	0.795	0.741	0.705	0.496	0.858

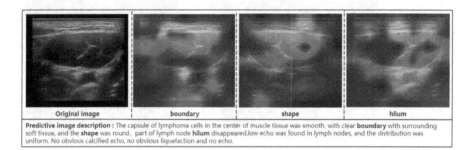

Predictive image description : The capsule of lymphoma cells in the center of muscle tissue was smooth, with clear **boundary** with surrounding soft tissue, and the **shape** was round, part of lymph node **hilum** disappeared.low echo was found in lymph nodes, and the distribution was uniform. No obvious calcified echo, no obvious liquefaction and no echo.

Fig. 3. Visual result presentation: Visualizations of image-text attention mappings between a specific Ultrasonography of lymphoma and generated reports from our model.

COATT designed for generating medical diagnosis reports, stable modules are designed and added in this paper to better focus on lymphoma rather than soft tissue background. According to the results in the Table 3, we can see that our model has improved to a certain extent compared to previous work. In addition, we also demonstrate the effectiveness of the model in the form of interpretability and sample analysis.

Interpretability Analysis. One of the most intuitive ways to interpret an image model is to visualize the pixel features that have a decisive influence on its decision making. For two random input ultrasound images of lymphoma, the model eventually generated a medical image description of length L. In this paper, by calculating the attention fraction of encoder output and prediction sequence in the cross attention layer of decoder, the attention diagram of dimension (L, 7, 7) is obtained as the final interpretable basis. The effect is shown in Fig. 3.

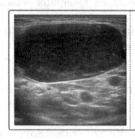

Ground-truth

The capsule of lymphoma cells in the center of muscle tissue was smooth with clear boundary with surrounding soft tissue and the shape was round.

Lymph node hilum disappeared. Low echo in lymph nodes relatively uniform distribution . no obvious calcification echo, no obvious liquefaction echo .

Ours

The capsule of lymphoma cells in the center of muscle tissue was smooth with clear boundary with surrounding soft tissue and the shape was round .

Part of lymph node hilum disappeared. Low echo was found in lymph nodes and the distribution was uniform . no obvious calcified echo, no obvious liquefaction and no echo

Fig. 4. An image description of reports from ground-truth, ours for lymphoma images

Sample Analysis. To further prove the effectiveness of our model, we selected a typical case from the test set for analysis. As shown in Fig. 4, we present an ultrasound image of the patient's lymphoma and its corresponding diagnostic description (ground-truth), and the image description from our model is listed on the right side of the image. We marked the corresponding medical terms in different colors in the picture. From the picture, we can see that our model can effectively characterize the branch structures of grammar tree, such as "smooth envelope", "clear decomposition", "oval shape" and "disappearance of lymphatic hilum structure". The image description generated by the model is similar to the ultrasound doctor's diagnosis content and has certain validity.

4   Conclusion

In this paper, we propose a model for the generation of lymphoma ultrasound image description. This model uses Transformer framework [11] to generate ultrasonic image description based on chain rule. In the model, we incorporate deep stable learning to make the model more focused on lymphoma, and replace Resnet with Resnest [14] to improve the ability of extracting pixel features. Experiments on the data set from Shanghai Ruijin Hospital show that the proposed model can generate meaningful ultrasound image descriptions containing necessary medical terms and is interpretable to some extent.

Acknowledgements. This work was supported by the National Key R&D Program of China under Grant 2019YFE0190500.

References

1. Fukumizu, K., Gretton, A., Sun, X., Schölkopf, B.: Kernel measures of conditional dependence. In: Conference on Neural Information Processing Systems, pp. 489–496 (2008)

2. He, K., Zhang, X., Ren, S., Sun, J.: Deep residual learning for image recognition. In: 2016 IEEE Conference on Computer Vision and Pattern Recognition (CVPR) (2016)
3. Hendricks, L.A., Akata, Z., Rohrbach, M., Donahue, J., Schiele, B., Darrell, T.: Generating visual explanations. In: European Conference on Computer Vision (2016))
4. Jie, H., Li, S., Gang, S., Albanie, S.: Squeeze-and-excitation networks. In: 2018 IEEE/CVF Conference on Computer Vision and Pattern Recognition (2017)
5. Jing, B., Xie, P., Xing, E.: On the automatic generation of medical imaging reports (2017)
6. Lu, J., Xiong, C., Parikh, D., Socher, R.: Knowing when to look: adaptive attention via a visual sentinel for image captioning. In: 2017 IEEE Conference on Computer Vision and Pattern Recognition (CVPR) (2017)
7. Rennie, S.J., Marcheret, E., Mroueh, Y., Ross, J., Goel, V.: Self-critical sequence training for image captioning. Int. J. Res. Eng. Sci. Man. 1 (2016)
8. Shen, Z., Cui, P., Zhang, T., Kunag, K.: Stable learning via sample reweighting. Proc. AAAI Conf. Artif. Intell.34(4), 5692–5699 (2020)
9. Smilkov, D., Thorat, N., Kim, B., Viégas, F., Wattenberg, M.: Smoothgrad: removing noise by adding noise (2017)
10. Strobl, E.V., Zhang, K., Visweswaran, S.: Approximate kernel-based conditional independence tests for fast non-parametric causal discovery. J. Causal Infer. 7 (2017)
11. Vinyals, O., Toshev, A., Bengio, S., Erhan, D.: Show and tell: A neural image caption generator. In: 2015 IEEE Conference on Computer Vision and Pattern Recognition (CVPR) (2015)
12. Xie, S., Girshick, R., Dollár, P., Tu, Z., He, K.: Aggregated residual transformations for deep neural networks. In: 2017 IEEE Conference on Computer Vision and Pattern Recognition (2016)
13. Xu, K., et al.: Show, attend and tell: neural image caption generation with visual attention. In: Proceedings of the 32nd International Conference on Machine Learning, pp. 2048–2057 (2015)
14. Zhang, H., et al.: ResNeSt: split-attention networks. arXiv preprint arXiv:2004.08955 (2020)
15. Zhang, X., Cui, P., Xu, R., Zhou, L., Shen, Z.: Deep stable learning for out-of-distribution generalization. In: 2021 IEEE/CVF Conference on Computer Vision and Pattern Recognition (CVPR) (2021)
16. Zhang, Z., Xie, Y., Xing, F., Mcgough, M., Yang, L.: Mdnet: A semantically and visually interpretable medical image diagnosis network (2017)

Computer Graphics (Modeling, Rendering, Algorithm Simplification and Acceleration Techniques, Realistic Scene Generation, 3D Reconstruction Algorithm, System and Application, etc.)

Accelerated Photon Mapping for Homogeneous Participating Media Based on Octree

Bo Hou and Chunmeng Kang[✉]

Shandong Normal University, Ji'nan 250014, China
kcm89kimi@163.com

Abstract. Rendering participating media using photon mapping has been a hot subject in computer graphics, but the rendering process generally needs much time cost. In this paper, we propose an octree-based photon storage structure and a corresponding photon query algorithm to solve this problem, which can be used to reduce the time for rendering homogeneous participating media. Our algorithm is based on the traditional photon mapping. Firstly, the photons in the volume medium are recursively divided according to their spatial positions, and the divided data are stored by bounding boxes. All bounding boxes are organized to generate an octree structure, and finally a cluster of photons is stored in the leaf nodes of the octree. Using the octree structure to store photon information can reduce the complexity of the data structure. At the same time, the spatial localization of arbitrary sampling points in the ray can be performed to quickly find the group of photons contributing to these points, because of the octree structure during the collection process. Therefore, our algorithm reduces the time cost of photon queries and finally improves the efficiency of the photon mapping algorithm for rendering the participating media.

Keywords: Photon mapping · Participating media · Octree

1 Introduction

The participating medium is the natural phenomena such as clouds, smoke, fog, etc., which are common in our daily life, and includes human skin, translucent materials such as jade and milk. In the film industry, in addition to expressing natural phenomena in specific scenes, the addition of additional media in the scene can form visual effects to enhance the beauty and artistic sense of the picture. When light enters these media, it will be scattered or absorbed a lot greatly and finally spread to our eyes. Due to the complexity of simulating light in participating media, it has been a popular research field in how to render participating media efficiently.

In a related paper by Fong [1], the participating medium is considered as an ensemble containing particles at the molecular level, and when light passes through the medium there is a chance that it will be scattered by any of the particles and change the propagation direction of the light or be absorbed and disappear, and these light losses along the original path eventually form the occlusion phenomenon. It is obviously impossible to simulate

Y. Wang et al. (Eds.): IGTA 2022, CCIS 1611, pp. 235–245, 2022.
https://doi.org/10.1007/978-981-19-5096-4_18

every particle in a computer, so many algorithms use probabilistic models [2] to model the interference of light by a medium in a region.

The photon mapping algorithm [3] calculates the radiance value of a sample point by caching photons and estimating the density of photon. Compared with the path-tracing algorithm, the photon mapping algorithm can better handle the caustics and the propagation of light in the medium, its shortcoming is bias, the solution is to increase the photons in the photon map, but this will slow down the efficiency of the photon mapping algorithm.

In this paper, we provide an improvement to the photon mapping algorithm [4] for rendering homogeneous participating media.

- Firstly, this paper adopts the octree to manage all the divided scene regions, compared to the KD tree, which can divide the spatial structure according to the maximum dimension. The octree can perfectly allocate the whole scene space by continuously dividing the child nodes downward, so that the photons cached in the scene medium can be arranged in the bounding box.
- The octree structure in this paper manages all photon information by using the leaf nodes, and all non-leaf nodes manage the range of spatial region division. We set the optimal number of photons that a leaf node can store to limit the height of the tree.
- During the calculation of radiance values, we query photons by ray marching. By emitting query rays from screen pixel points and generating sampling points on the rays, the corresponding leaf node can be located in the octree structure according to the position of the sampling points simply, and multiple photons contributing to the viewpoint can be queried in the leaf node immediately.

Since the height of the octree managing the same number of photons is lower than that of the KD tree and the query process does not need backtracking, the efficiency of rendering participating media using photon mapping algorithm is improved.

2   Related Work

2.1   Path Tracing

The path tracing (PT) algorithm [5] is a Monte Carlo method whose main contribution is to emit a query ray from an image pixel location like a real ray, bounce it around the scene and eventually intersect with the light source. Compared to path tracing, bidirectional path tracing (BDPT) [6] can simulate more complex scenes, especially scenes where the light source is hidden. With the improvement of computer performance, path tracing is a widely used technique in the related film and television industry [7]. In Pharr [8] et al.'s theory, path tracing algorithms maintain an important position in the rendering field due to their accuracy and solid theoretical foundation for light simulation.

2.2   Photon Mapping

Jenson [4] first proposed the use of photon mapping algorithm. The method caches the radiance values in the scene with an efficient storage and query data structure, and then collects the radiance values inside the medium generated by internal scattering using ray marching along the direction of the viewpoint ray. Kang *et al.* [9] summarized previous work related to photon mapping algorithms and combined it with parallel algorithms. Jarosz [10] proposed a method to collect photons only once along the viewpoint ray as the in-scattered radiance of the whole ray and proposed a comprehensive framework in a subsequent paper [11] that refined the theory related to beam samples and beam queries. Bitterli [12] and Xi Deng [13] further proposed higher-dimensional photon samples based on beam samples to improve the accuracy of photon mapping estimation. Georgiev [14] proposed a photon mapping method for bi-directional path tracking with Monte Carlo sampling, and Kvrivánek [15], in order to exploit the corresponding different rendering scenes of each algorithm's potential, the different algorithms are combined by means of importance sampling and also constitute different radiosity estimation functions. In addition to the study of photon samples, Hao Qin [16] proposed an unbiased photon collection algorithm, which generates an unbiased path sample by collecting each photon independently and connecting it to the corresponding viewpoint ray.

2.3   Caching Data Structure

In the field of image rendering, effective data structures can greatly improve rendering efficiency. Methods and techniques related to raytracing acceleration structures are summarized in the literature by Arvo [17]. In an early example of ray intersection with tuples, a bounding box structure is needed to store various complex geometric tuples. By the way of intersecting with the bounding box first and then with the tuples in the bounding box, unnecessary intersection calculations can be reduced, thus improving the efficiency of ray tracing [18]. If the ray does not intersect with the bounding box, then it must not intersect with the tuples. One of the more mainstream structures includes square bounding box and sphere bounding box. KD tree was first proposed by Jensen to construct an accelerated structure for storing photons [10]. KD tree mainly divides the photons in an ensemble by recursion, and then efficiently reads the contents in each node. In the related method of beams query, by changing the original structure into the structure of hierarchical bounding boxes, that is, adding a bounding box for each node on the basis of the original structure, the bounding box of the parent node should contain its children. In our study, we found that the distribution of photons in homogeneous media is uniform to a certain extent, so that using octree to store photons and to calculate radiation values would be a better solution than KD tree.

3   Light Transport in Participating Media

Light transport in the participating media can be divided into four different ways, including absorption, out-scattering, in-scattering, and emission, as shown in Fig. 1.

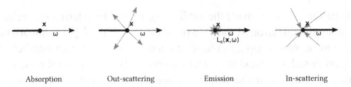

| Absorption | Out-scattering | Emission | In-scattering |

Fig. 1. Light transport in medium.

Absorption and out-scattering indicate a loss of light energy, in-scattering can be seen as an enhancement of light energy, and emission generally refers to flame-like media. In a scene with medium, the radiance from the $\overrightarrow{w}$ direction, arriving at the viewpoint x, can be expressed as:

$$L(x, \overrightarrow{w}) = T_r(x, \overrightarrow{w})L(x_s, \overrightarrow{w}) + \int_0^s T_r(x)\delta_s(x_t)L_i(w_t, \overrightarrow{w})dt, \tag{1}$$

where T_r is the transmittance between two points, s is the distance from the viewpoint to the nearest object surface, and t is a relevant parameter. The radiance on the surface of the object and can be solved using the rendering equation. $L_i(x_t, \overrightarrow{w})$ represents the in-scattering of the medium, which can be further expressed by Eq. (2),

$$L_i(x_t, \overrightarrow{w}) = \int_{4\pi} p(x_t, \overrightarrow{w}, \overrightarrow{w_t})L(x_t, \overrightarrow{w_t})d\overrightarrow{w_t}, \tag{2}$$

where p is the phase function that determines the direction of light scattering in the medium.

It is a difficult task to calculate these equations analytically. The photon mapping algorithm solves the radiative transfer equation precisely by density estimation, photon tracking, and collecting photons along a ray. In the process of this algorithm, a lot of photons are emitted from the light source, which scatter or reflect a certain number of times and eventually stay in the medium or on the surface. Then, these photons are stored using the KD tree. In the rendering stage by emitting query rays in a specified direction from the viewpoint, the computational process of the radiance can be simulated by ray marching [4]. Thereby Eq. (1) can be numerically approximated as:

$$L(x, \overrightarrow{w}) \approx T_r(x, \overrightarrow{w})L(x_s, \overrightarrow{w}) + \sum_{t=0}^{s-1} \int_0^s T_r(x)\delta_s(x_t)L_i(w_t, \overrightarrow{w})\Delta t, \tag{3}$$

Δt is the length of the line segment and $x_0,\ldots, x_s$ are the samples on the ray. $L_i(x_t, \overrightarrow{w})$ is the most computationally expensive part of the equation because it contains contributions from all possible directions around the sampling points. The same density estimate can be used to calculate the radiance at any sampled point.

$$L_i(x_t, \overrightarrow{w}) \approx \sum_{i=1}^n \frac{p(x_t, \overrightarrow{w}, \overrightarrow{w_i})\Delta\varphi_i}{\frac{4}{3}\pi r^3}, \tag{4}$$

where $\Delta\varphi_i$ is the energy of the i-th photon and, $\overrightarrow{w_i}$ is the direction of incidence of the i-th photon.

4   Render Participating Media Using Octree

In this paper, the complexity of the photon storage structure is reduced by changing the storage data structure to achieve the goal of arranging the photons by spatial position. The octree structure manages its 8 child nodes, which exactly corresponds to the region in the stereoscopic space by each dimension. After completing the construction of the photon map, we propose an algorithm for estimating the corresponding radiance based on the structure of the octree. Firstly, by generating and tracking the photons emitted from the light source, we can obtain a collection of photon information, which we use to build an Octree based on a bounding box. Secondly, by casting a query ray through the pixel from the viewpoint during the rendering time, the samples are set on this ray. Each sample point falls within a region managed by an octree leaf node. Finally, the radiance values of the sampling points on the ray are calculated by collecting the photons inside the leaf nodes directly through a density estimation method, and the radiance information on this ray is integrated to draw the colors of the pixel points. The process is shown in Fig. 2.

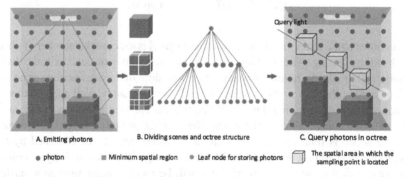

A. Emitting photons   B. Dividing scenes and octree structure   C. Query photons in octree

● photon   ▦ Minimum spatial region   ● Leaf node for storing photons   ⬚ The spatial area in which the sampling point is located

Fig. 2. Process of this paper.

4.1   Establishment of Octree

The photon map used in this paper is a tree structure based on a Bounding-Volume Hierarchy (BVH). This structure was used to manage photon data with radius information in Jaroze's paper [10], where the BVH structure is used to store photons in a pattern of each parent node recursively manages two children downward, and each parent node's bounding-volume can accommodate all its children. Our octree structure is also a hierarchical bounding box in which the parent node contains all its children, but each internal node has eight children. The internal nodes are only used to divide the space and do not store any photon information.

After the photons are emitted in the medium, we use the information about the 3D position coordinates of these photons to construct a photon map with an octree structure. A scene can be treated as a box, and we need to divide this space in a way that does not consider any geometry surface. Firstly, a midpoint segmentation method can be used, which recursively classifies the photons in the whole scene at the midpoints of the x, y

and z dimensions, marking the photons in different region with 0–7. Until the number of photons in each marked region is less than a given threshold K' or the depth of recursion is greater than $2 * \log_8 N$, where N is the total number of photons emitted in the medium, and K' is taken as half of the user-set K-NN search value (default 120). The different methods of dividing the space we show in Fig. 3.

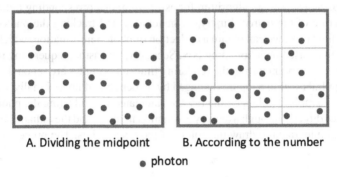

A. Dividing the midpoint   B. According to the number

● photon

Fig. 3. Two different way of dividing.

In contrast to the midpoint division, another method is to count the number of photons on each axis by sorting. After sorting and counting the photons on each axis, the division position tries to make the number of photons on both sides of the axes as same as possible.

Compared with the A method in Fig. 3, the B method can be well adapted to scenes with non-uniform photon distribution. When translucent media such as cloud, smoke, steam, etc. is scattered all over the scene, the number of body photons distributed in the whole scene is relatively uniform, and a balanced tree can be obtained by using the midpoint division method in Fig. 3A, and the algorithm is relatively simple. For the scene contains caustics effects, photons will be more concentrated in a particular region, the use of balanced tree division will appear serious differences in the size of the bounding box. In this case, the light sampling in the irradiance calculation stage will result in multiple invalid sampling points that intersect with the same oversized box. If the scene contains scattering effects, our algorithm stops the tree building process based on the termination condition of the tree building, i.e., the number of photons in the node reaches the storage optimum or recursion reaches maximum depth. We no longer pursue the balance of the octree.

The data structure of this algorithm consists of two main parts, one is the nodes of the octree and the other is an array of photons stored according to subscripts. The final photon map consists of an octree structure and an array of photons, which can be queried by the data in the leaf nodes to find the photons in the corresponding array.

4.2 Radiance Calculation

At the stage of collecting photons to calculate radiance, the color value of a pixel point is determined by the photons in the direction of the viewpoint. The photons carry radiation values that illuminate their corresponding areas. Usually, n sampling points are set in this direction: the first sampling point starts from the viewpoint; the n-th sampling point will fall on the face surface of the scene; and the middle n-2 sampling points are in the medium of the scene. Our algorithm sets an adaptive number of light samples to ensure that there are samples in the bounding boxes of the octree through the r ay casting. The number of samples C is determined by the number of leaf nodes M in the octree division:

$$C = a^{\log_8 M}, \tag{5}$$

where a is 3. And label all the leaf nodes of the queried in photon map to avoid the repeat calculation. Each sampling point is estimated by photon density estimation of its radiance value, and finally the radiance values of all sampling points are combined to the color of the sampling point.

By searching the nearest-neighbor photons around each sampling point, their radiance values are estimated using photon density estimation. In the traditional photon mapping algorithm density estimation is done by querying K photons around the sample point in the KD tree, and dividing the sum of the energy of these photons by the volume around the sample point. This algorithm needs to find the K nearest photons to the sampling point in the KD tree sequentially, so the photon query is not efficient.

In our algorithm, we can directly calculate the searching range of photons by using the bounding box data of leaf nodes and get the number of photons in leaf nodes. Then, we filter the photons that contribute to the light by the distance between each photon and the light. Set a label for the leaf node when it has been checked to ensure that the second calculation does not produce when different sampling points fall into the same leaf node. The adaptive number of sampling points ensures that we collect most of the photons that have an impact on the calculation of the scattered radiation within the ray casting. According to the terminating condition of tree building, when the number of photons in the leaf node is less than the threshold K', we consider that the radiance of all photons in the leaf node can be exactly estimated as the radiance of the sampling point. Photons can be taken out at one time as a whole. At the maximum depth stopping tree division, the number of photons within the leaf node will be greater than the lookup value K. In this case, the nearest neighboring K photons are looked up in the leaf node.

The pseudo code of query photon in octree is as follows:

```
program Query (Output)
  {Assuming all photon has been collected in a octree};
  point sampling_point;
  vector<photon> photonArr;
  octree root node;
  begin

  query()
  if root_node->leaf != true;
    root_node get into next_node;
  else
    photons=photonArr[root_node->offset];
    calculate radiance using Equation6;
    return radiance
  end.
```

For the K' photons in the bounding box corresponding to the collected sampling point x, the radiance is calculated as:

$$L_i(x_t, \overrightarrow{w}) \approx \sum_{i=1}^{K} \frac{p(x_t, \overrightarrow{w}, \overrightarrow{w_i}) \Delta \varphi_i}{d_i^3}, \tag{6}$$

where d_i is calculated as the average of the different edge lengths of the bounding box in three dimensions.

The distribution of photons in participating media is relatively uniform, so the distribution of photons in each divided region is also relatively uniform. As the number of emitted photons increases, the division of the leaf region is gradually decreased, and then the more accurate the value of the internally scattered radiation obtained by sampling is.

5 Results

The experiments in this paper were run on the PC mitsuba renderer [19] with the following PC configuration: Intel (R) Core (TM) i9-9900K 3.60 GHz CPU, 64 G RAM, NVIDIA GeForce RTX 2080 Ti GPU and window10. There are four test scenes, including cbox, caustic, living-room1 and living-room2, all scenes in this paper are from one website [20] and all of which have an additional homogeneous participation medium in addition to the model itself.

The most intuitive representation of the medium in the experiment mainly contains two parameters—the absorption σ_a and scattering σ_s of light by the medium. The parameters set in different scenes are shown in Table 1.

Table 1. Parameter of absorption and scattering.

Scene	σ_s	σ_a
Cbox	0.8	0.1
Living room1	0.6	0.1
Caustic	0.8	0
Living room2	0.5	0

After determining the parameters of each scene, we rendering the scenes with different levels of photon emission using the traditional photon mapping algorithm and our method and recorded the plotting time. The time used is also recorded for comparison experiments. In Fig. 4, we compare the rendering results of our method with the conventional photon mapping algorithm at 250,000 photons, and it can be seen that with a certain number of emitted photons, the results of medium with less noise using our method.

Traditional photon mapping   The algorithm in this paper

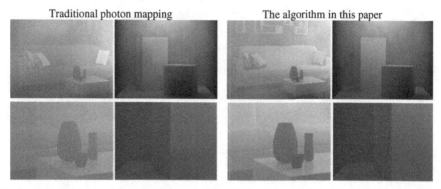

Fig. 4. We compare traditional photon mapping (left) with our method (right) in two different scenes with 250000 photons.

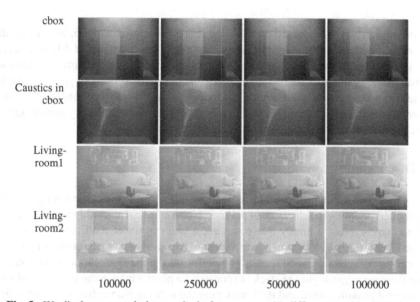

Fig. 5. We display our rendering results in four scenes with different number of photons.

The theoretical analysis in Sect. 3.2 shows that the increase in the number of photons is beneficial to improve the accuracy of our rendering method, so we set different number gradients for our experiments. Figure 5 correspond to the four scenes of cbox, caustic, living-room1 and living-room2 from top to bottom, respectively, and the number of photons in each scene increases from left to right, 100,000, 250,000, 500,000 and 1,000,000, respectively, which can be seen that as the number of photons increases, the drawing results are gradually optimized and some of the noise.

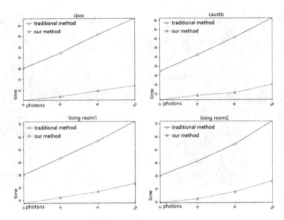

Fig. 6. Time for rendering different scene using our and traditional method.

In addition, we also counted the time, the results are shown in Fig. 6. We can see that our method outperforms the traditional photon mapping algorithm for different scenes and different numbers of photons. The blue lines indicate the drawing time of traditional photon mapping methods for different scenes and different numbers of photons, and the orange lines indicate the algorithm of this paper. It can be observed that the obviously better time efficiency of the algorithm in this paper than the traditional method, and the average performance of the algorithm is greater than 70%.

6 Discussion

In this paper, an efficient algorithm for rendering homogeneous participating media is proposed by adapting the structure of photons. The traditional algorithm for constructing photon map is to use a binary tree structure, which can traverse all the photons to be queried, but it takes a lot of time when a photon map storing a great number of photons. In contrast, our method can be seen as first performing some aggregation of photons and using these aggregated photon stacks to construct a photon map in the form of replacing the original photon points, and then managing them through an octree structure, which aims to reduce the height of the tree and uses spatially located sampling points to remove the backtracking process, making the efficiency of photons in the query phase improved. However, the method requires a homogeneous distribution of photons in the scene to better divide the box space and can reduce the complexity of the algorithm, so future work can improve the probability of uniform distribution of photons in the scene during the photon emission stage, so that our algorithm will have a more robustness.

References

1. Fong, J., Wrenninge, M., Kulla, C., Habel, R.: Production volume rendering: SIGGRAPH 2017 course (2017)
2. Novák, J., Georgiev, I., Hanika, J., Jarosz, W.: Monte Carlo methods for volumetric light transport simulation. J. Comput. Graph. Forum **37**(2), 551–576 (2018)

3. Jensen, H.: Global illumination using photon maps. In: Pueyo, X., Schröder, P. (eds) Rendering Techniques 1996. EGSR 1996. Eurographics, pp. 21–30. Springer, Vienna (1996). https://doi.org/10.1007/978-3-7091-7484-5_3

4. Jensen, H., Christensen, P.: Efficient simulation of light transport in scenes with participating media using photon maps, pp. 311–320 (1998)

5. Kajiya, J.: The rendering equation. Comput. Graph. **20**(4), 143–150 (1998)

6. Lafortune, E., Willems, Y.: Rendering participating media with bidirectional path tracing. In: Pueyo, X., Schröder, P. (eds) Rendering Techniques 1996. EGSR 1996. Eurographics, pp. 91–100. Springer, Vienna (1996). https://doi.org/10.1007/978-3-7091-7484-5_10

7. Christensen, P., Jarosz, W.: The path to path-traced movies. J. Found. Trends Comput. Graph. Vision. **10**(2), 103–175 (2016)

8. Pharr, M., Humphreys, G.: Physically Based Rendering: From Theory to Implementation. Morgan Kaufmann Publishers Inc., Burlington (2016)

9. Kang, C., Wang, L., Xu, Y., Meng, X.: A survey of photon mapping state-of-the-art research and future challenges. J. Front. Inf. Technol. Electron. Eng. **17**(3), 185–199 (2016)

10. Jarosz, W., Zwicker, M., Jensen, H.: The beam radiance estimate for volumetric photon mapping. C. Comput. Graph. Forum. **27**(2), 557–566 (2008)

11. Jarosz, W., Nowrouzezahrai, D., Sadeghi, I., Jensen, H.: A comprehensive theory of volumetric radiance estimation using photon points and beams. J. ACM Trans. Graph. **30**(1), 5 (2011)

12. Bitterli, B., Jarosz, W.: Beyond points and beams: higher-dimensional photon samples for volumetric light transport. J. ACM Trans. Graph. **36**(4), 1–2 (2017)

13. Deng, X., Jiao, S., Bitterli, B., Jarosz, W.: Photon surfaces for robust, unbiased volumetric density estimation. J. ACM Trans. Graph. **38**(4), 1–12 (2019)

14. Georgiev, I., Krivanek, J., Davidovic, T., Slusallek, P.: Light transport simulation with vertex connection and merging. J. ACM Trans. Graph. **31**(6), 192 (2012)

15. Krivánek, J., et al.: Unifying points, beams, and paths in volumetric light transport simulation. J. ACM Trans. Graph. **33**(4), 1–3 (2014)

16. Qin, H., Sun, X., Hou, Q., Guo, B., Zhou, K.: Unbiased photon gathering for light transport simulation. J. ACM Trans. Graph. **34**(6), 1–4 (2015)

17. Arvo, J., Kirk, D.: A survey of ray tracing acceleration techniques, pp. 201–262 (1990)

18. Popov, S., Georgiev, I., Dimov, R., Slusallek, P.: Object partitioning considered harmful: space subdivision for BVHs, pp. 15–22 (2009)

19. Mitsuba renderer. http://www.mitsuba-renderer.org

20. Rendering resources. https://benedikt-bitterli.me/resources/

Visualization and Visual Analysis
(Scientific Visualization, Information
Visualization and Visual Analysis.)

A Survey of Literature Analysis Methods Based on Representation Learning

Qinghui Zhang and Yi Chen[✉]

Beijing Key Laboratory of Big Data Technology for Food Safety, School of Computer Science and Engineering, Beijing Technology and Business University, Beijing 100048, China
chenyi@th.btbu.edu.cn

Abstract. The analysis of massive scientific literature collections can help researchers capture potential knowledge, understand disciplinary insights, and discover opportunities for academic collaboration. However, the huge volume of literature data becomes a major problem for human analysis and computer processing, which prevents scholars from rapidly obtaining disciplinary knowledge. Representation learning methods can effectively handle large-scale text and graph data, which have excelled in literature analysis tasks. In this study, we introduce the types of literature data and several typical academic networks. Then, we review the representation learning models and classify these methods into (a) word representation learning-based, including word2vec, GloVe, ELMo, Bert, etc.; (b) graph representation learning-based, including matrix factorization-based, random walk-based and deep learning-based methods, such as DeepWalk, node2vec, GCN, etc. Finally, we discuss the opportunities and present three challenges of representation learning-based approaches for literature analysis.

Keywords: Literature analysis · Representation learning · Bibliometrics

1 Introduction

With the advent of the Internet era, scientific literature data is becoming more and more available. The analysis of literature data can reveal the nature [1] and condition of the research object, which can help investigators form a general impression about the research object and facilitate a historical and dynamic grasp of the research object [2, 3]. Literature-based discovery [4] is a knowledge extraction technique that allows scientific discovery by connecting what already exists in the literature. Most of the methods involved in existing review studies are out-of-the-box literature analysis tools (e.g., CiteSpace [5], etc.) and some traditional data mining methods (e.g., TF-IDF [6], etc.), which are more suitable for small-scale data. However, scientific literature collections have the common "5V" characteristics, not only the large volume of data, complex data structure and many data items, which makes the above tools and methods unable to handle the problem effectively. Therefore, it is a great challenge to reveal the research context, objectives and impacts, the cooperation patterns of research subjects and the structure and evolution of disciplines from the huge amount of complex literature data.

© The Author(s), under exclusive license to Springer Nature Singapore Pte Ltd. 2022
Y. Wang et al. (Eds.): IGTA 2022, CCIS 1611, pp. 249–263, 2022.
https://doi.org/10.1007/978-981-19-5096-4_19

Existing methods of representation learning (RL) perform well in dealing with large amounts of complex unstructured data and provide great help in analyzing and mining literature data [7–9]. The method has become a prevailing trend to extract a large amount of effective information mining from massive results nowadays.

This paper reviews the RL-based literature analysis work in recent years, summarizes the data sources of this literature analysis work, divides the literature data into text data and relational data according to the features of literature data and puts forward a category of RL-based literature analysis methods. According to the data features, the RL-based literature analysis methods are divided into word representation learning-based and graph representation learning-based. Finally, the challenges of literature analysis and future research are put forward. This paper's overview is shown in Fig. 1.

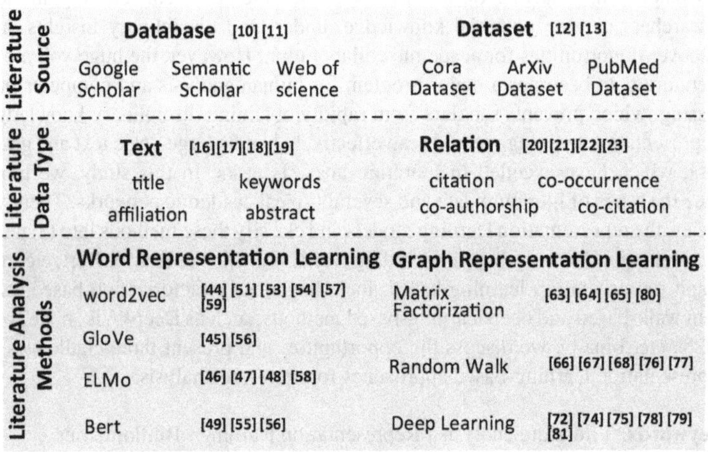

	Database [10] [11]			Dataset [12] [13]		
Literature Source	Google Scholar	Semantic Scholar	Web of science	Cora Dataset	ArXiv Dataset	PubMed Dataset
Literature Data Type	**Text** [16][17][18][19]			**Relation** [20][21][22][23]		
	title	keywords		citation	co-occurrence	
	affiliation	abstract		co-authorship	co-citation	
Literature Analysis Methods	**Word Representation Learning**			**Graph Representation Learning**		
	word2vec	[44] [51] [53] [54] [57] [59]		Matrix Factorization	[63] [64] [65] [80]	
	GloVe	[45] [56]				
	ELMo	[46] [47] [48] [58]		Random Walk	[66] [67] [68] [76] [77]	
	Bert	[49] [55] [56]		Deep Learning	[72] [74] [75] [78] [79] [81]	

Fig. 1. An overview of literature analysis research based on representation learning.

2 Sources and Type of Literature Data

2.1 Sources of Literature Data

Understanding the knowledge of a subject needs a lot of literature. The developed Internet has brought us facilities for accessing literature and literature is available from a wide range of sources. The common sources of literature data mainly include the following aspects:

(1) **Literature database** [10]. In addition to the popular databases such as *Web of Science, Elsevier, IEEEXplore, Semantic Scholar, Google Scholar*, etc., each country also has its own database platform, such as the Chinese *CNKI*, German academic search engine *Base*, etc. Williams et al. launched the digital library and academic literature search engine CiteSeerχ [11] integrates the massive literature data on the network and carries out data processing such as automatic extraction, clustering,

entity linkage and person name disambiguation. Researchers can filter and access literature metadata and publications from these off-the-shelf tools.

(2) **Literature dataset.** In the field of machine learning, the effect of an evaluation model often needs to be tested by a variety of public data sets [12] to compare a variety of indicators. For example, the commonly used dataset *Cora* [13] is one of the most commonly used literature citation network datasets. Its nodes are papers and its edges are the citation relationships between papers, as well as node types and label characteristics. In addition, there are public data sets for *ArXiv, PubMed, WebKb, Citeseer, Vispubdata* and *KGG* competitions. Compared with the literature metadata obtained from academic search engines, the open datasets are formatted. The open datasets are often used in tasks such as topic modeling, prediction, or node classification.

2.2 Types of Literature Data

With the flourishing of scientific research, more and more research results have emerged in various disciplines and at the same time, many interdisciplinary and new fields have emerged, which has led to the massive growth of scientific literature. Literature data is the record of these research results, including information about articles, authors, citation relationships, publication channels, etc. Analyzing the massive amounts of literature data can not only show the development of each discipline and help scholars understand the development trend of their fields, but also evaluate the academic achievements of authors to plan a more appropriate development path for themselves [14, 15]. According to literature analysis tasks, the literature data consists mainly of textual and relational data.

Textual Data: The most important component of literature data is text data, which contains a large amount of technical information, knowledge and potential value [16]. Using statistics, data mining, machine learning, deep learning and other means [17, 18] to extract valuable information from text data helps researchers fully understand the laws of technological evolution, research status and future development trends in relevant fields and effectively avoid the risk of infringement while avoiding blind research [19]. The text data in the literature data mainly includes title, abstract, figure title, figure title, keyword, publisher, etc. The analysis of literature text data can not only accelerate the speed of knowledge dissemination, facilitate the innovation of knowledge and promote academic research, but also help to implement the practical benefits of academic research on the ground.

Relational Data: In terms of academic benefit, information networks are an important form of expression of information. Effective and reasonable data analysis of complex information networks is a hot topic in academic research [20–22]. Mining the relationship between literatures is one of the main topics in academic research [23]. These relationships mainly include the relationships between papers, words [24], authors and so on. They are not only of great importance to the academic community of academic evaluators and the sound development of national science and technology and the improvement of original innovation capability, but also closely related to the personal interests of researchers in terms of entry, promotion of titles and acquisition of grants and awards. The exploration of this graph data can assist researchers in understanding potential connections between literature and insights. Literature relational data can mainly form co-occurrence networks, co-citation networks, citation networks and co-authorship networks. The following are details of several typical academic networks.

(1) **Citation network**: Citations in scientific papers constitute complex citation networks [25, 26] that have received a lot of attention in application areas such as retrieving similar topics, recommending high-impact authors, high-impact papers and predicting the number of authors and citations of papers. Rosvall [27] uses random walk to analyze citation networks, exploring the distribution of research knowledge in journals and mining the relationship between the topics of published papers across journals. By using citation networks, Lu et al. [28] propose a time-cost-compressed method for recommending authors and papers. CiteRivers [29] provides a new user-friendly model for researchers to comprehend citation patterns and mining trends. The potential relationships in citation networks help in information retrieval, finding similar topics, high level papers and providing innovative points.

(2) **Co-occurrence network**: It is a common approach for using word co-occurrence to establish the relevance of scientific terms [30]. It simulates relationships between text sources based on words contained in context (e.g., documents, paragraphs, sentences, etc.), as well as relationships between words within and across contexts, reflecting relationships between words that are similar. Interesting connections between keywords may also stimulate new research ideas. Benito-santos et al. [31] propose to use bag-of-words technique (BoW) to capture co-occurrence network knowledge and discovers the works of other authors in the field. As can be seen, co-occurrence networks can help researchers not only to extract similar topics, but also to explore collaboration between interdisciplinary communities and experts.

(3) **Co-authorship network**: Successful publications often require the collaboration of several researchers, thus creating a data structure of connections and collaborations that can help in the analysis, i.e., a co-authorship network [32]. Y. Li et al. [33] define six evaluation metrics for co-authorship networks to translate co-author information into cognitive capital to measure the impact of an author. Existing studies [34, 35] use random walk, neural network and visualization techniques to recommend potential collaborators, discover novel topics and predict potential collaborations.

(4) **Co-citation network**: Co-citation network is often used in information retrieval [36]. The citation relationship of a document reflects that the research directions or research topics are closely related to each other. The co-citation relationship exists between a pair of documents cited by a third document and the more frequently the two documents are co-cited, the stronger the correlation between their academic research directions. For co-citation networks, existing studies [37–39] use techniques such as logistic regression and graph embedding to achieve information retrieval, topic modeling and link prediction of documents.

3 RL-Based Literature Analysis Methods

As the volume of literature data has increased in recent years, earlier manual methods have become increasingly difficult to satisfy the work of literature analysis. The word RL-based method is a dimensionality reduction method that can embed massive text data into a vector of finite dimensionality. Such vectors can embed high-dimensional document data features into the latent space, transforming the similarity problem of documents, topics, and collaborations into the similarity problem of the embedding vectors. Thus, a large number of word RL-based methods [40] are used to automate the knowledge discovery process.

3.1 Word RL-Based Literature Analysis Methods

With the advent of the Internet era, scientific literature data is becoming increasingly available and the hundreds of references usually included in a literature survey require advanced models for effective analysis. Among these, textual data is a type of data that takes up fewer resources and has greater information meaning. The calculation of natural language similarity helps to determine the search for relevant documents. The most fundamental problem of natural speech processing is text representation, i.e., representing text in a form that can be parsed by a computer, with the uniqueness of text and its semantic information. Text representation is divided into word RL, sentence representation, paragraph representation and document representation. Different granularities of text representation have different focuses, but the commonality is that they all need to represent the semantic features of text to the maximum extent.

It is the mainstream research direction to use deep learning and neural networks to solve Natural Language Processing (NLP) problems [41]. The development of neural networks can be traced back to the early 19th century, but due to the limitations of models and computational power, neural networks at that time could only handle simple linear problems. With the continuous updating of technology and the gradual increase of machine computing power, neural network models with deep learning have been realized. Deep learning mainly refers to enhancing the computational depth of the model in the neural network model to better fit the model by increasing the computational power. The advent of deep learning has enabled neural networks to work better. Bridging neural network models into NPL can improve the effectiveness of text representation. In recent years, scholars have focused on neural network-based word representation learning models for specific tasks in NLP [42], such as sentiment analysis, topic extraction and automatic summarization. The underlying input forms for these tasks are inseparable from their textual feature representation.

Typical Word RL Models. Word RL models take advantage of the excellent learning capabilities of deep learning and are widely used for language modeling and feature learning. The models transform words in natural language into computable dense vectors, i.e., in the form of word embedding vectors, which convert text from a high-dimensional original feature space to a low-dimensional vector space, facilitating the use of computers to mine features between words and sentences in text. Word embedding is a method to associate words with real vectors. The characteristics of various word representation learning models are shown in Table 1. Earlier **one-hot** models constructed word vectors that lacked potential correlation between them, were independent of each other and were prone to dimensional disasters when the corpus had too many words. In 2003, Bengio et al. [43] proposed the NNLM (neural network language model), a framework for building statistical language models using neural networks and introduced the concept of word embedding, which uses a multilayer neural network to predict the next word given a representation of words and documents in a low-dimensional vector space. In 2013, Mikolov et al. [44] drew attention to **word2vec**, an approach that captures not only grammatical correctness but also semantic features. While word2vec only considers the local information of the word and does not consider the connection between the word and words outside the local window, **GloVe** (Global Vectors for Word Representation) makes use of co-occurrence matrices and considers both the local information and the overall information [45]. Word2vec and GloVe have the problem that the vector representation of words in different contexts is the same for both models. Then, **ELMo** (Embeddings from Language Models) [46] is put forward to address this point so that the model can learn the complex properties of word usage and the variations of these complex usages in different contexts. However, ELMo uses the LSTM Transformer [47]. There are two main problems with sequential models like LSTM, one is that it is unidirectional. Even **BiLSTM** [48] only does a simple summation at loss, which means it does inference sequentially and there is no way to consider the data in the other direction; second is that it is a sequential model, it has to wait for the previous step to finish the computation before it can compute the next step and the ability of parallel computation is poor. **Bert** (Bidirectional Encoder Representation from Transformers) [49] not only combines the Transformer structure but also changes the game of NLP completely. Traditional NLPs have four major categories of tasks, including sequence annotation, classification, sentence relation judgment, generative tasks. Bert has designed simple downstream interfaces for the first three tasks, eliminating the need for complex network structures. It has achieved substantial improvements in the overall experimental results. Thus, Bert can create contextualized word embeddings, which generate word RL that are closely related to the words around a word. Table 1 shows the commonly used word RL models, which involves the advantages, disadvantages and references. It can be seen that word2vec is the most popular model to be applied in NLP, which is due to word2vec's adaptation to universal data and tasks.

Application. In some recent studies, word representation models have been applied to the field of document analysis [50]. Deep natural language models are used to have outstanding achievements in extracting topic information, cross-domain disciplinary understanding, literature similarity retrieval, and disambiguation of domain ambiguity. Zhang et al. [51] apply word2vec and Doc2vec models to quantitatively represent the content of patent science citations. Then, they use clustering methods to analyze the scientific and technical topics of patent science citation content for association. Sun et al. [52] use representation learning model to analyze the association of patents at the semantic level, which compares the similarities and differences between the scientific citation themes of patents in China and the U.S. In addition, similarity-based word RL methods can help with information retrieval and knowledge inference. The previous

Table 1. The advantages and disadvantages of typical word RL models.

Model	Advantage	Disadvantage	Reference
word2vec	Capturing the grammar by bag-of-words (BoW)	Missing global information and context information	[44, 51, 53, 54, 57, 59]
GloVe	Using co-occurrence matrix to assemble local and overall text information	Missing context information	[45, 56]
ELMo	Getting the complex features of word usage and its variation in different contexts by using LSTM	The model is unidirectional and have poor parallel computing capability	[46–48, 58]
Bert	Attention mechanism is added; Better solution for information extraction of long sequences	Multiple parameters	[49, 55, 56]

TF-IDF and LDA, can perform similarity matching and topic modeling problems, but it has problems such as low efficiency and many parameters. The pre-trained Transformer structure similarity matching, topic modeling and paper classification have been successful in tasks. Wang et al. [53] mapped the corresponding keywords to a low-dimensional vector space by word2vec. The keyword vectors are used to calculate the magnitude of the relationship between keywords and obtain quantitative keyword co-occurrence relationships. Extracting potential interdisciplinary cross-knowledge and interdisciplinary keyword co-occurrence relationships provides a new research idea to explore interdisciplinary knowledge discovery methods and to discover potential interdisciplinary growth. Kanakia et al. [54] implemented a paper recommendation system and processed incomplete citation information based on word2vec for Microsoft Academic Graph (MAG), alleviating the cold-start problem. Narechania et al. [55] use a combination of Transformer self-supervised pre-training on academic abstracts, SPECTER, to embed visual domain literature and improve the performance of tasks such as academic literature recommendation and topic classification. Tu et al. [56] design a transformer-based based fine-tuning method for neural networks that directs attention to learning domain-specific lexical relations and uses these keys to construct new word networks. This approach focuses on the importance of words when propagating information in the network. Tshitoyan et al. [57] propose a method for extracting knowledge and relationships from a large amount of scientific literature, which uses word2vec for mining potential knowledge in scientific literature, effectively encoded as information-intensive word embeddings and eventually from materials science literature finds that potential knowledge about the future relies heavily on past publications. Sun et al. [58] use Bi-LSTM to extract words from biochemical literature data that have the key role in the field. Chen et al. [59] use Semantic word RL to understand the impact of situational variations of words in the scientific domain on facilitating interdisciplinary communication. Currently, these applications of word RL models provide a convenient tool for understanding large-scale textual data, greatly reducing costs and improving efficiency.

3.2 Graph RL-Based Literature Analysis Methods

The scholarly network [60] is a network system composed of association relationships in literature data, which reflects the temporal and spatial change relationships and logical structural relationships in literature data. The nodes in academic networks can be different papers, authors, countries, regions, institutions, journals, disciplines, subject terms and keywords, etc. Literature graph data has a complex structure, diverse attribute types and multi-level learning tasks. Hence, an efficient graph data representation method [61] is required to take full advantage of graph data. This essentially corresponds to a nonlinear structure of graph data due to intrinsic associations. This non-linear structure complements the data and, at the same time, it poses a great challenge for learning the data. Therefore, Similar to the important position of word RL methods in text analysis, graph RL models have become a very popular research topic in the field of graph learning.

Typical Graph RL Models. Graph representation models embed nodes into a low-dimensional vector space and maximize the preservation of the original network topology and its properties, aiming to complete various graph mining tasks [8]. Graph data not only contains complex network structures, but also includes diverse node features. For different networks and application scenarios, the embedding space is needed to preserve the network structure, labels, symbols [62] and other information. The graph RL methods are classified into three types: matrix factorization-based [63–65], random walk-based [66–68] and deep learning-based [69–71]. Among them, **DeepWalk** [66] samples node sequences by performing truncated random walks on the network. It uses Skip-Gram for training to learn representation vectors by maximizing the probability within a certain window. **LINE** [67] designs objective functions for first-order similarity and second-order similarity of the network, respectively. The first-order and second-order vector representations are learned by optimizing the objective function and finally the two are combined as the final representation vector. These methods can well aggregate the structural information of the graph. Graph RL models based on deep learning, graph neural network [72] is a very powerful model for graph data, which can easily aggregate the graph's feature and structural information. These two-dimensional representations can preserve the relative proximity of nodes in the graph even without any training. After **GCN** was proposed [73], many deep graph RL models have appeared, such as **GraphSAGE** [74], **GAT** [75], etc. There are the graph RL models' category, typical graph RL models, characteristics of each type and their references in the Table 2.

Application. Graph representation models can perform potential machine learning tasks, such as node classification, link prediction, community detection, subgraph similarity detection, etc. Paper classification, similar topic paper retrieval and matching, reference link prediction and etc., can be achieved by computing the similarity between

Table 2. The category of typical graph RL models.

Category	Typical model	Characteristic	Reference
Matrix factorization	Odd matrix Non-negative matrix Random odd matrix	Treating topological relations as high-dimensional sparse matrices	[63–65, 80]
Random walk	DeepWalk node2vec LINE	Topological relations are obtained by random walk	[66–68, 76, 77]
Deep learning	GCN GraphSAGE GAT	Aggregating node features and structural features at the same time	[72, 74, 75, 78, 79, 81]

embedding vectors. The emergence of Paper2vec [76] makes it possible to measure the similarity of papers by distributed representations learned from the citation context of papers. The success of graph representation learning techniques for network embedding has promoted more academic network analysis and mining techniques based on graph representation learning. Ganesh et al. apply DeepWalk to co-author networks and propose Author2vec [77], which combines author information and co-author relationships, making authors with similar content and sharing similar network structures in the embedding space. Qin et al. [78] propose E-GCN, which learns the appropriate network topology for semi-supervised learning by connecting estimated labels and given labels in a centralized network framework. Jeong et al. [79] combine the advantages of GCN and Bert for perceiving context to construct a document encoder and a context encoder to improve the accuracy of citation recommendation. Wu et al. [80] design a metric function for co-citation network information and proposed a higher-order similarity preserving network embedding model that can preserve asymmetric transferability well. Yadati et al. [81] make HyperGCN applied to hypergraphs such as co-authored networks and co-citation networks. The method makes an outstanding contribution to solving real literature data. Hamioton et al. [74] proposed GraphSAGE to generate node embeddings for paper classification tasks. In conclusion, the graph RL models provide effective methods for the analysis of massive literature relational data and greatly improve the efficiency of mining domain knowledge.

4 Opportunity and Challenge

With the rapid increase in the number of published papers, exploring the massive amount of academic data not only shows the development of each discipline and helps scholars understand the development trend of their fields, but also allows them to evaluate the authors' academic achievements to plan a more appropriate development path for themselves. The emergence of text mining and the rise of graph mining techniques has made deep learning techniques more and more widely used in downstream tasks of literature analysis, solving the problems of topic clustering, paper classification, knowledge extraction, literature information retrieval and recommending academic collaboration opportunities in the context of big data.

Opportunities. Many current studies [82] have outstanding contributions in textual and web data analysis of literature and more and more studies express interest in text mining and contextual scenario mining. Currently, knowledge graph-based literature analysis methods [83] are prominent in literature analysis and these methods provide new channels for the organic integration of textual information and related structural information.

Challenges. The existing RL applications to mine and analyze literature data currently suffers from the following problems in general:

(1) The data, RL-based methods used, are often already cleaned, which have perfect attribute features for easy computer processing, but realistic literature data are often unlabeled such as topics. In particular, the knowledge graph is composed of tri-ads, such that standard literature data is difficult to obtain, which will be a major challenge in solving literature analysis problems.
(2) Although powerful RL methods can process literature data efficiently, RL methods are black-box and we can only observe the validity of their results through qualitative metrics and quantitative visual views, but whether the embedding vectors have learned the original graph features is unconvincing.
(3) Most of the literature knowledge analyzed by existing representation learning methods is limited, mostly to information retrieval, paper classification, link prediction, etc. Therefore, this paper does not provide a detailed classification of the downstream tasks of representation learning. This is due to the fact that much of the existing research uses literature datasets to test the models after improving the representation learning methods rather than looking at the deficiencies of the literature analysis tasks to find realistic solutions to the problems. These issues will be the direction of future research to be considered.

5   Conclusion

This paper surveys recent advances in representation learning techniques in a literature analysis. From the perspective of large-scale literature data analysis, the sources of literature data are counted. According to the characteristics of literature data, complex literature data is divided into two types: textual data and relational data. Textual data is mainly divided into the study of words, sentences and paragraphs, while relational data is often constructed into a network for analysis. Based on a comprehensive analysis of the characteristics of literature data and existing research on representation learning, we divide the representation learning methods applied to literature analysis into word RL-based literature analysis methods and graph RL-based literature analysis methods. RL-based literature analysis methods are sorted out. Finally, the opportunities and challenges of RL-based literature analysis methods are presented. We hope that this survey can provide an overview of the research on representation learning methods for literature analysis, help to understand the state-of-the-art in this field and provide guidance for future research.

Acknowledgments. This work is supported by the National Natural Science Foundation of China (61972010); National Key R&D program of China (2018YFC1603602).

References

1. Zhang, C., Li, Z., Zhang, J.: A survey on visualization for scientific literature topics. J. Vis. **21**(2), 321–335 (2017). https://doi.org/10.1007/s12650-017-0462-2
2. Federico, P., Heimerl, F., Koch, S., Miksch, S.: A survey on visual approaches for analyzing scientific literature and patents. IEEE Trans. Vis. Comput. Graph. **23**, 2179–2198 (2016)
3. Onwuegbuzie, A.J., Leech, N.L., Collins, K.M.T.: Qualitative analysis techniques for the review of the literature. Qual. Rep. **17**, 56 (2012)
4. Thilakaratne, M., Falkner, K., Atapattu, T.: A systematic review on literature-based discovery: general overview, methodology, & statistical analysis. ACM Comput. Surv. **52**, 1–34 (2019)
5. Chen, C.: CiteSpace II: detecting and visualizing emerging trends and transient patterns in scientific literature. J. Am. Soc. Inform. Sci. Technol. **57**, 359–377 (2006)
6. Yetisgen-Yildiz, M., Pratt, W.: Using statistical and knowledge-based approaches for literature-based discovery. J. Biomed. Inform. **39**, 600–611 (2006)
7. Chen, F., Wang, Y.C., Wang, B., Kuo, C.C.J.: Graph representation learning: a survey. APSIPA Trans. Signal Inf. Process. **9**, e15 (2020)
8. Gao, J., Li, D., He, X., Wang, Y.Y., Duh, K., Liu, X.: Representation Learning Using Multi-Task Deep Neural Networks. US20170032035A1 (2017)
9. Bengio, Y., Courville, A., Vincent, P.: Representation learning: a review and new perspectives. IEEE Trans. Pattern Anal. Mach. Intell. **35**, 1798–1828 (2013)
10. Jacso, P.: Academic search engines: a quantitative outlook. Online Information Review (2000)
11. Williams, K., Jian, W., Choudhury, S.R., Khabsa, M., Giles, C.L.: Scholarly big data information extraction and integration in the CiteSeerχ digital library. In: IEEE International Conference on Data Engineering Workshops. IEEE (2017)
12. London, B., Getoor, L.: Collective classification of network data. Data Classif. Algorithms Appl. 399–416 (2014)
13. Cecile, C., Antoine, G., Karina, V.S., Mathieu, H., Pierre-Yves, L.T.: The CORA dataset: validation and diagnostics of in-situ ocean temperature and salinity measurements. Ocean Sci. **9**(special issue: The MyOcean project: scientific advances for operational ocean monitoring and forecasting), 1–18 (2013)
14. Annarelli, A., Battistella, C., Nonino, F., Parida, V., Pessot, E.: Literature review on digitalization capabilities: co-citation analysis of antecedents, conceptualization and consequences. Technol. Forecast. Soc. Chang. **166**, 120635 (2021)
15. Hausberg, J.P., Korreck, S.: Business incubators and accelerators: a co-citation analysis-based, systematic literature review. In: Handbook of Research on Business and Technology Incubation and Acceleration (2021)
16. Liu, S., et al.: Bridging text visualization and mining: a task-driven survey. IEEE Trans. Vis. Comput. Graph. **25**, 2482–2504 (2019)
17. Kevork, E.K., Vrechopoulos, A.P.: CRM literature: conceptual and functional insights by keyword analysis. Mark. Intell. Plan. **1**(1), 48–55 (2019)
18. Siddiqi, S., Sharan, A.: Keyword and keyphrase extraction techniques: a literature review. Int. J. Comput. Appl. **109** (2015)
19. Gopalakrishnan, V., Jha, K., Xun, G., Ngo, H.Q., Zhang, A.: Towards self-learning based hypotheses generation in biomedical text domain. Bioinformatics **34**, 2103–2115 (2018)

20. Chen, Y., Lv, C., Li, Y., Chen, W., Ma, K.-L.: Ordered matrix representation supporting the visual analysis of associated data. Science China Inf. Sci. **63**(8), 1–3 (2020). https://doi.org/10.1007/s11432-019-2647-3

21. Chen, Y., Sun, M., Wu, C., Sun, X.: Visual associative analysis of big data in food safety: a review. Big Data Res. **7**, 61–77 (2021)

22. Du, X., Chen, Y., Li, Y.: TransGraph: a transformation-based graph for analyzing relations in data set. J. Comput.-Aided Des. Comput. Graph. **30**, 79–89 (2018)

23. Chen, Y.: A survey on visualization approaches for exploring association relationships in graph data. J. Vis. **22**, 625–639 (2019)

24. Radhakrishnan, S., Erbis, S., Isaacs, J.A., Kamarthi, S.: Novel keyword co-occurrence network-based methods to foster systematic reviews of scientific literature. PLoS ONE **12**, e0172778 (2017)

25. Butun, E., Kaya, M.: Predicting citation count of scientists as a link prediction problem. IEEE Trans. Cybern. **50**, 4518–4529 (2020)

26. Choe, K., Jung, S., Park, S., Hong, H., Seo, J.: Papers101: supporting the discovery process in the literature review workflow for novice researchers. In: IEEE Pacific Visualization Symposium, pp. 176–180 (2021)

27. Rosvall, M., Bergstrom, C.T.: Maps of random walks on complex networks reveal community structure. Proc. Nat. Acad. Sci. USA **105**, 1118–1123 (2008)

28. Lu, M., Qu, Z., Wang, M., Qin, Z.: Recommending authors and papers based on ACTTM community and bilayer citation network. China Commun. **15**, 111–130 (2018)

29. Heimerl, F., Han, Q., Koch, S., Ertl, T.: CiteRivers: visual analytics of citation patterns. IEEE Trans. Vis. Comput. Graph. **22**, 190–199 (2016)

30. Li, H., An, H., Wang, Y., Huang, J., Gao, X.: Evolutionary features of academic articles co-keyword network and keywords co-occurrence network: based on two-mode affiliation network. Physica A **450**, 657–669 (2016)

31. Benito-Santos, A., Sanchez, R.T.: Cross-domain visual exploration of academic corpora via the latent meaning of user-authored keywords. IEEE Access **7**, 98144–98160 (2019)

32. Abdelaal, M., Heimerl, F., Koch, S.: ColTop: visual topic-based analysis of scientific community structure. In: 2017 International Symposium on Big Data Visual Analytics, BDVA 2017 (2017)

33. Li, E.Y., Liao, C.H., Yen, H.R.: Co-authorship networks and research impact: a social capital perspective. Res. Policy **42**, 1515–1530 (2013)

34. Park, I., Yoon, B.: Technological opportunity discovery for technological convergence based on the prediction of technology knowledge flow in a citation network. J. Informetr. **12**, 1199–1222 (2018)

35. Érdi, P., et al.: Prediction of emerging technologies based on analysis of the US patent citation network. Scientometrics **95**, 225–242 (2013)

36. Eto, M.: Extended co-citation search: Graph-based document retrieval on a co-citation network containing citation context information. Inf. Process. Manag. **56**, 102046 (2019)

37. Shiau, W.L., Dwivedi, Y.K., Yang, H.S.: Co-citation and cluster analyses of extant literature on social networks. Int. J. Inf. Manag. **37**, 390–399 (2017)

38. Shin, H., Perdue, R.R.: Self-service technology research: a bibliometric co-citation visualization analysis. Int. J. Hosp. Manag. **80**, 101–112 (2019)

39. Verma, S., Bhattacharyya, S.S.: The intellectual core and structure of mergers and acquisitions literature: a co-citation analysis. Int. J. Bus. Innov. Res. **20**, 305–336 (2019)

40. Chen, J., Gong, Z., Wang, W., Wang, C., Liu, W.: Adversarial caching training: unsupervised inductive network representation learning on large-scale graphs. IEEE Trans. Neural Netw. Learn. Syst. **2021**, 1–12 (2021)

41. Wu, S., et al.: Deep learning in clinical natural language processing: a methodical review. J. Am. Med. Inform. Assoc. **27**(3), 457–470 (2020)

42. Gysel, C.V., Rijke, M.D., Kanoulas, E.: Neural vector spaces for unsupervised information retrieval. ACM Trans. Inf. Syst. (TOIS) **36**(4), 1–25 (2017)
43. Bengio, Y., Ducharme, R., Vincent, P.: A neural probabilistic language model. In: Advances in Neural Information Processing Systems, vol. 13, pp. 1–7 (2003)
44. Mikolov, T., Sutskever, I., Chen, K.: Distributed representations of words and phrases and their compositionality. In: The 26th International Conference on Neural Information Processing Systems, pp. 3111–3119. ACM Press, New York (2013)
45. Pennington, J., Socher, R., Manning, C.D.: GloVe: global vectors for word representation. In: Proceedings of the 2014 Conference on Empirical Methods in Natural Language Processing, pp. 1532–1543 (2014)
46. Peters, M., Neumann, M., Iyyer, M., Gardner, M., Zettlemoyer, L.: Deep contextualized word representations (2018)
47. Vaswani, A., et al.: Attention is all you need. In: Advances in Neural Information Processing Systems, vol. 30 (2017)
48. Xu, G., Meng, Y., Qiu, X., Yu, Z., Wu, X.: Sentiment analysis of comment texts based on BiLSTM. IEEE Access **7**, 51522–51532 (2019)
49. Devlin, J., Chang, M.W., Lee, K., Toutanova, K.: Bert: pre-training of deep bidirectional transformers for language understanding. arXiv preprint arXiv:1810.04805 (2018)
50. Tafti, A.P., Wang, Y., Shen, F., Sagheb, E., Kingsbury, P., Liu, H.: Integrating word embedding neural networks with PubMed abstracts to extract keyword proximity of chronic diseases. In: 2019 IEEE EMBS International Conference on Biomedical and Health Informatics (BHI), pp. 1–4 (2019)
51. Zhang, J., Wan, Y., Hu, Y.: Analyzing sci-tech topics based on semantic representation of patent references. Data Anal. Knowl. Discov. **3**, 52–60 (2019)
52. Sun, X., Chen, N.: Analysis of Patent Science Relevance Based on Representation Learning, vol. 41, pp. 10–18 (2021)
53. Wang, W., Yao, C., Qiao, Z., Cui, W., Du, Y., Zhou, Y.: Method of discovering interdisciplinary knowledge of the national natural science foundation of China based on word embedding: a case study on artificial intelligence and information management. J. China Soc. Sci. Tech. Inf. **40**, 15 (2021)
54. Kanakia, A., Shen, Z., Eide, D., Wang, K.: A scalable hybrid research paper recommender system for Microsoft academic. In: WWW (2019)
55. Narechania, A., Karduni, A., Wesslen, R., Wall, E.: VITALITY: promoting serendipitous discovery of academic literature with transformers & visual analytics. IEEE Trans. Visual Comput. Graphics **28**, 486–496 (2021)
56. Tu, Y., Xu, J., Shen, H.W.: KeywordMap: attention-based visual exploration for keyword analysis. In: 2021 IEEE 14th Pacific Visualization Symposium (PacificVis), pp. 206–215 (2021)
57. Tshitoyan, V., et al.: Unsupervised word embeddings capture latent knowledge from materials science literature. Nature **571**, 95–98 (2019)
58. Sun, C., et al.: A deep learning approach with deep contextualized word representations for chemical–protein interaction extraction from biomedical literature. IEEE Access **7**, 151034–151046 (2019)
59. Chen, B., Ding, Y., Ma, F.: Semantic word shifts in a scientific domain. Scientometrics **117**(1), 211–226 (2018). https://doi.org/10.1007/s11192-018-2843-2
60. Yun, J.: Generalization of bibliographic coupling and co-citation using the node split network. arXiv preprint arXiv:2110.15513 (2021)
61. Hu, A., Chen, H.: Data visualization analysis of knowledge graph application. In: 2021 2nd International Conference on Artificial Intelligence and Information Systems, pp. 1–10 (2021)

62. Ribeiro, L.F., Saverese, P.H., Figueiredo, D.R.: struc2vec: learning node representations from structural identity. In: Proceedings of the 23rd ACM SIGKDD International Conference on Knowledge Discovery and Data Mining, pp. 385–394 (2017)
63. Wang, X., Cui, P., Wang, J., Pei, J., Zhu, W., Yang, S.: Community preserving network embedding. In: Thirty-First AAAI Conference on Artificial Intelligence (2017)
64. Tu, C., Zhang, W., Liu, Z., Sun, M.: Max-margin deepwalk: discriminative learning of network representation. In: IJCAI, vol. 2016, pp. 3889–3895 (2016)
65. Zhang, D., Yin, J., Zhu, X., Zhang, C.: Collective classification via discriminative matrix factorization on sparsely labeled networks. In: Proceedings of the 25th ACM International on Conference on Information and Knowledge Management, pp. 1563–1572 (2016)
66. Perozzi, B., Al-Rfou, R., Skiena, S.: Deepwalk: online learning of social representations. In: Proceedings of the 20th ACM SIGKDD International Conference on Knowledge Discovery and Data Mining, pp. 701–710 (2014)
67. Tang, J., Qu, M., Wang, M., Zhang, M., Yan, J. Mei, Q.: Line: large-scale information network embedding. In: Proceedings of the 24th International Conference on World Wide Web, pp. 1067–1077 (2015)
68. Grover, A., Leskovec, J.: node2vec: scalable feature learning for networks. In: Proceedings of the 22nd ACM SIGKDD International Conference on Knowledge Discovery and Data Mining, pp. 855–864 (2016)
69. Wang, D., Cui, P., Zhu, W.: Structural deep network embedding. In: Proceedings of the 22nd ACM SIGKDD International Conference on Knowledge Discovery and Data Mining, pp. 1225–1234 (2016)
70. Gu, Y., Sun, Y., Li, Y., Yang, Y.: Rare: social rank regulated large-scale network embedding. In: Proceedings of the 2018 World Wide Web Conference, pp. 359–368 (2018)
71. Dong, Y., Chawla, N.V. Swami, A.: metapath2vec: scalable representation learning for heterogeneous networks. In: Proceedings of the 23rd ACM SIGKDD International Conference on Knowledge Discovery and Data Mining, pp. 135–144 (2017)
72. Gallicchio, C., Micheli, A.: Fast and deep graph neural networks. In: Proceedings of the AAAI Conference on Artificial Intelligence, vol. 34, pp. 3898–3905 (2020)
73. Kipf, T. N., Welling, M.: Semi-supervised classification with graph convolutional networks. arXiv preprint arXiv:1609.02907 (2016)
74. Hamilton, W., Ying, Z., Leskovec, J.: Inductive representation learning on large graphs. In: Advances in Neural Information Processing Systems, vol. 30 (2017)
75. Veličković, P., Cucurull, G., Casanova, A., Romero, A., Lio, P., Bengio, Y.: Graph attention networks. arXiv preprint arXiv:1710.10903 (2017)
76. Tian, H., Zhuo, H. H.: Paper2vec: citation-context based document distributed representation for scholar recommendation. arXiv preprint arXiv:1703.06587 (2017)
77. Ganesh, J., Ganguly, S., Gupta, M., Varma, V., Pudi, V.: Author2vec: learning author representations by combining content and link information. In: WWW (Companion Volume) (2016)
78. Qin, J., Zeng, X., Wu, S., Tang, E.: E-GCN: graph convolution with estimated labels. Appl. Intell. 51(7), 5007–5015 (2021). https://doi.org/10.1007/s10489-020-02093-5
79. Jeong, C., Jang, S., Park, E., Choi, S.: A context-aware citation recommendation model with BERT and graph convolutional networks. Scientometrics 124(3), 1907–1922 (2020). https://doi.org/10.1007/s11192-020-03561-y
80. Wu, Y., Wang, B., Cui, Y., Tong, X.: Study on co-citation enhancing directed network embedding. Comput. Sci. 47, 279–284 (2020)
81. Yadati, N., Nimishakavi, M., Yadav, P., Nitin, V., Louis, A., Talukdar, P.: Hypergcn: a new method for training graph convolutional networks on hypergraphs. In: Advances in Neural Information Processing Systems, vol. 32 (2019)

82. Ganesh, J., Gupta, M., Varma, V.: Doc2Sent2Vec: a novel two-phase approach for learning document representation. In: SIGIR, pp. 809–812 (2016)
83. Agarwal, V., Joglekar, S., Young, A.P., Sastry, N.: GraphNLI: A Graph-based Natural Language Inference Model for Polarity Prediction in Online Debates. arXiv preprint arXiv:2202. 08175 (2022)

Applications of Image and Graphics (Image/Video Processing and Transmission, Biomedical Engineering Applications, Information Security, Digital Watermarking, Text Processing and Transmission, Remote Sensing, Telemetering, etc.)

A MobileNet SSDLite Model with Improved FPN for Forest Fire Detection

Yulei An, Jialin Tang, and Yongfeng Li[✉]

Beijing Institute of Technology, No. 6 Jinfeng Road, Tangjiawan, Zhuhai, GuangDong, China
{an_yl,01068,18139}@bitzh.edu.cn

Abstract. In recent years, the number and intensity of forest fires have been increasing due to climate change, causing great ecological and property losses. The recent advances in deep learning and object detection have made it possible to use efficient models to detection forest fires. To further improve the detection speed and accuracy of early forest fires, the deep learning-based methods are increasingly adopted. Considering the detection speed and accuracy, the MobileNet SSD model has a good performance. However, it does not perform well when detecting small objects, such as fire in the initial stage. To enhance the model's detection performance for small objects, we proposed an improved feature pyramid network. To achieve real-time speed, replace SSD (Single Shot MultiBox Detector) with SSDLite, forming a MobileNetV2_SSDLite_FPN model. The experimental results indicate that this model achieves 89.7% mean Average Precision (mAP), 2.3 MB parameters, and 0.013 s average running time on our fire dataset.

Keywords: Forest fire detection · SSDLite · MobileNet · Feature pyramid network

1 Introduction

Forest fires are becoming a global problem due to global warming. Forest fires bring serious economic and ecological losses and endanger human life. In March 2019, a forest fire occurred in Liangshan, Sichuan, China, killed 30 people. In 2020, a forest fire broke out in Australia, which burned for more than 210 days. The fire killed about 3 billion animals. Firefighters did their best but Australia still suffered heavy losses. Since 2020, the area devastated by wildfires in California has exceeded 1 million hectares, and more than 3700 buildings have been destroyed. The earlier a fire is detected, the better it is for reducing the damage caused by the fire. As a result, there are many studies and papers on early fire detection. Forest fires detection methods can generally be divided into two categories [1–7], one is based on flame and smoke sensors, and the other is based on image and video processing. Sensor-based fire detection methods have the following drawbacks: First, the fire must be large enough to trigger the sensor to send a warning signal, thus the best time to put out the fire will be lost. Second, these sensors are difficult to function in outdoor spaces such as forests and grasslands.

Nowadays, CCTV surveillance systems with cameras are ubiquitous, and drones with cameras are becoming more and more popular, and fire detection approaches based

Y. Wang et al. (Eds.): IGTA 2022, CCIS 1611, pp. 267–276, 2022.
https://doi.org/10.1007/978-981-19-5096-4_20

on image and video processing will have good application prospects. There are two main categories of fire detection methods based on image and video processing. One based on traditional image features such as shape, color, and texture [5–8]. The features extracted based on traditional target detection methods are more intuitive, easier to understand, and have certain pertinence. For forest fire, may have large differences in shape, color, texture etc. Therefore, traditional methods lead to unsatisfactory results. For example, when detecting by color features, sunsets, lanterns, and other similarly colored objects can be misjudged as flames.

In 2012, Alex Krizhevsky used deep convolutional neural network [9] (CNN) to classify 1.2 million high-resolution images in the ImageNet LSVRC-2010 contest, and won the championship. Since then, various convolutional neural network-based target detection models have emerged. Approaches based on deep learning have their own unique advantages in solving these kinds of problems. Deep learning models can extract features that contain much deeper semantic information than traditional approaches, therefore the detection accuracy is higher. Zhang et al. [10] compared different deep learning models, and they found that SSD was better than Faster R-CNN as well as Yolo in terms of detection accuracy and efficiency. Kim et al. [11] used Faster R-CNN, combined with long short-term memory (LSTM) for detecting fires and improving the reliability of detection results. Lee, Y [12] proposed a fire detection model, which employed Faster R-CNN to locating fire areas in images. But this method is not satisfactory in terms of detection speed. Wu et al. [13] proposed a fire detection method that combines deep learning model and principal component analysis (PCA), and the combination of the two models improves the positioning accuracy of fire areas. Squeeze Net can detect, locate, and semantically interpret an image of fire at the same time. Muhammad [14] proposed a CNN model derived from the Squeeze Net and make use of it for fire detection. Peng et al. [15] proposed a real-time forest smoke detection approaches using hand-designed features combined with deep learning. To summary, there have been many study achievements in forest fire detection, but there is still a need for faster, more accurate, and more lightweight models.

2 Related Works

In the past few years, new detection models have been proposed to solve the detection speed problem of R-CNN and its successors and to improve real-time detection performance. The most famous ones are YOLO [16] (You Only Look Once) and SSD [17] MultiBox (Single Shot Detector). Due to its good detection accuracy and fast detection speed, the SSD model has been widely concerned by researchers. SSD adopts multi-scale convolutional layers to extract feature maps and combined with default boxes for detection. Using the features extracted by different convolutional layers, SSD can detect objects of different sizes in an image. However, the SSD model is built on the VGG-16 [18] architecture, which suffers from a massive number of parameters and a large storage space occupation, and the real-time performance of the detection is not good enough. The lightweight model SSDLite [19] is obtained by replacing the regular convolution in the SSD model with the depthwise separable convolution. Table 1 shows the comparison of SSD and SSDLite in terms of number of parameters and volume.

Table 1. Comparison of SSD and SSDLite in terms of number of parameters and volume.

Model	Billion Mult-adds	Million parameters
SSD	1.25	14.8
SSDLite	0.35	2.1

There are no regular convolutional layers in the MobileNet [20] model, instead depthwise separable convolutional layers, combined with SSDLite, reduces the amount of computation and model size, and greatly improves the detection speed. MobileNet V2 [19] is an improved version of MobileNet network. Compared with MobileNet V1, MobileNet V2 adds a residual structure to the network and removes part of ReLU, thereby preserving feature diversity, making full use of feature information, and improving accuracy. In this paper, MobileNet V2 is used as the basic network structure of our model. The basic structure of a MobileNet SSD is depicted in Fig. 1. It consists of two modules: a MobileNet V2 CNN model for extracting features from input images, and an SSD, using full convolution, for region-of-interest (ROI).

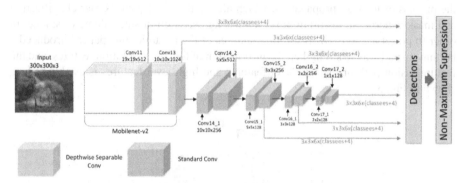

Fig. 1. MobileNet SSD structure

FPN [21] is used to fuse features of different scales. Experiments show that combining FPN with Fast R-CNN and RPN respectively can improve the detection accuracy, especially for small-scale objects [22]. The feature pyramid network connects high level features with low level features through top-down trajectory, which makes it semantically strong at all scales, as shown in Fig. 2. It is very important that introducing FPN into the backbone network does not degrade the performance of the network.

Fig. 2. FPN approach

3 Our Method

3.1 Improved Feature Pyramid Network

Figure 2 depicts the inner working of the FPN at a high level. The bottom-up path is the encoding part where the image is converted to a low-resolution feature map. For the decoding part, the feature map combines these low-resolution feature map that has semantically strong features, with the previously upsampled image that has the semantically low features.

Due to the long fusion path between the low-resolution features and the high-resolution of the pyramid network, the bottom feature information is seriously lost in the process of forward propagation, which affects the subsequent border classification and mask generation, resulting in some missing detection of small flame or smoke. In order to preserve more low-resolution features of the pyramid, this paper introduced a bottom-up pathway to strengthen the information of the low-resolution features, and the feature fusion path of the low level features and high level features is established, as shown in Fig. 3.

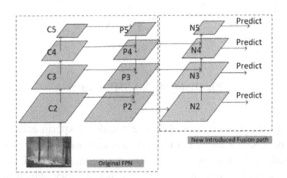

Fig. 3. Improved feature pyramid network, the dashed box on the right is the newly introduced fusion path

As shown in Fig. 3, the original FPN outputs P2, P3, P4 and P5 feature map layers, and this paper introduced new layers N2, N3, N4, and N5, where N2 is P2. While N3, N4 and N5 layers mainly include the features of their respective layers, they also merge the high-level features and low-level features to form a new pyramid structure. The newly introduced fusion operations are shown in Fig. 4. The operation to generate N3, N4 and N5 is shown in Eq. 1, where K represents the convolution kernel.

$$\begin{cases} N_2 = P_2 \\ N_{i+1} = (N_i \otimes K_{size=3}^{stride=2} + P_{i+1}) \otimes K_{size=3}^{stride=1} \end{cases} \tag{1}$$

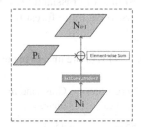

Fig. 4. Feature fusion operations

3.2 MobileNet_SSDLite with FPN

Our approach is based on MobileNet SSDLite because it is accurate and fast. On top of that we added the improved feature pyramid network to improve the ability to detect small fires. This is shown in Fig. 5. There are two parts of our model, MobileNet SSDLite and the FPN with and the newly introduced feature fusion path. In order to improve the detection ability of small fires, we selected the sixth convolutional layer, which contains shallow features, also selected the 12th and 13th convolutional layers to construct the FPN, in addition, other convolutional layers are also used.

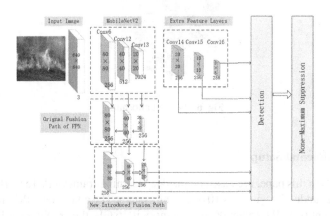

Fig. 5. The structure of our model

4 Evaluation

4.1 Dataset

For fire detection methods based on deep learning, an important issue is to have enough samples to improve the generalization ability of the model. One of the datasets provided by Salim Said AL-Ghadani et al. [23] contains 8982 fire images. We eliminated the part of the images that were not forest fires or grassland fires. We also extracted frames from fire videos and used web crawlers to get more forest fire images (Table 2).

Table 2. Details of fire images in our dataset

Dataset	Forest fire images	Grassland fire images	Total
Our fire dataset	8534	4523	13,057

The training data were divided into training and validation sets, which accounted for 84.2% and 7.9% of the total images respectively. In total, there are training set, validation set and test set. We used 84.2% of the total images as training set, and the remainder of the images are divided equally into 2 parts, one for the test set and one for the evaluation set, as shown in Fig. 6. Some of the images in our dataset are shown in Fig. 7.

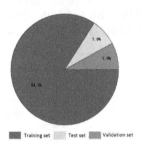

Training set   Test set   Validation set

Fig. 6. Dataset allocation

4.2 Experimental Setup

The methods in this paper are based on the deep learning framework TensorFlow, which is carried out under the windows 10 operating system. The computer CPU model used in the experiment is AMD R5 5600G, the memory is 16 GB, the graphics card is NVIDIA GTX1070 with 8G video memory. The basic parameter settings for training are shown in Table 3.

Fig. 7. Some of the images in the dataset

Table 3. Setting of training parameters

Terms	Value
epochs	250
bach_size	32
optimizer	SGD
momentum	0.99
learning rate	10^{-5}

4.3 Evaluation index

In this section, we designed experiments to evaluate our model and compare it with MoblileNet SSD. Typically, the mean accuracy (mAP) is used as a standard measure of object detector performance. We need the following metrics shown in Table 4 to obtain the mAP. The mAP is obtained with Eq. 2 where the AP is calculated from all classes and M is the number of classes. In addition, we have evaluated the real-time performance of the model for detecting forest fires through the FPS (Frames Per Second).

$$mAP = \frac{1}{M} \sum_{i=0,1} AP_i \qquad (2)$$

4.4 Experimental Results

We evaluated the proposed method and MobileNet SSD using the same dataset, and the results show that the proposed model can reach 89.1% of the mAP, which is better than the 76.8% result of MobileNet SSD. In terms of detection speed, the FPS value of the proposed model is 75, which is also better than MobileNet SSD's result of 31. Wang [24] used YOLOv4 to detect fires and both mAP and FPS lagged behind with our method. Table 5 shows the comparison of the accuracy and speed of these three models.

We specifically selected pictures with relatively small fires to evaluate our model's ability to detect small fires and compared it to the MobileNet SSD model. As shown in

Table 4. Metrics for evaluating object detection models

Terms	Short	Description
True positives	TP	Number of correctly proposed predictions
False negatives	FN	Number of missed predictions
False positives	FP	Number of falsely proposed predictions
Recall	R	R = TP/(TP + FN)
Precision	P	P = TP/(TP + FP)
Average precision	AP	Area Under the Precision-Recall Curve

Table 5. Differences in speed and accuracy between the three models

Models	mAP	FPS
YOLOv4	82.5	21
MobileNet SSD	76.8	31
Ours	89.1	75

Fig. 8, the right images are the detection results of MobileNet SSD, and the left images are the detection results of our approach. The approach in this paper has a better detection effect on small fires.

Fig. 8. Comparison of detection results (left: results of our method, right: results of MobileNet SSD)

5 Conclusion

This paper constructs a dataset for forest fire detection and proposed a forest fire detection method based on MobileNet SSDLite with an improved FPN. The newly introduced bottom-up feature fusion path enhances the model's ability to detect small fires. Experiments results show that our approach has improved in terms of detect speed and accuracy compared to MobileNet SSD. Next, we plan to test images of larger size and will validate the accuracy and real-time performance of our algorithms on an embedded platform.

Acknowledgements. This work was supported by Provincial Key Platforms and Major Research Projects of Universities in Guangdong Province under No. 2021ZDZX3012 and 2021KTSCX187. The authors gratefully acknowledge all these supports.

References

1. Fonollosa, J., Solórzano, A., Jiménez-Soto, J.M., Oller-Moreno, S., Marco, S.: Gas sensor array for reliable fire detection. Proc. Eng. **168**, 444–447 (2016). ISSN 1877–7058, https://doi.org/10.1016/j.proeng.2016.11.540
2. Lee, K., Shim, Y.-S., Song, Y., Han, S., Lee, Y.-S., Kang, C.-Y.: Highly sensitive sensors based on metal-oxide nanocolumns for fire detection. Sensors **17**(2), 303 (2017)
3. Sowah, R.A., Ofoli, A.R., Krakani, S.N., Fiawoo, S.Y.: Hardware design and web-based communication modules of a real-time multisensor fire detection and notification system using fuzzy logic. IEEE Trans. Ind. App. **53**(1), 559–566 (2017)
4. Kr Kruger, S., Despinasse, M.C., Raspe, T., Kai, N., Moritz, W.: Early fire detection: are hydrogen sensors able to detect pyrolysis of household materials. Fire Safety J. **91**, 1059–1067 (2017)
5. Çelik, T., Özkaramanlı, H., Demirel, H.: Fire and smoke detection without sensors: image processing based approach. In: 15th European Signal Processing Conference (EUSIPCO 2007), 3–7 September 2007
6. Seebamrungsat, J., Praising, S., Riyamongkol, P.: Fire detection in the buildings using image processing. In: Proceedings of the 2014 Third ICT International Student Project Conference (ICT-ISPC), pp. 95–98, IEEE, Bangkok, Thailand, March 2014
7. Foggia, P., Saggese, A., Vento, M.: Real-time fire detection for video-surveillance applications using a combination of experts based on color, shape, and motion. IEEE Trans. Circuits Syst. Video Technol. **25**(9), 1545–1556 (2015)
8. Bi, F., Fu, X., Chen, W., Fang, W., Miao, X.: Fire detection method based on improved fruit fly optimization-based SVM. Comput. Mater. Cont. **62**(1), 199–216 (2020)
9. Krizhevsky, A., Sutskever, I., Hinton, G.E.: ImageNet classification with deep convolutional neural networks. In: Pereira, F., Burges, C.J.C., Bottou, L., Weinberger, K.Q. (eds.) Advances in Neural Information Processing Systems 25, pp. 1097–1105. Curran Associates Inc., Red Hook (2012)
10. Wu S., Zhang L.: Using popular object detection methods for real time forest fire detection. In Proceedings of the 11th International Symposium on Computational Intelligence and Design (ISCID 2018), Hangzhou, China, 8–9 December 2018; pp. 280–284
11. Kim, B., Lee, J.: A video-based fire detection using deep learning models. Appl. Sci. **9**, 2862 (2019)

12. Lee, Y., Shim, J.: False positive decremented research for fire and smoke detection in surveillance camera using spatial and temporal features based on deep learning. Electronics **8**(10), 1167 (2019). https://doi.org/10.3390/electronics8101167

13. Wu, S., Guo, C., Yang, J.: Using PCA and one-stage detectors for real-time forest fire detection. J. Eng. **2020**, 383–387 (2020)

14. Muhammad, K., Ahmad, J., Lv, Z., Bellavista, P., Yang, P., Baik, S.W.: Efficient deep CNN-based fire detection and localization in video surveillance applications. IEEE Trans. Syst. Man Cybern. Syst. **49**(7), 1419–1434 (2019). https://doi.org/10.1109/TSMC.2018.2830099

15. Peng, Y., Wang, Y.: Real-time forest smoke detection using hand-designed features and deep learning. Comput. Electron. Agric. **167**, 105029 (2019). ISSN 0168–1699, https://doi.org/10.1016/j.compag.2019.105029

16. Redmon, J., Divvala, S., Girshick, R., Farhadi, A.: You only look once: unified, real-time object detection. In Proceedings of the IEEE Conference on Computer Vision and Pattern Recognition, pp. 779–788 (2016)

17. Liu, W., Anguelov, D., Erhan, D., Szegedy, C., Reed, S., Cheng-Yang, F., Berg, A.C.: SSD: single shot multibox detector. In: Leibe, B., Matas, J., Sebe, N., Welling, M. (eds.) Computer Vision – ECCV 2016. LNCS, vol. 9905, pp. 21–37. Springer, Cham (2016). https://doi.org/10.1007/978-3-319-46448-0_2

18. Simonyan, K., Zisserman, A.: Very Deep Convolutional Networks for Large-Scale Image Recognition. CoRR, abs/1409.1556

19. Sandler, M., Howard, A., Zhu, M., Zhmoginov, A., Chen, L.-C.: MobileNetV2: inverted residuals and linear bottlenecks. In: 2018 IEEE/CVF Conference on Computer Vision and Pattern Recognition, pp. 4510–4520 (2018). https://doi.org/10.1109/CVPR.2018.00474

20. Howard, A.G., et al.: MobileNets: Efficient convolutional neural networks for mobile vision applications. arXiv preprint arXiv:1704.04861 (2017)

21. Lin, T.-Y., Dollár, P., Girshick, R., He, K., Hariharan, B., Belongie, S.: Feature pyramid networks for object detection. In: Proceedings of the IEEE Conference on Computer Vision and Pattern Recognition, pp. 2117–2125 (2017)

22. Li, Q., Lin, Y., He, W.: SSD7-FFAM: a real-time object detection network friendly to embedded devices from scratch. Appl. Sci. **11**, 1096 (2021)

23. AL-Ghadani, S.S., Jayakumari, C.: Innovating fire detection system fire using artificial intelligence by image processing. Int. J. Innov. Technol. Explor. Eng. (IJITEE) **9**(11) (2020). ISSN: 2278–3075

24. Wang, G.: Fire detection method based on transformer improved YOLO v4. Intell. Comput. App. **11**(7), 86–90 (2021)

Applications of Photogrammetry and Remote Sensing Technologies in Tianwen-1 Mission

Jia Wang[1], Guolin Hu[1], Xiaofeng Cui[1], Ziqing Cheng[1(✉)], Shaoran Liu[1],
Zuoyu Zhang[1], Shaojin Han[1], Qian Xu[1], Zhao Huang[1], Sheng Gou[2],
and Wenhui Wan[2(✉)]

[1] Beijing Areospace Control Center, Beijing 100094, China
masterhgl@sina.com, cuixf@pku.org.cn, yzlunehlzu@163.com
[2] State Key Laboratory of Remote Sensing Science, Aerospace Information Research Institute,
Chinese Academy of Sciences, Beijing 100101, China
gousheng@aircas.ac.cn, wanwh@radi.ac.cn

Abstract. Tianwen-1 represents China's first effort to explore Mars. The developed technologies of interest include orbiter image mapping based on a strict geometric model, lander localization based on a two-step method, and telepresence reconstruction based on multi-source data. These technologies have been developed to directly support day to day operations of the Zhurong rover. This paper presents a brief overview of the applications of photogrammetry and remote sensing technologies in the Tianwen-1 mission. To provide context for the analysis and interpretation of the in situ measurements, the basis of this study is the use of available multi-source remote sensing data to demonstrate the analysis of Martian geomorphic characteristics within 60 km^2 of the landing area. Combining the scientific payloads of the orbiter and rover, the comprehensive exploration of the landing area in terms of morphology, mineralogy, stratigraphy, and climatology will greatly promote understanding of the geological evolution of the largest impact basin on Mars, Utopia Planitia, in the planetary science community.

Keywords: Tianwen-1 · Zhurong rover · Landing site · Photogrammetry · Remote sensing · Detection

1 Introduction

China's first Mars exploration mission, Tianwen-1, was launched from Wenchang Space Launch Site in the Hainan Province on July 23, 2020 [1]. On February 24, 2021, the probe successfully entered Mars parking orbit by applying near-Mars braking [2]. On May 15, 2021, the probe implemented "entry, descent and landing" (EDL) successfully landed in the candidate landing area in the south of Utopia Planitia [3, 4], and released the Zhurong rover on the same day. On June 12, 2021, the National Space Administration held a press conference to announce the success of the Tianwen-1 mission in terms of orbiting, landing, and patrolling Mars. These achievements were not only indicative of China's scientific and engineering capabilities, but also its entry into the advanced ranks of the field of planetary exploration [5].

© The Author(s), under exclusive license to Springer Nature Singapore Pte Ltd. 2022
Y. Wang et al. (Eds.): IGTA 2022, CCIS 1611, pp. 277–291, 2022.
https://doi.org/10.1007/978-981-19-5096-4_21

After having gone through key stages (i.e., Mars capture, separation, landing, and patrol), the Tianwen-1 probe has now reached the final remote sensing detection stage [6]. Using the near-Mars drift caused by orbit perturbation, the orbiter will conduct a global and comprehensive remote sensing exploration of Mars. At the same time, the probe will continuously provide communication services for the Zhurong rover [7]. Under the guidance of remote sensing survey, the Zhurong rover has always maintained an efficient mobile detection mode [4]. Together with the orbiter, it collects high accuracy scientific data with different perceptual scales for five main scientific targets [8].

Photogrammetry and remote sensing technology have been developed and applied to topographic mapping, rover positioning, mineral retrieval and other fields, which have greatly supported the engineering implementation and scientific research of the Tianwen-1 mission.

2 Tianwen-1 Landing Site and Data

2.1 Landing Site

For selection of the landing site, safety concerns and scientific interests were taken into account [4]. Before the launch of Tianwen-1, two preselected landing areas with large scope and important research value were preliminarily selected according to engineering constraints [9–11] (Fig. 1a). These areas were selected after thorough evaluation of slope, rock distribution, thermal environment, and feasibility of establishing and maintaining a stable communication channel with Earth. Once all these considerations were made, the preliminarily selected areas in the southern Utopia Planitia and the western Elysium Mons were finally classified as primary and alternative candidate landing areas, respectively (with an area of 150×60 km^2) [4] (Fig. 1b). Three months before the Zhurong rover landed on Mars, the Tianwen-1 orbiter conducted detailed remote sensing of the primary candidate landing area via the High Resolution Imaging Camera (HiRIC). On the basis of these data, the primary candidate landing area was further reduced to an ellipse of 56×22 km^2 [4]; and on May 15, 2021, the Zhurong rover successfully landed in this area (red box in Fig. 1b).

Figure 2 shows topographic features surrounding the landing site of Tianwen-1 (20 km radius). On the 200 m scale, the overall terrain of the landing area is high in the south and low in the north, with an elevation of -4119 ± 54 m and a slope of $0.4 \pm 0.5°$ (Fig. 2b). The terrain of the landing area is gentle, making it ideal for the Zhurong rover to easily conduct follow-up inspections and explorations.

2.2 Data

While the Tianwen-1 probe was in the parking orbit, it performed detailed remote sensing imaging of the pre-selected landing area by means of multi orbit in a linear sweep mode with HiRIC [4, 12]. The high-resolution digital orthophoto map (DOM) and digital elevation model (DEM) of the landing area were then produced and provisioned by Key Laboratory of Lunar and Deep Space Exploration, National Astronomical Observatories, Chinese Academy of Sciences.

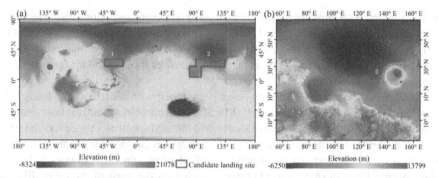

Fig. 1. Preselected landing areas of Tianwen-1 mission. Base image from MOLA DEM (http://astrogeology.usgs.gov/search/details/Mars/GlobalSurveyor/MOLA/Mars_MGS_MOLA_DEM_mosaic_global_463m). (a) Two wide-range candidate landing areas of China's Mars Exploration Mission. (b) The primary and the alternative landing area are presented by red and green boxes respectively, and they correspond to the area marked 2 in Fig. 1a.

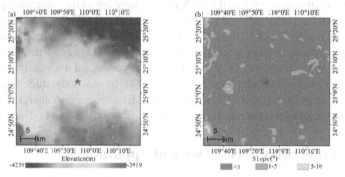

Fig. 2. Topographic features within 20 km of the landing site of the Zhurong rover (marked by the red star): (a) elevation; (b) slope. (Color figure online)

The lander's Guidance Navigation and Control (GNC) system has an optical sensor, named Descent Camera, which is mounted close to the bottom edge of the lander platform. It has a field of view (FOV) of 58° and an image size of 2048 × 2048 pixels [12]. It is deployed for imaging landing area during the EDL phase. The first received single descent image, captured at a height of about 80 m estimated by the lander's GNC system, has a very limited coverage area and a much higher ground resolution comparing with the orbiter image, which led to great difficulties in direct image matching to conduct localization [12, 13]. Other descent images were sent back to the ground control station throughout the relay of the orbiter for 10 days after the first descent image was downlinked.

Binocular Navigation Terrain Cameras (NaTeCam) were installed on the mast of the Zhurong rover, which can rotate in the yaw and pitch directions. Two pairs of hazard avoidance cameras (HazCams) were attached to the front and rear of the rover [14], and fisheye lenses were used to provide a larger FOV for the front and rear wheel areas respectively. Before launch, the internal parameters and installation parameters of

NaTeCams and HazCams are accurately calibrated on the ground. Along the traverse, the rover obtains stereo NaTeCams and HazCams images at every waypoints and acquires 360° panorama NaTeCams images at some waypoints. These stereo images have been routinely used in detailed topographic mapping and rover localization to support ground teleoperation task planning.

Besides NaTeCams, the Zhurong rover is equipped with other five playloads [11]. Mars Surface Composition Detector (MarSCoDe), combining active laser-induced breakdown spectroscopy with passive short wave infrared spectroscopy, covers the spectrum from visible light to medium wave infrared, which can provide scientific data for the species, content and spatial distribution of Martian mineral resources [11]. The Multispectral Camera (MSCam) [11] was installed on the mast of the rover, like the NaTeCams. It can obtain high-resolution multispectral images of the surface of Mars in the visible and near-infrared bands, and provide information about the morphological characteristics and material type distribution of the landing area.

We also used the background camera (CTX) and high resolution imaging science experiment (HiRISE) images carried by Mars Reconnaissance Orbiter (MRO). After years of cumulative observation, the CTX images have basically completed global coverage. Dickson [14] et al. produced and released the global CTX mosaic image of Mars with a spatial resolution of 5 m/pixel. HiRISE can obtain high-definition images with a width of approximately 6 km, a length of approximately 60 km and a resolution of up to 0.25 m/pixel at an orbital height of 300 km [15]. It conducted high-definition imaging of the landing area of Tianwen-1 on June 6, 2021 [4]. In this study, three sets of remote sensing images (from the HiRIC, CTX and HiRISE) were used to analyze and present the topographic and geomorphic characteristics of the landing area of Tianwen-1.

3 Photogrammetry Technology and Applications

3.1 Landing Site Mapping Using Orbiter Images Based on Rigorous Geometric Model

In the parking orbit, the Tianwen-1 orbiter used the HiRIC to image the primary candidate landing area (the red rectangular in Fig. 1b) 21 times [4]. Each image has a width of ~11 km in the east-west and 170 km in north-south direction [4]. These data realized multiview stereo coverage of the 150×60 km^2 primary candidate landing area [4].

First, a rigorous geometric model of HiRIC image was established based on the geometric calibration parameters and orientation parameters of the Tianwen-1 orbiter, including its position and attitude. Then, the images within the whole candidate landing area are partitioned, and the images in each partition were adjusted to solve the geometric deviation between the images in the partition and the geometric inconsistency between the image and the control data [16]. During this period, CTX image and MRO Mars Orbiter Laster Altimeter (MOLA) terrain data were used as the control points of plane and elevation respectively [4]. On this basis, the orthophoto correction and image mosaic of the images in the partition were completed. Owing to the resolution limitation of the reference source, some positional inconsistencies of the DOM mosaics between neighboring subareas persisted. Therefore, a thin plate function (TPS) model-based image registration was applied to the generated DOM mosaics of each subarea.

Finally, a seamless DOM product of the entire candidate landing area was generated via mosaicking [16].

Key Laboratory of Lunar and Deep Space Exploration, National Astronomical Observatories, Chinese Academy of Sciences used these data to produce and provision the DEM and DOM of the primary candidate landing area. The DOM and DEM, having a resolution of 0.7 m/pixel and 3.5 m/pixel respectively [4]. According to the photogrammetric adjustment results, the standard deviation (s.d.) of the horizontal dimension of the preselected landing area topographic data is dimension 0.4 m, and the s.d. of the elevation dimension is dimension 1.0 m [4]. The topographic data played an important role in the high precision localization of the landing site, the environmental assessment of geological science in the landing area, the analysis of topographic and geomorphic characteristics and the subsequent plan for movement of the Zhurong rover.

3.2 Lander Localization Based on a Two-Step Method

Combined with the characteristics of the Tianwen-1 mission, the visual localization of the lander based on multi-source images (including HiRIC images, descent camera images and NaTeCam images) was adopted to realize the localization of the lander in two steps, coarse, then fine [12, 13].

First, the 12 images captured atop of landing platform by the left NaTeCam were used to generate a 360° panorama with image stitching. In the panorama, the peaks and discontinues of the skyline were considered as candidate landmarks to be identified and matched in the orbiter DOM. The image coordinates of landmarks in original NaTeCam images were obtained using the stitching transformation parameters. The azimuth angle of each landmark was calculated with the EOPs of the NaTeCam images and the collinearity equation. However, owing to the great difference in observation directions, it was very challenging to match the corresponding landmarks between orbiter DOM and NaTeCam panorama. An image simulation system was introduced to generate simulated NaTeCam images at multiple view angles. The simulated images facilitated verification of the identities of the corresponding landmarks [12].

To obtain the azimuth angles of the landmarks with respect to the lander, the image points of identified landmarks in panorama were converted to the points in the original NaTeCam images using the transformation parameters of image stitching. The exterior orientation parameters (EOPs) of each NaTeCam image in local landing site coordinate system were obtained with the rover orientation and 3 joint rotations of rover mast. Using the simulated images for verification, the corresponding landmarks in the orbiter DOM were identified to obtain the geographic coordinates of landmarks [12, 13].

Guided by the rough positioning results, 4 descent images without plume effects are selected for image matching, and they are registered with the HiRIC DOM, as shown in Fig. 3a. To further refine the localization results, the NaTeCam DOM was matched with the landing image [12], as shown in Fig. 3b. On June 6th 2021, HiRISE released the image of the landing area of the Tianwen-1 [17], and our lander localization results were verified by comparison (Fig. 3c).

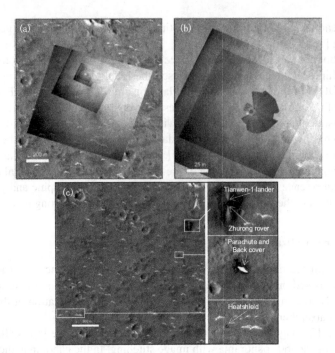

Fig. 3. Localization results and verification based on image matching methods. (a) Image matching among the sequential descent images and the HiRIC DOM [12]. (b) Triangulation, descent image matching, and NaTeCam DOM matching based localization results, represented as the green, yellow and red points, respectively [12]. (c) Orbital image with the visibility of the lander and Zhurong rover. (Color figure online)

3.3   Telepresence Reconstruction Based on Multi-source Data

Given the limited tracking, telemetry, and command (TT&C) resources of the mission along with the complex and changeable environment of the Mars surface and the large communication delay [18], the Zhurong rover adopted a control mode combining "ground teleoperation planning + semi autonomy on board" [13]. The ground teleoperation center completed the telepresence reconstruction and working-status assessment based on the rover images and telemetry data, which were the basis and premise for the implementation of the teleoperation plan for the next sol day [19]. The technical process steps are illustrated in Fig. 4.

Because of the extremely limited number of information transmission channels in the Tianwen-1 mission, the Zhurong rover adopts a set of schemes, using a field programmable gate array with a digital signal process block to compress the image [14, 20]. Therefore, the ground teleoperation center began by pre-processing the compressed stream (as shown in the blue box in Fig. 4). Then, detailed topographic mapping and rover localization were performed using rover images through photogrammetry techniques of feature extraction and matching, bundle block adjustment (BA), dense matching, 3D point cloud generation, DEM interpolation, image ortho-rectification, etc.

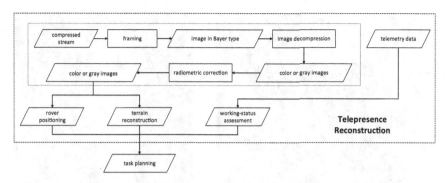

Fig. 4. Telepresence reconstruction based on multi-source data.

After the "release and separation" were completed, the Zhurong rover began to work with greater mobility [8]. By adopting the relay movement mode of "blind walking + autonomous obstacle avoidance", the daily moving mileage was expanded from 10 m to about 20 m [13]. In order to precisely localize the rover, we adopted a combination of "on-board autonomy + ground correction" [13]. The latter mainly relied on the ground engineers using visual positioning: continuous cross-site relative localization based on the BA. During the period, absolute localization, based on the matching of the NaTeCam DOMs and the HiRIC or HiRISE DOMs, was used to regularly correct the cumulative error of the relative localization [13, 21]. Visual positioning was completed in a near real-time manner, which could provide more accurate positioning results.

As of the first 100 sols, the accumulated mileage of the rover exceeds 1 km [22], and all stations have been continuously located using the BA method, as shown in Fig. 5a [13]. At some sites, the rover captured 360° panorama, and we obtained absolute localization (as shown in the red mark in Fig. 5b). It can be seen that the corrected localization of the rover is almost completely consistent with the tracing rut. The visual positioning method based on multi-source images has been successfully applied to the localization of the Zhurong rover. The high-precision positioning results effectively ensure the safe and efficient movement of the Mars rover on the Mars surface [13].

Local DEMs and DOMs with 0.02 m/pixel were routinely generated using NaTeCam images at each waypoint by the ground teleoperation engineers. In the blind spot caused by using the topographic data derived from NaTeCam images, the images of the front HazCam will also be used for detailed topographic analysis, ensuring safe and efficient traversing on the rugged Mars surface.

The Zhurong rover, is a six-wheeled, solar-powered robot with rocker-bogie suspension [8]. When moving, it has various modes of movement, making it versatile across various terrain [25]. One of these modes is known as crabbing and it enables the rover to move laterally; this configuration is achieved by turning the steering wheels by 90°. Creeping mode is also available for overcoming surface depressions and steep slopes. This mode is realized by decreasing or increasing the angle of main rocker arm, coordinated with the movement of other wheels. This range of modes greatly enhanced the rover's mobility. At the same time, in order to maximize the inspection and exploration results of the designed 90-sol primary mission, a relay movement mode is used to

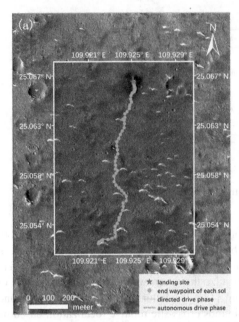
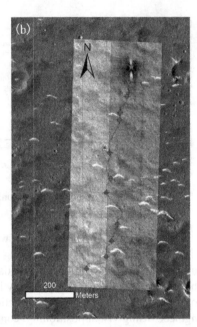

Fig. 5. The path of the Zhurong rover for the first 100 sols. The base map is HiRISE [23]. (a) The routing path of the Zhurong rover, the green dots represent the end waypoints on each sol based on BA. (b) The image matching and rectification between NaTeCam DOMs and HiRISE DOM, where the red marks represent the position of the absolute correction, and the small picture in the middle is the track of the Zhurong rover acquired by HiRIC onboard the Tianwen-1 orbiter [24]. (Color figure online)

increase the potential mileage of each sols. Because slippage was a prominent problem encountered by the rover during traversal and exploration, the ground engineers will carefully compare the ruts of the rear HazCam images after each movement, to evaluate the completion of the movement [19].

4   Remote Sensing Technology and Applications

4.1   Geomorphic Features of the Landing Zoom

Using available remote sensing images (including images from CTX and HiRISE) and related terrain products, this study analyzed the geological characteristics within the 75 × 60 km² landing area of the Tianwen-1 mission. At least five geomorphic features within the landing area have been preliminarily identified (Fig. 6).

(1) Impact Crater

The most remarkable feature of the Tianwen-1 landing area is that it contains various types of impact craters. In the northwest of the landing area, there are not only indistinguishable ghost craters, but also a large number of secondary craters. These secondary impact craters are mainly distributed in a chain running northwest to southeast, indicating that the impact direction of the original impact crater may be northwest to southeast [2]. In addition, there are two distinct rampart craters at the north and south

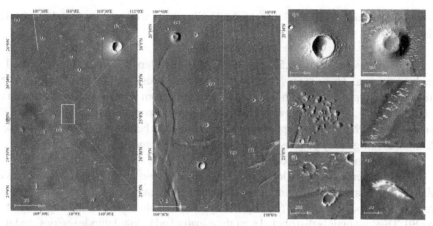

Fig. 6. Geomorphic features in the 75 × 60 km² landing area, among them, the base map of (a), (b) and (d) is CTX [26], the rest are HiRISE [23], and (b), (c), (d), (e), (f) and (g) are enlarged view of the red boxes in Fig. 6a. (b) a typical rampart crater northeast of the landing site (diameter: 8.4 km; location: 110.7°E, 26.0°N). (c) an isolated pitted cone northwest of the landing site (location: 109.9°E, 25.2°N). (d) a cluster of cones south of the landing site (location: 109.7°E, 24.8°N). (e) a polygonal trough about 1.2 km northwest of the landing site (location: 109.9°E, 25.1°N). (f) a ridge about 42.7 km southeast of the landing site (location: 110.0°E, 25.0°N). (g) a Transverse Aeolian Ridge (TAR), enlarged in the red box in Fig. 6f. North is up in all images. (Color figure online)

ends of the landing area. Among them, the northern one (Fig. 6b) is approximately 67 km away from the landing site, with a diameter of approximately 9 km and a depth of approximately 1 km. Rampart craters are generally considered to be the product of interaction between underground water ice rich strata and hypervelocity impactors. It is an important research objective to analyze the current and past groundwater ice on Mars [26].

(2) Cones

Another typical landform of the Tianwen-1 landing area is the cone [2], one of the most significant and controversial landforms in Utopia Planitia [4]. Cones are also found in other areas of the Martian surface, such as Chryse Planitia, Isidis Planitia and Asidaria Planitia [2]. There are often crater-like depressions at the top of cones, which are very similar to ice mounds on Earth. Relatively lighter-toned materials are exposed on the rim of the summit crater, and relatively darker-toned materials are present on the upper flank [27]. About 7 km northwest of the landing site of Tianwen-1, we found some typical isolated pitted cones (Fig. 6c). To the south of the landing site, we also observed clusters (Fig. 6d). At present, the origin of cones remains controversial, candidates include mud volcano, cinder cones and rootless cones [2, 4].

(3) Troughs

Tens of giant troughs have been identified in these area. The length of the troughs varies from ~1.2 to ~10 km [4], and the width range is ~150 to ~500 m [2]. Trough depths vary between ~1 and ~20 m [4]. They occur throughout Utopia Planitia, and the nearest polygonal trough is ~1.2 km from the Tianwen-1 landing site (Fig. 6e). It is oriented in a NE-SW direction. Parallel aeolian bedforms occur in the trough with crest lines oriented perpendicular to it. Within 50 km^2 of the landing area, we have not found a complete giant polygonal trough [2].

(4) Ridge

Some ridges between ~0.59 and ~12.6 km [4] in length can also be observed in the landing area. These ridges usually have rounded crests and relatively symmetrical cross-sectional profiles, which is distinctly different from wrinkle ridges often seen on volcanic plains. Figure 6f shows a cliff-like ridge approximately 5 km southeast of the landing site, with a length of approximately 3.3 km and a height of 4–10 m. In the Utopia Planitia, the ridge may be caused by tectonism and volcanism [4, 28].

(5) Transverse Aeolian Ridge

The Transverse Aeolian Ridge (TAR) is one of the unique aeolian sand landforms on Mars, and they are common within the landing area of Tianwen-1[2], especially in some troughs and impact craters [4] (Fig. 6g). They have a height of meters and a spacing of 10 m [29]. They are mainly distributed near the equator and in low-latitude regions, and they are more in the southern hemisphere than in the northern hemisphere. Higher albedo and symmetric cross-sections are their most remarkable characteristics, which are similar to the cross-sectional shape of giant sand ripples and reverse dunes on Earth [30]. The grain size composition of TAR sediments generally has bimodal characteristics. The surface layer is covered by coarse sand, but the thermal inertia is low [30]. Most TARs in the landing area run toughly in the east-west direction, indicating that the local wind was predominantly north–south in the past [8].

Research on the distribution, morphological characteristics and sediment composition of the TARs can provide important clues for the analysis of paleowind field and paleoenvironment in the landing area [2, 4]. It is difficult to completely measure their length, width, spacing, height, and trend from the CTX and HiRISE images alone, so these need to be supplemented by the in situ investigations of the Zhurong rover.

The above analysis shows that there is abundant topography featuring a wide varity of landforms within the Tianwen-1 landing area, and the geological environment of the landing area can be roughly outlined through remote sensing images. However, limited by the low resolution of hyperspectral images and/or the lack of absorption features of the surface materials, the compositions and abundances of the minerals in the landing area are currently unknown. Thus, the in situ investigations of the Zhurong rover are especially important.

4.2 On-board Application of the in Situ Detection by the Zhurong Rover

The Tianwen-1 mission will combine remote sensing and detailed in situ detection to promote our understanding of Mars. The in situ detection modes of the Zhurong rover includes three modes [19]: mobile detection, in situ detection and environment detection. Mobile detection refers to the start-up detection of the Mars Rover Penetrating Radar (RoPeR), Mars Climate Station (MCS) and Mars Rover Magnetometers (RoMAG). In situ detection refers to the use of Mars Surface Composition Detector (MarSCoDe), Multispectral Camera (MSCam) and NaTeCams to perform detection when the rover approaches high-value detection objects such as sand dunes, stones, impact craters, mud volcanoes and so on. Environmental detection refers to the use of RoMAG and MCS for joint detection.

So far, the TAR, trough and cone to the south of the landing site have been selected as nominal and short-term extended detection targets respectively [4], and has achieved some preliminary results.

Figure 7 shows the first TAR encountered by the Zhurong rover after landing on the Mars surface. Under the control of the ground teleoperator, the rover finally arrived near it (Fig. 7c) after navigating for approximately seven sols (curve in Fig. 7b). During this period, a stone was in detected in situ (marked by the yellow box in Fig. 7c), and the detection results of the MSCam were partially enlarged. In order to make a relatively complete image of this TAR, subsequently, the ground teleoperator navigated to the south and used the NaTeCamera to capture it again (Fig. 7d). The TAR is crescent-shaped, with a length of ~40 m, a width of ~8 m, and a height of ~0.6 m [4]. These images were captured ~210 m from the landing site.

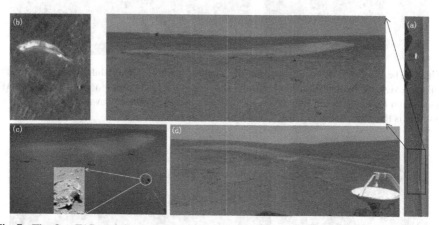

Fig. 7. The first TAR and the route of the detection encountered by the Zhurong rover. (a) The shooting point is about 30 m away from the TAR, corresponding the red dot marked in Fig. 7b. (b) the detection route. (c) the shooting point is about 9 m away from the TAR, surrounded by stones of different sizes, and the enlarged view is the result of MSCam. (d) move to the south side of the TRA and image again, corresponding to the green dot in Fig. 7b. (Color figure online)

Figure 8 shows the second TAR encountered by the Zhurong rover, when its mileage exceeded 1 Huali (509 m). The TAR is in the shape of light and dark overlapping water ripples, with a length of ~51 m and a width of ~9 m. According to [17], dark materials are composed mostly of coarse sand and rich in olivine. During this period, MarSCoDe, MSCam, RoMAG and MCS were used to comprehensively detect the TAR's mineral composition and surrounding environment, and mineralogical and environmental information such as mineral abundance of sediments were collected.

After completing the scientific exploration of the second TAR (Fig. 8), the Zhurong rover continued southward and arrived at a complex and rough area with dense stones, impact pits and sand dunes (Fig. 9). The ground teleoperator completed the movement plan of the rover and navigated across this complex area safely according to the NaTeCam images obtained every sol-day.

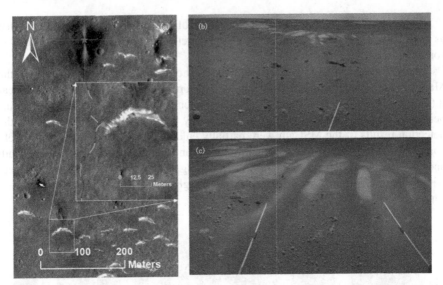

Fig. 8. The second TAR encountered by the Zhurong rover. (a) The white box represents the enlarged view of the detection route. (b) the shooting point is about 30 m away from the TAR, its position is the red dot in Fig. 8a. (c) the shooting point is about 4 m away from the TAR, its position is the green dot in Fig. 8a. (Color figure online)

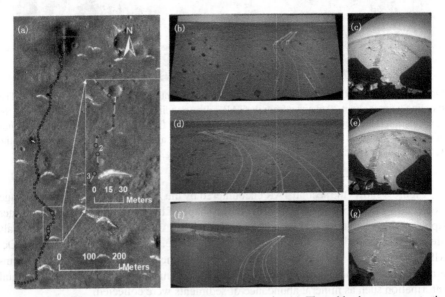

Fig. 9. The Zhurong rover began to cross complex terrain. (a) The white box represents the enlarged view of the travel route. (b), (d) and (f) are the three ground planned moving routes marked with numbers 1, 2 and 3 in Fig. 9a. (c), (e) and (g) are the ruts captured by the rear HazCam after each movement.

As of January 31, 2022, the Tianwen-1 has been ongoing for 557 days, 325 million km away from the Earth. The Zhurong rover has worked for 255 sols and traveled 1524 m in total [31]. At present, the Tianwen-1 has relayed back approximately 600 GB of scientific data, and the two devices are in good condition [31]. Under the guidance of remote sensing data, the Zhurong rover continues to travel south, and the medium-term exploration target is a trough about 1.7 km away from the landing site. In the future, the mud volcano, which is about 20 km away from the landing site, is a planned detection target.

5 Conclusions

The Tianwen-1 Mars exploration mission has opened the pace of China's deep space exploration, greatly promoting the development of China's space science, especially planetary science. Through the Tianwen-1 mission, we have obtained multi-element first-hand Martian scientific data, detailing Martian topography, surface material composition, underground structure, magnetic field, meteorology, and space environment. This provides a basic guarantee for planetary scientific research. With the joint support of photogrammetry and remote sensing technology, the Zhurong rover has successfully completed the main mission phase. This paper introduces the application of these methods in detail and shows preliminary results describing the surface characteristics of the landing area.

In the future, the orbiter will measure the global topographic and geomorphic characteristics of Mars and obtain high-precision morphological data of typical areas through remote sensing. It will detect the types and global distribution of Martian soil, search for ice information; while simultaneously supporting research looking into the genesis and evolution of Martian geological structure and the layered structure of Martian soil profiles. The Zhurong rover will continue to travel to the suspected ancient ocean-land junction in the south of Utopia Planitia, seeking clues to uncover the mystery of the origin and evolution of Mars.

Acknowledgments. This study was supported by National Key R&D Program of China (No. 2018YFB1305004); National Natural Science Foundation of China (grant Nos. 42172265, 41771488). The Tiawen-1 mission was carried out by the Chinese Planetary Exploration Program. We thank the Lunar and Deep Space Exploration Science Applications Center of the National Astronomical Observatories for providing the HiRIC DOM and DEM.

References

1. Wan, W.X., Wang, C., Li, C.L., et al.: The payloads of planetary physics research onboard China's First Mars Mission (Tianwen-1). Earth Planet. Phys. 4(4), 331–332 (2020)
2. Gou S, Yue, Z.Y., Di, K.C., et al.: Geological characteristics of the landing area of the Zhurong rover at Utopia Planitia, Mars. J. Remote Sens. (2019). https://doi.org/10.11834/jrs.20211403
3. Mallapaty, S.: China has landed its first rover on Mars-here's what happens next. Nature **593**, 323–324 (2021)

4. Liu, J.J., Li, C.L., Zhang, R.Q., et al.: Geomorphic contexts and science focus of the Zhurong landing site on Mars. Nature Astron. (2021). https://doi.org/10.1038/s41550-021-01519-5
5. http://www.gov.cn/xinwen/2021-06/12/content_5617394.htm
6. https://www.chinanews.com.cn/sh/shipin/2021/11-09/news906610.shtml
7. https://new.qq.com/rain/a/20211109A085VZ00
8. Ding, L., Zhou, R.Y., Yu, T.Y., et al.: Surface characteristics of the Zhurong Mars rover traverse at Utopia Planitia. Nat. Geosci. (2022). https://doi.org/10.1038/s41561-022-00905-6
9. Ye, P.J., Sun, Z.Z., Rao, W., et al.: Mission overview and key technologies of the frst Mars probe of China. Sci. China Technol. Sci. **60**, 649–657 (2017)
10. Dong, J, Sun, Z.Z., Rao, W., et al.: Mission profile and design challenges of Mars landing exploration. Int. Archives Photogramm. Remote Sens. Spat. Inf. Sci. XLII-3/W1, 35–39 (2017)
11. Li, C., et al.: China's mars exploration mission and science investigation. Space Sci. Rev. **217**(4), 1–24 (2021). https://doi.org/10.1007/s11214-021-00832-9
12. Wan, W.H., Yu, T.Y., Di, K.C., et al.: Visual localization of the Tianwen-1 lander using orbital, descent and rover images. Remote Sens. **13**(17), 3439–3450 (2021)
13. Wang J, Li, D.F., He X.M., et al.: High precision localization of Zhurong rover based on multi-source images. J. Deep Space Explor. **9**(1), 62–71 (2022)
14. Liang, X., Chen, W., Cao, Z., et al.: The navigation and terrain cameras on the Tianwen-1 mars rover. Space Sci. Rev. **217**, 37 (2021)
15. Dickson, J.L., Kerber, L.A., Fassett, C.I., et al.: A Global, Blended CTX Mosaic of Mars with Vectorized Seam Mapping: A New Mosaicking Pipeline Using Principles of Non-Destructive Image Editing In: Proceedings of the 49th Lunar and Planetary Science Conference. The Woodlands, Texas: Lunar 648 and Planetary Institute, vol. 2480 (2018)
16. McEwen, A.S., Eliason, E.M., Bergstrom, J.W., et al.: Mars reconnaissance orbiter's high resolution imaging science experiment (HiRISE). J. Geophys. Res. **112**(E5), E05S02 (2007). https://doi.org/10.1029/2005JE002605
17. Jia, M.N.: High-resolution large-area digital orthophoto map generation based on multi-coverage lunar orbital images and its science application. University of Chinese Academy of Sciences, Beijing (2019)
18. Website of Nature: Flurry of photos capture China's Zhurong rover on surface of Mars. https://www.nature.com/articles/d41586-021-01588-6. Accessed 12 June 2021
19. Wang, J., Yu, T., Yuan, J., Li, L., Peng, M., Wu, F., Liu, S., Wan, W., He, X.: Mapping methods in teleoperation of the mars rover. In: Wang, Y., Song, W. (eds.) IGTA 2021. CCIS, vol. 1480, pp. 252–264. Springer, Singapore (2021). https://doi.org/10.1007/978-981-16-7189-0_20
20. Zhang, H., Lu, H., Yu, T.Y., et al.: Teleoperation technology of zhurong mars rover. J. Deep Space Explor. **8**(6), 582–591 (2021)
21. Zhu, J.B., Xu, Y., Wang, C.L., et al.: Image compression software design for zhurong mars exploration rover. J. Deep Space Explor. **8**(5), 503–510 (2021)
22. Liu, Z.Q., Wan, W.H., Peng, M., et al.: Remote sensing mapping and localization techniques for teleoperation of Chang'e-3 rover. J. Remote Sens. **18**(5), 971–980 (2014)
23. http://www.scpublic.cn/news/wx/detail?newsid=526157
24. https://www.uahirise.org/dtm/dtm.php?ID=ESP_069665_2055
25. https://mp.weixin.qq.com/s/ls1RxFW53Jx6l7_in0Gz2g
26. Pan, D., Jia, Y., Yuan, B.F., et al.: Design and verification of the active suspension mobility system of the Zhurong Mars rover. Scientia Sinica Techonologica (2021). https://doi.org/10.1360/SST-2021-0483
27. Gou, S., Yue, Z.Y., Di, K.C., et al.: Rampart craters in the Isidis Planitia, Mars: remote sensing analysis and environment implications. J. Remote Sens. **25**(7), 1374–1384 (2021)

28. Zhao, J. N., Xiao, Z. J., Huang J, et al.: Geological characteristics and targets of high scientific interest in the Zhurong landing region on mars. Geophys. Res. Lett. **48**, e2021GL094903 (2021)

29. Lanz, J.K., Wagner, R., Wolf, U., et al.: Rif zone volcanism and associated cinder cone feld in Utopia Planitia, Mars. Geophys. Res. Planets **115**, E12 (2010)

30. Berman, D.C., Balme, M.R., Rafkin, S.C.R., et al.: Transverse Aeolian Ridges (TARs) on Mars II: distributions, orientations, and ages. Icarus **213**(1), 595 116–130 (2011)

31. Dong, Zh. B., Ping, L., Li, C., et al.: Unique Aeolian Bedforms of Mars: transverse Aeolian Ridges **35**(7), 661–677 (2021)

32. https://www.sohu.com/a/520133371_121118995

MRI Brain Tumor Classification Based on EfficientNet with Non-rigid Transformations

Chengyang Gao[1,2], Zhenwei Wang[1,2], Wei Wang[1], and Jianxin Zhang[1,2(✉)]

[1] School of Computer Science and Engineering, Dalian Minzu University,
Dalian 116600, China
jxzhang0411@163.com
[2] Institute of Machine Intelligence and Bio-computing, Dalian Minzu University,
Dalian 116600, China

Abstract. Computer-aided MRI brain tumor analysis technology plays an important role in brain tumor diagnosis. Recently, with the great progress of deep learning in various medical image tasks, MRI brain tumor classification methods using deep learning have also attracted widespread attentions. In this work, we present a novel brain tumor classification method mainly based on the recently proposed EfficientNet model, i.e., a lightweight model that well balances network depth, width, and resolution with brilliant performance in natural image tasks. More specifically, we utilize the pre-trained EfficientNet B2 model to capture brain image features for brain tumor classification. Besides, to address sample imbalance as well as network generalization problems, we further introduce the augmentation method using non-rigid transformations combined with oversampling strategy, which effectively improves the model performance. We perform experiments on the public Figshare dataset to evaluate the given model, and it achieves the optimal five-fold cross-validation accuracy of 99.15%, demonstrating the effectiveness for this medical image task.

Keywords: Brian tumor classification · EfficientNet · Oversampling strategy · Non-rigid transformations · Data augmentation

1 Introduction

The brain is one of the most important and complex organs of human beings. As a type of cancer, brain tumor can seriously affect brain function and endanger physical health. Therefore, the early and effective diagnosis of brain tumors is very important. There are many medical imaging techniques that can be used to detect and diagnose brain tumors. Magnetic resonance imaging (MRI) is a commonly used detection technique that can obtain relatively clear soft tissue structures without causing radiation damage. The traditional diagnosis method mainly relies on doctors with very rich professional knowledge and experience, which is inefficient. Therefore, the use of computer technology to assist doctors in diagnosis has become a mainstream trend. Improving physician productivity by using computer-aided analysis of MRI brain tumor images [1].

Recently, with the breakthrough success of deep learning in various computer vision and medical image analysis tasks, deep learning related models have also become the mainstream of MRI brain tumor classification, showing significant performance improvements compared with traditional machine learning models. Some researchers have tried to reorganize the convolutional neural network (CNN) structure to distinguish brain tumors. Badža and Barjaktarović [2] propose a simple CNN model which mainly consists of two convolutional blocks and a fully connected (FC) layer for brain tumor classification. Anaraki et al. [3] utilize genetic algorithm to reconstruct the CNN structure to completed classification of brain tumors. Meanwhile, in order to further improve classification efficiency, Wadhah Ayadi et al. [4] propose a deep CNN model with different layers using different sizes and softmax classifiers for MRI brain tumor classification. For the problem of limited training samples for brain tumor classification, some researchers have introduced transfer learning strategy to transfer the prior knowledge learned on other datasets to this task to achieve a more robust network [5]. Rehman et al. [6] introduce pre-trained AlexNet and GoogleNet to train on the brain tumor dataset and augment the data to complete tumor classification. Khan Swati et al. [7] utilize pre-trained VGG19 model for classifying brain tumors from Figshare brain MRI dataset. Adopting the concept of transfer learning, Talo et al. [8] and Kumar et al. [9] employ pre-trained Resnet34 and Resnet50 models respectively to classify MRI brain tumor. In order to train a more generalized model, Ghassemi et al. [10] use a new deep learning method, the deep neural network was first pre-trained as a discriminator in Generative Adversarial Networks (GAN) on different MRI images datasets to extract robust features of MRI images, and then replaced the full connection layer to train the entire deep network as a classifier to distinguish between the three tumor types. A more detailed processing method is proposed [11], which segment the tumor part first and fine-tune the pre-trained CNN model, for brain tumor classification, which achieved good results.

The existing CNN related models have shown obviously performance improvements over the traditional works, achieving more and more attentions in this field. Following their merits, we attempt to propose a novel CNN-related model to achieve more promising classification accuracy. Considering characteristics of MRI brain tumor samples, we utilize the recently proposed lightweight network EfficientNet [12]. The EfficientNet utilizes neural network search technology to explore the reasonable configurations, and it well balances network depth, width, and resolution, which helps capture discriminant brain tumor image features for classification. More specifically, we take an EfficientNet B2 model trained on the large-scale ImageNet benchmark [13] and then fine-tuned on the brain tumor classification task. In addition, since the collection and labeling of MRI pathological images are not as easy as natural images, there is often a large gap in the amount of data between categories. To solve this problem, we use an oversampling strategy to add more samples. At the same time, to ensure that the network has a stronger generalization ability, data augmentation technology is used to increase the number of samples after oversampling, so that the data samples are more diverse to suppress the occurrence of overfitting. In the practical application of medical images, due to the complex structure of various parts of the human body, it is difficult to describe the complex deformation and local feature information of these structures by simple rigid transformation. These information are the important basis for experts to diagnose and clinically treat patients, so non-rigid medical image registration methods are more suitable for practical applications. We introduce three non-rigid transformation methods from the Albumentations library [14], namely ElasticTransform, GridDistortion and OpticalDistortion. The overall flowchart of the proposed model can be shown in Fig. 1. We conduct experiments on the publicly available Figshare dataset [15] to evaluate a given model, achieving an average accuracy of 99.15% under five-fold cross-validation, the best result we know. The method is demonstrated to be effective for this medical image task.

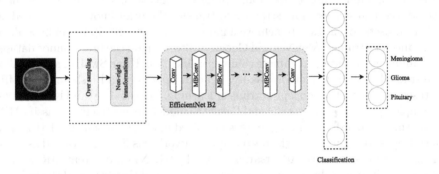

Fig. 1. The overall flowchart of the given brain tumor classification method.

2   Method

In this section, we will describe the details of our EfficientNet-based method for MRI brain tumor classification. Firstly, we introduce the overall architecture of the given method. Then, a basic description of EfficientNet will be given, followed by an introduction of non-rigid transformations and transfer learning.

2.1   Overall Architecture

As shown in Fig. 1, considering characteristics of MRI brain tumor classification task, we employ the lightweight EfficientNet model to capture discriminant image features for classification. As it is difficult to achieve the large-scale brain tumor image dataset, transfer learning is adopted to improve the model performance. Specifically, we use the EfficientNet B2 model pre-trained on ImageNet and redefine the classifier at the end of the network to make it suitable for the task of brain tumor classification. Besides, to achieve the more robust classification result, we also introduce the augmentation method for non-rigid transformations including ElasticTransform, GridDistortion and OpticalDistortion [14], as well as oversampling strategy before data augmentation, which solves the sample imbalance issue to a certain extent.

Table 1. The structure of EfficientNet B2.

Stage	Operator	Output size	Channel	Layer
1	Conv3 × 3	260 × 260	32	1
2	MBConv1, k3 × 3	130 × 130	16	2
3	MBConv6, k3 × 3	130 × 130	24	3
4	MBConv6, k5 × 5	65 × 65	48	3
5	MBConv6, k3 × 3	32 × 32	88	4
6	MBConv6, k5 × 5	16 × 16	120	4
7	MBConv6, k5 × 5	16 × 16	208	5
8	MBConv6, k3 × 3	8 × 8	352	2
9	Conv1 × 1 & Pooling & FC	8 × 8	1408	1

2.2 EfficientNet

EfficientNet, proposed by Tan and Le in 2019 [12], is among the most efficient models with promising accuracy on image classification tasks. The overall structure of a typical EfficientNet model is shown in Table 1. EfficientNet is mainly composed of a series of inverted bottleneck MBConv given in MobileNetV2 [16], but its usage is different from MobileNetV2 due to the increased FLOPS (floating point operations per second) budget. The MBConv block is mainly composed of 1 × 1 convolutional layers, SE modules, depthwise separable convolutions and shortcuts, as shown in Fig. 2. This inverted residual structure can enable depthwise separable convolution to obtain more feature information. The depthwise separable convolution convolves each layer of the input features individually and then uses a 1 × 1 convolution kernel to exchange information between feature channels. Therefore, after the dimension is increased, the features extracted by the depthwise separable convolution will be more abundant and the performance will be improved. Compared to traditional layers, using depthwise separable convolution reduces the computation by a factor of almost k^2, where k is the kernel size and represents the width and height of the 2D convolution window [16].

Besides, EfficientNet employs a simple and efficient composite scaling method that makes it easy to extend the baseline CNN to any target resource constraint in a more principled way, while keeping the model efficient. It utilizes a compound coefficient ϕ to uniformly scales network width, depth, and resolution as follows:

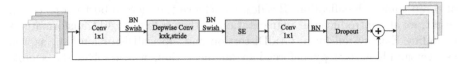

Fig. 2. Mobile inverted residual bottleneck block.

$$depth : d = \alpha^\phi$$
$$width : w = \beta^\phi$$
$$resolution : r = \gamma^\phi \tag{1}$$
$$\alpha \geq 1, \beta \geq 1, \gamma \geq 1$$

where α, β, γ are constants which can be determined by grid search. ϕ is a user-specified coefficient that controls how many resources are available for model scaling, while α, β, γ specify how to allocate these additional resources, network width, depth, and resolution, respectively.

2.3 Non-rigid Transformations Augmentation

Image augmentation is a common implicit regularization technique to prevent networks from overtraining on smaller datasets, which effectively improves the network performance. As brain tumor datasets are small in size due to the difficulty of data collection and labeling of samples, most deep learning frameworks implement basic transformations. However, they are usually limited to flip, rotate, zoom, and crop [2,6]. To add the diversity of sample images and improve the model generalization, this work adds non-rigid transformations for the brain tumor classification network. Non-rigid transformations augmentation can be thought of as locally rigid or affine transformations, and they do not need to preserve any quality and can move each pixel in the image independently [17]. The detailed non-rigid transformations augmentation used in this work are ElasticTransform, GridDistortion and OpticalDistortion [14]. Since the dataset used in this paper is annotated at the image level, spatial-level transformations will not affect its results.

ElasticTransform refers to multiplying the displacement field through Gaussian convolution by the scale factor that controls the deformation intensity to obtain an elastic deformation displacement field. Finally, this displacement field is applied to the image after affine transformation to obtain the final elastic deformation enhanced data, and make the image shake [18]. GridDistortion is an image warping technique which is driven by the mapping between equivalent families of curves, arranged in a grid structure. Change the size of each small block of the image. OpticalDistortion is any apparent change in the geometry of an object, as seen through transparent materials or specular reflections. The effect of the non-rigid transformations is shown in Fig. 3. Increasing the size of dataset through data augmentation and image synthesis generally makes them more robust and the corresponding models generalize better. Besides, due to the class imbalance problem, we also utilize an oversampling strategy [19] before the augmentation, which effectively avoids the learned weights being biased towards a certain class due to the excessive number of samples.

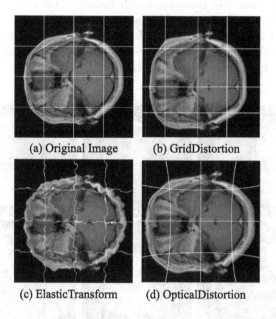

(a) Original Image   (b) GridDistortion

(c) ElasticTransform   (d) OpticalDistortion

Fig. 3. Non-rigid transformations augmentation.

2.4 Transfer Learning

Transfer learning is regarded as an effective machine learning strategy that well solve the problem of limited training samples for obtaining more robust network. It gains useful priori knowledge by training model on a large-scale labeled image dataset, and then transfers the model information into another different domain [20]. As it is difficult to achieve enough labeled brain tumor images, we also utilize the transfer learning strategy in this task. More specifically, we employ the EfficientNet B2 [12] model pre-trained on ImageNet [13], and only the final classifier is redefined and transferred to the task of brain tumor classification. Then, it is finetuned by using limited MRI brain tumor images to achieve more robust performance for this medical image task.

3   Experiments and Results

3.1   Dataset

We evaluate the proposed model on the public Figshare brain tumor dataset [15]. The Figshare dataset includes 3064 T1-weighted contrast augmentation images collected from 233 patients, which mainly consists of three categories: meningioma (708 slices), glioma (1426 slices), and pituitary tumor (930 slices). The data format of the dataset is MATLAB (".mat") format, and each MAT file includes information such as label and image data of brain tumor. Some typical image examples from this dataset are shown in Fig. 4.

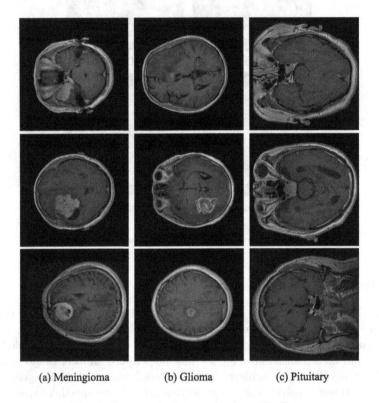

(a) Meningioma   (b) Glioma   (c) Pituitary

Fig. 4. Some typical examples from Figshare.

3.2   Experiment Settings

In the experiments described in this paper, we first divide the entire Figshare dataset into training, validation and test sets in a ratio of 60:20:20 to verify the effectiveness of the augmentation method for non-rigid transformations for brain tumor image classification results influence. In the use of data augmentation, the image data is perturbed before segmentation and a random seed is set to ensure reproducible results. Meanwhile, in order to adapt to the input size of the EfficientNet B2 model, we downscale the spatial resolution of the original image from 512×512 pixels to 260×260 pixels. For other experimental settings, we used cross-entropy loss as the loss function and stochastic gradient descent algorithm for updating the weights. The initial learning rate was set to 0.01, and trained for 200 epochs using cosine learning rate decay and warm-up strategies. For the final experiment, we adopt five-fold cross-validation to obtain statistical results. All programs are implemented through the Pytorch [21] deep learning framework and run on a single GeForce GTX 1080Ti GPU.

3.3 Experiment Metrics

We employ the most commonly used accuracy metrics to test the performance of a given method. Besides, precision, specificity, sensitivity(recall), and $F1 - score$ metrics are also utilized for further evaluation. These metrics are computed by the following equations:

$$Accuracy = \frac{TP + TN}{TP + TN + FP + FN} \tag{2}$$

$$Precision = \frac{TP}{TP + FP}$$

$$Specificity = \frac{TN}{TN + FN} \tag{3}$$

$$Sensitivity = \frac{TP}{TP + FN}$$

$$F1 - score = \frac{2 * Precision * Sensitivity}{Precision + Sensitivity} \tag{4}$$

where TP, TN, FP and FN are true positive, true negative, false negative and false negative values, respectively.

3.4 Experiment Results

First, we conduct experiments using a partitioned dataset of 60:20:20 to evaluate the impact of three non-rigid transformations (ElasticTransform, OpticalDistortion and GridDistortion) on the accuracy, and the effect of different combinations of the three augmentation methods on the experimental results. The experimental results are shown in Table 2, and they are the results of using an oversampling strategy and a pre-trained EfficientNet B2 model.

As shown in Table 2, when the non-rigid transformations is not used, the accuracy of the model reaches 98.69%, and we use this model as the baseline. When ElasticTransform was introduced, its accuracy increased by 0.49% over the baseline. At the same time, using GridDistortion alone can also achieve a slight

Table 2. Comparison of different Non-rigid transformations augmentation on the test set

ElasticTransform	OpticalDistortion	GridDistortion	Accuracy
×	×	×	98.69%
√			99.18%
	√		98.53%
		√	98.86%
√	√		98.20%
√		√	98.69%
	√	√	99.02%
√	√	√	99.67%

accuracy gain, reducing the performance of the model by 0.16% when only OpticalDistortion was used. The accuracy of the model dropped by 0.49% when combining ElasticTransform and OpticalDistortion. When combining GridDistortion and ElasticTransform, the accuracy of the model did not change. When combining GridDistortion and OpticalDistortion, the accuracy of the model increased by 0.31%, and finally when the three methods were combined, the accuracy of the model increased by 0.98% and the accuracy reached 99.67%. Experiments demonstrate that the combination of three non-rigid transformation methods is effective for brain tumor classification.

Then, we compare the given method with some representative works. Here, we perform experiments on two different protocols, where the first one is at the ratio of 60:20:20, and another is based on the five-fold cross-validation strategy. The compared results are reported in Table 3. EfficientNet* represents the pretrained EfficientNet B2 model combined with the oversampling strategy and the non-rigid transformation methods.

Table 3. Comparing the training and testing results of different network architectures on the original dataset

Reference	Data division	Method	Accuracy
Cheng et al. [15]	Five fold	BOS-SVM	91.28%
Anaraki et al. [3]	75:25	GA-CNN	94.2%
Badža and Barjaktarović [2]	60:20:20	Four-layer CNN	97.39%
W.Ayadi et al. [4]	Five fold	CapsNet	94.74%
Khan Swati et al. [7]	Five fold	VGG-19 (Transfer learning)	94.82%
Ghassemi et al. [10]	Five fold	CNN based Gan	95.60%
R Lokesh Kumar et al. [9]	Five fold	Resnet-50+fine-tuning	97.48%
Arshia Rehman et al. [6]	Five fold	GoogleNet+fine-tuning+augmentation	98.04%
Proposed	60:20:20	EfficientNet	98.37%
	Five fold	EfficientNet	98.16%
	60:20:20	EfficientNet*	99.67%
	Five fold	EfficientNet*	99.15%

As can be seen from Table 3, when only using the pre-trained EfficientNet B2 model, the accuracy under 60:20:20 partition reaches 98.37%. Meanwhile, its five-fold cross-validation accuracy achieves the high performance of 98.16%. When introducing the oversampling strategy and non-rigid transformations, the given model shows more robust performance, with the optimal results of 99.67% (60:20:20) and 99.15% (five-fold cross-validation). Its five-fold cross-validation accuracy is 1.11% higher than the GoogleNet related model given by Arshia Rehman et al. [6], and outperforms the ResNet related model [9] by 1.67% gains. The comparative experimental results well illustrate the performance of the proposed model on the MRI brain tumor classification task.

Because in medical image experiments, it is not enough to only use the accuracy rate as an evaluation inden. To further test the effects of the proposed method, we also show the confusion matrix in Fig. 5. Based on the confusion matrix and formula 2, the accuracy, sensitivity, specificity and F1 score are calculated and listed in Table 4. It can be seen from the table that Meningioma has achieved promising results in various indicators, with accuracy values larger than 99.5%. Meanwhile, though Glioma and Pituitary tumor are slightly worse, they also achieve 98.4% precision and 98.6% sensitivity, respectively. The above experimental results once again demonstrate the effectiveness of our method.

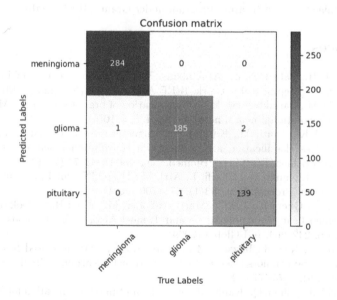

Fig. 5. Confusion matrix of the proposed model on the test set.

Table 4. Accuracy metrics in terms of precision, recall, specificity, and F1 score.

Tumor type	Precision	Sensitivity	Specificity	F1 score
Meningioma	1	0.996	1	0.998
Glioma	0.984	0.995	0.993	0.989
Pituitary tumor	0.993	0.986	0.998	0.989

4 Conclusion

In this work, we present a novel lightweight brain tumor classification method mainly based on the EfficientNet B2 model. Meanwhile, the non-rigid transformations augmentation combined with oversampling strategy are introduced to address sample imbalance and network generalization problems. We perform experiments on the public Figshare brain tumor dataset, and it achieves the optimal five-fold cross-validation accuracy value of 99.15%, demonstrating competitive performance with the representative CNN models on this task.

Acknowledgements. This work was supported in part by the Young and Middle-aged Talents Program of the National Civil Affairs Commission, and the University-Industry Collaborative Education Program under Grant 201902029013.

References

1. Sultan, H.H., Salem, N.M., Al-Atabany, W.: Multi-classification of brain tumor images using deep neural network. IEEE Access **7**, 69215–69225 (2019)
2. Badža, M.M., Barjaktarović, M.Č: Classification of brain tumors from MRI images using a convolutional neural network. Appl. Sci. **10**(6), 1999 (2020)
3. Anaraki, A.K., Ayati, M., Kazemi, F.: Magnetic resonance imaging-based brain tumor grades classification and grading via convolutional neural networks and genetic algorithms. Biocybern. Biomed. Eng. **39**(1), 63–74 (2019)
4. Ayadi, W., Elhamzi, W., Charfi, I., Atri, M.: Deep CNN for brain tumor classification. Neural Process. Lett. **53**(1), 671–700 (2021)
5. Olivas, E.S., Guerrero, J.D.M., Martinez-Sober, M., et al.: Handbook of Research on Machine Learning Applications and Trends: Algorithms, Methods, and Techniques, pp. 242–264. IGI Global (2009)
6. Rehman, A., Naz, S., Razzak, M.I., et al.: A deep learning-based framework for automatic brain tumors classification using transfer learning. Circuits Syst. Signal Process. **39**(2), 757–775 (2020)
7. Swati, Z.N.K., Zhao, Q., Kabir, M., et al.: Brain tumor classification for MR images using transfer learning and fine-tuning. Comput. Med. Imaging Graph. **75**, 34–46 (2019)
8. Talo, M., Baloglu, U.B., Yıldırım, Ö., et al.: Application of deep transfer learning for automated brain abnormality classification using MR images. Cogn. Syst. Res. **54**, 176–188 (2019)
9. Kumar, R.L., Kakarla, J., Isunuri, B.V., Singh, M.: Multi-class brain tumor classification using residual network and global average pooling. Multimedia Tools Appl. **80**(9), 13429–13438 (2021). https://doi.org/10.1007/s11042-020-10335-4

10. Ghassemi, N., Shoeibi, A., Rouhani, M.: Deep neural network with generative adversarial networks pre-training for brain tumor classification based on MR images. Biomed. Signal Process. Control **57**, 101678 (2020)

11. Sajjad, M., Khan, S., Muhammad, K., et al.: Multi-grade brain tumor classification using deep CNN with extensive data augmentation. J. Comput. Sci. **30**, 174–182 (2019)

12. Tan, M., Le, Q.: Efficientnet: rethinking model scaling for convolutional neural networks. In: International Conference on Machine Learning (ICML), pp. 6105–6114 (2019)

13. Deng, J., Dong, W., Socher, R., et al.: Imagenet: a large-scale hierarchical image database. In: IEEE Conference on Computer Vision and Pattern Recognition (CVPR), pp. 248–255 (2009)

14. Buslaev, A., Iglovikov, V.I., Khvedchenya, E., et al.: Albumentations: fast and flexible image augmentations. Information **11**(2), 125 (2020)

15. Cheng, J., Huang, W., Cao, S., et al.: Enhanced performance of brain tumor classification via tumor region augmentation and partition. PLoS ONE **10**(10), e0140381 (2015)

16. Sandler, M., Howard, A., Zhu, M., et al.: Mobilenetv2: inverted residuals and linear bottlenecks. In: Proceedings of the IEEE Conference on Computer Vision and Pattern Recognition (CVPR), pp. 4510–4520 (2018)

17. Durech, E.F.: Deep Convolutional Neural Network for Non-rigid Image Registration. arXiv preprint arXiv:2104.12034 (2021)

18. Simard, P.Y., Steinkraus, D., Platt, J.C.: Best practices for convolutional neural networks applied to visual document analysis. In: International Conference on Document Analysis and Recognition (ICDAR), pp. 958–963 (2003)

19. Chawla, N.V., Bowyer, K.W., Hall, L.O., et al.: SMOTE: synthetic minority oversampling technique. J. Artif. Intell. Res. **16**, 321–357 (2002)

20. Weiss, K., Khoshgoftaar, T.M., Wang, D.D.: A survey of transfer learning. J. Big Data **3**(1), 1–40 (2016). https://doi.org/10.1186/s40537-016-0043-6

21. Paszke, A., Gross, S., Massa, F., et al.: Pytorch: an imperative style, high-performance deep learning library. In: Advances in Neural Information Processing Systems, pp. 1–12 (2019)

Design and Implementation of the Search System Based on the Airborne Multi-mode Imaging Cloud Platform

Chuandong Yang, Yibo Gao, Ziwen Sun, and Chong Ling[✉]

Ammunition Technology Office, PLA Army Academy of Artillery and Air Defense, Hefei 230031, Anhui, China
1363338649@qq.com

Abstract. A search system based on the airborne multi-mode imaging cloud platform is designed. The system consists of imaging detection subsystem, 2D map reconstruction and image cross-matching subsystem, and ground station subsystem and three key technologies are proposed: multimode cloud platform design, image cross-matching, and deep learning-based target recognition, which provides a feasible solution to the current problem of unexploded submunitions searching.

Keywords: Multi-mode cloud platform · Target recognition · Deep learning · Search system

1 Introduction

Due to the small and unstable feature of unexploded submunitions, it is a highly dangerous task to search and exclude the submunitions. In recent years, the frequency of live-fire exercises has rapidly increased, which leads to higher pressure for searching the submunitions, and the intelligent search for unexploded submunitions has become an urgent problem [1]. At present, the main detection methods include magnetic method detection, radar detection, explosive chemical detection, and image detection [2]. The false alarm rate of magnetic detection is high; Radar detection detects the metal shell. When detecting small targets, high-frequency electromagnetic waves are vulnerable to environmental interference; explosive chemical detection usually using biological, thermal neutron and other mediums, it is not suitable for rapid detection of large area target range [3]; The detection method based on visible light/infrared realizes the detection of unexploded submunitions by detecting the different spectral characteristics of unexploded submunitions. According to the different detection platform, it can be divided into on-board, individual soldiers, airborne and other detection methods [4]. Considering that unexploded submunitions usually fall on the shallow surface and spread widely, this paper proposes an unexploded submunitions search system based on UAV multi-mode imaging. According to the multispectral images taken from the bomb drop area, the unexploded submunitions exposed on the ground can be quickly detected and located through the target recognition technology based on deep learning, which can complete the search and detection task in a lower detection cost and safer way.

2   System Design

2.1   Composition of the System

The system is divided into three subsystems according to the technical correlation, including: imaging detection subsystem, 2D map reconstruction and cross-matching subsystem, and ground station subsystem, as shown in Fig. 1.

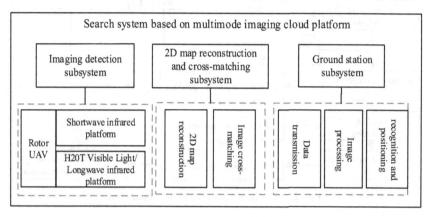

Fig. 1. System composition block diagram

The imaging detection subsystem is mainly used to realize the predetermined track flight, real-time image acquisition and image wireless transmission in the landing area. The multimode imaging cloud platform is mounted on the rotor UAV, which is responsible for the acquisition of bullet landing area images in real time. The 2D map reconstruction and image cross-matching subsystem is mainly used for 2D map reconstruction of falling areas, cross-matching of the same region images in different time periods, and rapid positioning and detection of suspected targets. The ground station subsystem is mainly used for accurate recognition and accurate positioning of suspected targets, including image reception, target recognition, target positioning, and instruction sending modules.

2.2   Process of the System Operation

The implementation of the system is mainly divided into two stages: suspected target detection and accurate target recognition and positioning, as shown in Fig. 2.

In the suspected target detection stage, the imaging detection and unmanned payload platform subsystem needs to complete the scanning of the bomb drop area before and after shooting according to the scheduled flight route, two-dimensional map reconstruction and image cross matching subsystem according to the two scanning results (save image data and geographic coordinate data), and according to the reconstructed two-dimensional digital map image cross matching, to achieve rapid detection and positioning of suspected target.

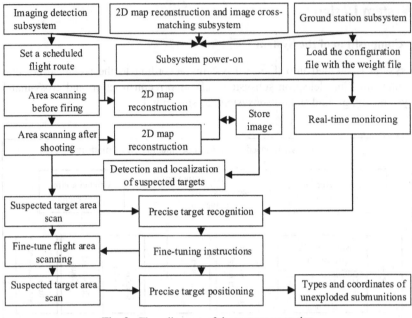

Fig. 2. Flow diagram of the system operation

In the stage of accurate target recognition and positioning, the imaging detection and unmanned load platform subsystem scan the suspected target area one by one, and transmit the image to the ground station subsystem in real time, complete the ground station subsystem in real time, and send control command to adjust the flight position of the unmanned load platform, and finally complete the precise positioning of the target.

3   Key Technology of the System

3.1   Design of the Multi-mode Cloud Platform

The core of the imaging detection subsystem is the design of multi-mode platform, including short-wave infrared platform, H20T dual-optical platform, M300 UAV and other parts. Through the controller circuit design and the image remote control data transmission design, the three-light (short-wave infrared, long-wave infrared, visible light) imaging cloud platform based on the M300 four-rotor data transmission UAV is realized (Fig. 3).

DJI H20T dual-light camera equipped with zoom and wide Angle camera and long wave infrared refrigeration thermal imaging camera movement, can be in high rate zoom screen, wide Angle images, long wave infrared images quickly switch, with the official interface, facilitate communication and power supply, can directly obtain visible light images and long-wave infrared images.

DJI has no official shortwave cameras, so it needs customized development. Short-wave infrared camera development is conducted based on the DJI xport open-source cloud platform controller (Fig. 4).

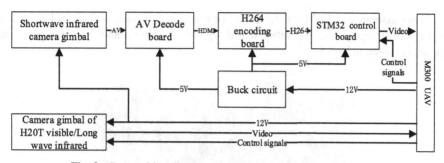

Fig. 3. Composition diagram of the imaging detection subsystem

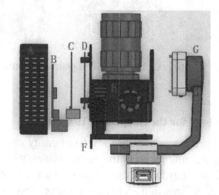

Fig. 4. Shortwave infrared camera cloud platform

3.1.1 Design of the Video Signal Scheme

The analog AV video output from the short-board infrared camera needs to be converted to video streaming in the H264-encoded format for the M300 drone transmission. From analog video to HDMI board to digital HDMI video output, the HDMI video is video compressed in H264 format to the M300 UAV through the HDMI coding board, and the UAV is transmitted to the ground station receiving terminal by remote map for display and processing.

3.1.2 Design of the Cloud Platform Control

Cloud platform control uses chip STM32F407 to run DJI PSDK2.2.1 development package, communicate with M300 aircraft, and execute cloud platform control. Use basic features such as PSDK for information acquisition, data transfer, and power management, as well as advanced features such as camera, cloud platform, load collaboration, and precision positioning. At the same time, the 12 V power supply output by DJI M300 UAV can directly power the camera and power the STM32 controller, H264 encoder and analog transfer HDMI board through the 5 V buck circuit.

After assembly to DJI UAV for center of gravity adjustment and control precision and optical imaging test, the subsystem design is completed, and the cloud platform mount is shown in Fig. 5.

Fig. 5. Multi-mode imaging cloud platform mount map

3.2   Detection Technology for the Suspected Target Area

Suspected target area detection is usually for a fixed entity object, analyzed and compared by remote sensing technology in continuous timelines. It is a more common remote sensing data analysis technology, which can be divided into two processes: image cross-matching and image change detection according to the processing process. Image cross-matching completes the pre-processing of the two-time phase image (i.e., to correct the geometric radiation deformation), allowing it to form an image pair with a unified coordinate system. Image change detection uses some strategy to generate difference maps for the two-time phase images, and performs similarity judgment and binary classification of the difference images, so as to obtain the final change difference map.

3.2.1   Cross-matching Technology of Image

For matching images of falling areas taken twice before and after shooting, this system proposes a SIFT UAV image registration algorithm based on internal point maximization and redundant point control. First, detect the feature point under a threshold according to the basic principle of SIFT [5], and then, based on the SIFT dynamic threshold model and local background structure similarity to build accurate and reasonable the scene image stretched to the target image, finally, use the dynamic Gaussian kernel to control the displacement distance of the feature point, make the image transformation from rigid to non-rigid, complete the image preprocessing correction (registration).

3.2.2   Change Detection Technology of Image

The target fast detection algorithm based on a deep neural network first generated a similar neighborhood pixel matrix, filtered by the FCM, and then pretrained the similarity feature joint matrix by DNN. Finally, the multiphase images were tested using DNN to classify the final detection graph.

3.3 Target Recognition Technology Based on Deep Learning

Target recognition module is the core module in the ground station subsystem to complete the accurate target recognition and positioning order. It is responsible to preload the configuration files and weight files, and recognize the received images in real time to determine whether the suspected target is unexploded submunitions, and mark the target in a visual way. The core technology of the target recognition module is a deep learning-based image target recognition method, usually composed of the target recognition model, model training and reasoning process.

3.3.1 Design of the Target Recognition Model

In terms of model selection, the recognition model can be divided into two-stage methods based on the regional recommendation network (Region Proposal Network, RPN) and a single-stage method based on whether the foreground and background candidate box are initially screened during the target recognition process. Considering the memory cost, computational amount, and speed, the single-stage target recognition model based on the YOLO series was selected as the unexploded submunitions target recognition method [6].

The recognition model includes feature extraction network, feature pyramid prediction module, decoupling detection head, NMS post-processing module, training loss function, and the detection framework is shown in Fig. 6.

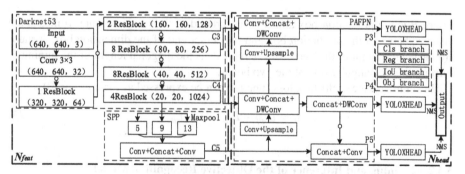

Fig. 6. The target recognition model framework

Using darknet53 as a feature extraction network, SPP pooling fused graph local features with global features, enriching the expression power of the feature maps and covering a larger range of receptive fields. Drawing from the path fusion feature pyramid PAFPN [7] adds a low-to-high-level channel, directly transfers the low-level information upward, improves the utilization rate of the underlying information, and obtains the multi-scale prediction feature map of fusion location information and semantic information at three different scales. The decoupling detection head is divided into target classification branch, coordinate prediction branch, and target confidence branch. By decoupling the detection head of the yolo algorithm, each branch is responsible for only one prediction task can improve the detection effect.

Cross-entropy loss was trained on category and confidence branches, and GIoU loss was trained on positional branches.

Category predicted loss L_{cls} and target confidence loss L_{obj} are achieved through a binary cross-entropy loss, Eq., if, for example (1).

$$L_{cls} = \sum_{i}^{N} \sum_{c=1}^{C} BCE(y_i^c, \hat{y}_i^c)$$

$$L_{obj} = \sum_{i}^{N} BCE(p_i, \hat{p}_i) \tag{1}$$

$$BCE(y_i, \hat{y}_i) = -y_i \log \sigma(\hat{y}_i) - (1 - y_i) \log(1 - \sigma(\hat{y}_i))$$

where σ is the activate function for the sigmoid, y_i^c means the predicted probability that i is category c, The corresponding true value confidence $\hat{y}_i$ indicates whether there is a target at the grid, the same boundary box loss, and the target confidence only considers the largest matching prior box with the true box IoU. If a target exists, the confidence truth of P_i takes the intersection ratio of the prediction box and the truth box, the coordinate error L_{box} is realized by calculating the DIoU distance deviation between the predicted boundary box and the ground-truth box,

$$DIoU(B, \hat{B}) = 1 - IoU(B, \hat{B}) + \frac{\rho(b, \hat{b})}{c^2} \tag{2}$$

where B is the prediction box and $\hat{B}$ is the ground-truth box coordinate, ρ means the distance between the prediction box and the center end of the dimension box, b and $\hat{b}$ are the central point of the two boxes. c represents the diagonal length of the minimum surrounding rectangular box of the two boxes.

In summary, the multi-task loss function can be expressed as formula for (3).

$$L = L_{obj} + L_{cls} + \lambda_{box} L_{box} \tag{3}$$

3.3.2   Training and Inference of the Objective Recognition Model

Model training includes two processes: forward propagation and backpropagation, inputting the data in the training data set into the training network by the batch, assigning the network parameters with pretraining weight or weight initialization. After the feature extraction network, multiscale prediction branch structure activation and loss function loss calculation, calculate the gradient backpropagation, update the network parameters through the optimization algorithm, and finally output the trained weight file. After training, the model can be used for target recognition tasks. The inference process only forward propagation and filters the results through a non-maximum suppression algorithm output directly.

The experiment used a server configured with DGX A100, and the operating system is ubuntu 20.04 to program the algorithm model based on the pytorch deep learning framework. For the established unexploded submunitions dataset, trained using the SGD

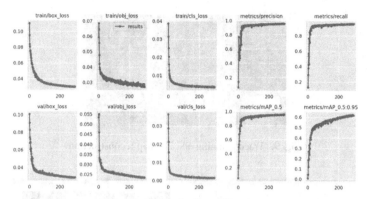

Fig. 7. Change in the training loss

optimization method, the initial learning rate was 210-4, a total of 300 rounds, and the training process loss changes in Fig. 7.

The trained models were tested for accuracy. Model accuracy and recall at different confidence values are shown in Fig. 8(a), (b) and see Fig. 8(c) for PR plots. It can be seen that the average detection accuracy of the model reaches 95.6%, with high detection accuracy, and a detection speed of 50 fps at ground stations.

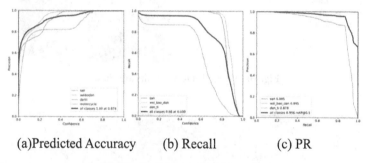

(a)Predicted Accuracy   (b) Recall   (c) PR

Fig. 8. Model accuracy test results

4 Experiments

The designed search system is used to search and test the submunition model in the test area according to the operation process. Track planning and 2D map reconstruction are completed through Dajiang intelligent map, as shown in Fig. 9.

The suspicious region can be obtained by image cross matching using the twice reconstructed map. Then, target detection and positioning can be carried out in the ground station, as shown in Fig. 10.

The video detection effect is shown in Fig. 11. It can be seen that accurate detection frames can be given for submunition targets in different optical video frames, and it has good stability in long-term detection.

Fig. 9. Trace planning and 2D map reconstruction

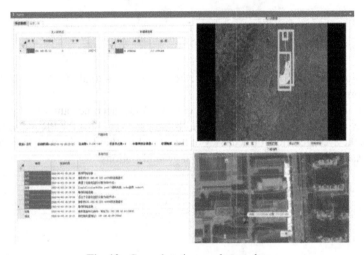

Fig. 10. Ground station results are shown

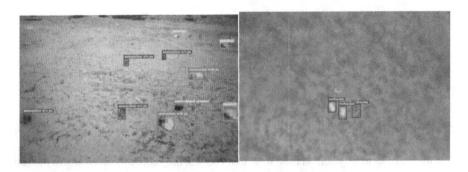

(a) Visible light   (b) Long-wave infrared

Fig. 11. Results of the video detection

5 Summary

In this paper, a search system for unexploded submunitions based on an airborne multi-mode imaging cloud platform is designed. We focus on key technologies such as multimodal cloud platform design, image cross-matching, and deep learning-based target recognition, which provides a feasible solution for an efficient, safe and rapid search for unexploded submunitions.

References

1. Qiudong, Q., Qingtao, W., Haoyong, Q.: Analysis of the explosion possibility of metal/explosive composite structure under laser irradiation. In: Proceedings of the Chinese Mechanics Congress (CCTAM 2019), pp. 2907–2916 (2019)
2. Qinggui, M., Wei, G., Qing, S.: Global UXO status and geophysical detection systems. In: Proceedings of the 2017 China Joint Annual Conference on Earth Sciences (31)—Topic 59: Advances in the Application and Research of Environmental Geophysical Technologies, Topic 60: Advances in Shallow Surface Geophysics, pp. 6–8 (2017)
3. Xin, C., Xiu, L.: Ultra-low altitude aviation transient electromagnetic shallow buried depth anomaly is being simulated. In: Proceedings of the 2017 China Joint Annual Conference on Earth Sciences (31)—Topic 59: Advances in The Application and Research of Environmental Geophysical Technologies, Topic 60: Advances in Shallow Surface Geophysics, p. 99 (2017)
4. Cong, H., Xiaohui, H., Shao, F., Lu, G., Wang, J.: Detection of unexploded bombs based on Faster R-CNN. J. Electromech. Product Develop. Innov. 34(05), 105–107 (2021)
5. Lowe, D.G.: Distinctive image features from scale-invariant keypoints. J. Int. J. Comput. Vis. 2, (2004)
6. Chengji, X., Xiaofeng, W., Yadong, Y.: Attention-YOLO:YOLO detection algorithm that introduces attention mechanisms. J. Comput. Eng. Appl. 55(06), 13–23+125 (2019)
7. Liu, S., Qi, L., Qin, H., Shi, J., Jia, J.: Path aggregation network for instance segmentation. In: Proceedings of the IEEE Conference on Computer Vision and Pattern Recognition (CVPR), vol. 3 (2018)

Method for Imaging Quality Evaluation of Onboard Camera of Image-Guided Projectile

Chuandong Yang, Ziwen Sun, Song Xue, Yibo Gao, and Xiaolong Zhang(✉)

Ammunition Technology Office, PLA Army Academy of Artillery and Air Defense,
Hefei 230031, Anhui, China
1092850034@qq.com

Abstract. As the key device of image-guided projectile seeker, the performance of onboard camera directly affects the hit accuracy. An imaging quality evaluation method is proposed. Firstly, four independent core attributes are extracted, which are image clarity, color difference, dynamic range and geometric distortion. Modulation transfer function (MTF), color difference ($\triangle E$), dynamic range (DR) and distortion rate (GD) are selected as evaluation indexes and a linear weighted evaluation model is proposed. Finally, the tested cameras are evaluated and the results can be used to guide the onboard camera design and evaluation.

Keywords: Onboard camera · Imaging quality · Evaluation method · Image-guided projectile

1 Introduction

Visible light image-guided projectile [1] is an important part of emerging force in artillery weapons. It uses the onboard camera of image-guide projectile to obtain the image of the target area, which is processed by the onboard image processor in real time to control the projectile to hit the target. With its advantages of low cost, strong anti-interference ability, intuitive image information, it has attracted great attention at home and abroad [2]. The onboard camera is an important device to ensure the projectile target. Affected by the motion characteristics of Strapdown projectile (high-speed rotation, violent jitter) and different weather and time (cloud, illumination, etc.), Its working environment is poor, and it needs to be processed such as automatic exposure, white balance, image correction, image stabilization and enhancement. The quality of imaging affects the completion of the strike task.

Therefore, it is essential to objectively evaluate the imaging quality. Imaging quality evaluation has attracted much attention in remote sensing, smart phone and other fields. Xu [3] used MTF as the imaging performance index to measure the image quality. Gao [4] proposed an imaging quality evaluation model for mobile phone imaging module. At present, there are few relevant evaluation standards in the field of onboard cameras. Therefore, the establishment of corresponding imaging quality evaluation method has high application value for developing high-performance onboard camera and improving the combat efficiency of ammunition.

Y. Wang et al. (Eds.): IGTA 2022, CCIS 1611, pp. 314–325, 2022.
https://doi.org/10.1007/978-981-19-5096-4_24

2   The Establish of Imaging Quality Evaluation Model

As an important part of the image seeker, the onboard camera is mainly composed of the lens, CMOS image sensor, filter, image processing board, anti-high overload component, etc. In order to ensure that the onboard camera can withstand an overload environment of no less than 12000 gravitational acceleration, the high-overload resistance component is added to the overall structural design, and the lens is usually selected to focus at infinity. The light in the target area is adjusted through the lens and imagined in the image sensor through the filter. The image sensor is to convert the light signal into an electrical signal, which is usually divided into CCD and CMOS.

Due to the advantages of fast imaging speed, low cost and low power consumption, CMOS is applied in the onboard camera. The image data obtained by CMOS is then input to the image processing circuit through the communication interface to obtain the final clear image and output it for subsequent tasks such as the target detection and tracking. The structure of the onboard camera is shown in Fig. 1.

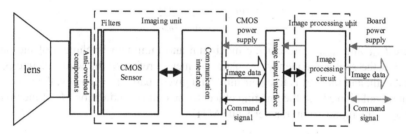

Fig. 1. Vehicle-loading camera structure

Imaging quality evaluation is not only an internal problem of industrial standard formulation, but also affects the reliability and advanced nature of the weapon system. The scientific, reasonable and objective evaluation of onboard camera imaging quality not only needs to select specific image evaluation indexes according to onboard imaging environment and operational requirements, but also needs a comprehensive evaluation method considering multiple indexes.

2.1   Quality Evaluation Index of Onboard Camera

The image quality obtained by the imaging system refers to the relevant international standards of digital cameras (such as GB/T19953S, ISO15739, ISO12233, etc.) [5], Which can be characterized by image definition, noise, color, dynamic range, geometric distortion, uniformity, exposure time, and measured scientifically and accurately through instruments and equipment. Firstly, all kinds of attributes are summarized, and the representative index is selected combined with the specific use tendency of the onboard camera.

2.1.1 Image Clarity

The definition of images acquired by the camera is an important attribute of image quality, which is crucial for image guidance projectile discovery and capture targets, and is the primary indicator of the imaging quality evaluation of bullet-borne cameras. Clarity is the ability to distinguish the differences between lines in an image. Camera with higher clarity can produce richer image details and deeper contrast ratios [6]. Representative attributes that can usually represent clarity include MTF (Modulation Transfer Function), SFR (Spatial Frequency Response), etc. Since image processing algorithms such as noise reduction and image sharpening affect the measurement of the SFR, MTF is chosen as the clarity indicator.

Affected by the diffraction and aberration of the imaging system, the input optical signals of different frequencies will be modulated to a certain extent, making the amplitude of the corresponding spatial frequency spectrum decrease and the phase offset. The MTF reflects the modulation loss of the spatial frequency. The ratio of the optical signal brightness amplitude to the average brightness is recorded as the adjustment system:

$$M = \frac{I_{max} - I_{min}}{I_{max} + I_{min}} \tag{1}$$

where I_{max} and I_{min} represent the maximum and minimum brightness of the optical signal at the spatial frequency v. Spatial frequency refers to the width of line pair in unit length, and the unit is line pair/mm. At a given spatial frequency v, the ratio of the input modulation M_w of the imaging object to the output modulation M_x of the imaging system is the modulation transfer value MTF.

$$MTF(v) = \frac{M_x}{M_w} \tag{2}$$

The MTF curve of the imaging system can be obtained by plotting all frequencies in the spatial frequency range v with the corresponding MTF. The 10% frequency value reaching the red dotted line in the figure is the limited resolution, which is called MTF10. Correspondingly, in the space frequency response of less than 50%, MTF50 is its largest spatial frequency (Fig. 2).

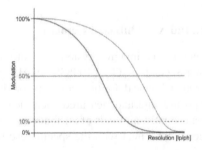

Fig. 2. Schematic representation of the MTF curve

2.1.2 Color Difference

Influenced by the light source, imaging target, lens, CMOS and preprocessing algorithms, there must be certain differences between the actual color obtained by the onboard camera and the perception of human eye vision. The color difference reflects the true degree of the imaging system for reflecting the actual color, and represents the ability of the camera to restore the color. It has a great influence on the identification and tracking of image guidance and the observation intervention of operators, which is an important indicator for the imaging quality evaluation of onboard cameras.

In order to quantify the degree of color deviation accurately and scientifically, a reasonable quantification of color space should be needed. At present, there are mainly RGB, YCbCr, XYZ, Lab and other color space. RGB color space is based on color mixing space, strong correlation between three primary color channels and small color change [7]; while the human eye feels objects through color, saturation and brightness, there is nonlinear relationship with three primary color, poor visual effect is not conducive to quantitative color analysis. The YCbCr color space is represented by the luminance, the blue color difference signal, and the red color difference signal, which can be transformed linearly with the RGB color space. The XYZ color space specifies three new three primary colors X, Y, and Z instead of R, G, and B, so that colors at any wavelength in visible light can correspond to a combination of positive weights. Lab quantitatively describes the difference between colors, and is a device-independent color system based on human visual sensing. L indicates the brightness of the pixels, a represents the range from red to green, and b represents the range from yellow to blue with a wider color gamut. With Lab color space, the spatial distance between two color samples can be used to quantitatively evaluate the difference between colors, which is color difference ΔE_{ab}:

$$\begin{cases} \Delta E_{ab} = \sqrt{\Delta a^2 + \Delta b^2} \\ \Delta a = a_{reference} - a_{sample} \\ \Delta b = b_{reference} - b_{sample} \end{cases} \tag{3}$$

Among them, Δa and Δb represent the chromaticity difference between the two colors, and ΔE represents the color difference between the two colors.

2.1.3 Dynamic Range

Influenced by the high-speed motion of projectiles, the illumination changes widely and rapidly in the receiving area of the camera, which result in changes in the dynamic range between the resulting image sequences; For a single image, when the CIS field of view contains high-intensity areas, such as the sun's reflections on the surface of the sea, low-intensity areas such as shadows, resulting in a wide dynamic range feature of images [8]. Wide dynamic range will greatly interfere with the target's clear image, affecting subsequent detection tasks.

Dynamic Range (DR) describes the range of light intensity that the camera CIS can detect from the darkest to the brightest part, the maximum scene contrast that can be restored [9]. Ideally noiseless, the dynamic range is the bit depth of the camera digital-to-analog converter, such as 12 bits or 8 bits. The actual dynamic range needs to consider the circuit output noise of the sensor and the noise occurring in the whole digital image processing process. The high noise means the low dynamic range.

Methods to calculate the dynamic range based on the Opto-Electronic Conversion Functions (OECF) are provided in the ISO19894 [10]. The OECF function describes the characteristics of the camera for converting the input brightness into numerical values. Measurements using a specific test plate, the brightness L of a density D of a gray scale block is calculated as follows:

$$L = 10^{-D}E/\pi \tag{4}$$

Among them, the unit of D is in Kandra/Square meter (cd/m^2), E is the illumination incident on the test panel, and the unit of e E is Lux (lx). The dynamic range can be calculated by Eq. (5):

$$DR = \frac{[log(L_{sat}) - log(L_{min})]}{log(2)} \tag{5}$$

where L_{sat}, L_{min} are set brightness value and minimum brightness value.

2.1.4 Geometrical Distortion

Geometrical distortion refers to the phenomenon that the geometry of the target image taken by the camera is not similar to the actual target plane projection. When image guided projectile is imaging in the air, the degree of imaging geometric distortion of the target area obtained has a significant impact on the accuracy of target recognition and guidance control command, so it is necessary to measure the degree of distortion [11]. Image distortion originates from the non-linearity of the optical system caused by lens surface error, optical processing accuracy, design combination of lens and CMOS, mechanical assembly and so on in the camera optical system.

As a result, the reflected light from the target does not conform to the ideal projection imaging model, which changes the relative position relationship between the corresponding points between the objects and images. At the same time, the more the light deviates from the main optical axis, the more obvious the position offset caused by refraction. Radial lens distortion is the main consideration in the distortion evaluation, which can be divided into occipital distortion and bucket distortion (Fig. 3).

Distortion can be expressed as (6):

$$GD = 100 \times \frac{(H' - H)}{H} \tag{6}$$

Among them, H is the position of the point without distortion, and H' is the distance from the point to the center of the image. The geometric distortion of a grid location is the value between the radial distance H' of the actual grid location and H of the ideal grid location divided by the ideal grid location H. H' less than H denotes negative distortion (barrel distortion), and H' greater than H indicates positive distortion (pillow distortion).

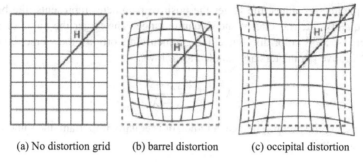

(a) No distortion grid   (b) barrel distortion   (c) occipital distortion

Fig. 3. Schematic diagram of the distortion

2.2 Imaging Quality Evaluation Model of Onboard Camera

The evaluation of imaging quality of shell-borne cameras involves many indexes from different angles. The evaluation methods of the indexes are different and the dimensions of each index are not consistent. In order to evaluate the image quality comprehensively and objectively, it is necessary to set up a single index evaluation algorithm and set up a unified evaluation model in a reasonable way.

2.2.1 Establishment of Model

The essence of quality evaluation model is multi-index statistical analysis. For the image quality of the onboard camera, this paper chooses four independent and independent parameters corresponding to MTF, $\triangle$E, DR and GD from four aspects: image sharpness, color difference, geometric distortion and dynamic range. The four evaluation indexes can not only characterize the image quality from different aspects, but also have no correlation among each other, which makes it easy to use an intuitive and feasible weighted evaluation model. This section is intended to be evaluated using evaluation models based on linear weighting methods:

$$V = X_1\lambda_1 + X_2\lambda_2 + X_3\lambda_3 + X_4\lambda_4 \tag{7}$$

Among them, V indicates the value of camera imaging quality evaluation, $X_1, ..., X_4$ are four independent evaluation indicators and λ means the corresponding weight of each indicator, $\sum_{i=1}^{4} \lambda = 1$.

Considering that the dimensions of evaluation indexes are not unified and the order of magnitude of each index parameter is quite different, it is necessary to normalize the parameters in different dimensions and directions. For the positive index, the parameter value is normalized to [0, 1] by linear transformation.

$$X' = \frac{X - X_{\min}}{X_{\max} - X_{\min}} \tag{8}$$

where $X_{\max}$ and $X_{\min}$ are the maximum and minimum values corresponding to multiple camera test parameters X respectively. In order to solve the problem of positive and negative parameter values, the larger the positive parameter represents, the better the imaging quality, such as clarity and dynamic range. The larger the value of negative parameters (such as color difference and geometric distortion), the worse the imaging quality. Negative parameters are handled as follows:

$$X' = \frac{X_{max} - X}{X_{max} - X_{min}} \tag{9}$$

Considering the premise that each indicator is equally important, the same weight is used for each attribute.

2.2.2 Realization of the Evaluation Index Measurement Method

2.2.2.1 Index Measurement Method of MTF

Siemens stars simulate established spatial frequencies by lines with different radial frequencies, and the MTF decreases with the difference between the black and white lines. Break the Siemens star into eight parts to measure the camera MTF from eight different directions, as shown in Fig. 4.

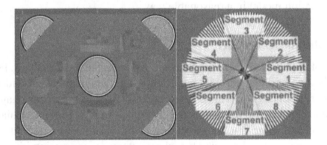

Fig. 4. Siemens star used for measurement

The measurement process is shown in Fig. 5.

Fig. 5. Calculation flow chart of MTF

2.2.2.2 Index Measurement Method of $\triangle E$

The color block area is obtained by collecting the standard color chart, and the imaging color difference of the camera is calculated. The color block of the chart is shown in Fig. 6. Since the color space output by the missile borne camera is RGB, it is necessary to continue the operation of color space conversion to calculate the color difference.

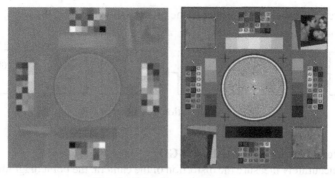

Fig. 6. Color block recognition

Measurement process is shown in Fig. 7:

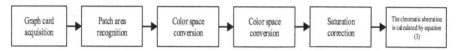

Fig. 7. Flow chart of color difference calculation

2.2.2.3 Index Measurement Method of DR

The DR of the camera can be measured by photographing a group of gray-scale blocks with known density, as shown in Fig. 8.

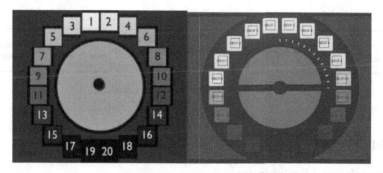

Fig. 8. Gray-scale block identification

Measure and calculate according to the process shown in Fig. 9.

Fig. 9. Calculation flow chart of DR

2.2.2.4 Index Measurement Method of GD

In order to accurately measure the distortion of the camera, the point diagram is selected for distortion test, and the difference between the actual image height and the ideal image height is used to represent the distortion result of a certain part (Fig. 10).

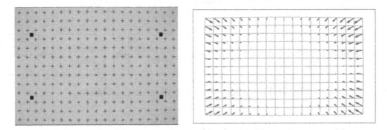

Fig. 10. Distortion card and identification

The calculation flow is shown in Fig. 11.

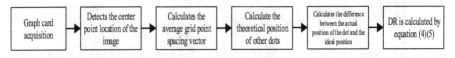

Fig. 11. Flow chart of distortion calculation

3 Experiments

3.1 Experimental Environment

In this paper, there are four groups of cameras tested: camera A using filter 1 preprocessing algorithm 1, camera B using filter 2 and preprocessing algorithm 1, camera C using filter 1 and preprocessing algorithm 2, and camera D using filter 2 and preprocessing algorithm 2. The optimal image preprocessing algorithm is selected and tested. In order to obtain accurate evaluation parameter results, a darkroom measurement laboratory conforming to IEEE standard is built. The surrounding environment of the laboratory is black or 18% neutral gray to prevent the light of other colors from affecting the test results. Two 45° vertical xxx graphic card lighting sources are used to ensure uniform light on the surface of the graphic card and avoid insufficient exposure by fine adjusting the light intensity, color temperature and position of the light source. The chart card is arranged on the chart card support, TE42 comprehensive chart card and TE251 distortion measurement chart card are selected respectively to measure the specific values of relevant indicators. During DR index measurement, LG3 transmission light box and TE270X transmission gray scale test chart card are used alone, including 20 gray scale blocks in a circle, and the measurable dynamic range can reach 80 dB. The test software uses IQ anaylaer laboratory environment, as shown in the Fig. 12.

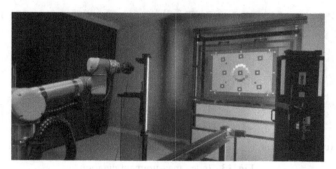

Fig. 12. Laboratory environment

3.2 Evaluation Results of Measurement

The absolute value results of each index of the tested camera a are shown in Fig. 13. Figure 13(a) shows the MTF of the eight parts of the central Siemens star. The y-axis represents the modulation rate and the x-axis represents the spatial frequency. The red vertical dotted line indicates the Nyquist frequency. The red horizontal dotted line indicates the modulation at a specific limit resolution. Figure 13(b) shows the pixel value changes of 20 density decreasing blocks in R, G, B and Y channels respectively. Figure 13(c) shows the color difference value measured by 96 color blocks. The darker the color, the more serious the color difference deviation is. Figure 13(d) divides the image into four quadrants. The x-axis represents the distance to the center and the y-axis represents the distortion rate. The curve represents the best fit line of the grid position.

The index of the four cameras was tested and evaluated by the model (7) for the final evaluation score, as shown in Table 1. It can be seen that the camera D adopts the filter 2 and the image preprocessing algorithm 2 to achieve the optimal imaging quality.

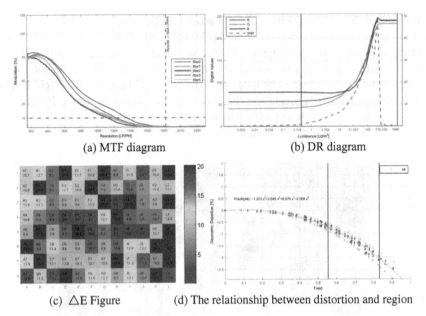

(a) MTF diagram

(b) DR diagram

(c) △E Figure

(d) The relationship between distortion and region

Fig. 13. Index measurement diagram

Table 1. Results of the imaging quality evaluation indicators

Tested cameras	MTF (%)	DR (dB)	△E_mean	GD_mean (%%)	V
cameraA	67.8	62.37	12.3	−1.0	2.09
cameraB	83.7	65.19	6.7	−0.8	1.88
cameraC	76.1	61.63	10.6	−0.6	1.14
cameraD	90.1	69.56	5.1	−0.7	2.25

The imaging results of the onboard camera in the air are shown in Fig. 14.

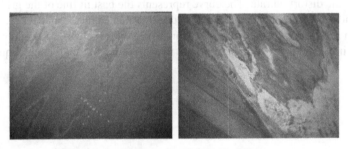

Fig. 14. Imaging results of the onboard camera

4   Conclusion

It is crucial to evaluate the imaging quality of onboard camera, which is the key component of image guided projectile seeker. Firstly, this paper analyzes the four aspects of image clarity, color difference, dynamic range and geometric distortion that the onboard camera focuses on. Secondly, it selects MTF, $\triangle$E, DR and GD as independent evaluation indexes, and gives the measurement method. Finally, this paper puts forward an evaluation model based on linear weighting. Through the evaluation of the camera to be tested in the built laboratory environment and used to guide the design of onboard camera and the evaluation of imaging effect, it has high application value for improving the operational efficiency of ammunition.

References

1. Qian, L.Z.: Study on the Key Technique of the TV-Guided Projectile Weapon System, pp. 2–6. The University of Science and Technology of China, D. He fei (2006)
2. Wen, S.l., Song, Y.R.: Research on seeker cost transfer program of DARPA. J. Tactical Missile Technology **002**, 5–9 (2016)
3. Xu, N.S., Ren, G.Q., Huang, Y.M.: Correlation analysis between visible light remote sensing imaging performance index and image feature parameter. J. Foreign Electron. Measure. Technol. **40**(5), 114–120 (2021)
4. Gao J.: Quality Evaluation Method for Smartphone Imaging Modules, pp. 18–21. Hangzhou University of Electronic Technology, D. Hangzhou (2018)
5. ISO 17850–Geometric distortion (GD) measurements
6. Xu, W.W., Zhang, L.M., Si, X.L., Yang, B.Y., Wang, J.X.: Research on image quality evaluation method of high resolution optical satellite sensor based on radial target. J. Opt. **39**(09), 346–351 (2019)
7. Huang, J.J., Ke, W., Wang, J., Deng, Z.M.: Color difference detection and rating system of denim clothing based on computer vision. J. Textile **40**(05), 163–169 (2019)
8. Cheng, H.: Research on tone mapping algorithm of high dynamic range image. D. University of Chinese Academy of Sciences (Institute of optoelectronic technology, Chinese Academy of Sciences) (2019)
9. Feng, X.B., Chen, X., Min, H.N., Wu, W., Wang, S.P., Wu, G.H.: Dr image enhancement of aeroengine Guide Vane Based on improved CLAHE. J. Aeronaut. Power 1–12 (2021)
10. ISO 14524–Opto-Electric Conversion Function (OECF)
11. Liu, D., Qian, H., Wang, Z.F.: Reconstruction of distorted signal with limited innovation rate based on LSTM feature extraction. J. Electron. 217–225 (2021)

Stroke Based Painting with 3D Perception

Yiren Song, Zhongliang Jing[✉], and Minzhe Li

Institute of Aerospace Science and Technology, Shanghai Jiaotong University,
Shanghai 200240, People's Republic of China
{songyiren,zljing,liminzhe}@sjtu.edu.cn

Abstract. Generation of stroke-based non-photorealistic imagery is an important problem in the computer vision community. Existing stroke-based rendering algorithms are based on minimizing the difference between the input image and the output image. However, human painter artistry emphasizes creation based on 3D prior information rather than simply reproducing input images. To better simulate the painting process of human painters, this paper presents a novel solution by introducing 3D perception into 2D painting tasks. A perception network and an interactive rendering agent are designed to obtain attractive rendered pictures with enhanced details. Then, a Bi-level painting agent based on reinforcement learning transfers the rendered images into stroke sequences with oriental ink style. Compared with existing algorithms, our method is superior to others in texture quality and user evaluation. Ablation study and user study demonstrate the effectiveness of the proposed method, the results show that our method is superior in style and detail quality compared with baseline methods.

Keywords: Stroke-based painting · 3D perception · Neural painting

1 Introduction

Teaching machines to paint like humans is an important research content of computer vision. Some scholars use style transfer to generate artistic works [2], which refers to the mapping of a style from one image to another by preserving the content of a source image, while learning lower-level stylistic elements to match a destination style [5,12] presents a Neural Abstract Style Transfer method for Chinese traditional painting. However, the output image of style transfer has many artifacts and the process lacks interaction so the artist cannot participate (Fig. 1).

© The Author(s), under exclusive license to Springer Nature Singapore Pte Ltd. 2022
Y. Wang et al. (Eds.): IGTA 2022, CCIS 1611, pp. 326–341, 2022.
https://doi.org/10.1007/978-981-19-5096-4_25

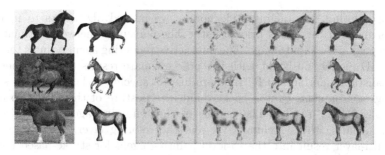

Fig. 1. Given a natural horse image as input, our algorithm can produce an oriental ink painting with the process by drawing one stroke every time. (a) Input image, 3D perception and (b) rendering result, painting process created by (c) our method.

Stroke-based rendering (SBR) is a method of non-photorealistic imagery that recreates images by placing discrete drawing elements such as paint strokes or stipples on canvas. Placing brushes on the canvas one by one to simulate the input pictures and by adjusting the parameters of the brushes, different styles of paintings can be obtained. Most SBR algorithms solve the stroke decomposition problem by Greedy Search [11,13] on every single step. Recent deep learning-based solutions adopt the use of recurrent neural networks for stroke decomposition. However, these methods, like Sketch-RNN [6], require access to sequential stroke data which is hard to obtain. StrokeNet [28] addresses this limitation by using a differentiable renderer. [4] and [9] introduced RL for the sketch synthesis task. The reward functions are designed to make the model learn which strokes will decrease the loss between the painting and the target image. However, what existing stroke based Neural Painters can do is just imitate the input image, but cannot create beyond the input image. The difference between various renderers is only the difference in the degree of fitting approximation. What those SBR methods achieve is more similar to the original image rather than more attractive. Some work studies the effects of using different stroke designs [5] to simulate different styles. But the concept of style in painting is very broad, only by simply adjusting parameters such as stroke color and texture, the style we can imitate is limited. What's more, users cannot determine the output effect through interactive control in the process of painting.

Before the birth of electronic products, human painters used models and still life to assist in painting. In the process of copying a photo, experienced painters will quickly construct a 3D model of the copied object in their mind to assist them in expressing the relationship of position, perspective, light, and shadow. In the digital age, we still cannot do without model reference. Many digital artists tend to 3D-assisted painting. Compared with the 2D image, 3D assets contain more information useful for painting. Through 3D modeling, they can get the accurate shape, perspective relationship, satisfactory composition, and add material to the objects in the picture to increase the details of the picture. Inspired by this, this paper presents a novel solution by introducing 3D perception into 2D painting tasks. Our method consists of three parts: perception network, interactive rendering agent, and Bi-level painting agent. For the specific task of painting oriental ink style horses. we invited 3D artists to make 3D models and textures as 3D prior. Firstly, The perception network estimates the horse's pose in the input image. The interactive rendering agent adjusts the bone-driven 3D model consistent with the pose estimate results and then performs non-realistic rendering (NPR) that produces a specific style. Users can set the lighting environment, canvas background, the posture of the model to obtain more satisfactory results. The output of the rendering agent is divided into layers, including the sketching layer and the coloring layer. Finally, we input the multi-layer result into the Bi-level painting agent for stroke-based painting to get the final result.

Our method have significant advantages compared with style transfer [2,5] or other image translation algorithms [9,18,30]. Firstly, through the pose estimation and 3D reconstruction of the object in the input image, the network can acquire 3D prior information, which is essential to enhance the visual quality. Secondly, unlike traditional 2D edge detection methods based on filters, rendering-based 3D edge detection methods can obtain accurate model edge detection results without being affected by texture. The 3D edge detection results can be used as the sketching layer after post-processing [24]. Thirdly, the interactive rendering agent allows users to edit 3D assets and rendering parameters to determine the final effect. Through a comparative experiment and user study, we verified that the proposed method has advantages over baseline methods. Ablation experiment prove the effectiveness of the 3D perception module.

The contribution of our paper is summarized as follows:

- We propose a stroke-based painting method with 3D perception, innovatively introduce 3D perception into a 2D painting task. To our best knowledge, there are few previous works have been done on this topic.
- An interactive rendering agent which allows human interaction is achieved. We design a powerful tool based on deep learning for designers and artists rather than replacing them with a massive data-driven and complex network.
- We propose a Bi-level painting agent based on deep reinforcement for oriental ink style painting generation and achieve state-of-the-art visual quality.

2 Relate Work

2.1 Image Translation and Style Transfer

Image translation, which means translating images from one domain (e.g., real photos) to another (e.g., artworks) is very popular in recent years. GAN-based image translation such as Pix2Pix [5], CycleGANs [21] are of great significance in tasks such as style transfer and also have been applied to computer-generated arts. In addition to the GAN-based method, neural style transfer has also played an important role in stylized image synthesis and is widely used for artwork creation [2,5]. But the above methods all generate paintings in a pixel-by-pixel manner, unlike humans use brushes to paint stroke by stroke.

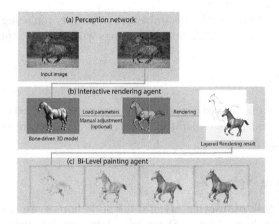

Fig. 2. Overview of Stroke base painting with 3D perception Pipeline. Our SBR method with 3D perception pipeline consists of three parts. The perception network (a) complete key point detection and pose estimation. Interactive rendering agent (b) render 3D perception result into sketching layer and coloring layer. Finally, Bi-level painting agent (c) turn rendered image into Stroke sequence.

2.2 Stroke Based Rendering

Stroke-based rendering (SBR) is a method of nonphotorealistic imagery that recreates images by placing discrete drawing elements such as paint strokes or stipples on canvas. Traditional methods usually devise heuristic painting strategies [11] or greedily select a stroke that minimizes difference from the target image step by step [13]. Recent works use RNN and RL to improve the stroke decomposition of images. [6] proposed an RNN-based solution to generate strokes for sketches. [4,29] introduced RL for the sketch synthesis task. [27] elaborate on the design of actions and stroke and explored the RL method for ink painting. [24] accomplish an image-to-pencil automatic drawing algorithm. [22] introduce content loss into SBR process which make the brush stroke planning of the painting agent more human-like. [14] formulate the task as a set prediction problem and propose a novel Transformer-based framework. However, the above methods didn't use images' prior information and what they realized is fitting the input image as much as possible.

2.3 3D Pose Estimation

Recent works have made significant advances in the frontier of skeleton-based 3D human pose estimation from single image, with many approaches achieving impressive results [15,16,23,25]. Those methods can be divided into two categories: regression-based methods and optimization-based methods. The result of model-based pose estimate methods is smooth and accurate, which is what painting task require. [19] builds on a state-of-the-art human pose-estimation algorithm allow user extracting the poses of animals without using markers. Our perception network is designed to estimate horses'3D pose and adjust a bone-driven model fit the input image. Our method is universal, by simply replacing the perception module and 3D assets, we can achieve paintings with different themes.

3   Approach

Our method consists of three parts, they are perception network, interactive rendering agent and Bi-level painting agent. The architecture of our method is shown in the Fig. 2.

3.1   Perception Network

For the specific task of drawing oriental ink style horses, we train a perception network based on bone-driven 3D models, detecting key points of bones and estimating the pose of the target object. The Perception network is a two-stage network, which architecture is shown in Fig. 3 below.

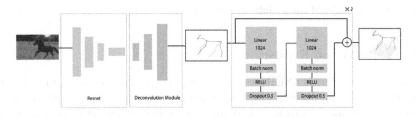

Fig. 3. A diagram of perception network architecture.

The first stage estimates the key points of the horse's 2D pose from a single picture, and the second stage uses the input image and the 2D pose estimate result to generate the 3D pose detection result. ResNet [8] is a most common backbone network for image feature extraction. It is also used in [20,26] for pose estimation. Our method simply adds a few deconvolutional layers over the last convolution stage in the ResNet. We adopt this structure because it is arguably the simplest to generate heatmaps from deep and low resolution features and also adopted in the state-of-the-art Mask R-CNN [7]. By default, three deconvolutional layers with batch normalization and ReLU activation are used. Each layer has 256 filters with 4×4 kernel. The stride is 2. A 1×1 convolutional layer is added at last to generate predicted heatmaps $\{H_1 \ldots H_k\}$ for all k key points. Now we have 2D keypoints detection results, our goal is to estimate body joint locations in 3-dimensional space given a 2-dimensional input. [15] provides a 2D to 3D baseline, that given 2d joint locations, predicts 3d positions through a neural network. Input is a series of 2d points $x \in \mathbb{R}^{2n}$, and our output is a series of points in 3d space $x \in \mathbb{R}^{3n}$. We aim to learn a function $f^* : \mathbb{R}^{2n} \to \mathbb{R}^{3n}$ that minimizes the prediction error over a dataset of N poses:

$$f^* = \min_f \frac{1}{N} \sum_{i=1}^{N} \mathcal{L}\left(f\left(\mathbf{x}_i\right) - \mathbf{y}_i\right) \tag{1}$$

Figure 3 shows a diagram with the basic building blocks of Stage two. Our approach is based on a simple, deep, multilayer neural network with batch normalization, dropout, and Rectified Linear Units, as well as residual connections. The residual block is repeated twice, which means that we have 6 linear layers in total.

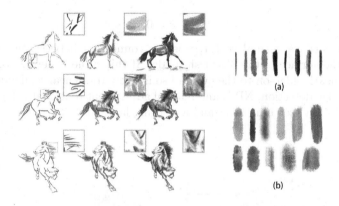

Fig. 4. The process of human artist create oriental ink style horse, it can be seen from the zoomed-in areas that different strokes are used in the sketching and coloring stage. Some stroke shapes are used in the sketching layer (a) and coloring layer (b).

3.2   Interactive Rendering Agent

In this section, we developed an interactive rendering agent, taking the pose estimate result as input, and rendering it in Euclidean space. The TigDog [3] dataset labels 18 bone key points for each horse, but it's not enough to fit the horse's rich posture in nature. As shown in Fig. 2, Our rendering agent added 11 control points such as tail and ankle joints, expands the number of bone key points to 29, allow user to adjust the horse's posture more finely based on the result of 3D perception. We design an interactive interface that allows users to adjust the light environment, target object posture, NPR parameters and camera parameters such as focal length, position, and angle to obtain more satisfactory rendering results. We believe that it is necessary to involve experienced artists in the creative process, art-directed tools take time to develop, but the rewards justify the effort. Practical interactive tools can increase the creative involvement of artists who can validate the quality of the algorithm and highlight potential intrinsic problems [17].

Line rendering technique play an important role in simulating the human painting process. Traditional 2D edge detection methods are based on filters such as the Sobel filter and Laplacian filter. The above methods based on detecting gray gradient changes will produce some false results that are difficult to eliminate. The rendering-based 3D edge detection method can obtain accurate model edge detection results without being affected by texture. The results can be used as the sketch of the painting after post-processing. Specifically, for a 3D mesh model, the dot product between the direction to the viewpoint and the surface normal can be used to give a silhouette edge.

$$f \cdot x = 0 \tag{2}$$

where f is surface normal vector, x is the connection between the eye and a point on the surface of the 3D mesh model. If this value is near zero, then the surface is nearly edge-on to the eye and so is likely to be near a silhouette edge. After 3D edge detection, NPR, and manual adjustment (optional), the rendering result contain a sketching layer and a coloring layer.

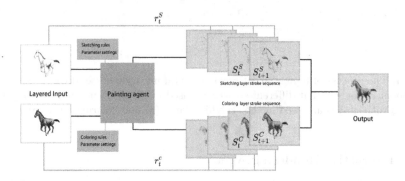

Fig. 5. Overview of Bi-level painting agent. The input are layered rendering result of the Interactive rendering agent, output is stroke sequence.

3.3   Bi-level Painting Agent

The proposed work builds on the deep reinforcement learning framework from [9]. In order to better simulate oriental ink painting, we improve the previous method into a Bi-level painting agent, which use different strategies to draw sketching layer and coloring layer.

We formulate the procedure of adding a stroke as a Markov Decision Process (MDP) consisting of a tuple $(\mathcal{S}, \mathcal{A}, p_{\mathrm{I}}, p_{\mathrm{T}}, R)$, where s is a set of continuous states, a is a set of continuous actions, p_{I}, is the probability-density of the initial state,

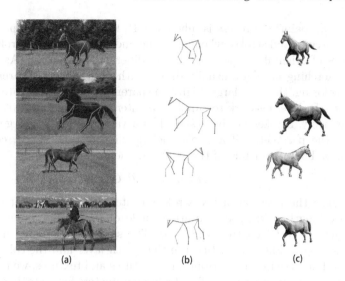

(a)   (b)   (c)

Fig. 6. Example output of perception network. (a) Input image from TigDog dataset and groundtruth, (b) 2D pose estimate result, (c) 3D perception result.

$p_T(s' \mid s, a)$ is the transition probability-density from the current state $s \in \mathcal{S}$ to next state $s' \in \mathcal{S}$ when taking action $a \in \mathcal{A}$, $R(s, a, s')$ is an immediate reward function for the transition from s to s', by taking action a.

Let $\pi(a \mid s; \boldsymbol{\theta})$ be a stochastic policy with parameter θ, which represents the conditional probability density of taking action a given state s. Let $h = (s_1, a_1, \ldots, s_T, a_T, s_{T+1})$ be a trajectory of length T. Then the return (i.e., the discounted sum of future rewards) along h is expressed as

$$R(h) = \sum_{t=1}^{T} \gamma^{t-1} R(s_t, a_t, s_{t+1}) \tag{3}$$

where $\gamma \in [0, 1)$ is the discount factor for the future reward. The expected return for parameter θ is defined by

$$J(\boldsymbol{\theta}) = \int p(h \mid \boldsymbol{\theta}) R(h) \mathrm{d}h \tag{4}$$

where

$$p(h \mid \boldsymbol{\theta}) = p(s_1) \prod_{t=1}^{T} p(s_{t+1} \mid s_t, a_t) \pi(a_t \mid s_t, \boldsymbol{\theta}) \tag{5}$$

To make the final canvas resemble the target image, the agent should find the optimal policy parameter $\boldsymbol{\theta}^*$ that maximizes the expected return $J(\theta)$:

$$\boldsymbol{\theta}^* \equiv \operatorname{argmax} J(\boldsymbol{\theta}) \tag{6}$$

The human painting process is inherently Bi-level [22]. Human painters use different strategies and strokes when sketching and coloring. Brushstrokes In different stages of oriental ink painting have a different distribution. As shown in Fig. 5(a), sketching layer are usually drawn with dark, low-transparency lines, and when coloring, they use large, high-transparency strokes. Motivated by this, we propose a Bi-level network to simulate painter's sketching and coloring process, respectively. Strokes are be designed as a variety of curves or geometries. In general, the parameter of a stroke include the position, shape, color, and transparency. The parameters of the stroke are defined as follows:

$$a_t = (x, y, n, h, w, \theta, t, R, G, B)_t \tag{7}$$

where (x, y) is the position of the stroke's center, n is stroke shape number, (h, w, θ) are length, width, and rotation angle of the stroke, t means transparency, and (R, G, B) controls the color. The stroke shapes used in the two layers are shown in Fig. 5(b,c). Because the sketch layer and the coloring layer have large differences in the distribution of features and textures, we modify the action bundle at to separately predict strokes parameters for sketching layer and coloring layer, i.e.

$$a_t = \{a_s, a_c\} \tag{8}$$

where a_s and a_c represent the parameters in sketching layer and coloring layer, respectively. Different initialization parameters (stroke shape, size range, transparency range) and rules are set for the two kinds of action bundle. When drawing sketching layer, we limit the number of stacked layers of strokes in the same position to obtain a more concise picture. At the same time, the transparency of the strokes is lower, the shape of the strokes are small slender lines, and choose the color with low saturation. When drawing the coloring layer, the brush strokes are allowed to be unrealistically large, e.g., more than a quarter the width of the canvas. The color selection is more flexible and allows multiple superimpositions of high-transparency brushstrokes to simulate oriental ink effects. For mathematical convenience alone, we define two distinct stroke map definitions Φ, Φ^c. $\Phi(a_t) \{\in [0, 1]^{H \times W}\}$ represents the stroke density map, whose value at any pixel provides a measure of transparency of the current stroke. $\Phi^c(a_t)$ is the colored rendering of the original stroke density map $\Phi(a_t)$ on an empty canvas. Next, given a painting agent Φ target image I_S (sketching layer) and I_c (coloring layer), the canvas state S_t is updated in the following stages.

$$s_{t+1}^s = s_t^s + \Phi^c(a_s) \tag{9}$$

$$M_{t+1} = M_t + \Phi(a_s) \tag{10}$$

$$s_{t+1}^c = s_t^c + \Phi^c(a_c) \odot [1 - M_{t+1}] \tag{11}$$

$$s_t = s_t^s + s_t^c \tag{12}$$

where $\odot$ indicates element-wise multiplication and $\Phi^c(a_c)$ is the colored rendering of the stroke density map $\Phi(a)$, M_t is the mask composed of the stroke sequence in s_t^s. The reward for each stroke type is then defined as,

$$r_t^s = D^{wgan}(I_s, S_{t+1}) - D^{wgan}(I_s, S_t) \tag{13}$$

$$r_t^c = D^{wgan}(I_c, S_{t+1}) - D^{wgan}(I_c, S_t) \tag{14}$$

The total reward function is the sum of r_t^s and r_t^c:

$$r_t = r_{t+1}^c + r_t^s \tag{15}$$

In the predicting stage, painting agent turn layered rendered images into stroke sequences. The final output is obtained by mixing the stroke sequences predicted by the two kinds of action bundle and then render them on an empty canvas.

Fig. 7. Ablation study on proposed 3D perception and Bi-level painting reward. (a) Input image, (b) full model, (c) without Bi-level painting reward,(d) without 3D perception, (e) with out 3D perception module and Bi-level painting reward.

4 Experiments

4.1 Dataset

In this paper, the perception network is trained on the TigDog [3] dataset to get the 2D pose estimate result. TigDog dataset contains video shots for three different classes: tigers, horses and dogs, it manually annotated the 2D location of 19 landmarks in each frame (e.g. left eye, neck, front left ankle, etc.). Due to the lack of 3D labeled datasets for horse pose estimation, we use the unity perception package to generate a 3D pose estimate dataset. Becourse both the human body and the horse body are highly symmetrical structures, there are many similarities between estimation of the human body and horse. We use the model trained on Human3.6M [10] as the pre-training weights and perform fine-tuning on the synthetic horse-3D dataset we have labeled.

4.2 Implementation Details

3D Perception. Our ResNet backbone network is initialized by pre-training on ImageNet classification task. In the training for pose estimation, the base learning rate is 0.001 and exponential decay. Mini-batch size is 32, optimizer is Adam. When predict 3D pose from 2D pose estimate result, since we do not predict the global position of the 3d prediction, we zero-centre the 3d poses around the hip joint.We train our network for 200 epochs using Adam, a starting learning rate of 0.001 and exponential decay, using mini-batches of size 32. Initially, the weights of our linear layers are set using Kaiming initialization. Interactive rendering agent is developed based on Unity3D, a popular engine for 3D related work. Thanks to Unity's powerful developer community, various styles of NPR and 3D assets can be used by the interactive rendering agent proposed in this paper.

Bi-level Painting Agent. We closely follow the architecture from [9], while designing the differentiable neural renderer Φ. Given a batch of random brush stroke parameters on the blank canvas, the network output rats is trained to mimic the rendering of the corresponding stroke on an empty canvas. The training labels are generated using an automated graphics module and the renderer is trained for 5×10^5 iterations with a batch size of 64. As to Loss function, we use Wasserstein-l distance [1], also known as Earth-Mover distance, which has great ability in measuring the distribution distance between the generated data and the target data.

4.3   Experiments Results and Analysis

In this section, we compare our results with two representative methods [9, 30] to prove the effectiveness of our algorithm. As can be seen from Fig. 7, what the two baseline methods achieve is fitting the input image. If the input image lacks detail like the second input image in Fig. 7, the result will be unsatisfying. But our method with 3D perception is not limited by the quality of the input image, which can achieve a more refined picture and texture. Huang's method uses the Bézier curve as stroke. Zou's method aims to simulate the style of oil painting, the stroke is two kinds of an opaque paintbrushes. Our method has a more abundant selection of brush strokes. Because we set up a brush library containing dozens of brush shapes for the sketching layer and the coloring layer respectively. Besides, we set the optional range for each parameter based on the artist's experience, which have played an important role in enhancing the effect of the picture. Because rules are set to constrain paint agent behavior, such as not allowing unrealistic large brush strokes to minimize the loss in the first few strokes, our method offers better resemblance with a human painter. In terms of background drawing, oriental ink paintings usually retain the color of rice paper, unlike oil paintings that fill the entire picture. These two methods are not good or bad, but from the results, the background of our method is cleaner than Zou's method.

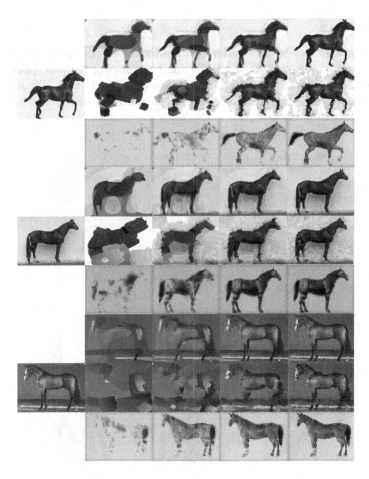

Fig. 8. Comparison with two baseline methods. The input image is on the left, and the painting process is on the right. For each input image, the first line is the result of [9], the second line is the result of [30], and the third line is the result of ourmethod.

4.4   Ablation Study

We present ablation study results to verify the effectiveness of the 3D perception module and Bi-level painting reward. The 3D perception module in this section means the sum of the 3D perception network and interactive rendering agent. As shown in Fig. 8, without the 3D perception module, the result is directly rendered by the Bi-level painting agent stroke by stroke. In order to ensure that the Bi-level painting agent is available, we replaced the Sketching layer with the 2D edge detection results. The result of the painting looks like a filter effect is used on the input image, but it is far from the oriental ink painting. Without Bi-level painting reward, the result lacks line details at the same time looks vague and dirty.

4.5   Gallery

This paper presents a novel solution by introducing 3D perception into 2D painting tasks. Our method is universal, by simply replacing the perception module and 3D assets, we can obtain paintings with different themes. Figure 9 shows some works of other themes created by our method, the effect is comparable to that of a human painter.

Fig. 9. Other subject paintings created by our method.

5   User Study

We carry out a user study to quantitatively evaluate the proposed method. 100 participants were investigated the preferences to our algorithm and two baseline methods. We mixed 50 paintings (10 from our method, 10 from [9], 10 from [30], and 20 from human painters and let participants find out the works of humans. The result is shown in Fig. 10(a), our algorithm is more likely to be mistaken for human work compared to the other two baseline methods, which means our results are more similar to the works of human painters. And then, ten sets of pictures are been given to every participant. Every set of pictures included an input image, the corresponding result of three SBR algorithms, and several pictures of the painting process. Participants didn't know the drawing was from which method and the ordering of three methods was shuffled in every set. Participants were asked to rate three algorithms from detail preference, style preference and overall prefernce, score range was 0 to 10. The feedback results are shown in Fig. 10(b). After completing the above survey, we let each participant choose their favorite algorithm and counted the number of people who voted for each algorithm. Then we showed our interactive rendering agent and encourage them to experience the interactive function. We informed participants that the other two methods couldn't allow user interaction and let them choose their favorite algorithm again. The survey results are shown in Fig. 10(c), more people voted for our method as their favorite after experiencing the interactive function.

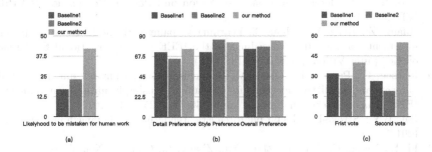

Fig. 10. Results of the user study. (a) Likelihood to be mistaken for human work, (b) participant's scoring results, participant's vote result for the favorite method.

6   Conclusion

This paper propose a 3D perception pipeline for the "learning to paint" problem. By introducing 3D prior information into the 2D painting task, state-of-the-art visual quality is achieved. Unlike other methods which resemble a black box, our method allows users to participate and improve the final effect. We innovatively design a Bi-level painting agent which turn rendered layers into a stroke sequence that closely resembles a human painter. The ablation study and user study verify the effectiveness of the method we propose.

References

1. Arjovsky, M., Chintala, S., Bottou, L.: Wasserstein generative adversarial networks. In: International Conference on Machine Learning, pp. 214–223. PMLR (2017)
2. Chen, D., Yuan, L., Liao, J., Yu, N., Hua, S.: Stylebank: An explicit representation for neural image style transfer. In: 2017 IEEE Conference on Computer Vision and Pattern Recognition (CVPR) (2017)
3. Del Pero, L., Ricco, S., Sukthankar, R., Ferrari, V.: Behavior discovery and alignment of articulated object classes from unstructured video. Int. J. Comput. Vis. **121**(2), 303–325 (2017)

4. Ganin, Y., Kulkarni, T., BabUschkin, I., Eslami, S., Vinyals, Q.: Synthesizing programs for images using reinforced adversarial learning. In: Proceedings of the 35th International Conference on Machine Learning, PMLR 80, pp. 1666–1675 (2018)

5. Gatys, L.A., Ecker, A.S., Bethge, M.:: Image style transfer using convolutional neural networks. In: 2016 IEEE Conference on Computer Vision and Pattern Recognition (CVPR) (2016)

6. Ha, D., Eck, D.: A neural representation of sketch drawings. arXiv preprint arXiv:1704.03477 (2017)

7. He, K., Gkioxari, G., Dollár, P., Girshick, R.: Mask r-CNN. IEEE Trans. Pattern Anal. Mach. Intell. (2017)

8. He, K., Zhang, X., Ren, S., Sun, J.: Deep residual learning for image recognition. 2016 IEEE Conference on Computer Vision and Pattern Recognition (CVPR). IEEE (2016)

9. Huang, Z., Heng, W., Zhou, S.: Learning to paint with model-based deep reinforcement learning. In: Proceedings of the IEEE/CVF International Conference on Computer Vision, pp. 8709–8718 (2019)

10. Ionescu, C., Papava, D., Olaru, V., Sminchisescu, C.: Human3. 6m: Large scale datasets and predictive methods for 3D human sensing in natural environments. IEEE Trans. Pattern Anal. Mach. Intell. 36(7), 1325–1339 (2013)

11. Lai, B.Y.: Stroke-based non-photorealistic rendering. J. Guangzhou Mar. Coll. (2012)

12. Li, B., Xiong, C., Wu, T., Zhou, Yu., Zhang, L., Chu, R.: Neural abstract style transfer for chinese traditional painting. In: Jawahar, C.V., Li, H., Mori, G., Schindler, K. (eds.) ACCV 2018. LNCS, vol. 11362, pp. 212–227. Springer, Cham (2019). https://doi.org/10.1007/978-3-030-20890-5_14

13. Litwinowicz, P.: Processing images and video for an impressionist effect. In: Proceedings of the 24th Annual Conference on Computer Graphics and Interactive Techniques, pp. 407–414 (1997)

14. Liu, S., et al.: Paint transformer: Feed forward neural painting with stroke prediction (2021)

15. Martinez, J., Hossain, R., Romero, J., Little, J.J.: A simple yet effective baseline for 3D human pose estimation. In: 2017 IEEE International Conference on Computer Vision (ICCV). IEEE Computer Society (2017)

16. MehtaD, D., et al.: VNect: real-time 3D human pose estimation with a single RGB camera. ACM Trans. Graph. 36(4), 1–14 (2017)

17. Montesdeoca, S.E., et al.: A framework for real-time expressive non-photorealistic rendering of 3D computer graphics. In: Proceedings of the Joint Symposium on Computational Aesthetics and Sketch-Based Interfaces and Modeling and Non-Photorealistic Animation and Rendering, pp. 1–11 (2018)

18. Nakano, R.: Neural painters: a learned differentiable constraint for generating brushstroke paintings. arXiv preprint arXiv:1904.08410 (2019)

19. Nath, T., Mathis, A., Chen, A.C., Patel, A., Bethge, M., Mathis, M.W.: Using deeplabcut for 3D markerless pose estimation across species and behaviors. Nat. Protoc 14(7), 1 (2019)

20. Papandreou, G., et al.: Towards accurate multi-person pose estimation in the wild. In: Proceedings of the IEEE Conference on Computer Vision and Pattern Recognition, pp. 4903–4911 (2017)

21. Sindel, A., Maier, A., Christlein, V.: Art2Contour: salient contour detection in artworks using generative adversarial networks. In: 2020 IEEE International Conference on Image Processing (ICIP) (2020)

22. Singh, J., Zheng, L.: Combining semantic guidance and deep reinforcement learning for generating human level paintings. In: 2021 IEEE/CVF Conference on Computer Vision and Pattern Recognition (CVPR) (2020)

23. Sun, X., Xiao, B., Wei, F., Liang, S., Wei, Y.: Integral human pose regression. In: Proceedings of the European Conference on Computer Vision (ECCV), pp. 529–545 (2018)

24. Tong, Z., Chen, X., Ni, B., Wang, X.: Sketch Generation with Drawing Process Guided by Vector Flow and Grayscale. AAAI (2020)

25. Tung, H.-Y.F., Tung, H.-W., Yumer, E., Fragkiadaki, Y.: Self-supervised learning of motion capture. arXiv preprint arXiv:1712.01337 (2017)

26. Xiao, B., Wu, H., Wei, Y.: Simple baselines for human pose estimation and tracking. In: ECCV (2018)

27. Xie, N., Hachiya, H., Sugiyama, M.: Artist agent: A reinforcement learning approach to automatic stroke generation in oriental ink painting. IEIE Trans. Inf. Syst. **96**(5), 1134–1144 (2013)

28. Zheng, N., Jiang, Y., Huang. D.: StrokeNet: a neural painting environment. In: International Conference on Learning Representations (2018)

29. Zhou, T., et al.: Terzopoulos. learning to sketch with deep Q networks and demonstrated strokes (2018)

30. Zou, Z., Shi, T., Qiu, S., Yuan, Y., Shi, S.: Stylized neural painting. In: Proceedings of the IEEE/CVF Conference on Computer Vision and Pattern Recognition, pp. 15689–15698 (2021)

Author Index

Printed in the United States
by Baker & Taylor Publisher Services